THE LOST PERSPECTIVE?

The Lost Perspective?
Trade Unions Between Ideology and Social Action in the New Europe

Volume 1
Ideological Persistence in National Traditions

Edited by
PATRICK PASTURE
JOHAN VERBERCKMOES
HANS DE WITTE

Avebury
Aldershot • Brookfield USA • Hong Kong • Singapore • Sydney

© P. Pasture, J. Verberckmoes and H. De Witte 1996

All rights reserved. No part of this publication may be reproduced, stored in a retrieval system, or transmitted in any form or by any means, electronic, mechanical, photocopying, recording or otherwise without the prior permission of the publisher.

Published by
Avebury
Ashgate Publishing Limited
Gower House
Croft Road
Aldershot
Hants GU11 3HR
England

Ashgate Publishing Company
Old Post Road
Brookfield
Vermont 05036
USA

British Library Cataloguing in Publication Data

The lost perspective? : trade unions between ideology and
    social action in the new Europe
    Vol. 1: Ideological persistence in national traditions. –
(Perspectives on Europe)
1. Trade-unions – Europe
I. Pasture, Patrick, 1961– II. Verberckmoes, Johan III. De
Witte, Hans
331.8'094

ISBN 1 85972 080 3

2 volume set: ISBN 1 85972 331 4

Library of Congress Catalog Card Number: 96-83269

Typeset by
Liesbeth Villa
Hoger Instituut voor de Arbeid
E. Van Evenstraat 2e
B-3000 Leuven
Printed and bound in Great Britain by Ipswich Book Co. Ltd., Ipswich, Suffolk

Contents

Introduction   1
Patrick Pasture, Johan Verberckmoes, Hans De Witte

1. The politics of ideological diversity in France   7
   Johan Verberckmoes

2. Between identity and pragmatism: Italian trade unionism on its way to Europe   52
   Giampiero Bianchi

3. Belgium: pragmatism in pluralism   91
   Patrick Pasture

4. The unattainable unity in the Netherlands   136
   Patrick Pasture

5. Germany: inner trade union diversity   180
   Johan Verberckmoes

6. The United Kingdom: between policy and party   215
   Johan Verberckmoes

7. Sweden: the emergence and erosion of a 'model'   245
   Bo Stråth

Contributors   281

Volume 2 contains the following contributions

Part 1 Historical legacy and actual significance of ideology for trade unions

1. The disarray of the trade unions in a state of crisis
   René Mouriaux
2. Who is afraid of ideology ?
   Frans De Wachter
3. From ideology to organization: the transformation of political unionism in Western Europe
   Bernhard Ebbinghaus
4. Union identities and ideologies in Europe
   Richard Hyman
5. Trade unions and ideology: unions and industrial relations systems
   Colin Crouch
6. Welfare state development, European integration and the lost perspective of inclusive trade unionism
   Anton Hemerijck
7. Trade unions and politics in Eastern and Central Europe: tripartism without corporatism
   Werner Reutter

Part 2 Ideology and cultural identity

8. The workers' movement and nationalism
   Lode Wils
9. Internationalism in European trade unions: a lost perspective or a new agenda ?
   Jelle Visser
10. Trade unions and migrant workers in Europe: a changing ideology as a reflection of variable principles
    Albert Martens
11. Feminine intrusions in a culture of masculinity
    Patrick Pasture

Part 3 The role of ideology in trade union participation

12. Ideology and union commitment
    Michael Gordon

13. Ideology and the social psychology of union participation
    Bert Klandermans

14. Are trade union members (still) motivated by ideology ? A review of the importance of ideological factors as determinants of trade union participation in (the Flemish part of) Belgium
    Hans De Witte

15. Trade union participation in the Netherlands: the role of ideology in trade union membership and participation in industrial actions
    Gerrita van der Veen

16. The 'new' service sector: employment status, ideology and trade union participation in the United Kingdom
    Jean Hartley

17. The importance of ideology in trade union participation in Sweden: a social-psychological model
    Magnus Sverke

Conclusion: reflections on the fate of ideologies and trade unions
Patrick Pasture

Contributors

Introduction

Patrick Pasture, Johan Verberckmoes, Hans De Witte

General perspectives

This book departs from an inquest into the concept of crisis and revolution which is emerging as the end of the century approaches. We all sense that we are experiencing a period of far-reaching social change. However, not only are we unable to comprehend its meaning, we also have the strong impression that the inherited certainties, orientations and distinguishing characteristics of the past century have disappeared or become irrelevant. The title of the book, 'The lost perspective?' refers to this loss, but also has a question mark, since the underlying discourse about the end of ideology and history sounds very familiar to the historian. At first sight, it appears to be the umpteenth variation on a theme that has been popular since the beginning of modern times. At present, the sounding is only more familiar, now that a new 'fin de siècle', the magical year 2000, is approaching. To a certain extent, the 'end of history' reminds us of the predictions by visionary prophets about the end of the world on the eve of the year 1000.

Over the past two decades, the study of the labour movement too has been imbued with the notion of crisis and farewell. Indeed, its support suddenly seemed to collapse. The social democratic political parties all over Europe lost heavily in elections and the fall in trade union membership was very sharp, especially in countries such as Great Britain, the Netherlands and France. At the same time, their overall standing in society weakened. Initially, the decline in the labour movement was linked to the differentiation of the working class and changes in the labour market. The link with the general 'mythology' about the end of ideology was not made in circles of those researching the labour movement.

This publication explicitly highlights the question of ideology with respect to the trade union movement. There are two points of departure. On the one hand, there is the popular-scientific argument about the end of ideology and related themes, as opened up for public debate by Francis Fukuyama's controversial essay *The End of History and the Last Man*, published in 1989. On the other hand, this theme is particularly relevant when confronted with developments in the trade union movement. After all, European trade unions not only have strong ideological ties, the ideological choices they make are especially important because translating these into social action is what trade unions are all about. In this sense, the trade union movement can be distinguished from political parties, normally the main topic for the study of ideology, as these are less concerned with practical considerations. Furthermore, the study of the ideology of trade union movements cannot be confined within one discipline. This book therefore is also an invitation to transcend the boundaries of our fragmented specialist fields.

Structure

The first volume of this book contains country analyses of the trade union movement's development in a number of European countries, from the perspective outlined. An attempt was made to introduce some logic into the sequence of the contributions, rather than simply working alphabetically. The second volume uses a number of themes to present the results of the thinking and analysis of some prominent social scientists on the relevance of ideology to the trade union movement, as formulated at the international and interdisciplinary colloquium on trade unions and ideology in Brussels in February 1995.

In our view, the country studies offer a substantial addition to existing literature, although they can also be read as general introductions to European trade union systems and cultures. The emphasis in these contributions is on recent history, from the end of the 1960s onwards. However, since the book focuses on the ideological dimension, a long-term perspective is expressly used. These studies are the result of three years of research involving Belgium and the Netherlands, France and Italy, Great Britain, (West) Germany and Sweden, in that order. This choice was largely motivated by pragmatic considerations and comprises both pluralist as well as unitary trade union systems and different traditions with respect to the organization of industrial relations and welfare provisions. The study is based mainly on material published by the trade unions, supplemented by literature. Significant use was made of material held by the European Trade Union Institute (ETUI) in Brussels, the International Institute of Social History in Amsterdam and the libraries and documentation centres of the trade unions studied and, in particular, the World Confederation of Labour and the documentation service of the Christian labour movement in Brussels. The staff of these institutes did everything they could to make our work the more easier: we owe them many thanks.

From the outset, we have attempted to streamline the contributions in this first volume by submitting to the authors a review with a definition of the problem and a number of specific questions, which they were, however, allowed to work out as they saw fit and as a function of specific national developments. In this way, the country-by-country analyses study the trade union movement in its wide social significance, with special attention paid to the ideological interpretation. For that matter, this is not merely the study of political ties, to which the ideological dimension of trade unions is often reduced. The complete trade union programme and its actions are taken into consideration. As a backdrop, we have major socio-economic and cultural changes, in particular the modified interpretation of the labour question as a result of the general increase in welfare, the differentiation of the working class, and the apparent blurring and increasing irrelevance of classic ideological cleavages. In this broad approach, focussing on both views and attitudes as well as trade union organization and practices, not only the standpoint of trade unions in the system of industrial relations is highlighted, but also their view of the expansion of the welfare state and their opinion of themselves in society, particularly in the working class and with respect to other social groups. Based on their ideological profile, the trade unions' reactions to the collapse of communism and the sweeping changes in Eastern and Central Europe are studied. One specific question concerns the significance of *gender* to the trade union movement and its ideology. In particular, an attempt is made to evaluate the influence women have on the ideology, organization and practice of the trade union movement. Incidentally, the country summaries take trade union pluralism as a basic premise and discuss both the differences and the parallels between different trade unions. Needless to say that the intention is certainly not to paint a more positive picture of one trade union current compared to another, nor to present pluralism as either an ideal or an aberration.

The second volume of the book contains the reworked contributions of the international trade union and ideology conference held in Brussels on 9 and 10 February 1995. The majority of the authors reflected on the historic meaning of ideology to the trade union movement. Firstly, René Mouriaux reminds us of the most important characteristics of 'the trade union crisis', where one of the striking aspects is that, in spite of all the changes of the past twenty years, the terms used to discuss the crisis have barely changed in that period. In other words, trade unions have not made much progress in their analysis or reaction. The other contributions elaborate more on the meaning of the 'lost perspective'. Frans De Wachter, a moral philosopher from Leuven, wonders whether the end of ideology myth relieves the trade union movement from any programme-based reformulations of its view of social reality - the answer is clearly negative. The fact that ideologies have played a major role in trade union development and that the trade unions themselves helped shape the workers' sense of identity is central to the contributions from Bernhard Ebbinghaus, Richard Hyman and Colin Crouch. In his well-documented study, Bernhard Ebbinghaus harks back to the Stein Rokkan theory of social cleavages, originally designed for explaining party formation systems. Ebbinghaus describes how socio-political and functional cleavages have a permanent influence on the formation and evolution of trade unions. Based on an analysis of the distinct attitude of the trade unions to a society-market-class triangle, Richard Hyman distils three major ideological traditions and observes a tendency towards convergence of the three poles. Colin Crouch concentrates on the interrelationship between ideology and the trade union movement in the industrial relations systems and arrives at a number of probing conclusions about the changing position of the trade union movement in society. Anton Hemerijck goes over the different views on the development of the welfare state and attempts to find possible new prospects for the trade union movement. According to Werner Reutter, trade unions in Central and Eastern Europe are in search of a new form of relationship with employers, the government and the other trade unions, largely inspired by their reaction against the situation during the 'communist era'.

At the aforementioned conference, ideology and the trade union movement were discussed from a cultural angle during a separate session. According to Lode Wils, the labour movement has always had close ties with national movements and, based on this finding, he puts the meaning of internationalism for the early labour movement into perspective. Jelle Visser agrees with this and gives a summary of the trade union movement's attempts to achieve international cooperation. He also observes that national traditions and sensitivities are major obstacles. With respect to the attitude of the trade union movement to immigrants, Albert Martens takes a closer look at its various successive trends, particularly the ambiguity between advocating a limit on immigration, on the one hand, and fighting for equal rights and working conditions on the other hand. Finally, Patrick Pasture analyzes the confrontation between class and gender and the way in which women are a challenge to the male class culture of the trade union movement.

However, trade union movement ideology is not only a matter for large programmes; it is also important to individual members and activists. This relationship is studied in the third part of the second volume by various social psychologists. The first two chapters are of a more general nature. In the four following chapters, results are reported concerning the importance of ideological factors for trade union participation in specific countries.

In a more theoretical introduction, American specialist Michael Gordon highlights the union commitment concept, considering this concept provides virtually the only link to union ideology among researchers from North America. After discussing the development of a measure of union commitment, he examines what industrial relations scholars and psychologists have said about ideology in order to generate proposals to revise the 'belief in unionism' subscale of the union commitment scale. In order to assess the precise role of ideology in trade union participation, an understanding of the social psychological dynamics of such participation is indispensable. Bert Klandermans therefore reviews the three guiding theoretical approaches in this field: frustration-aggression theory, rational choice theory and interactionist theory. He then develops a typology of four forms of participation, since the role of ideology is not necessarily the same for different forms of participation.

This typology of union participation is the starting point for a comparison of the importance of ideological factors as determinants of union participation in four European countries. In his review of the literature on the Flemish part of Belgium, Hans De Witte analyzes the role of socio-economic and socio-cultural (i.e. religious conviction and related aspects) ideology as determinant of the four kinds of participation distinguished by Klandermans. Referring to the Netherlands, Gerrita van der Veen looks at the role of ideology for membership and participation in industrial action. She adds commitment to the union to the two ideologies discussed by De Witte. Specific for her approach is a description of how the trade union movement has responded at organizational level to ideological trends in society. Jean Hartley also limits her analysis to membership and participation in actions in the United Kingdom. She focuses on employees in the 'new' service sector: mainly female white collar workers, working part-time in the finance industry. Because of the recent growth of employment in this area and because of the strong increase in part-time work, these workers represent an important target group for trade unions. Finally, Magnus Sverke analyzes the importance of ideology in trade union participation in Sweden. In doing so, he first develops a broader social-psychological model in which he integrates three different social action theories. This model is then used to analyze the four forms of participation mentioned by Klandermans. Only blue collar workers were interviewed in his research.

Acknowledgements

This book was made possible thanks to a three-year research project by the European Centre for Workers' questions (ECW) in Königswinter (Germany) and was funded by the European Commission. We are particularly indebted to ECW Secretary-General Joachim Herudek for his unstinting support and interest.

This project was conceived and coordinated by Dr. Patrick Pasture, senior research assistant at the National Fund for Scientific Research (NFWO-Belgium) and project manager at the HIVA. During the preparation of the colloquium an advisory committee was set up, comprising Dr. Hans De Witte (HIVA-KU Leuven), Prof. Albert Martens (KU Leuven), Jozef Mampuys (ACV), Dr. Patrick Pasture and Johan Verstraeten (World Confederation of Labour). Dr. Johan Verberckmoes, research fellow at the HIVA, made an important contribution to preparing for the conference and editing the book. Dr. Hans De Witte, head of labour sector at the HIVA took responsibility for the section involving the socio-psychological contribution. All the other texts were revised by Pasture and Verberckmoes, after which the authors reworked their own contributions.

Translations and linguistic revision (unless otherwise mentioned in a note) were entrusted to Vertaalbureau Deceuninck in Leuven. Liesbeth Villa of the HIVA secretariat designed the book with her usual expertise and flair, for which she deserves a special word of thanks.

1 The politics of ideological diversity in France

Johan Verberckmoes

Industrial relations in a strong State with a divided trade union movement

Since the French revolution of 1789, the State has dominated political, economic and social life. Through its simultaneously national and universal, self-imposed role of upholder of the revolutionary ideals of freedom, equality and fraternity, the French State has used legislation to sculpt an individual relationship between citizen and State. The church was resolutely declared a private institution. Throughout various constitutional changes, such active State action promoted an expansion of power on the part of the State administration. Paradoxically, the French trade union movement was not weakened by this. On the contrary, it rather strengthened the movement's revolutionary zeal. At the level of the organized defence of interests, French society always excelled at debate, unremitting ideological contrasts and organizational fragmentation. Moreover, the development of industrial relations was directly geared to the political situation. My argument in this chapter will be that the pursuit of an ideological opposition role - even internally - was the French trade union movement's answer to the age-old State initiative in controlling industrial relations. [1] With the strengthening of contractual procedures at company level over the past decade, these two opposing but complementary positions - State intervention and ideological dissension - seem in need of fundamental changes. As of yet, old patterns still prevail, however. In this introduction, a brief history of the development of French industrial relations will be given.

Then, the four large interprofessional confederations will be individually analyzed.

Since 1789 the French State has always taken the initiative in terms of governing industrial relations (overviews in Mouriaux, 1992 and 1994; Dufour, 1992; Goetschy and Rozenblatt, 1992; Howell, 1989; legal aspects in Weiss, 1988). The Le Chapelier law of 14 June 1791 forbade strikes and the formation of organizations based on profession. Thus, the position of the worker in the economic system was individualized. This was also expressed in the foundation, in 1806, of the *Conseils de prud'hommes*, which adopted their current form after the revolution of 1848: these are lay courts composed of elected employers and employees, intended to settle individual industrial disputes. Nonetheless, from the 1820s onwards, among the slowly expanding group of industrial workers, legal mutual welfare funds and cooperatives were set up, which sometimes served as covers for social action. The bloodily repressed rebellions of the canuts, silk weavers from Lyons, symbolized the struggle for life being fought by the emerging labour movement.

The lifting of the ban on *coalitions ouvrières* or workers' associations, by Napoleon III in 1864, paved the way for the legalization of trade union chambers, which were created in various places during the Second Empire and which were later grouped into professional or interprofessional federations. The Paris *Commune* of March-May 1871 was an important phase in the workers' struggle for emancipation, but ended in a bloodbath. In the long-term the *Commune* elevated the tensions between the conciliation-mutualist and the marxist-collectivist trends within the labour movement. The Waldeck-Rousseau law of 21 March 1884 gave everyone the right to become a member of a trade union. In the first instance, the law was followed by a deceleration in the creation of new trade unions, but later it stimulated the expansion of the trade union movement. On the other hand, by setting up local *Bourses du Travail* (trade union centres) from 1887 onwards, the State attempted to integrate the trade union movement, or at least to monitor it. However, encouraged by Fernand Pelloutier, these *Bourses du Travail* did especially enhance the unity within the labour movement, until they developed into the Confédération Générale du Travail (CGT) in 1895.

The CGT, the first French confederation, was initially under anarchic influence and used the general strike as its main weapon. However, it saw itself more as a historical variant of the revolutionary ideal of 1789 than as a movement which considered the class struggle of paramount importance. In addition, influenced by social Catholicism, a separate denominational trade union movement developed, which was consolidated in 1919 as the Confédération Française des Travailleurs Chrétiens (CFTC). It took its inspiration from the idea of cooperation between the classes, although without giving up its independence from the employers.

The weak link in the trade union movement was its institutional power. The French trade union movements have rarely and only temporarily succeeded in unionising more than a quarter of the working population. Not only did they have to cope with a strong State, but the employers were also unwilling participants. Furthermore, at the beginning of the twentieth century, France was chiefly still an agricultural country. It had a fragmented industrial infrastructure of companies, often run in a paternalistic manner. Industrial concentration did not increase until after the 1920s and large companies would not gain in importance until after the Second World War. The role which the trade union movement wanted to play in the development of that industry could only be exercised little by little. Although the law of 25 March 1919 did indeed implement the collective labour agreement, there was still no evidence of genuine negotiation in practice, with few exceptions. However, collective agreements did from then on take precedence over individual employment contracts, at least in theory.

The 1936 electoral victory by the People's Front (*Front populaire*) was probably the most influential social event in France this century. Subsequently, the confederations would continue to refer to it both explicitly and implicitly. Following a great wave of strikes, the Matignon agreement was concluded between the government and representatives of employers and workers. This took place in the official residence of prime minister Léon Blum, during the night of 7-8 June 1936. Some of the prominent results of this agreement were the 40-hour week, paid leave, complete trade union freedom and the creation of employee representatives (*délégués du personnel*) - elected by all employees to defend their individual interests in the company and to supervise compliance with the agreements entered into. However, '1936' also signified first and foremost recognition of the trade union movement as a public partner. Carrying on from the Matignon agreement, the law of 24 June 1936 regarding collective bargaining strengthened the institutional position of the trade unions. It was significant that the level of negotiation agreed in the law was that of the branch and not of the company, where the trade unions occupied a weak position. On the other hand, the legitimate position of the trade unions was also strengthened thanks to the stipulation that a collective labour agreement was valid as soon as it was signed by one representative trade union. This would later prove an important clause for the small trade unions such as the CFTC, Force Ouvrière (FO) and the confederation for executives founded in 1944, the Confédération Générale des Cadres (CGC).

During the Second World War the Vichy government imposed a corporatist order on industrial relations, with the *Charte du Travail* (Le Crom, 1995). This was not accepted by most trade unions. Both the CGT and the CFTC played a major role in the opposition. During the Liberation, in the summer of 1944, several factories were taken over by workers' councils, in a wave of revolutionary feeling. In an attempt to turn this mobilization to the benefit of the reconstruction of the country, in the initial post-war years various companies were nationalized, including the coal mines in Nord-Pas-de-Calais, Renault, electricity and gas companies, banks and insurance companies. These nationalized companies became important tools for the post-war Keynesian French State, which also attempted to govern economic life through modernization plans, about which the trade unions were consulted. The active participation of the workers in the reconstruction of the country was institutionalized in 1945/46 with the creation of works councils (*comités d'entreprise*). In these works councils, chaired by the employers, the workers' representatives were informed about and consulted on the social and economic situation of the company and the policy to be pursued, particularly with respect to the organization of labour.

Although the trade unions were able to get an institutional foot in the door of the company via the workers' representatives (*délégués*) and the works council, co-management and strong trade union power at that level were however not in evidence. The trade union movement was assigned the same kind of ambiguous role in the system of social security developed by the State in 1945/46. Trade union delegates can be elected to the administrative bodies of the social security funds, but these were themselves independent, so that the trade union movement is not involved further. Unemployment insurance did not come until 1958. During the *Trente Glorieuses*, the period from 1945 to 1975, the French economy grew spectacularly. The resulting unprecedented increase in welfare also benefited the workers, but the trade union movement was unable to turn it to its own advantage. The strike remained the supreme means of action. The law of 12 February 1950 opened up new possibilities for branch and company level collective agreements. It had some success, like the Renault agreement in 1955, but, in the end, the number of collective labour agreements remained limited.

For the trade unions, the breakthrough at company level came in May 1968. The law of 27 December 1968 allowed trade union delegates (*délégués syndicaux*) into the company and united them into company union divisions (*sections syndicales d'entreprise*). These delegates can negotiate within the company and conclude agreements. In 1971, the law of 1950 regarding collective labour agreements was adapted, so that the interprofessional and company levels gained in importance, next the branch level. However, after an initial sharp rise at the beginning of the 1970s, the number of company agreements was drastically reduced in the wake of the economic crisis of 1973. The most important incentive for the growth of trade union power in the company came in 1982, with the reforms of the socialist Minister of Work and Employment, Jean Auroux. From then on, companies with official trade union representation had to negotiate wages and working hours on an annual basis, without any obligation to reach an agreement, however. As a result, the number of company agreements increased sharply. In addition, the Auroux reforms also gave the employees the right to express themselves directly about working conditions and the organization of the company, through participation councils (*groupes d'expression*). This legal condition fitted in with the desire of some of the employers to try out new forms of worker participation in the organization of labour, in the light of a decline in Taylorism and Fordism.

Unfortunately, the Auroux reforms weakened rather than strengthened the confederations. The most important reason for this was that membership of the trade unions had begun to decline rapidly, making active trade union support at company level difficult from an organizational point of view. The consequence was that the works councils in particular, which had seen their possibilities of obtaining expert knowledge about the company's economic performance widen under the Auroux laws, became more important in collective bargaining at company level. On the other hand, the right to self-expression also gave employees greater possibilities for demanding a better status outside the trade union. The trade unions themselves were still mainly geared towards the national (interprofessional) and the branch level. The early Mitterrand presidency, on the other hand, actively intervened in social policy by reducing working hours to 39 in 1982, by dramatically altering the national minimum wage (*salaire minimum interprofessional de croissance*, SMIC) or through the legal conditions regarding increased flexibility in working hours, after interprofessional negotiations on the subject had ground to a halt in December 1984. Since the mid-1980s, however, industrial relations have been increasingly decentrally regulated, which compels both the State machinery and the confederations to review their roles.

From the start, French trade unionism has been ideologically divided and organizationally fragmented. On a national level, five confederations have been acknowledged as representative, on the basis of criteria outlined in the 1950 law on collective agreements. Four of them have distinct ideological origins and cover all categories of workers. They will be discussed in this chapter. The fifth, the Confédération Générale des Cadres (CGC), started in 1944 as an amalgamation of different federations of engineers and other cadre personnel. It had its roots mainly in social Catholicism and defended the specific interests of the cadres, advocating, for instance, the extension of an hierarchic salary scale. In the course of the 1960s the other confederations challenged the nearly monopolistic position of the CGC among senior officials by reviving their own unions for cadre personnel. The consequence was a lot of internal quarrelling in the CGC between a moderate majority and an anti-hierarchic minority. This finally ended in a relaunch of the organization in 1981 under the name of Confédération Française de l'Encadrement-Confédération Générale des Cadres (CFE-CGC). This CFE-CGC continued to restrict its action to senior officials. In the last decade it looked for closer cooperation with the other confederations, without, however, giving up its basic categorial orientation.

In addition to the five national representative confederations France also has dozens of 'autonomous' federations, representative at branch or company level. Moreover, 'independent' unions exist at national, branch or company level, some of which are conservative or even have connections with the far-right (Mouriaux, 1992, pp. 53-70). In 1981 ten autonomous federations (*le groupe des Dix*) met to coordinate actions and reflection. The group later enlarged and fuelled the discussion about the recomposition of French trade unionism. By far the most important of the autonomous unions is the Fédération de l'Education Nationale (FEN), recognized as representative in the education sector (Aubert a.o., 1985; Batsch, 1987). During the Liberation the Fédération Générale de l'Enseignement CGT transformed itself to become the FEN, thus stressing its wish to defend the categorial interests of the teachers as well as the lay school. In 1947 the FEN declared itself autonomous. It became firmly implanted in the public school sector. In 1987 the socialist majority in the FEN launched a moderately successful proposal for the recomposition of French trade unionism after the German and British model of a reformist, unitary trade union movement. In 1992 a split occurred in the FEN, which left the breakaway union, the Fédération Syndicale Unitaire (FSU) more powerful than the FEN itself (Mouriaux, 1994, p. 114). This split is based on a dissension between reformist socialists on the one hand and communists and minority leftist groups of different kinds on the other, a dissension which has troubled the FEN and its immediate predecessors since their origins. Perhaps, the recent split in the FEN symbolizes the re-emergence of strong ideological identities in France.

The Confédération Générale du Travail

The largest French confederation is the Confédération Générale du Travail (CGT), founded in Limoges in 1895. Although initially it was rather a loose amalgam of trade unions and *Bourses du Travail*, from 1902 onwards the CGT saw itself as an umbrella organization of trade unions, which can be structured both per branch or profession and regionally. Such a combination of vertical and horizontal divisions also characterizes the other French confederations. Up until the First World War, the CGT upheld revolutionary trade unionism in France, the principles of which were laid down in the Charter of Amiens (1906). Its outlook was radically anti-capitalist.

According to the Charter, the irreconcilable differences between workers and employers were the consequence of the class struggle typical of capitalism (Mouriaux, 1992, pp. 28-30). The capitalists exploited the workers, which generated opposition. The trade union attempted, through packages of demands, to improve working conditions, but in the long term they wanted the general emancipation of the working class, which would lead to the disappearance of the capitalist system. The general strike was used as the prime means of action. Despite its explicit political position, the Charter of Amiens also placed firm emphasis on the autonomy of the trade union movement. In order to be able to fulfil its role in economic life to the full, the trade union must not become involved with political parties. However, every trade union member was free, outside the trade union, to express his political leanings. However, the two elements which were still lumped together in this basic agreement - direct action and political independence - were the cause of continuing disunity within the non-Catholic French trade union movement after 1918.

Varying opinions on whether or not to intervene in the First World War and the October Revolution of 1917 led to the creation of a reformist majority and a revolutionary minority within the CGT during the inter-war period. The former group believed that cooperation with the

State was necessary to spark off a far-reaching process of change. Led by Léon Jouhaux, it promoted the development of a system of social insurance and the conclusion of collective labour agreements. The anarchist and communist revolutionaries, on the other hand, were ejected from the CGT in 1921 and had their own confederation until 1936, the Confédération Générale du Travail Unitaire (CGTU). The Bolshevists rejected all cooperation within the capitalist system and stressed the leading role of the Parti Communiste Français (PCF), founded in 1920, in the proletarian struggle against capitalism. Despite a temporary reunification between both tendencies in the *Front populaire* of 1936 and the prestige acquired by the communists in the opposition during the Second World War and during the period of national reconstruction, after 1945 the differences within the CGT again became clear. In 1947/48 a reformist minority split off and formed the Force Ouvrière (FO).

Within the CGT, with its continued communist majority, the Leninist view of the trade union as a mouthpiece of the communist party looked was implemented (Harmel, 1982, pp. 16-29). In this function, the CGT was there to mobilize the masses in favour of the political aims of the PCF. Nonetheless, it must be clearly Stated that, according to this Leninist view, the trade union itself is not communist, but the communist party does impose its views on the confederation. The high proportion of communists in the trade union machinery, their strong mutual contacts and their self-confident and active militantism ensure that links with the party are maintained within the trade union. Although this point of view may flagrantly contravene the principle of trade union independence contained in the Charter of Amiens, to the communists themselves there is absolutely no conflict between trade union freedom and political attitudes in favour of communism, since to them the PCF and the CGT are expressions of one and the same social class. Between 1947 and 1955, however, the CGT was totally subjected to the political strategy of the PCF which, in the context of the Cold War, pursued mainly international political options (Ross, 1982a).[2] In this period, it is true to say that the mouthpiece principle was rigorously applied. One specific consequence of this was that the CGT became isolated from the other confederations. No matter how close the links with the PCF may still be today, the CGT would no longer fulfil such a purely parapolitical role after 1955. Nevertheless, even in the early 1950s, internal pluralism was not discouraged in the CGT, with some worker priests being militants, for instance (Mouriaux, 1994, pp. 45-47).

In the 1960s, the strictly schematic thinking within the CGT was to make way for detailed analyses (Ross, 1982a, pp. 97-100 and 144-167). Pursuing a strategic alliance of the whole French left, in order to overthrow capitalism, was the new goal of the CGT. It also helped the union to distance itself somewhat from the PCF. While the related questions about joint trade union action and a democratic CGT posed at the 1957 congress could still be brushed aside by the doctrinal argument that there was only one working class and therefore trends within the trade union or other trade unions in theory had no raison d'être, six years later a plea for joint trade union action was uttered by Secretary-General Benoît Frachon himself. A sharp fall in the number of strikes in 1964/65 and differences between the CGT and the transforming CFTC/CFDT on the social action to be pursued, however, ensured that no immediate results were produced on the joint trade union front. The CGT believed in short strikes in the private sector and lightning strikes in public services, so as to gradually build up a broad opposition front against the Gaullist regime from a sympathetic base. By contrast, the new CFDT was aiming at enforced local strikes, which would end with a successful round of negotiations, and hard action geared towards concessions in the public sector.

Despite these strategic contrasts, on 10 January 1966 the CGT and the CFDT concluded an agreement on joint trade union action regarding professional and general economic demands. One of the most important explanations for the radical U-turn in interconfederal relations is undoubtedly the creation of the CFDT, which was seeking its own course. While the CFDT hoped to acquire some degree of legitimacy for its new, action-oriented and militant image through this agreement, the CGT mainly assumed that limited cooperation would in the long term lead to greater tactical and political convergence between the two confederations. However, the 1966 agreement and the ensuing joint days of action (*journées d'action*) had a more fundamental significance. Not only did the CGT regain its important position in French public life, following its ostracism since the Cold War, but the revival of revolutionary, protest-based trade unionism was also a clear indication that, despite the spectacular rise in prosperity, the workers had not ruled out the possibility of radical social change.

The months of May and June 1968, famous for their strikes, confronted the CGT with its own ideological options, in a way more brutal than the confederal leaders themselves had ever expected (Ross, 1982a, pp. 168-211; Groux and Mouriaux, 1991, pp. 61-63; Bridgford, 1989; Capdevielle and Mouriaux, 1988). Initially, the CGT was quite blasé about the noisy student protest, over which it had no control whatsoever, but following its appeal on 11 May for a 24-hour general strike on 13 May, the confederation took the initiative and attempted to immerse the student movement in a wider social movement. However, what the CGT failed to understand was that its quantitative economic demands concerning wages and working hours and, to a lesser extent the long-demanded legal recognition of trade union activities in the company, were entirely irrelevant in this case. The global ordinal words 'self-management' (*autogestion*) and 'structural reforms', which entirely characterized the protests of 1968, were dismissed by the CGT as pure rhetoric, although, on the other hand, workers control was practised under CGT-supervision, for instance at Nantes.

The sociological background to this lack of understanding points to a second sticking point confronting the CGT. The radical protests of 1968 had arisen chiefly in circles of students and employees from the middle classes, such as engineers or technicians, who had new qualitative demands. Although the CGT had relaunched its Union Générale des Ingénieurs et Cadres (UGIT) in 1963, it paid relatively little attention to these groups, since they were difficult to fit into the bipolar class system, unless they belonged to the ruling, capitalist class. Moreover, the CGT saw itself, during the turbulent months of May and June, as *la grande force tranquille* (the great calming force) - in the words of the new Secretary-General Georges Séguy - which used its control over the strikes to restore public order, threatened by violence and chaos, on behalf of a working class acting responsibly. During the night of negotiations on 26 May at the Ministry of Employment in the rue de Grenelle, the largest French confederation was therefore easily satisfied. This attitude was intended particularly to block the path of the successful radical new left-wing movements of Maoists and Trotskyists, mockingly known as *gauchistes*.

Despite the contradictions, the CGT saw May 1968 as a confirmation of its interpretation of the progress of the workers' struggle. Its interpretation? In fact it was the theory of State monopolist capitalism (*capitalisme monopoliste d'Etat*), as developed from 1966 onwards within the PCF and adopted by the CGT (Lazar, 1992, pp. 125-126; Ross, 1982a, pp. 240-242; Ross, 1982b, pp. 29-32).[3] According to CGT/PCF theory, capitalism in France had entered a new crisis phase because the large monopoly groups were increasingly turning to the State to increase their profits. This meant that not only were science and technology subordinated to a one-sided pursuit of profit, but also that the expansion of collective provisions was made more difficult. This theory forecast, as a consequence of this State-aided monopolization, increasing social unrest among the workers as well as among the centre groups of engineers, technicians and white collar workers. Since such problems were considered inherent in capitalism, according to classic marxist thinking, the French communists and the CGT could see good only in a '1936-style' Joint Left Front, which would achieve the radical transition to a socialist society.

In order to translate such high ideological expectations into practice, the CGT rejected the modernization of contractual procedures in the public sector, as introduced by prime minister Jacques Chaban-Delmas. Drastic interruptions in work, such as that at *Electricité de France* in November 1969, marked the CGT's opposition on principle to such collective bargaining at the government's request. On the other hand, there were clear signs that the CGT had not misunderstood the need for rejuvenation and renewal of its practices, expressed in May 1968. After all, in terms of membership the CGT had benefitted from '1968'. From 1970 onwards, therefore, the CGT began to sign agreements, including the interprofessional agreements concerning the monthly payment of wages (20 April 1970), continuing vocational training (9 July 1970), and paid maternity leave (2 July 1970) (Mouriaux, 1982, p. 114; Ross, 1982a, pp. 216-227). Such measures promoted both an immediate improvement in the lot of the workers as well as predisposing them towards the prospect of mass mobilization. These agreements were, however, always open to termination by the CGT because they were reached with class enemies. This had been the basic concept of the CGT since 1936, developed mainly by Benoît Frachon: 'mass and class trade unionism' (*syndicalisme de masse et de classe*) (Mouriaux, 1982, pp. 127-134; Ross, 1982a; Frachon, 1967-69). In the light of rising numbers (since the 1960s), following a continued slump in membership since the Second World War and a high level of strike activity in the first half of the 1970s, the CGT was again talking about 'the certainty of future victories'.[4]

On 1 December 1970 a new cooperation agreement based on a series of industrial demands was concluded with the CFDT, but it was unable to mask the persistent division. The debate which began between the two confederations in 1971 emphasized their mutual ideological differences, rather than erasing them. Nonetheless, a fair amount of cooperation still took place in practice. When the PCF and the PS signed the Joint Government Programme of the Left on 27 June 1972, the CGT immediately pledged its support. Important elements of that programme, such as the nationalization of the credit and insurance system and of a number of industrial groups, as well as democratic economic planning, were part of the package of demands which the CGT had formulated at its congresses since the second half of the 1960s, following in the footsteps of the PCF (Ross, 1982a, pp. 227-239; Bridgford, 1991, pp. 35-38 and 89-92).

This all seemed to bring the CGT gradually closer to achieving its ideological option of overthrowing the capitalist system. However, its politicized attitude brought problems for the trade union. In addition to the trade union militants, communists from the party were also active in the companies, with the aid of the CGT, and set up political cells within them. Furthermore, during pre-electoral periods the CGT sometimes suspended strikes so as not to prejudice the chances of the Left. National days of action acquired an openly political character. True, new life was breathed into joint trade union action with the CFDT in the summer of 1974, with a joint position on mass action and especially in the struggle against the strict austerity policy of the Barre government in 1976 and 1977 joint action grew in significance. However, it also suffered increasing damage as a result of the party-linked attitude of the CGT. In January 1978 this led to a refusal by the CFDT to continue the joint action, once the Parti Socialiste (PS) and the PCF had already withdrawn their cooperation from the Joint Government Programme in September 1977. Within the CGT, these events prevented a thorough consideration of the consequences of the economic crisis, which prevailed from 1974 onwards (Bridgford, 1991; Ross, 1982a, pp. 243-279; Ross, 1982b, pp. 45-51).

At its fortieth congress, held from 26 November to 1 December 1978 in Grenoble, the CGT had to face up to its failure to adapt to the dramatic changes in economic and social reality.[5] On the one hand there was a call for more democracy, while on the other hand pleas were heard for a re-sourcing of trade union action. Even Secretary-General Georges Séguy, a member of the political bureau of the PCF, called for self-criticism within the organization. For the first time in many years, critical noises were heard both before and during the congress about the voluntary subordination of the CGT to the aims of the French communist party. Nevertheless, the urgent appeal for modernization and a lifting of taboos did not lead to the creation of fractions or tendencies within the confederation. To non-communists too, trade union unity was more important than internal, institutionalized pluralism. On top of the political disenchantment after the electoral victory of the Right in March 1978, increasing doubts surfaced within the CGT about its effectiveness in the field of industrial relations. Not only had numbers been falling since 1976, but the increased unwillingness of the CGT to sign collective agreements during the 1970s had prevented the confederation from reaping the benefits of its militancy. It fought the fight, but its reformist colleagues, who did sign agreements, collected the benefits. The call in Grenoble was 'back to basics', and it was left to proposals for worker self-management (*autogestion*), workshop councils (*conseils d'atelier*) and structural reforms in the industry to give form to the new-look offensive approach. Joint trade union action would support these new trade union practices.

However, the fresh wind of re-sourcing soon turned into a stiff breeze of sectism. Even at the fortieth congress the modernization programme was unable to gain general approval and was shot to pieces at its first serious test, following an innovative CGT proposal for a restructuring of the French steel industry, because the CGT itself organized a March by steelworkers on Paris on 23 March 1979, which was nothing short of a rerun of the classical 'big slogan' demonstrations. Once again the greatest obstacle to a far-reaching development by the CGT was its faith in the PCF. The Soviet invasion of Afghanistan in January 1980 and the subsequent events in Poland involving Solidarity again isolated the CGT, with its pro-USSR stance, on the side of the PCF. This time, its renewed faith in the PCF also meant the kiss of death for joint trade union action. Accusing the CFDT of class collaboration, the CGT did not hesitate to dot the i's and cross the t's. No middle course was possible between revolutionary socialism and collaborating reformism. It was a question of fight or negotiate. However, this firm stance did not ease internal tensions.

Mitterrand's victory in the presidential elections of spring 1981 and the inclusion of communists in the government contributed further to the confusion among the ranks of the CGT. It explicitly approved the expansion of the nationalized sector, regional economic planning and a series of social measures, but at the same time criticized the inadequacy of some of the reforms, such as the (insufficient) increase in the minimum wage (SMIC). Such an attitude of critical support for the new Left-wing regime allowed the confederation, in the mean time, to further erase internal dissidence without seeming intolerant. At the congress of June 1982, Séguy was replaced as Secretary-General by Henri Krasucki, also a member of the political bureau of the PCF, but a hardliner, unlike Séguy.[6] The criticism from Jean-Louis Moynot, who had himself previously been dismissed from the confederal bureau and who wanted to continue the openness of the fortieth congress, was jeered at as an acceptance of a Left-wing strict austerity policy, such as that championed by the CFDT. In its own programme, the CGT stressed the old demands, such as the promotion of national economic growth and the strengthening of workers' purchasing power, but it also recycled several demands for modernization from 1978, relating to new forms of labour management and structural changes to the production process (Ross, 1984, pp. 79-88; Mouriaux, 1982, pp. 120-125; Kergoat, 1984).

The introduction of a harsh austerity policy by the Mauroy government in March 1983, which marked the failure of a policy of economic growth based purely on the stimulation of domestic demand, and restructuring processes in the coal and steel industry, which led to the loss of many jobs, led to heightened criticism of the CGT. The confederation repeatedly called for big demonstrations. Once the communists had left the Left-wing government in July 1984, the calls for social action became even louder. Hypermilitant actions with anti-socialist slogans, at Renault for example, showed that the CGT was not betraying its ideals. In the mean time, since the beginning of the 1980s, the CGT had become increasingly active at company level. In tandem with the increasing importance of company agreements - many of which were also signed by the CGT (59 per cent in 1983, 45.4 per cent in 1990) - this was a clear return to 'base', thus unexpectedly fulfilling the ambition of the fortieth congress for renewed trade union action. At national level, the CGT signalled its regained militancy by its stubborn opposition to any compromise in interprofessional negotiations on flexibility, which had to be held in 1984 and which came to nothing.[7]

Although membership fell drastically - from 2.3 million in 1977 to 1.2 million in 1985 - including retired workers - the CGT's analysis of the economic crisis remained virtually unchanged compared to the period before 1981. The only difference was that, in addition to the employers and the Right, the struggling Left was now also held responsible for the negative effects of the economic crisis, summarized by Henri Krasucki as a decline in civilisation (*un recul de civilisation*). The hedgehog position adopted by the CGT led to internal criticism from the socialist camp, but without any major consequences, as usual. Nonetheless, the adherence to old certainties also had favourable effects. The ideological leadership of the CGT was consolidated. More important still were the small changes to its action plan for the future. The working class was still referred to as the driving force behind the trade union movement, but in the second half of the 1980s, the CGT ultimately turned its attention more to executives, retired people, women, young people and immigrants. This was translated into detailed proposals for a revaluation of the minimum wage, a reduction in the retirement age, a reform of the system of family benefits, an increase in the number of nursery schools, a call for 'collective' child care facilities, etc.. In brief, at a time of crisis, social rights which had been acquired should not be questioned, but expanded. In this sense, the combination of fighting and negotiating was the best policy instrument. Or better still, as one delegate to the forty-second congress in 1985 put it, no more idle chit-chat about ideology (*plus de parlotes stériles sur l'idéologie*).[8]

The self-elected isolation in which the CGT pursued its action increasingly distanced it from its previous ideal of joint trade union action. Moreover, despite the rhetoric, there was no disguising the fact that a great deal of social unrest, such as that among students in 1986, railway workers in the winter of 1986-1987 or nurses in the autumn of 1988, was organized by *les coordinations* and not by the traditional unions (Hassenteufel, 1991). At the end of the 1980s, the CGT seriously began to worry about its waning power. The traditional truths had certainly not been renounced. Responsibility for the deepening crisis was now placed fully on Europe, a Europe which, according to the CGT, had always been an inhibiting factor standing in the way of its main priority - the development of the national, French economy (Rose, 1989). Without detracting from the marxist vision of the class struggle, the CGT frankly admitted that the roads to class consciousness among the workers could be extremely diverse and that the trade union would only have a coordinating and stimulating role.

The collapse of the communist regimes in Eastern Europe and the Soviet Union put marxism under a great deal of pressure, but both the PCF and the CGT continued to portray themselves as vigilant guardians of the inheritance. There are some indications, however, that the link with the PCF is being carefully loosened (Mouriaux, 1994, p. 117). Although the CGT signed a great many agreements at company level, it still considered them as a temporary solution to alleviate pressing needs. The fight against capitalism and imperialism remained the driving force behind the movement. During the preparations for its forty-fourth congress in 1992, the events taking place in the CGT closely mirrored those of the fortieth congress in 1978.[9] Now, it was Henri Krasucki, as outgoing Secretary-General, who criticized the orthodoxy which some believed they had to defend. However, no thorough debate ensued this time and the new Secretary-General, Louis Viannet, said from the podium in Montreuil in January 1992 that the confederation was continuing its fight against exploitation from the grassroots. The CGT had to stick to reality (*coller au réel*). Even though confrontation remained the point of departure for its social action, at the 1992 congress the CGT also looked for possible new foundations for its action. Since the second half of the 1980s, the CGT has after all always seen itself as the ultimate defender of social achievements. At least, it was the trade union which did not give in, neither where the curtailment of purchasing power was concerned, nor on the dismantling of the French production machinery or the public services, nor on the corrections to social security, nor on the unequal treatment of women and immigrants. By placing social requirements explicitly at the centre of its analysis ('needs are the cement of demands and the framework for social struggles' - *les besoins, ciment des revendications, charpente des luttes sociales*), perhaps the CGT developed a way out of its difficult position as an ideological pariah.[10]

The Confédération Française Démocratique du Travail

At an extraordinary congress in November 1964, a majority of just over two-thirds of the Confédération Française des Travailleurs Chrétiens (CFTC) decided to change the name of the confederation to the Confédération Française Démocratique du Travail (CFDT) and to remove all explicit references to Christian social doctrine from its statutes. In a programmatic preamble to its new statutes, the CFDT stipulated that 'respect for the dignity of the human being' was fundamental to its operation (*Liaisons sociales*, 1992, p. 76). This was a clear reference to its Christian origins and the personalism of Emmanuel Mounier. However, the new CFDT carefully argued that Christian humanism was only one of the forms of humanism from which it wished to draw its inspiration. By also emphasizing the freedom of the individual and his subjugation within the ruling economic system, the CFDT opened the way for other interpretations, which would give a broader intellectual and philosophical basis to the 'ideological trade union' which the CFDT wanted to be (Groux and Mouriaux, 1989, pp. 24-51; Branciard, 1990, pp. 97-101 and 186-194; Pasture, 1994, pp. 5-11; Tixier, 1992, pp. 239-277; Hamon and Rotman, 1984; Georgi, 1995).

The pedestal (Tixier, 1992) of the secularized CFDT was unmistakably personalism, despite the laicisation and the temptations of revolutionary collectivism. The development of the concept of personalism had been one of the central topics of discussion in the influential magazine *Reconstruction*, which had been published since 1946 and was the most important driving force for the *minorité* within the CFTC - the minority tendency which wanted to separate social action from any religious action and recognized the existence of the class struggle. Personalism signified respect for human dignity and freedom, the commitment of the individual and the willingness to enter into dialogue. That was a theme which, in this formulation, could be both a successor to Christian social doctrine and an upholder of universal humanism, as expressed in the Universal Declaration of Human Rights. The great sticking point in the transformation phase was the relationship between the person and the collectivity (Groux and Mouriaux, 1989, pp. 97-130; Branciard, 1990, pp. 195-220; Vignaux, 1980; Zimmerman, 1991).

How could the humanistic view of the new CFDT form part of a broader social project without falling into the traditional traps of corporatism or totalitarianism ? 'Democratic socialism' had to provide the solution. Essentially, this term referred to a legal situation of shared rights and duties, which guaranteed respect for the individual in a free society. Combined with the rejection of capitalism as an alienating economic system, that led to calls for more democracy, first and foremost in industrial relations. Workers had to be given the right to exercise control over the running of the company, as well as to participate in its management. More broadly, this democracy had to be achieved through democratic planning, a principle already accepted at the CFTC congress in 1959. In that concept, the conditions surrounding the production process were crucial: production is not intended to make a profit, but primarily to provide for collective needs. The free market did not have to vanish, but its investment must be publicly monitored.

These were the ideas, no matter how vague and ambiguous they were. But how could they be put into practice ? On this matter too, the CFDT cautiously sought a path of its own. Collective negotiation seemed to the confederation to be the appropriate way, but in the mid-1960s the government and the employers were extremely reluctant to start discussions. The CFDT therefore made an attempt at conciliation with the other confederations. Force Ouvrière refused to work with a trade union with Christian origins, but the CGT immediately jumped at the chance. On 10 January 1966 the two confederations concluded an agreement on joint trade union action. The ultimate goal of their coordinated action was 'to break the deadlock to genuine negotiations' (*de faire sauter le verrou fondamental pour l'ouverture de négociations véritables*), in the words of the Secretary-General of the CFDT, Eugène Descamps.[11] Ideologically speaking, both confederations stressed their own identities and diverging opinions. Politically, convergence between the CFDT and the non-communist Left increased after 1964, but many within the confederation continued to reject any political extension of trade union action.

The period of May-June 1968 was the first peak in ideological productivity for the CFDT (Groux and Mouriaux, 1989, pp. 120-130; Branciard, 1990, pp. 221-238). The CFDT recognized - almost immediately and in stark contrast to the CGT - that the students' protests were the same as those of the workers, although Paul Vignaud himself, the founder of *Reconstruction*, was very critical of the students' protest. In the storms of social discussion born out of the events of 1968, the term 'self-management' ('autogestion') became the rock on which the CFDT stood. Conceptually, this designation was still fairly empty and responded more to a feeling of what was underway. The full weight of the social action of the CFDT came to rest at the level of the company, where experiments involving self-management by the workers were carried out. Company sit-ins symbolized the will to bring about radical democratic change. The legal recognition of trade union rights in the company became the confederation's main point of conflict at national level. However, the fact that the new contractual procedures in the public sector, partly drawn up by former CFDT militant Jacques Delors, could often count on support from the confederation, was proof that even after 1968 the past had not been forgotten. However, this was not pure reformism, since the contracts were only considered temporary comprises to extract advantages and opportunities to consolidate one's own position.

The congress held by the CFDT from 6 to 10 May 1970 in Issy-les-Moulineaux was one of the most ideological in recent French history (Groux and Mouriaux, 1989, pp. 131-137; Branciard, 1990, pp. 238-250; Tixier, 1992, pp. 284-287; Georgi, 1995). The range of ideas became more radical even during preparations for the congress. At the congress itself, discussions and counter-proposals prevailed over the traditional virtual unanimity, on such occasions, on the policy proposal made by the confederal leadership. All this took place against a background of both post-May '68 militancy and a desire to convert the democratic principles, defended for more than a decade, into progressive applications. What at first sight appeared to be a mapped out transition to socialism was, in reality, a complex compromise of revolutionary positions and the legacy of personalism. There were accusations of inequality and alienation, two formulations which could be said to be both anti-authoritarian and personalist. Finally, three major lines were put forward: joint ownership of the means of production (*propriété sociale des moyens de production*), worker self-management, and democratic planning. The crux of CFDT ideology was an anti-hierarchic interpretation of what social relations would have to look like. The socialist ideal thus formulated was a new discovery by the CFDT. At political level, attempts were made to reconcile differences by talking about a committed autonomy for the trade union. This implied both the confederation's own political programme and inevitable cooperation with the Left-wing parties.

The consequences of this programme were far-reaching. Firstly, the congress of 1970 was permeated by the idea that the trade union did not simply defend workers' interests, but was first and foremost one of the most important links in the period of transition to a social democratic society. This utopia implied the rejection of all forms of co-management in the capitalist system, relied on wide social mobilization and again brought the CFDT closer to the CGT, with which a new cooperation agreement was concluded on 1 December 1970. On the other hand, the CFDT recoiled from statism along communist lines. Joint ownership of the means of production was therefore explicitly referred to, rather than nationalization, although it would amount to the same thing once it had been implemented. In a country where the State plays such an important role in governing industrial relations, the absence of any consideration of the role of the State, however, was noticeable. Last but by no means least, collective bargaining became considerably less important to the CFDT. While it had previously been the main means within the CFDT, it was now referred to as simply one of the means of action.

To the CFDT militants during the 1970s, the company became the site where the foundations were laid for their new model of the economy and society (Groux and Mouriaux, 1989, pp. 137-203; Branciard, 1990, pp. 251-302; Tixier, 1992, pp. 288-298; Mouriaux, 1984). Strikes were the most important means of making employers face up to the workers' demand for self-determination. During the first half of the 1970s in particular, drastic action was taken. Some of the actions which most appealed to the imagination were those at the Joint français in Saint-Brieuc, at Pennaroya (Lyons) and the Lip affair in Besançon, which was elevated to heroic status. These threw the CFDT as an organization into the spotlight of public opinion. Nonetheless, numbers would only increase slowly, peaking in 1976/77, so that the CFDT became the second largest French confederation, behind the CGT. The demands which the CFDT upheld during the 1970s were primarily qualitative in nature: improved working conditions, better safety at work, the right of the workers to express their opinions within the company. As far as wages were concerned, the CFDT developed its own point of view, at first disputed by the CGT, but which later found acceptance in the communist trade union after 1977, together with other CFDT opinions (Ross, 1982a, p. 229). The CFDT declared itself an absolute opponent of a thorough salary hierarchy by job classification. In order to bring wage scales closer together, the confederation proposed awarding uniform wage increases, from which the lower wages would initially benefit to a relatively greater extent.

A second priority in the anti-hierarchic attitude of the CFDT, in addition to the right to self-management, was the rejection on principle of all forms of inequality. The emphasis on more equality was a consequence of the attraction of the lively CFDT for various social groups, which were usually left high and dry by the trade union movement. While white collar workers had traditionally formed the mainstay of the confederation's membership, during the 1970s the CFDT was boosted primarily by uneducated workers, for example from the automotive or the textile industry, but also by technicians, women, young people and immigrants. Specific demands were put forward for each of these groups, each pressing its own position of independence. Women's demands included equal pay, mixed education, mixed vocational training, maternity leave on full pay and collective provisions for child care. Nonetheless, despite intense activity concerning these topics, the sensitivity to gender questions within the CFDT remained more a matter of principle, rather than leading to tangible results. The demands concerning young people were submerged in a broader package, including a call for non-denominational and democratic education, as well as a democratization of the army (without wanting to be anti-militarist). As far as immigrants were concerned, the same principle of equality was defended, albeit with some reticence when it came to political demands, such as participation in elections.

The question of how the CFDT could lift its struggle to a higher plane was strategically important for the achievement of its broad objectives (Bridgford, 1991; Ross, 1982a, pp. 243-279; Lewis, 1987). Joint trade union action with the CGT had been undergoing a revival since 1970 and would continue to flourish until 1977. In terms of ideology, the two confederations unmistakably moved closer together and their strategies converged, particularly once the economic crisis took off after 1974 and the basic requirements of the trade union movement relating to purchasing power and job opportunities were again the focus of attention, to the detriment of the CFDT's qualitative priorities. Nevertheless, the CFDT always made sure that it kept its distance from its partner. At political level, the CFDT was just as keen on its autonomy. Although the confederation could distinguish similarities between its points of view and those of the non-communist Left, it explicitly refused to take a stand in favour of the Joint Government Programme of the Left (1972-1977). The nationalization programme and the associated State centralism in particular were major stumbling blocks for the CFDT, as far as content was concerned. However, the CFDT's rapprochement with respect to the Parti Socialiste (PS) was unmistakable, especially after the CFDT had openly supported Mitterrand in the presidential elections of 1974.

In a little over a decade, the intellectually strong CFDT, through its over-confident course of rejuvenation, had succeeded in bringing about modernization in France and abroad, both for the trade union movement and on a political level, which responded to the fundamental changes in industrial society. In the second half of the 1970s, however, this same CFDT had to face the limits of that ability to adapt. That led to a 'recentring' of the confederation in 1978-1979. This quest for a centre position implied that pure trade union action was again the focus of attention within the confederation - an attitude which was translated into particular emphasis on collective bargaining as the appropriate means of action. From then on, the CFDT opted for the realism of the specific packages of demands rather than the utopianism of the self-management project. Various explanations can be advanced for this apparently radical change of track towards reformist moderation.

At first sight, the 'recentring' was the result of the political impasse in which the CFDT found itself, since the negotiations for adjustments to the Joint Government Programme of the Left had fallen through in September 1977, the union of Left-wing political parties had broken up and the Left had suffered another electoral defeat in March 1978. However, the problems essentially lay deeper and the CFDT was slowly becoming aware of this. The pluralism of the economic crisis in particular was analyzed by the confederation: it was not only economic, it was just as much political, social and cultural.[12] Based on the view that capitalism inevitably encouraged the alienation of the individual - reducing him to a performer of tasks and a willing consumer - the very concept of economic growth was questioned. Other criteria for measuring economic growth were sought, to replace those used by the consumer society: social benefit, the quality of life, greater equality, worker co-responsibility. This led to calls for a reduction in working hours, the improvement and expansion of the public services sector, and measures to combat youth unemployment. In the same context, a salary for mothers at home was rejected because this would deprive women of the right to work and therefore slow down their emancipation. In fact, 'recentring' therefore also meant that the CFDT had not succeeded in converting its ideal of self-management into social relations and that it was now trying to do it by formulating a broad cultural criticism of capitalism.

A third factor of change were the fundamental shifts taking place in the field of industrial relations. The increasing importance of white collar workers and executives on the labour market as a whole did not escape the attention of the CFDT. After the mid-1970s they were given more of a chance in trade union operations. Moreover, the Lip affair had not only been the prime symbol of modern revolutionary trade unionism - workers preventing the likely bankruptcy of their watch company by taking over production themselves and keeping it going for months - it had also encouraged the formulation of industrial counter-proposals by the trade union. Finally, new technologies confronted the CFDT with radical changes in the organization of labour, to which answers urgently had to be found.

At the thirty-eighth congress in May 1979 in Brest, the new confederal line was approved by a majority of 56.7 per cent of the votes in favour of the activity report and 63.4 per cent for the resolution with the action strategy.[13] These percentages did not represent a threat to the cohesion of the confederation. They rather reflected the open style of discussion which was usual in the CFDT. Despite an appeal from the extreme Left not to forsake the old ideals, no organized opposition to the trade union top surfaced at this congress. After all, the tide was turning for militantism and the CFDT was irrevocably sucked into this downward spiral of passiveness. In this sense, 'recentring' undoubtedly camouflaged a good deal of trade union disenchantment. One direct consequence was the floundering of the joint trade union action with the CGT in 1980, once the communist trade union had again tightened up its ideological course, and its mobilization policy in favour of the political Left was in increasingly sharp contrast with the new attitude of the CFDT.

However, lessons still had to be learned from the new strategy. One of the top priorities of the policy of 'recentring' was the question of the reduction in working hours (Groux and Mouriaux, 1989, pp. 209-222; Branciard, 1990, pp. 307-309 and 328-330; Autrand, 1987). The introduction of the 35-hour week would be able to further reduce inequalities between workers and at the same time make it possible for them to have more control and a greater say in their own working conditions.

In 1981 the 39-hour week was indeed introduced, but at the initiative of the government and after negotiations on it had come to a standstill. In the mean time, the debate had begun within the CFDT as to whether a reduction in working hours was possible without a wage cut. Within the confederation it became evident that much resistance still existed in this respect and it was not accepted, until the 1985 congress, that wage compensation could be negotiated if the creation of new jobs and the protection of low wages could also be included. To the CFDT, the core of the proposal for a reduction in working hours was the question of the redistribution of labour, against the background of rapidly increasing unemployment.

The fact that the CFDT had not gone back to a purely defensive position with its 'recentring' became clear, especially after the rather unexpected victory of Mitterrand in the presidential elections of May 1981. Thanks to the numerous and multi-faceted relations between the CFDT and the Left-wing government, many of the confederation's policies also found their way into politics. In that respect, the Auroux laws were the best known example. Nonetheless, the CFDT remained faithful to its former anti-statist and decentralized concepts. After an initial period of strong confidence in the politics of the Left, the CFDT quickly became more wary. The confederation expressed its criticism, particularly with respect to nationalization, the nuclear programme, the lack of progress in the award of rights to the workers and especially the wages freeze. The launch of a strict austerity plan by the Mauroy government, in spring 1983, without much hope of a way out of the economic crisis, accelerated that process. The CFDT urgently wanted to shake off the label of being the trade union of the government. Moreover, the confederation was increasingly losing members. In order to avoid further marginalization, the CFDT now made a resolute choice in favour of participative trade unionism which wanted to play a constructive role in the transition phase in which capitalism found itself. For the first time also, the CFDT advocated a recruitment strategy which did not emphasize ideological commitment (Bevort, 1994).

During this 'second recentring' all attention was again focused on the company (Groux and Mouriaux, 1989, pp. 222-282; Tixier, 1992, pp. 303-316; Leggewie, 1988; Segrestin, 1985; Tixier, 1985). After all, it was also in the interests of the trade union movement to increase competitiveness and therefore the chances of the company surviving. The entrepreneur's right to exist was explicitly recognized. The individual development of the wage-earners contrasted with the economic objectives of the entrepreneur. In other words, in place of the class struggle, the

CFDT accepted the existence of two opposing logics, which together shared power in the company. The cooperation between the two, however, could be nothing if not discordant. In order to settle these disagreements and to work towards both the desired modernization of the company and the creation of employment, negotiation was the appropriate method in each case. Increasingly, during the 1980s, the CFDT would therefore enter into collective bargaining in the company and in individual branches of industry. Interprofessional agreements were less important to the CFDT.

This 'adaptation' went a long way towards responding to a number of questions posed by the employers. The ideas of participative management were especially important in that respect. Nonetheless, the CFDT expressly Stated that it did not want to take part in co-management in the company, along German lines. It negotiated and assumed its own responsibility, but did not see itself subordinate to the economic logic of the company. However, in practice that difference was more theoretical. In addition, the CFDT expressed an interest in the introduction of new technologies as a means of creating better working conditions. The CFDT also believed that flexibility was acceptable under certain conditions, even inescapable, if the trade union movement did not want to retreat back into the ivory towers of those with a permanent job. For many, particularly the young, the only type of work available was temporary and insecure. As far as flexibility was concerned, the CFDT took a full and committed role in negotiations in 1984 with the employers' organization, the Conseil National du Patronat Français (CNPF) (Weber, 1986). Ultimately, however, the CFDT did not sign an agreement - nor, incidentally, did the other confederations, with the exception of the executives' trade union, the CGC - because it offered too few collective guarantees.

This modernist course, despite all the changes, still fitted in perfectly with the basic thinking of the CFDT. The autonomy of the individual in easing his collective laments was still strongly emphasized. Through debate, open confrontation and negotiation, the individual in the company realized his potential and gained emancipation. What did at first sight change fairly radically, but in fact was also deeply rooted in the CFDT, was the attitude of the confederation to politics. The CFDT distanced itself from an outspoken commitment to the Left and no longer categorically ruled out contacts with other political parties. This went hand in hand with a certain degree of loyalty not to make an issue of disputes. Moreover, the strike tool became increasingly known as the last resort within the CFDT. However, despite all the ideological justification, the shroud of declining union membership still cast its shadow on this far-reaching recentring. Typical in this context was the continued persistent appeal from the textile federation Hacuitex (clothing, leather, textiles) to revolutionary trade unionism, in its decades of opposition to the confederal line.[14]

An overall project for the confederation was now no longer deemed necessary for the achievement of social changes. The term 'socialism' was replaced by 'co-management' (*autogestion* !) and that was now defined as the prospect of permanent development of the capacity for self-determination of individuals and groups. Capitalism was no longer fundamentally questioned. As a result of the advancing internationalization of the economy, the CFDT believed it had become impossible to continue advocating immediate self-management by the workers in their company, because of their incomplete knowledge of all the economic implications. The market was a factor in modernization and was termed a guarantee of individual choice, but had to be corrected. The minimum wage and the conclusion of collective agreements were some of the ways in which these corrections were made. The CFDT's most important objectives were to combat unemployment (*chômage zéro*), to encourage change in the labour process, and social guarantees for all. Specifically, the CFDT took a great interest in small and medium-sized companies, where wage conditions were often inferior to those in the large companies, which were the traditional strongholds of the French trade union movement. Furthermore, the confederation advocated improved services in the public sector and collective provision for the underprivileged, young people and immigrants. In brief, individual emancipation and collective aspects could indeed be reconciled (Schinko, 1991).

At the beginning of the 1990s, the CFDT felt forced to further broaden its modernization argument into a general plea for democracy, where values such as freedom, responsibility, solidarity, individual development, social justice and ecological awareness took pride of place.[15] In order to defend that democracy, the confederation joined in the struggle against any form of social exclusion, both of immigrants and young people and of the unemployed and the retired. However, that could also be perceived as neglect of the traditional categories on which the trade union movement had always stood, i.e. the permanently employed. The fact is that increased tensions within the CFDT led to the early resignation of Secretary-General Jean Kaspar in October 1992. Kaspar had only succeeded Edmond Maire in 1988. He was replaced by Nicole Notat, the first ever female head of a French confederation.

A second way in which the CFDT attempted to rebuild the strength of the trade union movement was by explicitly joining the anti-communist camp. As a proponent of a democratic trade union movement, the CFDT called for closer coordination between the democratic trade unions, which could eventually lead to the formation of cartels along Italian lines. Although the convergence between the various confederations was of a highly temporary nature, from the autumn of 1993 onwards a greater willingness to take part in joint action against the Right-wing government became evident. Finally, the CFDT saw Europe as a third level where collective solidarity could be put into practice. The confederation called for a strong Europe, taking initiatives itself with respect to energy, farming, transport and the harmonization of social achievements.

Force Ouvrière

The CGT-Force Ouvrière (FO) was founded in 1947-1948 as heir to the reformist tradition in the CGT (Bergounioux, 1982; *Liaisons sociales*, 1987, pp. 77-86; *Liaisons sociales*, 1992, pp. 43-50; Bergeron, 1988). Against the backdrop of violent strikes supported by communists in 1946 and 1947, a number of independent trade unions were formed, which forced the opposition minority within the CGT, based around the magazine Force Ouvrière, into explicit anti-communism. In December 1947 the reformist group left the CGT, against the wishes of its figure-head Léon Jouhaux. They hoped they would soon regain a majority over the communists, as had been the case during the inter-war period, in order to be able to continue the (reformist) CGT. However, this time they were disappointed. The separation was to be final and Force Ouvrière would remain the little brother of the big CGT. One of the reasons for this was that, at the time of the division between the CGT and the CGT-FO, the Fédération de l'Education Nationale (FEN), the union for teaching staff in the public sector, opted for independence. In April 1948, the founding congress of the CGT-FO was held in Paris. FO wanted to defend the freedom of the West against communism and this against the background of the Cold War. Precisely for this reason, the brand new confederation could count on the material and moral support of other Western European trade unions and especially of the American Federation of Labor.[16] However, FO was not a powerful new trade union. Its low level of mobilization was undoubtedly partially due to its hazy profile. The confederation gave priority to the conclusion of collective labour agreements as the prime means of action, but it also played an active part in the great strikes of 1953 and 1963.

Influenced particularly by external circumstances, it was not until the end of the 1950s that the FO gradually started to formulate its own profile. A not unimportant factor in this respect was the foundation of the Fifth Republic in 1958, which institutionalized a sharp contrast between the trade union movement on the one hand, and the State machinery on the other hand. This allowed the FO to put its trade union independence into practice. Its point of departure in doing so was the collective labour agreement, which was seen by the FO as an agreement between two independent partners and, in addition, an agreement which was only ratified in retrospect by the State. Starting in the mid-1950s, the FO became highly active in pursuing collective bargaining. The confederation felt doubly justified in taking this contractual route when, at the beginning of the 1960s, a CFTC majority was transformed into a CFDT majority. Right from the start, the FO was highly sceptical of the militant CFDT. Firstly, it had an ideological objection. Based on its explicit neutrality and laicism, the FO mistrusted the Catholic breeding ground of the CFDT's ideas. Moreover, the CFDT appeared in favour of active involvement by the trade union in socio-economic life, both at company level and in a broader, socio-political context. Not only was the FO itself too weak to fulfil such a role, but the confederation saw this route as a threat to its strongly avowed trade union independence. When the CFDT and the CGT concluded an agreement on joint trade union action in 1966, the anti-communist FO felt it had an even stronger case against the CFDT.

Still, the modernization of the CFDT was also reflected within the FO, especially in a socialist trend which advocated a greater social role for the trade union movement. The chemical federation of the FO lent particularly in this direction, but this minority fraction was not a direct threat to the politics of the confederation as such. In 1972, Maurice Labi, leader of the chemical federation, would make the transition to the CFDT with just a few members. The existence of this type of minority trend within the FO was not unusual, however, since the confederation had been composed of various groups right from its foundation. In addition to the majority of reformists and socialists, militant anarcho-trade unionist revolutionaries, Trotskyists and right-wing conservatives were also active within the FO. This ideological pluralism even consolidated internal cohesion within the confederation, since the various tendencies all had a vested interest in being able to remain under the umbrella of the FO. Partly because the FO chiefly had links with the Section Française de l'Internationale Ouvrière (SFIO), the traditional socialist party founded in 1905, the modernization of the socialist movement - leading to the foundation of the Parti Socialiste in 1971 - passed the FO by largely unnoticed. This only increased the freedom of every militant to choose his own political party and the complete independence of the trade union from the political parties.

Although, in 1968, the FO explicitly reacted against all forms of violence and any politicization of the social struggle, the infamous year of strikes also represented a breakthrough for Force Ouvrière. Not only did its Secretary-General André Bergeron come to the attention of the media - a weapon which he would continue to use from then on - the FO also keenly encouraged the contractual politics introduced by the government itself. This was all the more important because it involved annual negotiations in the public sector, where the FO was the strongest. In addition, the FO made haste to vote on most of the interprofessional agreements concluded in the wake of 1968. The FO also strengthened its position institutionally, through the system of equal representation in the management of the social security funds introduced after 1967.

During the 1970s, the FO drew the boundaries within which it believed the reformism of the confederation had to be located (Moss, 1984, pp. 281-283; Bergounioux, 1984; Branciard, 1982, pp. 299-318). Although its position depicted strong continuity, the wording of its vision was, in more ways than one, a tribute to its opposition to the 'revolutionary' confederations, the CGT and CFDT, and their political strategy during that period. The FO did not deny the existence of the class struggle. It did not believe, however, in a revolutionary change to these unequal industrial relations, especially since the Soviet Union also had an oligarchic system. To the FO, the contrast between labour and capital was one which continued to exist, both in a capitalist and in a socialist society. Paraphrasing Proudhon, the federation declared that this contradiction could never be resolved except in a totalitarian State, and this it rejected, preferring democracy above all. Consequently, genuine change was only possible for the FO in stages. Furthermore, a power factor was involved. The power of the employers and the State was counteracted by the power of the workers, who could only be organized by the (independent) trade union.

The action policy of the FO was directly grafted on to this ideological profile. In the first instance, the function of a trade union was defined as the defence of the material and moral interests of the workers. The trade union did not work for a social project, but for the progressive improvement of the situation of the wage-earners. In this respect, the FO stressed the retention and, if possible, the increase of purchasing power, the protection of the minimum wage-earners through the revaluation of social security payments, the promotion of economic growth and employment. Secondly, the confederation continually stressed the need to seek compromise through collective bargaining. Finally, the existing division of power between capital and labour also implied that the FO was averse to any attempt to integrate the trade union movement into the company or the State.

The break-up of the left-wing front for the Joint Government Programme was confirmation to the FO of its independent and reformist course, even though the contractual policy was somewhat pushed into a corner by the economic crisis. From November 1977 onwards, the confederation demanded a fifth week of paid holiday, followed a few months later by demands relating to, for example, solutions to youth unemployment and a reduction in working hours, which were all intended to spark off more collective bargaining. The rising membership of the FO in the 1970s and in particular the unexpected success of the confederation in the elections for the *Conseils de prud'hommes* on 12 December 1979 seemed to indicate that the FO was much more valued for the 'permanent revolution' which it generated than for its frequently alleged wish to maintain a doctrinal status quo.[17] The left-wing electoral victory of 1981 did not change the strategy of the FO. As always, the trade union remained critical of political policy, even though it was pursued by a party which could count on a good deal of support from within the FO. One of the FO's greatest objections to government policy at the beginning of the 1980s concerned the matter of direct participation by the employees in the company, as outlined in the Auroux laws. The principle of co-management was after all directly at odds with the 'balance of power' position of the trade union movement, which the FO defended. At the other extreme of its horizon as a social organization, from 1980 onwards the FO pledged its active moral and material support for the independent Polish trade union, Solidarity.

On 19 October 1983 Force Ouvrière scored a resounding victory in the elections for the administrators of social security. With 25.16 per cent of the votes, the FO became the second most powerful confederation in France, only just behind the CGT (28.25 per cent). There was also cause for optimism when the FO federation for education saw some Trotskyist militants arriving who had left the FEN. Since 1948, the FO and FEN had had a tacit agreement not to fish in each other's waters. However, several problems arose during these years, which would be a heavy burden on the operation of the FO in the long term. First and foremost, after 1981 there was a reduction in the number of interprofessional agreements concluded. In parallel to this, company agreements increased in importance, particularly after the Auroux laws. These trends threw a spanner in the works for a small confederation like the FO, which always wanted to negotiate at as high a level as possible. Moreover, the government's strict austerity policy, the pay freeze and the breakdown of negotiations in the public sector led to an altogether poorer climate for the contractual policy. The workers' spending power declined, which the FO said only served to increase unemployment. From time to time, the confederation called strikes to defuse the situation.

Despite the far-reaching changes in the economic sphere, the FO continued to repeat its well-known principles. Modernization measures put forward by the employers, such as flexibility and forms of participative management, fell on deaf ears within the FO, although heated debates were held within the confederation on such matters. In addition, there was the question of a successor to André Bergeron, who began his last period in office in 1984. Since becoming Secretary-General in 1963, Bergeron's paternal and conciliatory style had gradually made him the prime binding agent between the various tendencies in the confederation. His departure threatened to disrupt this cohesion. In 1989, Marc Blondel was elected Bergeron's successor, at a confusing congress, partly thanks to the support of the Trotskyists within the confederation. Blondel's option was to place great emphasis on the demands upheld by the trade union movement. However, there was never any question of breaking with the ideology of the FO, since the new Secretary-General was firm in placing collective action within the framework of a refusal to join in with the logic of the company and of the economy as a whole. The aim of the independent Force Ouvrière was still to conclude contracts. According to Blondel, all that was needed was increased militancy, as a result of the greater unwillingness of the partners in the dialogue, to encourage development of the existing positions. And it did not stop at theory, because from 1989 onwards, the FO resolutely refused to sign several interprofessional agreements, including those regarding the redistribution of labour, temporary work and the modernization of the public sector. The FO was thus approaching the position of the CGT, while the rift between it and the reformist CFDT was widening. On 24 October 1991, Force

Ouvrière organized a general strike and on 12 October 1993 the CGT and the FO held a joint manifestation.

Despite Marc Blondel's emphasis on continuity, at the beginning of the 1990s several developments became evident, which seem to point to an ideological redefinition of the FO. What is particularly striking is a greater mistrust by the freemason Blondel of the Christian trade unionism of both the CFTC and the CFDT, compared to the old-school socialist Bergeron. Moreover, at the seventeenth congress of the FO in 1992, the principle of subsidiarity was swept from the table, the main reasons being that it would give the free market more power and the public sector would be left out in the cold.[18] This was to be detrimental to public services, collective social protection, laicism, European social law and interprofessional and branch negotiations. Individual decisions were threatening to replace collective contracts. The fact that this subsidiarity - defined by the FO as: the highest authority must not expand its action to a field where a lower authority is more competent - is a principle of Catholic social doctrine was a thorn in the side of the neutral FO. In as far as this principle of subsidiarity found acceptance at European level, the FO took a more anti-European position.

The FO also defended its neutral beliefs when it came to education. Grants to private schools were resolutely rejected by the federation and the secular chool just as fiercely defended, particularly when ministerial bills wanted to change the existing situation. Another principle attacked by Blondel and co. was that of the redistribution of labour. According to the confederal leadership, that was no different from the story of Peter, who tore his cloak in two to share it with Paul, with the result that both of them got cold.[19] The answer to the current problems which the FO believed did have to be given was, however, still the same as it had always been in the confederation: free wage negotiations to encourage spending, which, in combination with public investment in the industry, would lead to an economic revival.

The Confédération Française des Travailleurs Chrétiens

The CFTC is the smallest of the four French confederations with a clear ideological identity (Mouriaux, 1992, pp. 38-41 and 44-46; *Liaisons sociales*, 1987, pp. 105-114; *Liaisons sociales*, 1992, pp. 103-109). The first denominational trade union in France was the Syndicat des Employés du Commerce et de l'Industrie, founded in 1887 and shortly followed by other federations of railway and textile workers. Right from the start, both independence from the employers and peaceful cooperation between employers and employees within the company characterized French Christian trade unionism. In 1919 the Confédération française des travailleurs chrétiens (CFTC) was founded, as a confederation of Catholic and protestant trade unions, with its power base among white collar workers and in the regions of Alsace and Lotharingen. The social doctrine of the church, as defined in the encyclical *Rerum Novarum* (1891), was the main source of inspiration. After 1936 the CFTC made headway among blue collar workers, mainly thanks to the actions of the Jeunesse Ouvrière Chrétienne (JOC). Even before the Second World War, a group of teachers in State education with a neutral background, united in the Syndicat général de l'éducation nationale (SGEN) from 1937 onwards, sowed the seeds for the subsequent rift in the CFTC.

In 1947 the CFTC deleted references to *Rerum Novarum* from its new statutes, but it did still appeal to the principles of Catholic social doctrine. Against the will of its leader Gaston Tessier, two tendencies developed within the CFTC, the smaller of which grew to a majority, transforming the confederation into the CFDT. Immediately after the final vote at the extraordinary congress of 1964, a group of delegates left the auditorium. They wanted to maintain Christian trade unionism as such and founded the CFTC-maintenue, initially attracting approximately between 7 and 10 per cent of the members. The opposition to the reorientation being pursued by the CFDT came primarily from the federations in mining, private education and banking, and from the regions of Alsace, Nord and Paris. After a long legal battle, the CFTC-maintenue was permitted to keep its old logo after 1971. Jacques Tessier, Gaston's son, became Secretary-General of the confederation in 1964 and was its president from 1970 to 1981.[20]

At its refounding congress in the autumn of 1965, the CFTC established in its programme that it wanted to retain the legacy of French Christian trade unionism and the principles of Christian social doctrine (Tessier, 1992, pp. 157-167). Its crux was the supremacy of the human being. To the CFTC, human dignity, based on a Biblical interpretation, came above everything. Equality, peace, fraternity and freedom were important guidelines for its trade union action and ideas. The confederation thus advocated the right of workers to share in the results, ownership and labour organization of the company. Any disputes were preferably settled by mediation, so that the legitimate right to strike only had to be used in exceptional cases. Industrial relations also had to be more than purely a power struggle; joint responsibility was indispensable to the smooth operation of the company. Any political commitment by the trade union was rejected. The 1965 programme was not new in the least. As early as the inter-war period, ideas about the company as a community and the eligibility of a contractual policy within the CFTC had been developed (Groux and Mouriaux, 1989, pp. 3-17). After 1965 the CFTC continued to navigate by these coordinates.

Like the FO, the reformist CFTC had the wind in its sails after 1968. With its calls for a gradual transformation of society and its categorical rejection of the marxist ideology of the class struggle, the CFTC was clearly identifying with the reformists, who, thanks to the rise in collective bargaining, increased in importance in the French trade union movement as a whole. Moreover, the CFTC's views on the dignity of the human being were not necessarily Christian and the relationship between the confederation and the church hierarchy became extremely tense, so that the impression could be created that the CFTC was essentially a reformist trade union. However, the CFTC unmistakably stressed its own ideology. The anti-marxism of the confederation was thus explicitly accounted for by Secretary-General Jean Bornard, at the 1975 congress, on the basis of its Christian background. The spiritual breeding ground of the CFTC was clearly expressed in its reports, for example the report on 'the company at the service of the people' (*l'entreprise au services des hommes*) at the congress in 1973, where the community of interests between employers and employees in the company was founded on the principles of fraternity and equality. However, it was particularly in its family policy that the confederation showed its traditional Christian colours: the family as the basic component of society. At every congress, pleas were made for a social status for mothers staying at home to bring up children. The subject of the revaluation of family benefits was also a constant one, often linked to a debate on moral decline in modern society. During his closing speech in 1975, Jacques Tessier raised the idea that at general elections parents should have the right to receive extra ballot papers in proportion to the number of minor children in their care ![21]

Despite a slight rise in membership in the 1970s, the CFTC remained a small trade union, with approximately a quarter of a million members. As far as its 1965 programme points were concerned, precious little was achieved. Despite the call from the young people for more dynamism, the style of the confederation remained extremely conservative and hardly modern. The CFTC ran the risk of fossilizing in its minority position. It did not begin to align its identity in any way with the new political and social themes until after the left-wing electoral victory of 1981. It was particularly critical of what it believed to be excessive State intervention in economic life through the nationalization programme. According to the CFTC, the State should only orientate the economy in a general way. Further decisions were better left to lower levels, according to the principle of subsidiarity. In the same context, the confederation also reacted strongly against favouring of State education to the detriment of free education. After 1982, the CFTC stepped into the breach for the freedom to choose a school, which implied a recognition of the right to exist and the equality of free education.

At the forty-fourth congress of the CFTC in November 1991, Alain Deleu, a teacher in free education, became Secretary-General of the confederation, succeeding Guy Drilleaud, who became the new president. At that congress the CFTC explicitly confirmed its Christian identity, after not having been very explicit in that respect in preceding years. Christian social doctrine, the supremacy of the human being, the family as the basic component of society, the importance of intermediate groups in society, each allowing the other to develop its own possibilities, justice and solidarity with minimum wage earners were cited as the basic principles. All forms of monopolism and totalitarianism were rejected. This redefinition was symbolized by a new logo, the dove of peace, and a new slogan - *la vie à défendre* - which also became the title of its magazine. This phrase also underlined the strong moralist dimension of the CFT options: 'the defence of life' referred indirectly to its condemnation of abortion, a problem which was dealt with explicitly in some programme points, for example in the refusal to pay for an abortion through health insurance. At trade union level, the CFTC put its view into practice, for example, by reacting against Sunday working and night work for women, which jeopardize family life, and advocated putting people and the family first in defining economic requirements.[22]

This explicit ideological redefinition by the CFTC was set against a certain revival of Christian thinking on social matters. The centenary celebrations of *Rerum Novarum* in 1991 gave this movement an added boost. The CFTC's position was chiefly on the restorationist side of the brand of Catholicism encouraged by Pope John Paul II. Papal encyclicals and pronouncements were explicitly quoted by the CFTC. The confederation itself saw the fall of communism as confirmation that it was correct in believing that 'spiritual dimensions' in society could not easily be suppressed, as was the case in the former Eastern Bloc. Still, the CFTC attempted to give its ideology a universal touch, by referring to human rights and 'human ecology'. Similarities with other reformist trade unions in the first half of the 1990s related mainly to the neo-liberal offensive against the State which, to the CFTC too, remained the only true guarantee of the preservation of collective solidarity.

The politics of ideological diversity

French trade unions have been seriously affected by declining membership since 1978. Numbers have fallen drastically in an hitherto unprecedented downwards spiral (Table 1.1). In 1995, fewer than 1 in 10 wage-earners are still members of a trade union. The number of non-union members elected to the works council continually increased and at the beginning of the 1990s amounted to more than a quarter (Table 1.3). Since the 1980s, a level of absenteeism of 50 per cent and over has not been unusual in elections to both the *Conseils de prud'hommes* (Table 1.2) and the administrative commissions of the social security funds.[23] The survival of the French trade unions as such is questioned (Rosanvallon, 1988; Noblecourt, 1990; Labbé and Croisat, 1992; Groux and Mouriaux, 1990; Geiger and Waller, 1993). In recent literature, ideology is singled out as one of the main guilty parties responsible for the legitimacy crisis (Labbé, 1994). Ideological motivation would only play a very general and vague role in anyone's decision to become a member of a trade union. Oppositional attitudes in the trade unions, internal divisions and disputes would contribute directly to the collapse in membership. Even the much-lauded '1968' would rather have led to a fall in trade union numbers than to an increase.

But is it not too simplistic to use ideology as an umbrella term for differences of opinion ? Surely it was precisely as a result of the relative ideological homogeneity under the confederal secretaries that cohesion came about between all the centrifugal and decentralizing forces within each confederation ? Conversely, ideological options were not a simple conscious choice, but the result of specific historical developments. Somebody's choice of a particular confederation did after all frequently imply a rejection of the ideology of one or more of the others. Anti-communism and anti-clericalism played an important role in this respect. One was a specific twentieth-century factor, the other was a legacy of the revolutionary ideal of 1789. If sociological, organizational and political factors are taken into account, the ideological choices certainly seem to have produced varying results in the post-war history of French trade unionism.

Table 1.1
Trade union membership in France since the Second World War (in thousands)

Year	Total number	CGT		CFDT		FO		Level of membership of wage-earners
1949	11 777	3 887	(33%)	403	(3,4%)	1 000	(8,4%)	48%
1958	13 178	1 624	(12,3%)	525	(3,9%)	1 009	(7,6%)	27%
1968	15 282	2 302	(15%)	686	(4,4%)	799	(5,2%)	30%
1973	17 175	2 340	(13,6%)	847	(4,9%)	862	(5%)	29%
1978	17 915	2 193	(12,2%)	881	(4,9%)	983	(5,4%)	29%
1983	18 050	1 622	(9%)	763	(4,2%)	1 100	(6%)	25%
1988	18 038	918	(5%)	536	(3%)	760	(4,2%)	17%
1991	18 818	700	(3,7%)	571	(3%)	640	(3,4%)	14%

The figures are fairly accurate for the CGT and the CFDT for the actual number of members (including retired people). The figures for the FO are clearly overestimated and patently unreliable from the beginning of the 1980s onwards. The CFTC, since the 1970s, has referred to a membership fluctuating around 250,000; see *Liaisons sociales*, 1992, p. 110.

Source: Labbé, 1994, pp. 146-148; based on information provided by the confederations themselves.

Table 1.2
Elections to the 'Conseils de prud'hommes'

	1979	1982	1987	1992
CGT	42,0%	36,8%	36,3%	33,4%
CFDT	23,3%	23,5%	23,0%	23,7%
FO	17,3%	17,8%	20,5%	20,4%
CFTC	7,1%	8,5%	8,3%	8,6%
Abstentions	36,8%	43,6%	55,8%	59,7%

The organization was reformed under the law of 18 January 1979. The percentages for the confederations are calculated as a function of the electors who expressed a preference. Civil servants do not participate in these elections.

Source: B. Bouhet a.o., 1992, pp. 865-872 and Mouriaux, 1994, p. 109.

Table 1.3
Results from the confederations in the elections to works councils

Year	Abstentions	CGT	CFDT	FO	CFTC	Non-unionized
1968-69	27,2%	45,2%	18,9%	7,4%	2,9%	15,0%
1973-74	28,7%	42,1%	19,0%	8,1%	2,7%	16,8%
1978-79	29,7%	36,8%	20,5%	10,0%	2,9%	18,5%
1983-84	31,0%	29,0%	21,4%	12,6%	3,9%	21,2%
1989-90	35,0%	25,0%	20,5%	12,0%	4,1%	26,5%

Source: Labbé a.o., 1991, pp. 219-220 and, for 1989-90, *Liaisons sociales*, 1992, pp. 216-218. See also Labbé, 1991.

France is continually referred to as having a militant trade union movement with a highly assertive character. This image was, however, chiefly applicable to the CGT and the CFDT and mainly restricted, in terms of time, to the 1960s and the first half of the 1970s, with the exception of a few specific moments before and after that time. Incidentally, strikes are hardly regulated by law in France and are generally short, because the confederations do not award strike pay. The militant industrial ideology of both confederations was forged primarily from the end of the 1950s onwards when the metalworkers formed the heart of the membership of the CGT and the CFDT. The conflict strategy of these confederations can probably be attributed in part to this sociological basis although, in order to put this thesis into perspective, we must not forget that miners from the Nord region also formed a substantial core part of the moderate (but much smaller) CFTC. Conversely, the continued increase in the public sector's share in the membership of the confederations since the 1970s perhaps explains the less militant policy pursued since then. After all, in this public sector there were newly-won rights to be defended while, in the private sector, closures and restructuring programmes discouraged the continuation of hard-line collective actions. The relative success of the FO during the 1980s can, in the same context, largely be attributed to the fact that the FO was traditionally strong in the tertiary sector and among public officials.

The loss of the group of industrial workers as the glue holding together the class whose interests were ultimately defended by the trade unions presented major problems for the confederations (Verret, 1995; Noiriel, 1990; Terrail, 1990). To whom did they now turn - to specific groups or to an undifferentiated but increasingly diverse working class? The most important of these 'new' categories were women (Maruani, 1979; Jenson, 1984 and 1990). The CGT had since the Second World War always defended female wage labour, stressing the equal position of women to men, at home as well as at work. At the same time the confederation had never stopped considering women to be above all mothers and therefore had always pleaded for improved provisions for maternity leave, childcare and early retirement. In the CFDT *autogestionnaire*, in contrast, in the late 1960s female militants pushed through the view that the persisting subordinate position of women to men was above all due to long-standing patterns of domination, especially in the family. If inequality in the labour market was to be changed, the social position of women as such had to change first. It must be stressed that this view was not embraced wholeheartedly by the CFDT, rather the contrary. Yet, under the influence of a militant women's movement, both the CFDT and the CGT were feminized to an important extent in the course of the 1970s. Strategies did differ, however. The CGT argued that the women's struggle and the class struggle went hand in hand and that the battle must be fought on both fronts. Once the Union of the Left broke down, however, this argument was used to denounce women's pleas for a more democratic unionism; women were alleged to focus insufficiently on the class struggle. Symbolically, in 1982 the male leadership of the CGT took editorial control of the women's magazine *Antoinette*, in existence since 1955 and which would disappear in 1989. The CFDT of the 1970s, on the other hand, advocated an approach to the women's struggle beyond immediate workplace concerns, asking for better childcare, education and training and access to contraception and abortion. But the CFDT too changed its position after 1978 and abandoned the society-wide approach.

In the 1980s the CFDT simply dropped feminism. The CGT returned to its former position, insisting on women's economic independence. Neither confederation, therefore, paid much attention to the new economic reality of women being increasingly assigned part-time and temporary jobs. Similar problems of ambiguously incorporating diverse interests can be detected in the union's attitudes to foreign workers. Except for a brief period of active CFDT involvement in the 1970s, the French trade union movement has never taken a great interest in immigrant workers (Reid, 1993). Force Ouvrière even tried to make foreign employees as 'invisible' as possible in the union. The new social movements faced the same indifference among the trade unions. Whereas in particular the campaigns against nuclear energy and nuclear arms could formerly rely on CFDT support, under the Mitterand presidency the mobilization curves of the labour movement and the new social movements diverged considerably (Duyvendak, 1994). Concerning vocational training for the youth in the 1990s, the CGT was reluctant to encourage training in the company, whereas the CFDT was much more pragmatic, putting economic and social efficiency first (Lefresne, 1995). Thus, it seems the French trade unions have not renounced the unity of their target public.

What did change considerably over time, was the interunion cooperation. For both the CGT and the CFDT the late 1960s and 1970s were a period of active joint trade union action, although both maintained their own objectives. The CGT wanted organizational unity for the trade union movement, while the CFDT put all its efforts into preserving its independence and keeping a safe ideological distance from the CGT. When these tensions came to a head in the split of 1978, in the wake of the events involving Solidarity in Poland, the CGT became increasingly isolated from the CFDT, the FO and the CFTC, which all embraced Walesa and his followers for reasons of their own. Interunion rivalry was restored. In 1985/86 the FEN launched a proposal for the reshaping of the trade union landscape, but it had little in the way of specific consequences. The reformism which all confederations professed, with the exception of the CGT, was extremely diverse. Moreover, the strikes of *les coordinations* proved that the fragmentation of working class interests still continued. Although Italian-style cartel-formation, preserving the individuality of each organization, has been openly called for in recent years, the ideological differences still seem to outweigh the convergence. Only at company level cooperation between the trade unions is common practice.

The Auroux laws of 1982 occupied a special place in the development of industrial relations in France. They confirmed the strategy of both the CGT and the CFDT to pursue social action chiefly at company level. Unfortunately, the reforms came at a time when the influence of both confederations was waning and their industrial approach was questioned. In parallel with the attempt on the part of the State to decentralize industrial relations - ideologically entirely in line with the self-management concepts of the CFDT - the trade unions began, however, to give priority particularly to interprofessional and branch agreements, even though negotiations at these levels were often extremely difficult. Even on the eve of impending European unification and looking towards the third millennium, the French State remained the dominant factor in regulating social relations. This also had upward effects. Although the FO, CFTC and CFDT had been advocating European solutions on paper for decades, these same confederations showed little inclination to take action at international level.

Although '1968' has become the symbol of what is thought to be typically French revolutionary trade unionism, the most dramatic transformations in the French trade union movement took place mainly during the period from about 1974 to 1985. The rise of joint trade union action between the two large French confederations held the promise of a major political breakthrough with positive effects for industrial relations and workers' interests in particular. The CGT joined in with this unified strategy on the basis of its communist ideals of doing away with capitalism and the class struggle once and for all. The CFDT, with its Catholic background, was mainly inspired by ideas about social benefit and a fairer redistribution of income, together with an awareness of its duty to seek solutions to existing inequalities. When it became clear in the mid-1980s that this politicisation strategy had failed, the public domain in which the trade unions operated looked very different from that of a decade before. However, the CGT did not end its unique relationship with the PCF, it rather strengthened it, although the party dwindled much more quickly than the trade union. By the early 1990s the PCF was only a marginal political party, while the CGT was still the largest confederation in France, despite a massive fall in membership.

In the course of the 1980s, the CFDT became increasingly associated with the (often) ruling PS, although the union became increasingly critical, ideologically speaking, of political power. This fitted in with the anti-statist Catholic trade union culture of the CFDT, which distanced itself both from any form of State centralism along Soviet lines and from all forms of social-democratic interventionism. From that point of view, the principle of subsidiarity and the self-management concept in the utopian model of the basic Christian communities took on a more neutral, less politically charged significance. The CFDT was no longer interested in political changes to the existing society. From then on, it focused on the contractual middle course of gradually regulating a democratic, decentralized, free and equal society. Both the FO and the CFTC could plead that they had already plotted that course, even if it was true that the reformism of one of them was based on little more than a categorical rejection of the marxist doctrine of the class struggle, while that of the other saw reformism as a necessary consequence of its Christian principles of fraternity and a community of interests. At any rate, while the post-war system of trade union pressure on politicians via national strikes, rounds of negotiations or informal contacts falls increasingly into disuse, the trade unions seem to have little choice but to redefine their audience, their goals and their strategy.

Notes

1. I wish to thank René Mouriaux and Patrick Pasture for their comments on a first draft of this chapter.
2. Ross, 1982 is essential reading for the postwar history of the CGT, but is nonetheless insufficient as a result of an overly rigid analysis using the term 'strategy': the coherence of the confederal policy is so strongly expressed that the CGT is sometimes endowed with a greater role than it really had; e.g. see the chapter on May 1968.
3. The manual for this theory is the *Traité marxiste d'économie politique. Le capitalisme monopoliste d'Etat*, 2 volumes, Editions Sociales, Paris, 1971.
4. Report of the 38th congress of the CGT, *Le Peuple*, nos. 893-894 (1982). On the membership of the CGT, see *Liaisons sociales*, 1992, pp. 16-20; on the strike activity, see *Liaisons sociales*, 1991, pp. 88-90 and Mouriaux, 1992, pp. 98-99.
5. Report of the 40th congress of the CGT, *CGT-Informations*, no. 31 (1979); Mouriaux, 1982, pp. 118-121; Ross, 1982a, pp. 280-310; Ross, 1982b, pp. 60-64; Ross, 1984, pp. 74-79; Moss, 1984, pp. 275-280.
6. Report of the 41st congress of the CGT, *Le Peuple*, nos. 1135-1137 (1982).

7. *Liaisons sociales*, 1987, pp. 14-19 gives a detailed chronology of the CGT during the 1980s. Figures on company agreements in Mouriaux, 1992, pp. 104-107 and in *Liaisons sociales*, 1991, pp. 94-100; see also Jansen a.o., 1986.
8. Quoted by M. Noblecourt in *Le Monde*, 29 November 1985; report of the 42nd congress of the CGT, *Le Peuple*, nos. 1207-1209 (1985).
9. Report of the 44th congress of the CGT, *Le Peuple*, nos. 1346-1348 (1992).
10. *Le Peuple*, nos. 1373-1374 (1993).
11. Report of the 34th congress of the CFDT, *Syndicalisme CFDT*, no. 1162 (1967): response of E. Descamps to questions.
12. Report of the 37th congress of the CFDT, *Syndicalisme CFDT*, no. 1603 (1976).
13. Report of the 38th congress of the CFDT, *Syndicalisme-hebdo*, no. 1757 (1979).
14. Report of the 40th congress of the CFDT, *Syndcalisme CFDT*, no. 2071 (1985); report of the 41st congress of the CFDT, *Syndicalisme CFDT*, no. 2238 (1988).
15. Report of the 42nd congress of the CFDT, *Syndcalisme CFDT*, no. 2402 (1992).
16. Although substantial, American support was not a decisive factor in the breaking away of FO; see Kantrowitz, 1978 and MacShane, 1992, pp. 253-277.
17. *Immobilisme doctrinal ou révolution permanente*, special issue of *FO Hebdo*, supplement to no. 1596 (1979); see also Jansen a.o. (1986), pp. 163-165 and 236-243.
18. Report of the 17th congress of the FO, *FO Hebdo*, no. 2125 (1992); see also nos. 2145 and 2146; Goetschy and Rozenblatt, 1992, p. 410 and Mouriaux, 1992, pp. 36-38.
19. *FO Hebdo*, no. 2143 (1993), editorial by Marc Blondel.
20. Tessier, 1987 gives the view of the CFTC-maintenue on the split of 1964. Tessier, 1992 quotes documents in abundance which supposedly demonstrate that the explicit support of the Church was the main factor in the creation of the CFDT. This position is untenable; see Pasture, 1994, pp. 5-20.
21. *Syndicalisme CFTC*, no. 108 (1975) and Tessier, 1992, p. 279.
22. Report of the 44th congress of the CFTC (1990); report of the 45th congress of the CFTC (1993); *La vie à défendre. La magazine de la CFTC; Mensuel du bureau d'études de la CFTC*, no. 10 (September-October 1993).
23. For the elections to the social security funds, see Labbé a.o., 1991, pp. 180-192.

References

Aubert, V., a.o. (1985), *La Forteresse enseignante. La Fédération de l'Education nationale*, Fayard, Paris.

Autrand, A. (1987), *Les syndicats et le temps de travail. Revendications confédérales et pratiques des acteurs dans trois secteurs industriels*, CRESSY, Sceaux.

Batsch, L. (1987), *La FEN au tournant. De l'autonomie à la recomposition, 1947-1987*, La Brèche, Montreuil-sous-Bois.

Bergeron, A. (1988), *Tant qu'il y aura du grain à moudre*, Robert Laffont, Paris.

Bergounioux, A. (1982), *Force Ouvrière*, Que sais-je, Presses Universitaires de France, Paris.

Bergounioux, A. (1984), 'La stratégie syndicale de la CGT-FO', in Kesselman, M. and Groux, G. (eds.), *1968-1982*, pp. 113-125.

Bevort, A. (1994), 'Le syndicalisme français et la logique du recrutement sélectif: le cas de la CFTC-CFDT', *Le Mouvement social*, no. 169, pp. 109-136.

Bouhet, B., Groux, G., Mouriaux, R. and Pernot, J.-M. (1992), 'Les élections prud'homales', *Revue française de science politique*, vol. 42, no. 5, pp. 865-872.

Branciard, M. (1982), *Syndicats et partis. Autonomie ou dépendance, 2: 1947-1981*, Syros, Paris.

Branciard, M. (1990), *Histoire de la CFDT. Soixante-dix ans d'action syndicale*, La Découverte, Paris.

Bridgford, J. (1989), 'The Events of May: Consequences for industrial relations in France', in Hanley, D. and Kerr, A.P. (eds.), *May 1968: Coming of Age*, Macmillan, Basingstoke, pp. 100-116.

Bridgford, J. (1991), *The Politics of French Trade Unionism. Party-Union Relations at the Time of the Union of the Left*, Leicester University Press, Leicester/London/New York.

Capdevielle, J. and Mouriaux, R. (1988), *Mai 1968. L'entre-deux de la modernité. Histoire de trente ans*, Presses de la Fondation Nationale des Sciences Politiques, Paris.

Dufour, C. (1992), 'France', in IRES (ed.), *Syndicalismes. Dynamique des relations professionnelles*, Dunod, Paris, pp. 323-352.

Duyvendak, J.W. (1994), *Le poids du politique. Nouveaux mouvements sociaux en France*, L'Harmattan, Paris.

Frachon, B. (1967-69), *Au rythme des jours*, 2 vols., Editions sociales, Paris.

Geiger, P. and Waller, R. (1993), *Que reste-t il du syndicalisme ? Les syndicats dans les entreprises en France*, Ecole Nationale Supérieure des Mines de Paris.

Georgi, F. (1995), *L'Invention de la CFDT, 1957-1970. Syndicalisme, catholicisme et politique dans la France de l'expansion*, Editions de l'Atelier/CNRS Editions, Paris.

Goetschy, J. and Rozenblatt, P. (1992), 'France: The industrial relations system at a turning point ?', in Ferner, A. and Hyman, R. (eds.), *Industrial Relations in the New Europe*, Blackwell, Oxford, pp. 404-444.

Groux, G. and Mouriaux, R. (1989), *La CFDT*, Economica, Paris.

Groux, G. and Mouriaux, R. (1990), 'Le cas français', in Bibes, G. and Mouriaux, R. (eds.), *Les syndicats européens à l'épreuve*, Fondation nationale des sciences politiques, Paris, pp. 49-68.

Groux, G. and Mouriaux, R. (1991), *La CGT. Crises et alternatives*, Economica, Paris.

Hamon, H. and Rotman, P. (1984), *La deuxième Gauche. Histoire intellectuelle et politique de la CFDT*, Seuil, Paris.

Harmel, C. (1982), *La Confédération Générale du Travail 1947-1981*, Que sais-je, Presses Universitaires de France, Paris.

Hassenteufel, P. (1991), 'Pratiques représentatives et construction identitaire, une approche des coordinations', *Revue française de science politique*, vol. 41, no. 1, pp. 5-27.

Howell, C. (1989), *Regulating Labor: The State and Industrial Relations Reform in Postwar France*, Ph.D. thesis, Yale University.

Jansen, P., Kissler, L., a.o. (1986), *Gewerkschaften in Frankreich. Geschichte, Organisation, Programmatik*, Campus Verlag, Frankfurt/New York.

Jenson, J. (1984), 'Le problème des femmes', in Kesselman, M. and Groux, G. (eds.), *1968-1982*, pp. 203-223.

Jenson, J. (1990), 'Representations of difference: The varieties of French feminism', *New Left Review*, vol. 30, no. 180, pp. 127-160.

Kantrowitz, J. (1978), 'L'influence américaine sur Force Ouvrière: mythe ou réalité ?', *Revue française de science politique*, vol. 28, pp. 717-739.

Kergoat, J. (1984), 'De la crise économique à la victoire électorale de la Gauche. Réactions ouvrières et politiques syndicales', in Kesselman, M. and Groux, G. (eds.), *1968-1982*, pp. 337-365.
Kesselman, M. and Groux, G. (eds.) (1984), *1968-1982. Le mouvement ouvrier français. Crise économique et changement politique*, Editions Ouvrières, Paris.
Labbé, D., Bevort, A. and Croisat, M. (1991), *Effectifs, audience et structures syndicales en France depuis 1945 (le cas de la CTFC-CFDT)*, CERAT, Grenoble.
Labbé, D. (1991), *Vingt-deux ans d'élections aux comités d'entreprise (1966-67, 1987-88)*, CERAT, Grenoble.
Labbé, D. and Croisat, M. (1992), *La fin des syndicats ?*, L'Harmattan, Paris.
Labbé, D. (1994), 'Trade unionism in France since the Second World War', *West European Politics*, vol. 17, no. 1, pp. 146-168.
Lazar, M. (1992), *Maisons rouges. Les partis communistes français et italien de la Libération à nos jours*, Aubier, Paris.
Le Crom, J.-P. (1995), *Syndicats nous voilà ! Vichy et le corporatisme*, Editions de l'Atelier, Paris.
Lefresne, F. (1995), 'Les dispositifs d'insertion professionnelle des jeunes en France', *La Revue de l'IRES*, no. 17, pp. 97-133.
Leggewie, C. (1988), 'Französische Gewerkschaften auf dem Weg in die postindustrielle Gesellschaft ?', in Müller-Jentsch, W. (ed.), *Zukunft der Gewerkschaften. Ein internationaler Vergleich*, Campus Verlag, Frankfurt/New York, pp. 130-159.
Lewis, S.C. (1987), *Unions and Socialism. The CFDT and the Reconstruction of the French Left*, Massachussets Institute of Technology, Cambridge.
Liaisons sociales (1987), no. 10071, special issue *Syndicats,2: Organisations syndicales*.
Liaisons sociales (1991), no. 10995, special issue *Audience syndicale. Fonction des syndicats*.
Liaisons sociales (1992), no. 11320, special issue *Les organisations syndicales*.
MacShane, D. (1992), *International Labour and the Origins of the Cold War*, Clarendon Press, Oxford.
Maruani, M. (1979), *Les syndicats à l'épreuve du féminisme*, Syros, Paris.
Moss, B.H. (1984), 'Idéologie et politique revendicative. Les fédérations CGT, FO, CFDT', in Kesselman, M. and Groux, G. (eds.), *1968-1982*, pp. 275-293.
Mouriaux, R. (1982), *La CGT*, Seuil, Paris.
Mouriaux, R. (1984), 'La CFDT: de l'Union des forces populaires à la réussite du changement social', in Kesselmann, M. and Groux, G. (eds.), *1968-1982*, pp. 93-112.
Mouriaux, R. (1992), *Le syndicalisme en France*, Que sais-je, Presses Universitaires de France, Paris.
Mouriaux, R. (1994), *Le syndicalisme en France depuis 1945*, La Découverte, Paris.
Noblecourt, M. (1990), *Les syndicats en questions*, Editions ouvrières, Paris.
Noiriel, G. (1990), *Workers in French Society in the 19th and 20th Centuries*, Berg, New York/Oxford/Munich.
Pasture, P. (1994), *Christian Trade Unionism in Europe Since 1968. Tensions Between Identity and Practice*, Avebury, Aldershot.
Reid, D. (1993), 'The Politics of immigrant workers in twentieth-century France', in Guerin-Gonzales, C. and Strikwerda, C. (eds.), *The Politics of Immigrant Workers. Labor Activism and Migration in the World Economy since 1830*, Holmes & Meier, New York/London, pp. 245-277.

Rosanvallon, P. (1988), *La question syndicale: histoire et avenir d'une forme sociale*, Calmann-Lévy, Paris.

Rosanvallon, P. (1990), *L'État en France de 1789 à nos jours*, Seuil, Paris.

Rose, M.J. (1989), 'Les syndicats français, le jacobinisme économique et 1992', *Sociologie du travail*, no. 1, pp. 1-28.

Ross, G. (1982a), *Workers and Communists in France. From Popular Front to Eurocommunism*, University of California Press, Berkeley.

Ross, G. (1982b), 'The perils of politics: French unions and the crisis of the 1970s', in Lange, P., Ross, G. and Vannicelli, M. (eds.), *Unions, Change and Crisis: French and Italian Union Strategy and the Political Economy, 1945-1980*, George Allen & Unwin, London, pp. 13-93.

Ross, G. (1984), 'La CGT: crise économique et changement politique', in Kesselman, M. and Groux, G. (eds.), *1968-1982*, pp. 67-91.

Schinko, R. (1991), Die französische Gewerkschaft CFDT. Ihre interne *Krisenperzeption, das neue Programm und seine zukünftigen Realisierungschance*, Hans-Böckler-Stiftung, Düsseldorf.

Segrestin, D. (1985), 'Trade unions versus power: The French socialist experience after 1981', in Spyropoulos, G. (ed.), *Trade Unions in a Changing Europe*, European Centre for Work and Society, Maastricht, pp. 75-94.

Terrail, J.P. (1990), *Destins ouvriers. La fin d'une classe?*, Presses Universitaires de France, Paris.

Tessier, J. (1987), *La CFTC. Comment fut maintenu le syndicalisme chrétien*, Fayard, Paris.

Tessier, J. (1992), *Marxisme ou doctrine sociale chrétienne? Trente années de confrontation en France*, Fayard, Paris.

Thibault, M.-N. (1988), *Les militantes de la CFDT et le féminisme (1964-1982)*, CNRS-ATP Femmes, Paris.

Tixier, P.E. (1985), 'Participative management and labour unions in France', in Spyropoulos, G. (ed.), *Trade Unions in a Changing Workplace*, European Centre for Work and Society, Maastricht, pp. 49-62.

Tixier, P.E. (1992), *Mutation ou déclin du syndicalisme? Le cas de la CFDT*, Presses Universitaires de France, Paris.

Verret, M. (1995), *Chevilles ouvrières*, Editions de l'Atelier, Paris.

Vignaux, P. (1980), *De la CFTC à la CFDT: syndicalisme et socialisme. 'Reconstruction' (1946-1972)*, Editions ouvrières, Paris.

Weber, H. (1986), *Le Parti des patrons: le CNPF (1946-1986)*, Seuil, Paris.

Weiss, F. (1988), *Les relations du travail en France*, 2 vols., Cujas, Paris.

Zimmerman, B. (1991), 'Les premiers mai de la CFTC/CFDT: logique identitaire et pratique syndicale', *Le Mouvement social*, no. 157, pp. 87-102.

2 Between identity and pragmatism: Italian trade unionism on its way to Europe

Giampiero Bianchi

Introduction

On the face of it, the 'lost perspective' issue does not seem to be any different in Italy compared with other West European countries.[1] Trade unions, who until recently held the monopoly of representation, and who were recognized as bastions with the unassailable right to speak on behalf of all employees, have now lost a lot of their influence. In Italy too, the technological revolution has redefined the labour issue, and the living conditions of the working population are no longer rated as the most pressing social problem. Conservation of the environment, access to and control of information, for example, are now the important social issues. They are placed in a different setting, outside the domain of the struggle for the distribution of income and power within the modern company and the various production sectors. Furthermore, the old ideological contrasts are disappearing even in Italy.

The crisis inside the Italian trade movement seems to bear many points of resemblance to the crises observed elsewhere. However, the Italian situation also has its very own characteristics. The idea of social consensus was hardly thrown into disrepute at the end of the 1960s, since it had even failed to take root in Italy in the first place. What actually happened at that time was an upsurge of the traditional Italian inclination to protest, to overturn the establishment and eventually even to commit terrorism - effectively a return to the revolutionary model of Bakunin. Even so, the crisis did not culminate in a revolution. Since the crisis failed to find a social outlet, an attempt was made to resolve it in a more traditional, political way of smooth transformation, which ended in a project of coalition on a large scale, the so-called 'historical compromise'. Italy also knew a political period commonly known as *neo-liberista* or *neo-liberale*,[2] but it started very late. In fact, it only took hold at the time of the most recent parliamentary elections in 1994.

Because the lost perspective issue manifests itself in a clearly different way in Italy compared with other industrialized nations, we must start with a brief description of the socio-economic and political background, and dwell on the basic trends of the industrialization and democratization process, which had started in the beginning of the nineteenth century. Italy has indeed risen from its former position of 'latecomer' on the road to industrialization to the place of 'first comer' at the heart of the most developed economies - so much so that it has been allowed to join the league of the seven most industrialized countries of the world. Once the period of protectionism and a dramatic collapse of international trade during the two world wars was closed off, things developed rapidly. It actually started from the moment Italy was able to go along with the tide of innovations flooding the country after it became more involved in international trade. The speed of the economic miracle contributed to the big problems resulting from such an intense process. Phases of extreme unlimited growth alternated with sudden crises of variable proportions.

Guido Sapelli sums up the development of the Italian economy in this period as follows. In the 1950s, until the mid-1960s, there was development without inflation, with a modest growth of national consumption and large investments and profits, supported by export. After 1963, cycles of crisis and recovery occurred in rapid succession. From 1974 onwards the Italian economy stepped from a phase of salary increases, crumbling profits, decreasing investments and faltering business levels into a dangerous period of stagnation and inflation, combined with a deficit on the balance of trade and payments. The 1980s, however, are characterized by a decrease in salaries, employment and the burden of debt, and a recovery of profits and investments. From then onwards, the process of integration into Europe was a force to be reckoned with (Sapelli, 1994). The current debate and recent measures to drive back the overall deficit of the public sector, and the simultaneous decrease of the salary demands (obvious from the analysis for the collective agreements between government, trade unions and employers for the years 1991 to 1993 inclusive) are still too recent to allow one to anticipate how the economy and the political scene will handle the new challenge of international integration.

Next to these economic developments, the political evolution needs to be taken into account. During the entire post-war period until the most recent parliamentary elections, politics have had priority in Italy above civil society. In particular, politics have had an impact on the position and actions of trade unions, be it in varying ways and degrees (Farneti, 1979). Italy was in that sense a real party state, which later evolved into a state governed by the parties (Scoppola, 1990; Ginzburg, 1988; Lanaro, 1992). The main implication was that no important decision could be made, not even on economy or on social matters, without the approval, agreement and protection of the parties. It did not mean, however, that the parties were not under pressure from groups, clients and individuals when making decisions - far from it.

It all forms part of what can be regarded as the central problem in the Italian political system during the entire period. The problem has been dissected and studied under different names - political stagnation, incomplete two-party system, consociativism, neo-transformism, constitutional compromise, etc. In the interest of our research we should note that the two mass parties and the powers supporting those two parties managed to establish a modus vivendi, leading to a total and unassailable exercise of power. This hard rule could not be broken by anyone, not even the unions. In a number of areas (e.g. welfare provisions) the political class exercised a real prerogative, but its influence was also important in other domains.

The 1940s and 1950s: influence of national changes on trade union ideology and practice

The short unitary intermezzo

After the second World War, Italy promptly joined the international trade scene. All at once, the trade union movement had to face up to a new reality, an awesome task for which there were no precedents (Romani, 1988a, pp. 50-51; Horowitz, 1966, pp. 7-21). The Italian trade union movement had always been weak and strongly influenced by political ideologies and the factions embodying them (the socialist party, the Catholic movement, the anarchist-libertarian movement, and the communist party). At first, an organizational pluralism had existed, swiftly replaced by a compulsory and statutory trade union system in the trail of the national fascist party, which had eliminated the other parties and democracy itself for a period of twenty years.

Spurred on by the dramatic state of the country (there was little leeway for trade union policies over and above securing the guaranteed subsistence level), and, more importantly, encouraged by a new political situation which found all anti-fascist parties united in one government, the movement sprung into action. The acknowledged representatives of the most important factions within the trade union movement (viz. the communist, Christian-democratic and socialist factions) signed a 'Pact of trade union unity' in June 1944, with the intent of setting up a joint organization. It was a concise text which explicitly postponed the unsolved 'problems of a general nature' to a later date.[3] The decisive influence of the political parties on the new trade union was acknowledged in the text, and also apparent from the presence of political currents within the trade union. This agreement, justified by the signatories in a variety of ways, led to the only, brief Italian experience of a unitary trade union.

The ideological themes and strategic orientations of this unity would never be more closely defined, not even when the constitution of the new confederation was drawn up,[4] nor during its first national congress in Florence in May 1947. During the congress, big differences in opinion came to a head, among other things about the legitimacy of political strikes and the acceptability of fringe organizations like the Christian Associations of Italian Workers (Associazioni Cristiane dei Lavoratori italiani, ACLI) which represented the Catholic labourers.[5] The general feeling within the General Confederation of Italian Labour (Confederazione Generale Italiana del Lavoro, CGIL) was constantly disturbed by instances of intolerance and intimidation - power struggles and compromises prevailed (Lanzardo, 1989; Fondazione UIL, 1989; Carbognin and Paganelli, 1981; Carera, 1979).

As work began after the start of the post-war period on real reconstruction and therefore, the actual determination of economic, social and incomes policy, the contradictions became increasingly pronounced. The first marked clash took place in June 1946. Communists and socialists came out in favour of a strong impulse in public works, reduction of employment, higher taxes and universal pay increases. The Christian-democrats, however, made the fight against inflation and the protection of pay and employment their priorities. Eventually most of the socialist-communist viewpoint won through, but the episode was significant for the future (Galli, 1969, pp. 227-232). Shortly afterwards, the Marshall plan transformed the mainly latent controversy into two irreconcilable sides. On the one hand, the communist and socialist majority clearly opposed all union involvement with the European and Atlantic integration process. The Christian and secular reformist unionists, on the other hand, were prepared to cooperate with the implementation of the plan.[6] It was the beginning of a continuous dialogue between Italian and Western trade union leaders.

The eventual split in the CGIL came about in the Summer of 1948, after a general political strike called because of the assassination attempt on Palmiro Togliatti, leader of the Italian Communist Party, the PCI. After three unsettled months, the Catholic unionists supported by ACLI, which had called for a new non-denominational trade union, set up a new confederation, the Libera CGIL (Free CGIL). This organization was based on the principles of 'free and democratic' trade unionism and self-determination of the industrial categories (Saba & Bianchi, 1990). In the Spring of the following year, the small social-democratic and lay groups left the CGIL. They founded the Italian Labour Federation, FIL (Federazione Italiana del Lavoro). After long negotiations the leadership of the FIL decided to link up with the Libera CGIL and with other independent industrial unions in the Italian Confederation of Workers' Unions (Confederazione Italiana Sindacati Lavoratori, CISL). However, a section of the FIL did not back the amalgamation and founded the Union of Italian Labour (Unione Italiana del Lavoro, UIL), together with other small socialist trade union groups which had left the CGIL, and formerly left-wing fascist trade unionists (Turone, 1981; Forbice, 1981; Simoncini, 1986). The involvement of the USA trade union movement and government played an important role in these events, even though the Americans could not entirely achieve their dream of a united 'free' trade union movement against the communists (Romero, 1993). In 1950, Italy consequently returned to the original situation of trade union pluralism, with an organizational structure (CGIL, CISL and UIL) that was to remain largely unchanged to the present day.

CGIL, CISL and UIL facing up to big change

At the beginning of the 1950s, the Italian trade union movement for the first time in its existence had to deal with problems relating to rapid industrial development and the end of under-development. These were problems for which it was unprepared, mainly because the union movement was new to the collective bargaining process (Strinati, 1992; Starita, 1992). The same was true for the employers as well as for the political and social institutions. The CISL and the UIL were in favour of the main Atlantic and European choices (economic integration, monetary stability and production growth). The CGIL, however, was convinced of the inevitable decline and the unavoidable impoverishment of Italian capitalism, and it resisted any economic or social opening to the West. Together with the left-wing political opposition, it organized large-scale social and political campaigns.

Influenced by contacts with the American trade union movement in particular, the CISL, though largely consisting of Catholics, distanced itself from Catholic tradition and presented itself as a free and independent trade union. Ideologically, it adopted a pronounced personalistic manifesto, with human rights and workers' rights as key themes (Ciampani, 1991). It advocated trade union participation and gave priority to individuals and their support systems within the community, rather than to the role of the State. Its organization was based on the autonomy of industrial categories. This view was in fact more congruent with Catholic trade union tradition than CISL leaders of that time seemed to make out (Saba, 1980, pp. 3-23).

The CISL manifesto was presented at the first General Council in June 1950. In the CISL's view, Italy was definitely going through the universal capitalist transformation process, and trade unions, the government and business had to cooperate. The democratic State was to give the social forces free rein, and to ascertain that all parties concerned could fully participate in decision-making 'without dangerously restrictive legislation'.[7] With this last statement, the CISL resolutely rejected any form of legal regulation of trade union life and collective bargaining as laid down in the democratic Constitution (Izar, 1979). It equally denounced Catholic corporate tradition. The original character of the CISL was particularly obvious as far as collective bargaining was concerned (Zaninelli, 1981 and Saba, 1983). The CISL actually proposed a real 'social regulation of the Italian economy by means of collective bargaining aimed at establishing a social as well as an economic order' (Saba, 1988, pp. 151 ff).[8] This general strategy led to a few notorious successes, like the wages agreement about the *conglobamento*[9] in 1954 and victory in the elections of works councils in the years 1955-1956. Despite all its rhetoric, however, the CISL failed in its attempt to create a new climate of cooperation and shared responsibility between both sides of industry and the government.

Although its membership consisted mainly of Catholics, the CISL considered itself to be the centre of a new brand of trade unionism that wanted to overcome the old ideological differences. It wanted to be a serene forum for both Catholics and non-Catholics, and henceforth chose to join the International Confederation of Free Trade Unions (ICFTU) (Zaninelli, 1981; Saba, 1983).[10] It explicitly dissociated itself from the Christian trade unions allied in the International Federation of Christian Trade Unions (IFCTU) (Pasture, 1994). Furthermore, it emphasized its independence and justified its split from the CGIL because of its intention to liberate itself from interference by not just the communist party but all political parties. Nevertheless, the CISL could not function without political action, for which it depended on the renovated Christian Democratic Party (DC). Through this party it had its own members of parliament as well as experts on government committees. It formed its own 'current' (Forze Sociali, Social Forces) within Christian-democracy, through which it tried to alter government strategy and the internal balance of the party to the benefit of employees. This situation continued until 1958, when the historical leader of the CISL, Giulio Pastore, became prime minister, resigning the CISL leadership (Bianchi, 1985). A strong informal relationship with the DC kept existing, though, at least until the reorientations of 1969. It is obvious that this very ambiguous interpretation of the principle of autonomy, combined with the fact that the vast majority of the membership were Catholic and the unmistakable Catholic influence on the manifesto, reinforced the CISL's image as a Catholic trade union, regardless of the union leaders' efforts to distance themselves from the Catholic tradition (see also Bedani, 1995).

The CGIL defined itself as a general and a class trade union. In the early 1950s, for instance, it clearly aligned itself with the left-wing political opposition, sharing its analyses and tactical choices. It persistently refused to recognize the 1948-1949 split as an accomplished fact, and it sustained the internal subdivision into organized factions. Management posts on all levels were divided on that basis (Forbice and Favero, 1968; Pillon, 1972).[11] After the rejection of the Marshall plan and every form of European or Western integration (considered to bring about the country's industrial decline) at its 1949 congress, the CGIL proposed an alternative scheme for national development, the so-called 'Labour Plan' (*Piano del Lavoro*). Italy counted two million unemployed, and it was therefore necessary to create work for those people through large-scale public works and 'without appealing to foreign countries'. These public works would have had to be financed by a progressive tax on the affluent classes or by directing savings towards productive investments. Under those conditions, Giuseppe Di Vittorio claimed, the Italian working class would be prepared to make new sacrifices.[12] Despite the particular political scope of the plan, it can be considered as a first attempt to become involved into the new economic reality (Berta, 1987, p. 10; Ganapini, 1984, p. 2; Trentin, 1978, p. 198).

As far as trade union policy was concerned, the CGIL proposed wide-scale centralized action based on large demonstrations (against poverty, against extreme exploitation, against monopolies, etc.) and it militantly opposed the CISL's policy of productivity and cooperation, branding it an 'extreme exploitation' policy. The CGIL was as a rule suspicious of negotiations at company level, because they were considered a threat to the unity of the working class.[13] This attitude, however, led to humiliating defeats at the time of the ballots for the works councils (*commissioni interne*) in the most advanced companies. From 1955 onwards, the CGIL would revise its policy on trade union action within and outside companies, while remaining careful, however, to emphasize the overall continuity in its thinking. In the face of the increased power of monopolies and the increasing exploitation, the fight was to be continued with 'differentiated (...) and typical trade union demands, i.e. demands common to specific groups of employees'. The increased exploitation of the workers needed to be particularly fought off on company level. This about-turn did not mean that the CGIL had adapted its analyses of the fundamentals of economy nor of the duty of trade unions. These remained in essence antagonistic. The CGIL did not repeal its complete rejection of the negotiation philosophy of the CISL (Lama, 1971; Romagnoli, 1988, p. 313).

At its 1960 congress in Rome, the CGIL saw a clear 'aggravation of social differences' and a 'larger imbalance and increased internal conflicts in capitalist countries', even though the country went through an economic boom and consumption orientated production rapidly recovered. According to the CGIL, many historical contradictions remained, but under different guises. For those reasons, the CGIL especially turned against large monopolies. Nevertheless, it had started to adopt a different, more pragmatic approach to the European Community. It considered trade union cooperation on a European level important, even though it rejected any formal adhesion to European community institutions.[14] Under the influence of the changed economic climate and the drive by the CISL and the UIL, the CGIL redefined its tactics and interpretations, but it eventually stood by its basic plan of action and ideology (Trentin, 1962).

Next to the two other trade unions with such clearly defined beliefs and action plans, the third Italian trade union, the small UIL, struggled for a place in the centre (Auletta, 1979, p. 379). In fact, the UIL aligned itself with the CISL in the large battles of the 1950s, for instance about productivity, the Schumann plan or the *conglobamento*.[15] Heterogeneous factions happily co-existed within the group, partly because of the general theoretical common ground. The social-democratic influences won through to some extent as the 1950s developed, and therefore reformism was confirmed as the official ideology of the small trade union (Forbice, 1981).

After the failure of the idea to merge new autonomous trade unions and to use them as a bridge between the CGIL and the CISL, the UIL devoted more time in the 1960s to the socialists within the CGIL, partly as a result of the political merger between the socialists and the anti-communist social-democrats.[16] There was even talk of launching one single socialist trade union. The UIL remained sceptical about the 'Catholics' of the CISL, as if an invisible but real undertone of intense ideological rivalry continued to exist (Rossi, Valentini and Lodici, 1983, p. 275).

The 1960s: missed chances

In the course of the 1960s, the first attempts were made to regulate the economic and social scene in Italy, where intensive economic development and profound social changes were taking place. These attempts, largely backed by the CISL, remained unsuccessfull, and they were easily overthrown by the dramatic events at the end of the decade. While the main division lines within Italian political and trade union life had not changed, the reformation attempts notably followed the route of political regulation and planning instead of intervening in their own operational area, namely civil society. No new collective bargaining tradition emerged. Neither did the trade union movement (and other social actors) establish a culture of negotiation or a culture of economic compatibility, ever lacking in Italy (Berta, 1987). In that sense, the 1960s can be viewed as a series of missed opportunities. This failure underlies the schism occurring in the 1970s.

The analyses and the ideas of the CISL appeared popular at the beginning of the decade. The political context had changed and the economy was flourishing. The CGIL seemed to have toned down its stance, and a change of climate in public and private management seemed to be in the air (Romani, 1965, p. 129). This success was only superficial, however. Both sides of industry and institutions still harboured immense resistance to the concept of innovations. Their reservations became apparent on two accounts: the management of economic and social development, and collective bargaining.

The Vanoni plan in 1957, a first attempt at economic planning, was greeted by the CISL as an important step forward in Italian political tradition. Even so, the union criticized the abstract and centralist character of the plan, counter-proposing a view of planning as a meeting point and ground for cooperation between both sides of industry and the government.[17] The CISL's proposal included the suggestion that part of the pay increases obtained through collective bargaining would be spent on voluntary savings. The savings would be deposited in special accounts dedicated to financing investments (Carrera, 1979, p. 51). The CISL wanted to see the fundamental geographical and sectorial imbalances corrected by means of economic planning coordinated by the government.[18]

In October 1959, the CISL consequently asked the government to convene a congress for economic development based on the idea of 'active participation of the prevailing social forces'.[19] But at that congress in January 1961 it transpired that the CISL was virtually isolated in its views, and that the time was not yet right for a regulation of social and economic life. Prime Minister Fanfani (in the throes of forming a centre-left coalition at the time) had nevertheless claimed in his opening speech that a strategy for economic development was 'preeminently a unitary aspiration by politicians and trade unions alike'. But the employers from the private sector, united in Cofindustria, maintained that many problems would automatically be resolved as a result of the economic boom. The market forces were to be left unfettered. The employers did not believe it was appropriate to allow employees to obtain profit from increased productivity through negotiations within the workplace. The CGIL expressed pessimism about the national development potential. It opposed any constraints on individual wage increases. It objected to cooperation between trade unions and employers, on the grounds that it would lead to 'confusion of roles'.[20] The blockade was absolute, but shortly afterwards there were important new developments.

In March 1961, Fiorentino Sullo, Minister for Employment, proposed to both sides of industry to reach a 'major outline agreement' in order to regulate the Italian system of collective bargaining, not by law (as defined in article 39 of the Constitution), but by interconfederate agreement.[21] In July 1962, the trade unions and the public sector employer's association (Intersind) signed an agreement for the metalworking sector which included for the first time negotiations at company level. The private sector employers of Confindustria set aside their own reservations and they too accepted the agreement. It was the first important change to the negotiation process since the war.

In 1963-1965 a new centre-left political majority came to power while the country was being hit by recession. The political and trade union debate about planning was given a new lease of life. The trade unions widely differed in the way they felt the imbalance of the social and economic system could be monitored and corrected. However, regardless of their differences, both sides of industry reached an agreement in March 1965 in the National Council for Economic Affairs and Labour (Consiglio Nazionale dell'Economia e del Lavoro, CNEL) on a draft five-year government plan for economic planning and investment. The CNEL recognized that, as far as the relationship between wages and productivity was concerned, they could make allowances for the limits contained in the plan. Moreover, the responsibility shared between both sides of industry was considered to be of crucial importance to the economic future of the country.[22]

The CGIL had participated in setting up the agreement, but finally it abstained at the vote.[23] It felt deeply suspicious of the so-called 'Italian economic miracle', in the belief that it was hailed by the ruling classes to make the country forget its 'economic, social, historical and modern differences'. It also claimed that the programme for economic development for 1965-69 of the centre-left government granted complete freedom to a 'monopolist reorganization'. The CGIL consistently rejected any form of wage restrictions or government wage control. But it expected major advantages from wage increases, which would lead to improved employment conditions and increase the employees' spending power.[24] This issue concerning economic planning was one of the rare occasions on which the different schools of thinking within the CGIL came to blows. The socialists, who formed part of the government together with the DC, refused to oppose the development plan. On 27 January 1967, the leadership of the CGIL asked associate trade unionists who were members of parliament to abstain at the vote on the Plan. This solution by compromise led the leadership of the CGIL to declare that it kept clear of the 'logic of alliances with political parties', but it caused the CGIL to fall out with the other trade unions (Traverso, 1983, p. 59).[25]

On collective bargaining, the resistance against general regulation was very strong. Not only was the agreement of 1962 never put into practice, but the climate of renovation was never extended to other sectors. The most significant missed chance was the failure of a skeleton agreement for new rules for negotiations within companies, and for the relationship between the company and national deliberations. The decisive factor was the CGIL's strong opposition, which particularly originated with the Italian Federation of Blue-Collar Metalworkers (Federazione Italiana Operai Metalmeccanici, FIOM). The FIOM had thought long and hard before signing the 1962 agreement, and certainly did not wish to go any further down that route (Boni, 1993, p. 177). The recession of 1964-1965 caused a slowing-down of negotiations in all lines of industry, rendering the old-style centralized and uniform agreements - which had been tentatively replaced by individual workplace agreements - more prominent (Saba, 1988, p. 161). Despite agreements being signed, the general climate remained ominous: the government had accepted the differentiation between companies with great reservations, and the employers who had reluctantly allowed trade unions to operate in their companies tried to erode the trade union activities at the first opportunity.

In brief, the resistance to regulation seemed to gather force by the end of the 1960s through lack of a general stable framework. The demand for social regulation weakened (even within the CISL) and lost its attraction. New questions arose, such as the call for political regulation (proclaimed to be the only logical and successful way to change reality). Among the trade unionists, especially those in the CISL, a downcast mood prevailed for diverse reasons: the recession, the inflexible attitude adopted by the employees, the lack of experience workers had of industrial conflicts, and the disillusionment caused by the failure of the planning and incomes policy. Furthermore, there was growing social dissatisfaction with a situation both sides of industry seemed powerless to address: the new geographical and social imbalance (resulting from the transformations), the inadequate provisions made for the basic components of the Italian social state (pensions, health care, housing, transport) and finally the chronic failure of the state bureaucracy.

Against this background, the idea grew of an 'organic unity' between the various Italian trade unions. The CISL expressed this idea for the first time in public at its General Council meeting in March 1966.[26] From that moment on, the concept of an organic unity dominated the discussions between the three confederations. The CGIL, CISL and UIL had differing views on this matter from the beginning. As far as the CISL was concerned, the new organization would be 'the new trade union' which would give the entire Italian trade union movement a new base, a view which somehow clashed with the CISL's basic principles. The CGIL and the UIL saw it differently. The former reiterated a long-held belief in the advantage of a single organization for all employees without an explicit ideological agenda (but still strongly influenced by party lines).[27] The UIL, which was also divided into organized factions, had periodically declared its support for the trade union alliance of the working class, albeit in tactful ways so as not to upset its internal stability (Rossi, Valentini and Lodici, 1979).

Within the CISL a new political and cultural opposition was formed, supported by the Italian Federation of Metalworkers (Federazione Italiana Metalmeccanici, FIM) which questioned the leadership of Bruno Storti, Pastore's successor. The attacks mainly centred on the incompatibility of holding simultaneous positions of responsibility in union and party, and the autonomy of the professional associations. The FIM considered the procedural agreement as unauthorized unitarian interference in the sectorial collective bargaining process.

Despite the fact that the CISL continuously emphasized the enduring value of its body of thought, this minority displayed a clear ideological change of course by delivering scathing criticism of the 'moderate CISL of the early years'. In October 1968, the FIM described Italian society as a purely formal democracy in which the workers were seen as pawns to be manipulated. The ultimate cause was 'neo-capitalism' which increased the existing distances and inequalities in the country, and which threatened world peace by increasing the technological gap between developed and underdeveloped countries. The FIM suggested ways to reach a 'class and conflict perspective'. These views had obvious consequences for both the idea of economic planning and policies on pay and productivity. The FIM now turned its back to procedural agreements, contractual savings, and the idea of cooperation and shared responsibility between workers and employers.[28] It wanted to expand on the traditional autonomy of the CISL, putting the autonomy as a political actor first and foremost. The amalgamation with the CGIL and the UIL represented an opportunity to push through the process of trade union autonomy to its extreme point, turning the union into a real political actor. This was a far cry from the unitary point of view held by the communist movement in the CGIL who wanted to incorporate the current social change back into a general political strategy led by left-wing forces (Cella, Manghi and Piva, 1972; Treu, 1973, pp. 269-396; Baglioni, 1975; Saba, 1986, pp. 14-15).

At the congress of the CISL in Rome called 'Power against power' in June 1969, a split developed between the group of Secretary-General Storti and the FIM led by Pierre Carniti. The dispute was less about specific issues (such as the autonomy of industrial categories and the incompatibility between executive positions in the union and political parties) and more about a power struggle between two generations. The points of interest and opinions did not actually differ that much. One group stated its aim was to alter the structure of power in society, and the other group wanted to break through the historic subordination of the working class by using the trade union autonomy in a political way. Both supported organic unity as a tool of countervailing power by the trade unions, and their radical language in particular did not spare the DC.[29] A few months later, both adversaries reached an agreement and they formed the Carniti/Storti alliance which would lead the CISL during the 1970s.

At its congress in Livorno in June 1969, the CGIL showed little interest in the actions and themes of the student movement, but the influence of the general climate was clearly noticeable. The choice of local collective bargaining within the workplace was very cautiously confirmed. Bruno Trentin repeated his warning against the tendency to focus exclusively on the short-term objectives of plant-level bargaining, the so-called *aziendalismo*. Plenty of attention was paid to unitary rank and file committees spontaneously springing up within companies, overtaking trade unions and works councils, whereby much value was placed on 'direct democracy' and 'factory councils'. The government reforms were sharply criticized (even by socialist delegates). The communist Agostino Novella even talked of 'transcending the factions', which to the socialists only seemed feasible on a medium- to long term time scale. The CGIL also came out in favour of an imminent launch of the organic unity, and said it was prepared to support the incompatibility requested by the CISL.[30]

The 1969 congress of the UIL was completely marked by the socialist split which had occurred a few months earlier. Here also two movements took shape: on the one hand the socialists (unitarians) and on the other hand the social-democrats (opponents). The republican movement played an arbitrary role and Raffaele Vanni, one of its leaders, was elected to the position of secretary together with the social-democrat Lino Ravecca and the socialist Ruggero Ravenna (Turone, 1990, pp. 162-165).

At the end of the 1960s, a speedy launch of the organic unity, as well as the themes and methods of the radical and militant trade unionism surfacing in the factories were the two most influential, if not dominant attitudes in the Italian trade union movement.

The years of the split: 1969-1979

The outbreak of social dissent

The trade union congress of 1969 took place in the middle of a year marked by radical social dissent unlike any other in recent Italian history, culminating in the so-called 'hot autumn' (Pizzorno, 1974-1978; Accornero, 1992; 'A vent'anni dall'autumno caldo', 1989; Crouch and Pizzorno, 1977). The break with the previous decade and the attempts made at that time to set up a system of social regulation was clear-cut. After 1969, all joint responsibility in negotiations and 'economic compatibility' was refused (Berta, 1982, p. 10). A large social movement, violent at times, with strong anarcho-syndical leanings erupted in Italian factories and streets (see the prologue by Sapelli in Arisio, 1990 and Sapelli, 1989, pp. 67-85). As a matter of priority, the movement formulated what Pizzorno called 'non-negotiable aims'. These aims did not constitute a direct or indirect attempt at rationalization - on the contrary, the very idea of the need for a rational system of industrial relations was dismissed out of hand.

It could be argued that the country was not mentally geared up to the consequences of the big industrial transformation. The enormous demand for material growth (typical for countries barely surfacing from underdevelopment and deprivation) came hand-in-hand with a 'growing demand for political participation' (Romani, 1988b, pp. 292-294). These requests with a political and social content, rather than a trade union one, forced their way into business, where they found a fertile breeding ground in the shape of a weak trade union prepared to take them up.[31] However paradoxical it may appear, the success of Italian trade unions in those days was in that sense a clear sign of their weakness (Pizzorno, 1980, pp. 139-188). Unlike other trade unions in Europe, they were unable to control social movements in the workplace. Furthermore, the Italian trade unions had twenty years behind them during which they found it extremely difficult to get the factory workers actively involved, and the spontaneous dissent was just the thing many trade unionists had been waiting for. The Italian trade movement, particularly the CISL, contained numerous young intellectuals, which in itself suffices to explain the major influence of the rebellious themes of the student movement (Pizzorno, 1980, p. 140; Mershon, 1990). The Italian political situation, traditionally unswerving and consociate, complements the scene: it was a system in which 'the opposition was simultaneously formally immobilized and secretly sneaked into the power bases' (Pizzorno, 1980, p. 141). In this context, the trade movement managed to prove its appeal to the masses, as well as to show how trade unions would stand up and fight for general and common goals - which none of the political parties could.

It was the beginning of a ten year period of sharp social conflict, of 'permanent unrest' (Craveri, 1982, pp. 13-14; Regini, 1981, p. 48). The situation was brought to a head. No more talk now of 'skeleton agreements'; preference was given to 'reform strategies'. The 'welfare' idea was abandoned in favour of reforms which would be achieved through battles against the political authorities. The trade unions made demands (housing, pensions, transport, schools, etc.) and directed their demands relating to an alternative society to the politicians in power and to the business world (Craveri, 1982; Accornero, 1989). In the meantime, a deep economic recession took hold, which would engulf the country by the end of the century, bringing it to the brink of economic disaster, with an inflation rate of 20 per cent.

The trade union movement and the dissent

One of the first innovations which the period 1968-69 had brought for the Italian trade union movement was the change in its own base. The dissent had wiped out the old works councils (*commissioni interne*) and the new union workplace branches where they had been in place. Instead, workers' delegates and factory councils, often of a spontaneous anarchic character and unsympathetic to trade unions, had sprung up. However, the unions would manage to take controll over these bodies. Once the CISL had given up resisting it, the so-called Workers' Statute was accepted during the first few months of 1970, legally underpinning the new forms of representation. The mainstream trade union delegates laboured under the illusion that they could redress the balance of forces underlying the country's political, economic and social life by changing the political framework from the outside. From that viewpoint, the amalgamation of the three organizations was essential. But politics would take revenge precisely on the latter issue.

The backbone of the Italian trade union movement in the 1970s was hence formed by unitary employees organizations, while the trade unions maintained their independent role at provincial or industrial branch level. More often than not the battle was spearheaded by recently immigrated, industrial workers, egged on in turn by intellectuals. The ascendancy of these groups over the higher educated and skilled workers who had traditionally been at the centre of the Italian trade union movement probably explains why the struggle was conducted in such a reckless and often violent way (Sapelli, 1989, p. 108).

The trade union events between the end of 1969 and the Summer of 1972 were all affected by the situation. While Storti and the metalworkers in the CISL reached an agreement over the new trade union policy between January and July 1970, Parliament accepted the Workers' Statute. A congress of metalworkers unions which formed part of the CGIL, CISL and UIL was held to prepare for the amalgamation. Several general strikes were announced in the same period, the last of which in July toppled the government. In the Autumn, while the government and the unions came to an agreement regarding reforms to the Italian health service - an agreement which would take years before being transformed into law - the three confederations met in Florence to consider a proposal for unity in the trade union movement. Unification was described as 'the most suitable, imperative political answer that the Italian working class can give to the management, simultaneously reinforcing the autonomous role of the trade union'.[32] Within the CISL an anti-unitary minority organized itself by March 1971 (Romani, 1988a), but the launch of the confederation of the three unions seemed unstoppable so much so that the congresses for disbanding the three organizations were announced with the intention of setting up a new confederation by the beginning of 1973. However, the changing political climate would throw a spanner in the works.

In the consecutive elections between the end of 1971 and June 1972 the left had to concede ground to the centre-right every time. For the first time in ten years, a government was formed without socialists. This political change of tack had an immediate effect on trade union relations. The UIL already stated in March 1972 that a trade union alliance would not be feasible in the short term. After fierce internal conflicts, the CISL also decided with a slim majority on 27th May to put off the winding-up congress. In July, the three secretariats decided to launch a unitary Federation of the three confederations (Federazione Sindacale Unitaria) purely as a temporary venture, with its own powers and official body, but without infringing the sovereignty of each organization over non-delegated matters (relating to contract policies and social-economic policies).[33]

This is how the most stirring phase of the period after 1969 ended with a revenge of sorts by politics on the trade union movement's aspiration to seize power. A new period started, which saw the formal amalgamation between the three confederations in a new unitary federation. This period was not free of conflicts, but solutions were always found.

The attempt at political regulation

The economic and political cycle which had started in 1969 came to an end in 1973. The energy crisis which began during the second half of that year came as a stern warning of change: the widely scattered, total social conflict hit boundaries imposed by economic reality. All parties concerned had to rethink the organization of the production in a different light because of the new shortages.

The external context had also changed. The massive youth protest had died down, except for some small extreme groups on the left of the PCI, which would shortly afterwards turn to terrorism. The political system did not achieve an equilibrium. The new centre-right cabinet became bogged down almost immediately. In order to overcome the crisis and to make the country governable again, the idea of an 'historic compromise' between de PCI and the DC, envisaged as enabling an entirely new form of political regulation, gained ground. The PCI did a radical U-turn after 1973 and aspired to participate in government, but had no intention whatsoever to give up its identity and beliefs. Essential for this change of tack was a moderation by the trade unions through the CISL (Saba, 1987, p. 82; Savona, 1993). The amalgamation plan was given a new lease of life thanks to the communist faction of the CGIL, which saw the unity as a prerequisite to the 'historic compromise' with the centre parties and the employers. Anyway, after years of anarchy, the employers were looking forward to a 'social cease-fire' (Saba, 1985, pp. 24-25).

Even in 1973, the unions had confirmed their radical position. Only at the congress of the CISL did those wishing for change clash fiercely with those who did not. Eventually the left-wing view of Storti and Carniti, followed by the CISL since 1970, won the day: complete independence of the political forces, rejection of any agreement with the employers, as well as rejection of all negotiations in order to protect the employees' rights, equal pay increases for all categories of employees, and systematic pressure on the government to enforce social reforms.[34] At the congress of the CGIL, however, the decision to go for 'radical transformation of the economic and social structures and of political relations' was confirmed outright (Craveri, 1982, pp. 14-15). The same happened for the UIL. The Unitary Federation also confirmed the policy options adopted in 1969.[35] In January an agreement was reached on a system of index-linked pay scales, the *scala mobile*, which went along the road to automatic pay rises and egalitarianism.[36] This agreement was welcomed by the press as an important sign of 'political realism', which clearly showed that everyone was now convinced that the only way out of the crisis was the political one.

From 1975, the PCI, strengthened by election victories in 1975 and 1976, considered the programme of austerity as a historic chance for the left in Italy to obtain a structural change in society. On the other hand, the PCI presented itself to industry as the only force capable of achieving the industrial peace and consensus so badly needed for economic recovery. After the elections in 1976, there were governments so-called 'for national solidarity' for the first time since the war, with the PCI in the majority. As far as the trade unions were concerned, the CGIL's policy became clear at its 1977 congress in Rimini. In view of the serious recession and the new political situation, the CGIL not only showed employees the way of reforms and planning, but also austerity and how to protect employment. Cut-backs were now called 'an indispensable tool' to change economic and social structures. The new pay strategy would consequently be more concerned about the conservation of employment than about pay increases, and the welfare policy would equally be more preoccupied with its costs than with the expansion of rights.[37]

The UIL also went through a time of upheaval. After the socialist split in 1969 it had failed to receive clear leadership because of the continuous quibbling between the socialist and the social-democrat group. As soon as the two groups patched up their differences in 1976 they came to an agreement, and the young leader of the metalworkers, the socialist Giorgio Benvenuto, was elected Secretary-General (Turone, 1981, pp. 183-185; Simoncini, 1985, p. 214). The UIL remained loyal to its unitary line, but rediscovered after 1976 its own tradition and historic originality: the rejection of the DC-PCI dichotomy and the authentic representation of the secular and socialist part of the workers. Because of its strong political role, the UIL described itself as a new trade union. In his contribution to the Bologna congress in 1977, Benvenuto talked about the end of the atmosphere of conflict between the democratic state and trade unions, and about workers' control and participation.[38]

The CISL on the other hand remained internally deeply divided, coming dangerously close to a split. For the time being, the left wing was dominant. At the 1977 congress, the resolution proposed by the moderates defending the rolling back of the automatic pay rise system and the expansion of company-level bargaining (in order to curb inflation and the budget deficit) had to make way for a resolution based on the concept of a pluralistic and independent trade union defending the working class, inviting workers to fight for equality and workers' control.[39] In February 1978 the Unitary Federation of Trade Unions including the CISL, agreed to tailor trade union claims to the economic reality.[40]

The framework for national solidarity collapsed just a few months after the kidnapping and murder of Aldo Moro, the driving force behind the normalization of relations between PCI, the industrial employers and DC. Furthermore, neither the trade union, nor the communist party (PCI) were able to guarantee peaceful industrial relations within companies. Even in the years of national solidarity, the situation had actually worsened (Craveri, 1982).

As a result, the CGIL promptly reverted to antagonistic and contrary points of view. This in turn led to a big culture shock within the CISL. Paradoxically, the CISL confederation had just managed to overcome a long-running internal dispute. The federation of metalworkers gained control of the CISL, first with Luigi Macario (1977) and then Pierre Carniti (1978) as leader. The new leadership decided gradually to distance itself from the CGIL in view of what had happened since the joint meeting in February 1978. The CISL chose to gradually revert to type, picking up the thread of issues and views it had supported before 1969 (Saba, 1993, pp. 29-34).[41]

This development was significant for the run of events right up to the end of the unitary chapter. A number of notorious incidents poured oil on the fire of the theoretical and political recoil of the CISL. They caused many trade union leaders and activists alike, even outside the CISL, to question their beliefs. First, in July 1980, there was the controversy over the launch of a solidarity fund for investments in the *Mezzogiorno* (the South of Italy) with the savings of the workers. The fund had been agreed between the CGIL-CISL-UIL Federation and the government, but the PCI opposed it.[42] The CGIL consequently rejected the proposal. The communists claimed that no trade union movement should play a major part in policies of investment.[43]

In the meanwhile, events in Poland made a big impression. In August 1980, on the initiative of the CISL, the CGIL-CISL-UIL Federation put itself firmly on the side of the strikers of Gdansk. Networking with Solidarnosc was established, and kept up throughout the years of underground activity. Voices were raised about the autonomy of trade unions, the future of socialism, and the role played by religious motives or ideals in trade unions. The debate rippled through the various factions of the Italian trade union movement, causing many clashes. The differences were accentuated by the difference in dedication to the underground Solidarnosc by the CISL and UIL on the one hand and by the CGIL on the other hand.

The third incident was the Fiat dispute of 1980. It did not immediately cause discord between the three trade unions, but it is unanimously thought to have had such an important influence that the episode is seen as the swan song of the antagonistic and conflicting trade union policies of the 1970s (Turone, 1981; Accornero, 1992). While the three confederations were coordinating a national solidarity strike against the large-scale redundancies made by the FIAT board of directors, a coordinating committee of clerical workers and foremen organized a protest march in favour of a return to work. The impressive support given to the demonstration forced the unions to come to an agreement with the management. It was a crushing defeat, also psychologically. The trade union leaders were convinced they had reached the end of an era, even though no-one knew where to go from there.[44]

Ten years after the hot autumn of 1969, it became increasingly clear that the entire social and political model had failed. The strategy of wage moderation never became customary practice in sectorial collective bargaining, which could be seen in 1979, for instance. A much more profound change in industrial relations was needed to save Italian companies from the brink. The system of index-linked pay scales (*scala mobile*) was seen as a culprit, since it compressed salaries, limiting the scope for negotiations (Craveri, 1982, p. 18), not to mention the disastrous effect it had on inflation. During the following years, many conflicts ensued about whether the *scala mobile*, soon to be a symbol in itself, should be retained or modified.

The 1980s and 1990s: in search of consensus

Government, management and trade unions facing up to the crisis

At the height of the crisis at the beginning of the 1980s, with an inflation rate of 21.7 per cent in 1980, the political and social forces of the country tried to bring about a social consensus. The five-party governments (a new coalition ranging from centre-right to centre-left) took the initiative and encouraged both sides of industry to reach central agreements which would lay down the ground rules of their coexistence and restore the conditions for social peace.

The agreement of 1983 on curbing inflation was particularly important, not only because every trade union signed it, but also because it was an explicit bid to resolve the country's big economic and social problems, over and above collective bargaining and pay. The implementation of the agreement, however, was riddled with problems, because part of the trade union movement remained averse to the very idea of consensus. The second half of the 1980s and the beginning of the 1990s saw a radical change of climate, not only because the economy recovered surprisingly fast (the famous second Italian miracle), but also because the three unions accepted to play an important role in social regulation. Before the ratification of each annual budget, the government invited the unions to discuss the contents, often altering some points to the unions' satisfaction. Both sides of industry became implicitly involved in the social and economic regulation without even realizing it, and thus a delicate balance was struck.

The way out of the crisis (1980-1985)

At their congresses in 1981, the three trade union confederations had a chance to determine their position in the changed environment. But it proved to be too early for a clear decision to be made on tactics (Craveri, 1982, p. 32).

The 1981 CISL congress confirmed the newly found internal unity. The CISL saw the deep crisis as a transition instead of as a drama. The way out was through discussion, i.e. by imposing a system of three-way negotiations (management, trade unions and authorities) where the great reforms and the new economic and social policies could be mapped out. The importance accorded to central agreements pushed the traditionally relevant theme of plant bargaining somewhat aside, based on the belief that central negotiations would achieve a lot of economic and social regulation.[45] The title of the UIL congress in Rome, 'From antagonism to protagonism' was equally indicative of the watershed. At the congress, the UIL distanced itself from the 'lack of responsibility' of the 1970s. Instead, trade unions were to play a strong political role. The UIL proposed the formation of a broad front against inflation and was in favour of increased productivity.[46]

The CGIL opted for a defensive programme, more in the region of its former creeds. It indicated that the current system was powerless to achieve lasting, evenly spread growth. It opposed the stance that labour costs would be to blame for inflation and consequently fought to retain the *scala mobile*, as well as supporting equal wage increases for all categories of employees. It rejected privatisation of the social security system in any shape or form.[47]

This is how the three trade unions, in the Summer of 1981, started a major round of negotiations with the government and the management about the fight against inflation, leading to an agreement in January 1983 (Valcavi, 1989, p. 369; Treu, 1984). The UIL stated that a 'Social Pact' had been achieved at last. The CISL particularly stressed that there had been trilateral negotiations, as if the protocol had been a definite confirmation of what the CISL had recommended at its last congress. The CGIL, which had signed the final agreement with reservation, did not underwrite that interpretation at all (Treu, 1984). Hence different interpretations and contradictions soon came to light, sharpened during the further negotiations about the *scala mobile* which had been postponed by the January agreement. Fundamental discord appeared between the CISL and the communists within the CGIL. The CISL believed that the only way to control inflation would be by pre-determining the pay increases according to the *scala mobile*, while the communists felt that this would put the lowest-paid workers at a disadvantage.[48]

Firstly, the discord led to a definite rift within the Federate Pact that had existed between the CGIL, the CISL and the UIL since 1972. It was the end of an era in trade union history. Secondly, it caused fierce confrontations over labour costs and the *scala mobile*, first in parliament where the government introduced a bill based on the text of the disbanded agreement, and then in the country, because the PCI called on the workers and requested a referendum. The conflict resulted in an election defeat for the PCI after a fierce election campaign during which the CISL and the UIL aligned themselves with the government without engaging in direct confrontation with the CGIL. Another sign of how much the country had changed in ten years.

The trade unions in neo-industrial Italy

The second half of the 1980s was definitely a different story. The country which had unwittingly come through a crisis in the 1970s, knew a long period of political stability and intense economic growth. In 1986, the Milan stock exchange reached its high point, and the governor of the Italian national bank declared rather rashly that zero inflation was no longer an unattainable target. As if by miracle, the country had swiftly emerged from a dire crisis - a crisis which had contributed so much to changes of tack within the trade union movement - and it was now firmly on the road to what is generally called the post-industrial or neo-industrial phase of capitalism.

The trade union movement had reverted to its normal pluralism. The conflict and split during 1984-1985 did not lead to arguments and accusations, but paradoxically enough to a diffuse uniformity in its actions. The referendum was hardly mentioned after 1985. The unions each presented their lists of preferences to the government, - particularly when another national budget was to be ratified, but also relating to tax policies, economic and development policies - often to find their demands met. From 1985 onwards, it was a matter of systematic mutual consultation without exclusions or preferences for one or the other. It was a pragmatic course of action which consciously avoided the important national structural problems, for instance the issue of the welfare state.

Yet, the events of 1984 and 1985 have marked the three confederations to the very core. At its 1985 congress, the CISL returned to the historic and ideological roots of its own identity after travelling a long road of rediscovery. Carniti, who in the 1960s and 1970s had denied the 'moderate' tradition of the CISL, declared in January 1985 that he could identify, in a spirit of continuity, with the trade union project set up and carried out by Pastore. Even so, the political and organizational decisions that had been made in the 1970s were hardly the subject of criticism. On the contrary, those years were hailed as the golden era of the trade unions. The hatchet was buried within the CISL, while Carniti, leader of the old majority, was replaced by Franco Marini (previously heading the minority faction) at the congress which took place in Rome from 8 to 13 July 1985. At the congress, the CISL confirmed its independence and its belief in solidarity. It called for a social pact among trade unions against the undermining effects of neo-liberalism and a new pervasive corporate culture.[49]

By 1988, under the next government, the CISL felt that it had clearly made the right choices in 1983-1984, and that the facts were there to prove it.[50] The CISL reverted to many of its previous themes, such as the relationship between productivity and pay. Another topic was the idea of an integrated social security system which would combine a system run by the state with a private insurance system, based on the principle of subsidiarity (although this was not made explicit). Despite the mutual intention to cooperate, there were some fierce clashes with the CGIL. In 1986 they argued about whether the Catholic religion should be taught at school, in 1988 about the legitimacy of referenda in collective bargaining; two issues relating to each union's sense of identity. They also clashed about the associative character of the trade union, the right to pluralism and the respect for religious identity.[51]

At its 1985 congress, the UIL seemed intent on changing its image; the UIL model transcending the dichotomy between conflict and negotiations (Craveri, 1986, pp. 14-15). It rejected the culture of 'catastrophism and crisis' and advocated an entirely new approach as 'trade union of the citizens'. Trade union action would no longer centre on the workplace but on the citizens of a locality, and trade union services would be primarily targeted at the worker as citizen: 'Who will stand up for the citizen who's not a party member? Who will employ the youth without an influential father? Who will help the ill? (...) The answer is simple: the trade union should'.[52]

To the CGIL, a mere change of strategy to adapt to the changed situation, as occurred during the other big crisis in 1955-1956, did not seem sufficient this time after the defeat it suffered in 1984-1985. Hence the numerous bids to redefine itself and to return to some of its former beliefs, which have characterized its most recent ten years. On the eve of its eleventh congress and on the occasion of the fortieth birthday of the Pact of Rome, an issue was published of the *Quaderni di Rassegna Sindacale*, the CGIL's theoretical journal, about the historic development of the CGIL's philosophy. The real difference with the CISL and the UIL was shown to lie in the idea of general representation as opposed to associative representation. The future of collective bargaining depended on direct talks between both sides of industry. The trade union had to participate responsibly in regulation of the economy. Future care provision would be obtained from an appropriate balance of public and private care.[53]

All these themes and issues sounded very new, considering the CGIL's past, but the 1985 congress stuck to the traditional position and ideas. In connection with the fundamental issues about the associative or general character of the trade unions, the CGIL declared in 1986 that the trade union played the role of mediator between the organization of paid-up members on the one hand and the mass of non-subscribers on the other hand. This original vision did nothing to improve the dialogue with the other unions, despite several calls for organic unity.[54]

In 1988, the unsolved internal problems led to a crisis within the CGIL. The leader of the metalworkers, Bruno Trentin, was appointed Secretary-General and given as a brief the bringing of a new synthesis and order tot he CGIL's ideals and actions. Various steps were taken to that effect in what in the end was not a very successful process. The

CGIL's returned to the idea of dominant forces in the economy and Italian society at large.[55] It also called itself a 'programme trade union'.[56] Moreover, the communist faction was dissolved and the CGIL's unique stance as a general and class trade union was confirmed after the events in the Soviet Union in the Summer of 1991.[57] Finally, Trentin resigned in Chianciano in 1994. According to Trentin, who was the architect of the fundamental changes within the CGIL, the central problem remained that the CGIL, as a programme-based trade union, neglected to come to terms with its past, despite all the rigorous reforms.[58]

Trade union policy in development

The most significant innovations made to trade union activity after the watershed of 1984-1985 were in the area of collective bargaining. After the split of the 1970s, the Italian system of industrial relations finally abandoned its anomie and aversion to regulation. For the first time, an institutional structure was set up to control the negotiation process (Saba, 1988; Berta, 1987). The transition had a theoretical result too: the three organizations switched over from a belief in conflict to a belief in 'the trade union of participation'. Only a minority in the CGIL were not prepared to abandon its militant style. The above concepts were given diverse interpretations and there was still a lot of resistance. The resistance could be felt in actual trade union actions, also embodying the spirit of the 1970s (never 'reviewed') which continues to exist with a generation of leaders and militants who were trained in those years (Mershon, 1990). It is important, though, that the themes of flexibility and new technologies were accepted without problems in all company-level and industry-wide agreements.

Researchers into industrial relations have so far attached great significance to the uniqueness of the Italian situation, but it is losing credibility. The recent history of industrial relations in Italy should be seen as the history of the Europeanization of these relations rather than as a history showing specific Italian characteristics and deviations, even though those were present, of course (Saba, 1988; Craveri, 1982). The main outlines of the Europeanization in the second half of the 1980s and the beginning of the 1990s are the following. In May 1986, a general agreement was signed between Confindustria and the three large trade unions. This agreement put a stop to the ambiguous interpretations in connection with the *scala mobile* and wages, which arose after the agreement of February 1983.[59] On 16 July of the same year, the trail-blazing 'Intersind-Protocol' was signed, involving the trade unions in the reorganization and development of the Institute for Industrial Reconstruction (*Istituto per la Ricostruzione Industriale*, IRI), the most important public holding.

The main residue of the old system was the *scala mobile*. It had been adopted in 1945 and was later, in 1983-1984, only partly reversed. In June 1989, negotiations started between trade unions and the Confindustria about the global revision of the system of collective bargaining. The negotiations dragged on for four years, with various interim agreements, consecutive discussions and conflicts, particularly between the CISL/UIL and the CGIL. The *scala mobile* was eventually abolished. On 3 July 1993, for the first time in Italian history, a general agreement was reached on a new system of industrial relations. Trade union representation in the workplace remained in theory the same, but by mutual agreement the procedures surrounding meetings, dialogue and cooperation were now tightly regulated.[60]

When moving on from collective bargaining to other aspects of trade union activities to see how the various trade union factions coped with the fundamental transformations in Italian society, other, less obvious innovations can be found. Firstly, the various organizations responded differently to the fact that the spotlight is no longer on the labour issue or the living conditions of the working population. The UIL chose the most radical interpretation, claiming it wants to be a 'trade union of citizens', protecting and serving both employees and those not working, both in the workplace and outside. The CGIL, as 'general and programme trade union', practical as ever, is moving the centre line of its own organization to regional level, directing its attention to new movements and organizations (of unemployed, pensioners, workseeking youths, women, etc.). The CISL seems to focus its attention foremost on the workers, even though it is setting up numerous services open to all. Anyway, the CISL was originally set up and organized as an industrial and occupational union, and it can't abandon this at a time when various signs become apparent of a new demand by most skilled workers and clerks for a professional and workers' identity. The problem of the CISL lies rather with striking the right balance between the centre and the federations, between strong occupations and weak social groups, between interdependence, solidarity and strong local identity and workers' identities.

Following on from there, the health service and welfare provision deserve some attention. The Italian health service was substantially reformed as late as 1978, when services became more generally available and more widely spread. The reforms took place against the background of a previously chaotic system, containing elements of insurance and supplementary benefit. From then onwards and throughout the 1980s, the unions were at pains not to block any attempt at a counter-reform. There was a continuous stream of annual corrections at the time of the national budget. The numerous proposals for reform were opposed and never carried out. With the country moving towards a slimmer welfare system - in which the State would only take care of a few essential services, encouraging people to provide for their own needs - the efforts of the trade unions, channelled through the federations of pensioners, were concentrated on a defence of the current pensions. With reservation (from the CGIL) and stimulation (from the CISL) a policy of 'integrated pensions' was established along the principles of subsidiarity.

Perspectives for a trade movement in a country in political transition

In the first half of the 1990s, Italy was once again plunged into a period of profound changes, especially of a political nature. The ideological block formation which characterized the post-war period and hence the entire political system, collapsed in a spectacular way. The changed international situation with the visible bankruptcy of the communist regimes in Central and Eastern Europe and the collapse of the Eastern Block and the Soviet Union itself justified qualms about political relationships. At this moment, the persistent unwillingness of politicians and trade unions alike to deal with Italy's big problems (such as the economic and cultural divide between the industrial north and the underdeveloped south of the country, and the unsavoury aspects of the patronage system which had created openings for the underworld to penetrate the machinery of government) wreaked absolute havoc. It transpired that the ideological and political front often covered up immoral practices.

The old political parties were practically wiped out by the new political forces. However, on closer inspection, these forces turned out to be less new than they themselves pretended. That is clearly the case for the relaunched neofascist movement which undoubtedly has its roots in the period between the wars, regardless of how it chooses to disguise itself by name or appearance and despite the ideas in its actual programme on the free market and democracy. The Lega Nord can be considered as a new format for the old Italian regionalism, a problem which has never been taken seriously by the political class and which today has emerged with particular strength. Though the most important political formation to date, personified by media-mogul Silvio Berlusconi, presents itself in a non-ideological way, it is on closer inspection the product of the old system and the exponent of political and economic neo-liberalism.

The previously active political movements are not yet capable of a meaningful response. The once so powerful Christian-democratic movement, in particular, is out for the count, splintered and torn by nostalgia for power, by widely divergent social views, and by its inability to rebuild its own perspective despite a bid to hark back to the democratic tradition of the Partito Popolare from the 1920s. Communism still lives as an ideology in various forms and shapes bearing a neo-marxist hallmark. It still exists as a faction within the Democratic Left Party (Partito Democratico della Sinistra, PDS), the latter ensuring some continuity from the past by way of the sickle and hammer at the foot of an oak in its emblem. But the perspective of a protagonist party vying for power on behalf of the working class, backed by strong principles and an inheritance such as Antonio Gramsci's, is gone. With it have disappeared the grounds for the old sharp conflicts, in which the choices between good and evil and in defence of civilisation were forcefully stake.

What then are the consequences for the trade union movement of the recent changes in the social and political system, and more particularly of the political landslide ? It is still hard to tell. The political parties have not - so far - dragged the trade unions down with them in their fall, despite the fact that they have always been linked to them, even throughout the turbulent 1970s when they took their distance. On the contrary, the trade unions prove to be an opposition to be reckoned with, as appeared from the massive reactions against the pension plan of the Berlusconi government. Nevertheless, the representative power of the unions has been affected. The membership of the confederations, especially the CGIL, is decreasing, even though the movement has not completely collapsed. A referendum in June 1995 also decided to abrogate some pro-union laws. On the other hand, the new regionalist movements try to raise a universal popular movement, and the trade unions can play a role in this process. The Lega Lombarda, for instance, launched its own trade union, SAL (Sindacato Autonomo Lombardo), not without success in a few industrial counties in the North. Particularly in the public sector, militant rank and file committees (*cobas*) are pushing themselves forward in competition with the established trade unions, even though the latter try to usher in these groups as they did in the 1970s. The question remains whether the trade union landscape is threatened with fragmentation (Ferner & Hyman, 1992).

The CGIL is trying to tackle the threat to its level of representation, particularly by internal reorganization and renewal of its policies (Di Nicola, 1993, n. 31; Galantini and Nardini, 1994). The fact that it has not yet fully come to terms with its past is undoubtedly causing some problems. The CGIL still shares some common ground with the PDS, especially after the disappearance of the socialist party, its traditional competitor for the leadership in the CGIL. The origins of its leadership on all levels, the same grassroots support, a common cultural development all point to this close alliance between the CGIL and the PDS. There is little doubt, however, that the symbiosis will never be as absolute and explicit as it has been in the past.

The CISL still seems wrapped in a contrary attitude, presenting itself as the trade union that always emphasized its independence from politics. It thereby completely ignores the far-reaching personal and institutional entwining between the DC and the CISL in the 1950s and 1960s (the distance created between both in the 1970s is being interpreted by domestic as well as foreign observers as a rift). The latest evolution shows at the one hand a CISL longing back to the original idea of a trade union as a free association, independent of any political interference. On the other hand, at the end of the 1980s, a few trade union leaders from the CISL took the place of Christian-democratic politicians who had disappeared from the public scene after the *mani pulite* (clean hands) actions.

Recently the potential unification of the three trade unions has reappeared on the agenda. As we have seen before, substantial ideological differences, explicit as well as implicit ones, remain between them. Nevertheless, formal ritual declarations of belief in unity were made time and again throughout the history of the Italian trade movement, even in periods of fierce conflict. The CISL, CGIL and UIL do not always approach problems in their own way. The differences hence only surface sporadically, and they often remain hidden thanks to negotiations among the leaderships. On the other hand, it is often the problems that cause the solutions to run concurrently, and the general trend is towards an increasingly intensive cooperation. In view of the most unstable character of the Italian political system, a serious prognosis about the viability of trade union pluralism during the years to come is impossible.

Table 2.1
Membership of Italian trade unions (1950-1991) (in thousands)

Year	Total	CGIL	CISL	UIL
1950	5,830.4	4,640.5	1,189.9	?
1955	5,536.4	4,194.2	1,342.2	?
1960	3,907.6	2,583.2	1,324.4	?
1965	4,010.9	2,542.9	1,468.0	?
1970	5,530.1	2,942.5	1,807.6	780.0
1975	7,707.5	4,081.4	2,593.5	1,032.6
1980	9,005.8	4,599.1	3,059.8	1,346.9
1985	8,851.4	4,592.0	2,953.1	1,306.3
1990	10,144.6	5,150.4	3,508.4	1,485.8
1991	10,403.0	5,221.8	3,657.1	1,524.1

Source: 1950-1985: Visser, J. (1989), *European Trade unions in figures 1913-1985*, Kluwer, Deventer/Boston, p. 116.
1990-1991: C. Squarzon, 'La sindacalizzazione', in G. Baglioni, B. Liverani and S. Negrelli (eds.), *Le relazioni sindacali in Italia. Rapporto 1992-93*, Roma, 1994, p. 74.

Abbreviations

ACLI	Associazioni Cristiane dei Lavoratori Italiani (Christian Associations of Italian Workers)
CGIL	Confederazione Generale Italiana del Lavoro (General Confederation of Italian Labour)
CISL	Confederazione Italiana Sindacati Lavoratori (Italian Confederation of Workers' Unions)
DC	Democracia Cristiana (Christian Democratic Party)
FIM	Federazione Italiana Metalmeccanici (Italian Federation of Metalworkers)
FIOM	Federazione Italiana Operai Metalmeccanici (Italian Federation of Blue-Collar Metalworkers)
PCI	Partito Comunista Italiano (Italian Communist Party)
PSI	Partito Socialista Italiano (Italian Socialist Party)
UIL	Unione Italiana del Lavoro (Union of Italian Labour)

Notes

1. This paper is based on an essay by Giampiero Bianchi. It was abridged and slightly edited by Patrick Pasture. A contribution by Prof. Vincenzo Saba has been

incorporated in the introduction and the conclusion. Lina Waterplas provided a working translation of the Italian original and Anne Pieck translated the final version into English. Many of the references for this research were obtained from the library and the archives of the Fondazione Pastore. The author also thanks the management and personnel of the central libraries of the CISL and the CGIL for supplying him with other trade union material. Special thanks is due to many trade union colleagues who have enlightened and clarified many of the topics covered here with their witness testimonies, memories and observations.

2. In Italy, a distinction is made between *liberismo*, a purely economic term referring to the ideology of a free market, and *liberalismo*, referring to the moral awareness of the invidual taking preference over social forces. In this respect, political and economical liberalism are fundamentally different from each other and do not necessarily occur together (Amato, 1976; Bonelli, 1983).
3. The text only contained a few general principles (internal democracy, freedom of speech, independence of political parties) and intentions (reorganization of the trade union, protection of employees, fight against fascism, etc.) in preparation for an agreement on how to take over the existing fascist trade union structures.
4. *Lo statuto approvato all'unanimità al Congresso di Napoli, I congressi della CGIL*, vol. 1, ESI, S. Giovanni in Persiceto, 1970.
5. The ACLI were established in June 1944 under the impetus of Catholic church authorities to involve Christian employees in three areas: spiritual and moral education, witnessing to the faith at work, and active involvement in the unitary union. Pasini, 1974; Rosati, 1975; Boschini, 1975; Sala and Rosati, 1975; Sermani, 1978; Pozzar, 1985; Frigato, 1988.
6. With regard to the launch of Cominform in reaction to the Marshall plan and the instruction given to French and Italian trade union organizations on that occasion to call their members up for action, see Gibianskij, 1993, pp. 489-516. About board meetings at the CGIL, about the Marshall plan, see *Notiziario CGIL*, 30 December 1947, p. 2, and *Notiziario CGIL*, 1 March 1948.
7. La 'Mozione sulle linee di indirizzo e sugli obiettivi dell'azione sindacale', *Bollettino di Informazioni Sindacali*, no. 7, 1950.
8. See CISL (ed.), *Documenti ufficiali dal 1950 al 1958*, CISL, Roma, 1959, pp. 7-23 and CISL (ed.), *I lavoratori difendono l'Italia. L'Italia difenda i lavoratori*, CISL, Roma, 1951, pp. 44-47.
9. *Conglobamento*: criterion for comparing the provisions of the collective agreement with those of the individual contract of employment whereby, in order to establish which conditions are the more favourable for the employee, the comparison is made not clause by clause (...) but between groups of clauses which govern the same subject and which are regarded as inseparable in collective-bargaining terms (Treu, 1991, p. 62).
10. On the reasons underlying the CISL's choice not to join the IFCTU, also see 'La CISL e le altre centrali sindacali internazionali', *Sindacalismo*, nos. 2-3, 1951, pp. 131-132.
11. The communists represented 70 per cent of the membership, the socialists 23 per cent and the independents 7 per cent (*L'Unità*, 1990, p. 19).
12. 'Il Rapporto dell'On. Di Vittorio sull'attivita e le lotte della CGIL', in *I congressi della CGIL*, vol. III, ESI, S. Giovanni in Periscato, 1970, pp. 12-60.

13. See *Crociata di solidarietà nazionale contro la miseria*, in *Orientamenti e direttive di lavoro dal II al III Congresso*, Roma, Ufficio stampa e propaganda CGIL, 1952, pp. 16-17; 'I lavori del Convegno nazionale contro il supersfruttamento', *Notiziario della CGIL*, no. 8, 1 May 1951. At its 1952 congress in Naples the CGIL approved the workers' status in the enterprise (Atti, in *I congressi della CGIL*, vols. 4-5, pp. 36-39).
14. 'Intervento di A. Novella', in *I congressi della CGIL*, vol. 6, pp. 11-59.
15. See note 9.
16. In the 1960s, after the PSI participation in the center-left government, a minority group left the party and founded the PSIUP (Partito Socialista di Unità Proletaria). The majority of the PSI, on the other hand, merged with the social democratic party to form the PSU. After the 1968 election, the PSU was split up again in two parties: the PSI and the PSDI (Partito socialdemocratico italiano).
17. 'Mozione relativa all'attuazione del piano Vanoni... (CISL, Consiglio Generale, 10-11 October 1956), in *La CISL e la programmazione dello sviluppo*, Ufficio Studi e Formazione, Roma, 1964, pp. 54-56.
18. 'Mozione al III congresso (13 maggio 1959)', in *La CISL e la programmazione*, pp. 115-119.
19. 'Mozione sulla politica di sviluppo (CISL, Consiglio Generale, 14-15 October 1959)', in *La CISL...*, op. cit., pp. 119-125.
20. *Atti della Conferenza triangolare tenutasi nella Sala della Maggioranza al Ministero delle Finanze nei giorni 13-14 gennaio 1961*, Tip. Operaia Romana, Roma, 1961.
21. 'Lettera del Ministro del Lavoro alle organizzazioni dei lavoratori e degli imprenditori', in Pirzio Ammassari, 1976, pp. 329-331).
22. Text in 'Parere del Cnel sul programma per il quinquennio 1965-1969 (Cnel, Assemblea del 25 marzo 1965)', *Provasi*, 1976, pp. 229-234.
23. *Osservazioni presentate al Rapporto del prof. Saraceno dal rappresentante della CGIL, on. A. Novella, e dall'esperto dott. Andreina nella Commissione nazionale per la programmazione economica*, CGIL, Roma, 1964, pp. 169
24. 'Intervento di A. Novella', in *I congressi della CGIL*, vol. 7, pp. 15-17.
25. Text in *Rassegna Sindacale*, nos. 104-105, 1967, p. 13.
26. Document in 'Prospettive di unità sindacale' (CISL, Consiglio generale, 7-9 March 1966), *Sindacalismo*, no. 3, 1966, pp. 111-113.
27. See in particular 'Il documento della CGIL sui rapporti tra Stato e società', *Rassegna Sindacale*, no. 113, 1967.
28. See in particular 'Mozione sulla posizione della CISL nella politica di programmazione (8-9 April 1968)', in CISL (ed.), *Documenti ufficiali dal 1962 al 1969*, CISL, Roma, 1970, pp. 149-153 and the report of the General Council meeting of the CGIL in Dec 1968 in Berta, 1982, pp. 2-8.
29. 'Storti-rapport', in CISL, *Per una politica sindacale degli anni '70, Potere contro Potere. Atti del VI Congresso Confederale, Roma, 17-20 luglio 1969*, Roma, January 1970, p. 45.
30. See *I congressi della CGIL*, vol. 7, part 1, ESI, Roma, 1970. The minutes of the committee meetings can be found in *I congressi della CGIL*, part 2, ESI, Roma, 1970. See also Traverso, 1983, pp. 201-210 and the Settimo congresso in *Comunisti e socialisti*, pp. 105-128.
31. See the comment of Berta on Accornero, 1989 in *Ventesimo Secolo*, nos. 5-6, 1992, pp. 274-281.

32. 'Proposta-appello approvata dai Consigli Generali CGIL CISL UIL a conclusione dei lavori della I Assemblea unitaria (26-29 oktober 1970)', *Rassegna Sindacale*, nos. 169-170, 1970, appendix.
33. *Dal 6° Congresso al Patto federativo*, CISL, Roma, 1972, pp. 101-106.
34. La 'Mozione numero 1', in *Atti del VII Congresso Confederale, Roma, 18-21 giugno 1973*, Roma, January 1974, pp. 590 ff.
35. For example, by proposing to expand the model of the workers' councils to the entire trade union reality, and in connection with collective bargaining. Relazione di Lama, in 'I Lavori del Direttivo della Federazione Cgil Cisl Uil', *Ausi*, 12 Dec 1974.
36. 'Testo dell'accordo', *Ausi*, 25 January 1975.
37. 'Relazione introduttiva', in *I congressi della CGIL*, vol. 10, ESI, Roma, 1978, pp 45-49.
38. In connection with the 1977 congress, see 'Un sindacato di partecipazione per l'unità tra i lavoratori, i disoccupati, i giovani e le donne', text of the *Relazione di Bologna*, in G. Benvenuto, *Oltre la crisi. Come la UIL è venuta delineando, in tre congressi, un nuovo modello di sindacato*.
39. *Verso l'8° congresso*, complete edition of the two resolutions submitted to congress in *Conquiste del Lavoro*, 14 March 1977, p. 59.
40. 'Per una svolta di politica economica e di sviluppo civile e deocratico', document, amended and approved at the EUR-meeting, in *Atti CISL 1978-1981*, Edizioni Lavoro, Roma, 1981, pp. 623 ff. Statements made by the leaders in *Ausi*, 8 January 1977.
41. See for instance *Il 30° anniversario della costituzione CISL*, appendix with no. 54, July 1980.
42. This fund would be managed by the trade unions and financed by a central tax of 0.5 per cent levied on the workers' wages.
43. See the paper by the Minister for Employment, *Fondo di solidarietà dei lavoratori. Documentazione*, Istituto Poligrafico dello Stato, Roma, 1981, p. 72.
44. See the reactions of the Secretary-Generals of the CGIL, the CISL and the UIL in *L'Unità*, 17 October 1980 and P. Carniti in *Ausi*, 3 November 1980; G. Benvenuto in *L'Avvenire*, 21 October 1980; and Garavini, in *L'Unità*, 23 October 1980.
45. *Capire il nuovo, guidare il cambiamento. Atti del IX Congresso CISL. Roma, 7-12 ottobre 1981*, CISL, Roma, 1982; see also B. Manghi, *Rileggendo le carte. Le mozioni conclusive del IX Congresso*, in *CISL: 1981-1985*, EL, Roma, 1985, pp. 99-111.
46. *Anni '80: dall'antagonismo al protagonismo*, Roma, 10-14 June 1981.
47. 'Relazione di Luciano Lama', in *I congressi della CGIL*, Ediesse, Roma, 1986, p.19 and 'Mozioni finali', pp. 650-702.
48. See *Rassegna Sindacale*, nrs. 5-6, February 1984, monographic number and 'Nota sull'incontro tra le segreterie CGIL CISL UIL e la Confindustria, 23 luglio 1983', in *La CISL* and 'Consiglio Generale, Roma, 12/13 dicembre 1983', in *La CISL* , pp. 575-578. Regarding the CGIL one should remember that it was still divided in factions. In 1972 the communist faction represented 61 per cent, the socialists 33 per cent and others 6 per cent. See *L'Unità difficile tra dosaggi e rotture*, p. 19.
49. The resolutions of the congress in *La CISL dal X al XI Congresso, Documenti*, EL, Roma, 1989 and the interventions and reports in Conquiste del Lavoro, supplement, July 1985.

50. 'Relazione, Replica e Mozioni approvati all'XI Congresso Confederale CISL', of July 1989, in *Conquiste del Lavoro*, nos. 166, 173-174 and 179-180, of 1989.
51. *Risoluzione sull'uso del referendum*, in *La CISL dal X al XI Congresso*, pp. 367-368. *Nota sull'insegnamento della religione cattolica*, ibid., p. 529.
52. Report by G. Benvenuto, 'Volgersi al nuovo', in Benvenuto, *Oltre la crisi*. See also *Sindacato e terzo polo*, Milano, F. Angeli, 1987 and on the further implementation of this notion of the union as 'citizens' league' see Scheggi Merlini, 1985.
53. See 'CGIL, bilancio di 40 anni', *Quaderni di Rassegna Sindacale*, nos. 114-115, October 1985.
54. See L. Lama, 'Relazione introduttiva', in *I congressi della CGIL*, Ediesse, Roma, pp. 15-36.
55. B. Trentin, 'Autonomia e progetto', *Nuova Rassegna Sindacale*, 12 December 1988. The ideas expressed in this reorientation were already present in his book *Le dottrine neocapitaliste* from 1962.
56. *Percorso per un programma*, Ediesse, Roma, 1990 and *Atti della Conferenza di Chianciano*, 12 April 1989.
57. See in particular the introduction in *I congressi della CGIL*, XII Congresso Nazionale, Ediesse, Roma, 1993. On the motives of the dissolution of the socialist faction see 'Il convegno dei dirigenti comunisti', *Nuova Rassegna Sindacale*, November 1990.
58. B. Trentin, 'Le conclusioni' (Conferenza di Chianciano), *Nuova Rassegna Sindacale'*, June 1994, p. 61.
59. Text of the agreement in *Il Sole-24 Ore*, 8 May 1986.
60. Text of the agreement in *Il Sole-24 Ore*, 10 July 1993.

References

Accornero, A. (1992), *La parabola del sindacato. Ascesa e declino di una cultura*, Il Mulino, Bologna.
Amato, G. (1976), *Economia, politica e istituzioni in Italia*, Il Mulino, Bologna.
Amato, G. (ed.) (1972), *Il governo dell'industria in Italia*, Il Mulino, Bologna.
Arisio, L. (1990), *Vita da capi. L'altra faccia di una grande fabbrica*, Etaslibri, Milano.
Auletta, A. (1979), 'Soggetti e politiche delle relazioni industriali: la UIL', in Peschiera, F. (ed.), *Sindacato, industria e Stato negli anni del centrismo. Storia delle relazioni industriali dal 1948 al 1958*, Le Monnier, Florence, pp. 376-413.
Baglioni, G. (1975), *Il sindacato dell'Autonomia. L'evoluzione della CISL nella pratica e nella cultura*, De Donato, Bari.
Beccattini, G. (ed.) (1987), *Mercato e forze locali. Il distretto industriale*, Il Mulino, Bologna.
Berta, G. (1982), 'La produttività nella storia del movimento sindacale', *Industria e Sindacato*, no. 11, pp. 2-8.
Berta, G. (1987), 'La contrattazione come processo di adattamento', *Industria e Sindacato*, no. 6, pp. 9-11.
Berta, G. (1992), 'Originalità storica della via italiana', *Ventesimo Secolo*, nos. 5-6, pp. 274-281.
Bianchi, G. (1987), 'L'esperienza di "Forze Sociali" (1952-1958)', *Annali della Fondazione G.Pastore*, vol. 14, pp. 29-94.

Bonanni, G. (1985), 'Il Patto di Roma documenti inediti', *Quaderni di Rassegna Sindacale*, May-August, pp. 162-174.
Bonelli, F. (1983), 'Storia ed economia nell'industrializzazione italiana dalle origini al Welfare State', in *Atti del Convegno Governare l'economia*, Cedes, Roma, pp. 69-77.
Boni, P. (1993), *FIOM, 100 anni di un sindacato industriale*, Ediesse, Roma.
Boschini, A. (1975), *Chiesa e Acli*, Dehoniane, Napoli.
Carbognin, M. and Paganelli, L. (1981), *Il sindacato come esperienza. Ventidue militanti si raccontano*, EL, Roma.
Carera, A. (1979), *L'azione sindacale in Italia. Dall'estraneità alla partecipazione*, Vol. 2, La Scuola, Brescia.
Castronovo, V. (1992), 'L'economia italiana dal II dopoguerra ad oggi', *Rivista di Storia Contemporanea*, nos. 2-3, pp. 297-326.
Cella, G. P., Manghi, B. and Pasini, R. (1969), *La concezione sindacale della CGIL: un sindacato per la classe*, Acli, Roma.
Cella, G. P., Manghi, B. and Piva, P. (1972), *Un sindacato italiano negli anni '60. La FIM-CISL dall'associazione alla classe*, De Donato, Bari, pp. 216-223.
Ciampani, A. (1991), *Lo statuto del sindacato nuovo (1944-1951)*, EL, Roma.
Comunisti e socialisti nei congressi della CGIL (1984), Rapporti CESOS, no. 14, March, pp. 7-128.
Cova, A. (ed.) (1989), *La formazione dell'economia contemporanea. Vita e Pensiero*, Brescia.
Craveri, P. (1977), *Sindacato e istituzioni nel dopoguerra*, Il Mulino, Bologna.
Craveri, P. (1982), 'Dalla contrattazione graduale al contrattualismo senza gradualità', in Intersind, *Dieci anni di attività contrattuale 1958-1967*, in *Quaderni di Industria e Sindacato*, no. 7, pp. 6-26.
Craveri, P. (1986), 'Il progetto UIL nel contesto politico-istituzionale', in Benvenuto, G. (ed.), *Oltre la crisi. Come la UIL è venuta delineando in 3 congressi un nuovo modello di sindacato*, Politecnico, Roma, pp. 14-15.
Cristina Sermani, M. (1978), *Le ACLI*, Dehoniane, Napoli.
Crouch, C. and Pizzorno, A. (eds.) (1977), *Conflitti in Europa. Lotte di classe, sindacati e stato dopo il 1968*, Etas, Milano.
De Santis, G. (1993-1994), *I sindacati italiani e Solidarnosc 1980-1985*, tesa di laurea, facoltà di scienze politiche, Roma I, Storia dell'Europa orientale.
Di Gioia (1975), *La CGIL nei suoi statuti 1944-1974*, ESI, Roma.
Di Nicola, P. (1989), *Quarant'anni di tesseramento CGIL (1948-1988)*, Ediesse, Roma.
Di Nicola, P. (1993), 'La geografia della CGIL', *Nuova Rassegna Sindacale*, no. 31, pp. 25-29.
Ferner, A. and Hyman, R. (eds.) (1992), *Industrial Relations in the New Europe*, Blackwell, Oxford.
Ferrari, A. (1984), 'Itinerario di un disegno riformista: "Realtà sociale d'oggi e il magistero di M.Romani"', in Ferrari, A. (ed.), *La Civiltà industriale, colpa e redenzione*, Morcelliane, Brescia, pp. 81-109.
Foa, V. (1991), *Il cavallo e la torre*, Einaudi, Torino.
La Fondazione della UIL: I testimoni (1989), Oikos, Roma.
Forbice, A. (1981), *Scissioni sindacali e origini della UIL*, Edizioni Lavoro, Roma.
Forbice, A. and Favero, P. (1968), *I socialisti e il sindacato*, Palazzi, Milano.
Frigato, S. (1988), *I lavoratori cattolici tra testimonianza e politica. Storia teologica dei rapporti tra coscienza cattolica e impegno storico nelle ACLI e nell'MCL*, Elle di Ci, Torino.

Gabaglio, E. (1990), 'I sindacati italiani e la Polonia', in *L'Europa Ritrovata*, May-June, pp. 47-52.
Galantini, E. and Nardini, M. (1994),' Scommettere sul rinnovamento. Un'analisi dei dati per categorie e territori', *Nuova Rassegna Sindacale*, no. 10, pp. 36-43.
Galli, G. (1969), *I cattolici e il sindacato*, Palazzi, Milano.
Ganapini, L. (1984), 'I sindacati italiani dalla ricostruzione al 1968', intervento al convegno, *I sindacati occidentali dall'800 ad oggi in una prospettiva storica comparata*, testo dattiloscritto, Milano, 28 April.
Giacinto, E. (ed.) (1991), *1986-1990 cinque anni di sindacalizzazione*, E.L., Roma.
Gibianskij, L. (1993), 'La Costituzione del Cominform (alla luce dei nuovi materiali d'archivio)', *Storia Contemporanea*, no. 4, August, pp. 489-516.
Ginzborg, P. (1988), *Storia dell'Italia dal dopoguerra ad oggi. Società e Politica 1943-1988*, Einaudi, Torino, 2 vols.
Goodmann, E. and Bramford, J. (eds.) (1989), *Small firms and Industrial District in Italy*, Routledge, London.
Horowitz, D. (1966), *Storia del movimento sindacali in Italia*, Il Mulino, Bologna.
Izar, A. V. (1979), 'L'intervento dello Stato nel lavoro', in Peschiera, F. (ed.), *Sindacato, industria e Stato negli anni del centrismo. Storia delle relazioni industriali dal 1948 al 1958*, Le Monnier, Firenze, pp. 244-255.
La CISL e la programmazione dello sviluppo, a cura dell'Ufficio Studi e Formazione, Roma, 1964, pp. 54-56.
Lama, L. (1971), 'Dieci anni di processo unitario', *Quaderni di Rassegna Sindacale*, no. 29, pp. 3-28.
Lanaro, S. (1992), *Storia dell'Età repubblicana. Dalla fine della guerra agli anni '90*, Marsilio, Padova.
Lanzardo, L. (1989), *Personalità operaia e coscienza di classe. Comunisti e cattolici nelle fabbriche torinesi del dopoguerra*, F. Angeli, Milano.
Mershon, C. (1990), 'Generazioni di leader sindacali in fabbrica. L'eredità dell'autunno caldo', *Polis*, no. 2, pp. 277-323.
Nicola, P. (1989), 'La UIL rinnovata con maggiori adesioni', *Lavorosocietà*, no. 4, pp. 8-13.
Pasini, G. (1974), *Le ACLI delle origini*, Coines, Roma.
Pastore, G. (1955), in AA.VV., *I sindacati in Italia*, Einaudi, Torino.
Pasture, P. (1994), *Christian Trade Unionism in Europe Since 1968. Tensions Between Identity and Practice*, Avebury, Aldershot.
Pillon, C. (1972), *I comunisti e il sindacato*, Palazzi, Milano.
Pirzio Ammassari, G. (1976), *La politica della Confindustria*, Napoli, Liguori.
Pizzorno, A. (1980), *I soggetti del pluralismo. Classi partiti sindacati*, Il Mulino, Bologna.
Pizzorno, A. (ed.) (1974-1978), *Lotte operaie e sindacato in Italia, 1968-1972*, Vol. 6, Etas, Milano.
Pozzar, V. (1985), *Quarant'anni di ACLI*, Ed. ACLI/Formazione Lavoro, Roma.
Provasi, G. (1976), *Borghesia industriale e Democrazia cristiana*, De Donato, Bari.
Regini, M. (1981), *I dilemmi del sindacato*, Il Mulino, Bologna.
Riosa, A. (1975), 'Le concezioni sociali e politiche della CGIL', in *30 anni della CGIL*, Roma, pp. 8-32.
Romagnoli, G. (1980), *La sindacalizzazione tra ideologia e pratica. Il caso italiano (1950-1977)*, EL, Roma.

Romagnoli, U. (1988), 'Il secondo dopoguerra: della ricostruzione all' autumno 1969', in CGIL (ed.), *Il lavoro della Confederazione. Immagini per la storia del sindacato e del movimento operaio in Italia, 1906-1986*, Mezzotte, Milano, pp. 309-317.

Romani, M. (1988a), 'Tendenze e linee di sviluppo del movimento sindacale', in Zaninelli, S. (ed.), *M. Romani. Il risorgimento sindacale in Italia. Scritti e discorsi (1951-1971)*, F. Angeli, Milano, pp. 37-54.

Romani, M. (1988b), 'Il sindacalismo italiano ad una scelta', in Zaninelli, S. (ed.), *M. Romani. Il risorgimento sindacale in Italia. Scritti e discorsi (1951-1971)*, F. Angeli, Milano, pp. 287-323.

Romero, F. (1993), *The United States and the European Trade Union Movement. 1944-1951*, University of North Carolina, Chapel Hill.

Rosati, D. (1975), *La questione politica delle ACLI*, Dehoniane, Napoli.

Rossi, A., Valentini, A. and Lodici, C. (1979), 'I soggetti delle relazioni industriali: la UIL', in Peschiero, F. (ed.), *Sindacato, industria e Stato negli anni del centrismo*, vol. 2, Le Monnier, Firenze, pp. 376-413.

Rossi, A., Valentini, A. and Lodici, C. (1983), 'Soggetti e politiche di relazioni industriali: la UIL', in Peschiero, F. (ed.), *Sindacato, industria e Stato negli anni del centrosinistra*, vol. 3, Le Monnier, Firenze, pp. 272-306.

Saba, V. (1980), 'Dalla CIL alla CISL', in Baglioni, G. (ed.), *Analisi della CISL*, vol. 1, EL, Roma, pp. 3-23.

Saba, V. (1983), *Giulio Pastore sindacalista. Dalle Leghe bianche alla fondazione della CISL (1918-1958)*, Edizioni Lavoro, Roma.

Saba, V. (1985), *Essere CISL*, EL, Roma.

Saba, V. (1986), 'La FIM degli anni '50', *Lavoro e Sindacato*, no. 2, pp. 5-24.

Saba, V. (1986), 'Aldilà della crisi della Federazione unitaria. Presente e avvenire del sindacalismo in Italia', in FISBA CISL (ed.), *Verso una nuova era del sindacato*, EL, Roma, pp. 11-24.

Saba, V. (1987), *L'esperienza sindacale italiana dalla costituzione della CISL ad oggi*, EL, Roma.

Saba, V. (1988), 'Italia. Si tende all'europeizzazione', *Quaderni di Industria e Sindacato*, no. 24, pp. 37-54.

Saba, V. (1988), 'La dinamica dei rapporti fra impresa e sindacato', *Quaderni di Industria e Sindacato*, no. 23, pp. 145-171.

Saba, V. and Bianchi, G. (1990), *La nascita della CISL (1948-1951)*, Edizioni Lavoro, Roma.

Saba, V. (1993), 'La risposta alla crisi degli anni '70', *Progetto*, nos. 75-76, pp. 29-34.

Sala, F. and Rosati, D. (1975), *L'autocritica delle ACLI*, Dehoniane, Napoli.

Sapelli, G. (1989), *L'Italia inafferrabile*, Marsilio, Venezia.

Sapelli, G. (1994), *Economia, tecnologia e direzione d'impresa in Italia*, Einaudi, Torino.

Savona, P. (1993), 'Carli in Confindustria: una testimonianza', *Economia Italiana*, no. 3, pp. 361-368.

Scheggi Merlini, L. (1985), *Il ritorno del gigante*, F.Angeli, Milano.

Scoppola, P. (1990), *La Repubblica dei partiti. Profilo storico della democrazia in Italia (1945-1990)*, Il Mulino, Bologna.

Sermani, M.C. (1978), *Le ACLI*, Dehoniane, Napoli.

Simoncini, F. (1986), *Dall'interno della UIL (1950-1985)*, F.Angeli, Milano.

Starita, C. (1992), 'Problemi dello sviluppo e trasformazione della politica sindacale nella CGIL degli anni '50', *Studi Storici*, nos. 2-3, pp. 581-617.

Strinati, V. (1992), 'La sinistra italiana di fronte alle trasformazioni del capitalismo (1953-1963)', *Studi Storici*, nos. 2-3, pp. 555-582.

Tatò, A. (ed.) (1969), *Di Vittorio l'uomo e il dirigente*, Esi, Roma.

Traverso, V. (1983), 'Soggetti e politiche di relazioni industriali: la CGIL', in Peschiera, F. (ed.), *Sindacato, industria e Stato negli anni del centro-sinistra*, vol. 3, Le Monnier, Firenze, pp. 165-210.

'I tre interventi in inflazione, investimenti e unità sindacale: il Direttivo CGIL del 15-19 luglio 1946' (1976), *Quaderni di Rassegna Sindacale*, nos. 59-60, March-June, pp. 227-232.

Trentin, B. (1962), 'Le dottrine neo-capitalistiche e l'ideologia delle forze dominanti nella politica economica italiana', *Atti del Convegno*, Istituto Gramsci, Roma, pp. 97-144.

Trentin, B. (1978), in AA.VV., *Il Piano del lavoro della CGIL, 1949-1950*, Feltrinelli, Milano, pp. 196-199.

Trentin, B. (1993), 'Ricordando Di Vittorio', numero speciale di *Nuova Rassegna Sindacale*, no. 3, pp. 24-33.

Treu, T. (1973), 'La CISL degli anni 50 e le ideologie giuridiche dominanti', *Materiali per una storia della cultura giuridica*, Il Mulino, Bologna.

Treu, T. and Romagnoli, U. (1977), *I Sindacati in Italia. Storia di una strategie*, Il Mulino, Bologna.

Treu, T. (1984), *Il patto contro l'inflazione. Contenuti e documenti delle intese governo-sindacati*, EL, Roma.

Treu, T. (1991), *European Employment and Industrial Relations. Glossary: Italy*, Sweet and Maxwell, Office for Official Publications of the European Communities.

Turone, S. (1988), *Storia del sindacato*, Laterza, Bari.

Turone, S. (1989), *Il sindacato nell'Italia del benessere*, Laterza, Bari.

Turone, S. (1990), *Storia dell'Unione Italiana del Lavoro*, Franco Angeli, Milano, pp. 162-165.

'L'Unità difficile tra dosaggi e rotture' (1990), *Nuova Rassegna Sindacale*, no. 37, p. 19.

Valcavi, D. (1989), *Linee di sviluppo della contrattazione collettiva*, Isper, Torino.

'A vent'anni dall'autunno caldo' (1989), in *Prospettiva Sindacale*, pp. 3-264.

Zamagni, V. (1990), *Dalla periferia al centro. La seconda rinascita economica italiana 1861-1988*, Il Mulino, Bologna.

Zaninelli, S. (ed.) (1981), *Il Sindacato nuovo*, F.Angeli, Milano.

3 Belgium: Pragmatism in pluralism

Patrick Pasture

Belgium: a federal, pluralistic and neo-corporatist state

Although Belgium is deeply divided, it has managed to overcome these cleavages through a particular political system which has sometimes been labelled as 'consociatonal democracy' (H. Lijphart; K. Mc Rae; H. Daalder).[1] One major feature of this system is the actual division of society in mutual integrated networks of organizations with a common Weltanschauung, which are known as 'pillars'. The most important 'pillars' in Belgium are those elaborated by the Catholic and the socialist movements; there is also a less well-developed conservative-liberal pillar. On the Flemish-nationalist side there is a small network of organizations which some also refer to as a pillar.

At first sight this pillarization, in contrast to the situation in the Netherlands, has remained relatively unaffected to this day. Following a period of increasing cooperation in the 1960s, the old ideological cleavages were emphatically reinforced at the end of the seventies - including on a cultural level - and the different pillars actually began to diverge once again (Pasture, 1992, pp. 383-390, 1995c). However, all is not what it seems. Several authors have demonstrated that the ideological basis of these networks has been strongly watered down and that it is ultimately only the secondary features of the 'pillars', namely the organizational bloc-formation and the strategic jostling for power, which remain. In other words, the pillars have outlived themselves and have largely become 'empty boxes', within which there may well still be a common 'spirit', but which can of themselves no longer exert a binding force on their members and which certainly do not offer a mobilizing ideal (Huyse, 1984, 1987; Hellemans, 1990).[2] Moreover, since the start of the 1980s, new challenges have no longer been structured via the existing pillar organizations: as recent changes in the media landscape have shown, different fault lines have become more important (Pasture, 1995c).

To date, the trade union movement has continued to follow the main ideological cleavages.[3] There are three trade union confederations in Belgium: the Christian Trade Union Confederation (ACV/CSC), the largest of the three and particularly strong in Flanders; the socialist General Belgian Trade Union Confederation (ABVV/FGTB), which has its traditional power base in Wallonia; and the General Confederation of Liberal Trade Unions in Belgium (ACLVB/CGSLB), which can be seen as the little brother of the other two (membership figures in table 3.1, p. 127). These three confederations are virtually without competition, with the exception of unions representing middle managers and certain public services (e.g. the railways). The trade unions are closely attached via both formal and informal links to the other organizations in the pillarized labour movement - mutual health care funds, cooperative societies, etc. - and with the other pillar organizations, the political parties in particular, even when relations with the latter, especially within the Catholic pillar, are increasingly difficult.

In addition to being a pillarized country, Belgium is also divided along community lines. However, most institutions and also, in particular, the social and economic consultative bodies, remained national until the end of the 1960s. From the 1960s onwards, the problem of the dual communities, which found its focus mainly in the language issue, became a central political theme in Belgium. The labour movement partly supported this change. Historically, the Christian labour movement in Flanders had associated itself with the Flemish movement (Wils, 1986, 1992), although this seems to us to be less clearly the case for the trade unions, exception made for the Flemish white collar workers. The socialist movement in general for a long time adopted a more neutral stance in this respect. With the industrial decline of Wallonia since the late 1950s and the broad strike action against the so-called 'Unity Law' in 1960-61, however, the more radical leftist wing within the socialist trade unions argued for economic and political federalism in order to realize structural reforms at least in the southern part of the country (Deruette, 1991; Neuville and Yerna, 1990; Moreau, 1984). The successive constitutional reforms of 1970, 1980 and, in particular, 1988 and 1993, shifted more and more power to the regions or communities, including the power to determine economic policy, planning policy and urban development, matters concerning the living environment, housing, employment and public works and transport (1988). Since 1980 in particular, new regionalized socio-economic consultative bodies grew up alongside the existing organizations. The joint industrial councils, however, which form the cornerstone of the social consultative system, are still not split to this day (Stroobant, 1990). The trade unions adjusted their stance to match this evolution. But contrary to the political parties, which did split, they still retain a national structure, albeit with regional wings. In fact, the trade unions nowadays count among the mere 'unitary' forces of Belgium. Until the present day, the formulation of union ideology, fundamental objectives and programmes have continued to take place at national level. It is for this reason that this chapter adopts a largely unitary stance; where necessary, however, community-specific aspects will also be discussed.

The rate of unionization in Belgium is among the highest in the Western world, with only the Scandinavian countries having a proportionately higher rate (Visser, 1991). Moreover the Belgian trade unions also achieved a fairly high level of penetration in the service sector, not only in the public services but also in the private sector. This strong position of the trade union movement can be attributed to several factors. The trade unions undoubtedly owe their growth to a significant extent to their extensive service-provision, and in particular to their role in the organization of unemployment insurance; to this day unemployment benefit is paid out via the trade unions. The breakthrough by the trade unions in the inter-war period came about mainly as a result of the movement's response to mass unemployment during the economic crisis of the 1930s (Vanthemsche, 1994b). The trade union movement also continued to expand its service-provision after that time, and enjoyed the fruits of its efforts. The growth of the trade union movement immediately after the Second World War was due mainly to the introduction of compulsory unemployment insurance, the greater recognition the movement received as a result of the development of the joint consultative system, and the substantial increase in union power that resulted from it (Pasture and Mampuys, 1990; Pasture, 1992). The recognition of trade union representation in individual companies also offered the unions greater opportunities to provide services, whereby service and the promotion of both individual and collective interests went hand in hand. The continuing strength of the Belgian trade union movement in the 1980s also owed much to its strong position in the workplace, next to the payment of unemployment benefits (Hancké, 1993; Hancké and Slomp, 1993).

From the 1920s there were attempts to organize labour relations on a joint basis. The first joint committees (at sectoral level) date from 1919; their number increased considerably after the wave of strikes in 1936. After 1945 the principle of joint organization of labour relations was reinforced and extended to social security. Following the so-called 'Social Pact' of April 1944, the employers gradually recognized the trade unions as the representatives of the workers and as an equal partner, while the trade union movement expressed its respect to the economic authority of the employers (Luyten, 1995b; Pasture, 1993b; 1995c; Luyten and Vanthemsche, 1995). This principle led in 1948 to the setting up of a series of joint consultative bodies for social and economic affairs, both at industrial sector and national 'interprofessional' level, i.e. for all industries together. Within individual companies, the Works Councils (and the Health and Safety Committees) were given almost exclusive social powers. Trade union representation was recognized within companies and was accorded a service-providing and mainly combative function (1947). After an intermediate period government wage control in 1947 was handed over to the employers' and employees' organizations. In the practice of social consultation an 'exchange' process developed, in which the trade unions first consented in contributing to the increase of productivity in return of more explicit recognition in the companies (see for example the productivity aggreements of 1954 and 1957) and by the 1960s agreed to guarantee social peace in exchange for 'programmed' social benefits, recognizing the economic authority of the employers (Bundervoet, 1973, 1974). From this period onwards the government adopted a foreground role in economic life. New tripartite consultative bodies were formed in the context of economic programming, which were later also given a regional dimension. The new bodies did away with the distinction between economic and social powers which had characterized the consultative structure of the 1950s (Pasture, 1992).

At the start of the 1970s Belgium underwent a wave of 'wildcat strikes', during which, alongside pay demands and fears about unemployment, a strikingly large number of qualitative demands were raised. The 'established' unions responded - not without some hesitation - on the one hand by adopting a hard stance towards the strike leaders, and on the other hand by modifying their programmes, action resources and organization (Pasture, 1992, ch. 3; Brepoels, 1989, pp.

179-182). Finally, there was not the slightest threat to the existing structures.

What did pose a threat was the economic crisis of the 1970s and 1980s, and the underlying shifts in the industrial pattern. In these years, the government adopted a more regulatory stance, both in the context of its budgetary policies and in its socio-economic policy, in particular with respect to labour and employment. The trust between the social partners was lost: between 1975 and 1986 no new interprofessional social agreement could be reached, partly because the government had reduced the limits within which negotiations over pay could take place to virtually nil. A clear shift took place from negotiation at interprofessional level to negotiation at sector and, later, individual company level, partly as a result of reduced solidarity between employees and the relatively strong (or rather less weakened) position of some national (sectoral) unions (Hancké, 1991; Vilrokx and Van Leemput, 1989).

And yet the basic structure of the Belgian consultative model remained intact. Attempts to organize employee representation outside the trade unions failed, and since 1986 collective bargaining at interprofessional level has been taken up once again. Nevertheless, there has not been a complete recovery of the relatively good relations of the 1960s; the often highly anti-union stance adopted by some employers during the eighties has broken the trust. A section of the employers supported the neo-liberal offensive against the power of the pressure groups, and focused their efforts on reducing government responsibility on the socio-economic front. Despite the reviving economic climate after 1986, the trade unions - partly as a result of these developments, but also partly because of the continuing high unemployment - remained on the defensive. Moreover, the further evolution of labour relations towards the automation of companies and industrial groups was to undermine the impact of the trade union movement. Employers currently call upon judicial proceedings to break strike action, more and more using unilateral procedures which give the unions no opportunities of defence. Judges regularly complied with such proceedings and imposed high penalties upon the strikers, undermining the very right to strike itself. But even without these recent developments strike activity dropped considerably after 1982 (Martens, 1994; comp. Shalev, 1992).

Notwithstanding the gradual decline of unization in recent years (Ebbinghaus and Visser, 1995), the Belgian trade unions still continue to exert a strong power of attraction and do not face significant competition from new sector-specific unions. Their main feature in this respect is that they remain involved at different levels of collective action, even if emphasis is given at trade action at sectoral level.

The influence of the labour movement on Belgian society in general does appear to be very considerable. Via a system of formal and informal channels, which in fact constitute the pillar networks, the labour movement has a direct influence on the political decision-making process; the social ministries - in the first place the Ministries of Labour and Employment and of Social Affairs, but also the Ministries of Public Works, Transport, Welfare, Family and Regional Economy - are all staffed by ministers who have close links with the Christian or socialist labour movement. As a result of the far-reaching politicization, a consequence of the pillarization, the labour movement also has a very emphatic presence in the civil service, something which is reflected particularly in the system of recruitment and appointments (Hondeghem, 1990). Whether this also gives the trade union movement a great deal of power, however, can be discussed.

This politicization - which finally is tried, however, to push back, particularly since the political shake-up following the parliamentary elections of 24 November 1991 [4] ('Politieke benoemingen', 1993, pp. 6-17) - is an essential feature of Belgian society, in which the boundaries between government and pressure groups appear particularly diffuse and where the State cannot be viewed as a 'neutral third party' (Hellemans, 1988b, 1990). A number of functions which are normally taken up by the government are carried out by social organizations. This is particularly true of the organization of the social security system, which is financed partly by social contributions (from employers and employees) and partly by government funding, and which is administered jointly by employers and employees. The implementation of the system (i.e. the payment of benefits), however, is mainly in the hands of the social organizations; for unemployment insurance this means the trade unions, for health insurance the mutual health insurance funds, the so-called 'mutualities' (Vanthemsche, 1994b; Hellemans and Schepers, 1992, pp. 346-364).[5]

In fact, the government's role as a channel for financial transfers goes further than this. In order to maintain the various balances between the opposing groups and power bases, the Belgian pacification democracy has developed a system of compensations, in which the scope given to the pressure groups to develop their activities is guaranteed, and to a large extent financed, by the government.[6] The 'peace' was maintained not only between the pillars, but also between the two language communities, by extensive 'compensation' operations, particularly in the 1970s and early 1980s. Moreover, the emphasis at that time fell squarely on the financial contribution by the State, whereas in the 1950s and 1960s the ideological input was of much greater importance. The most important compensation operations since the 1970s, however, were concerned with language community problems, in which totally different issues were linked in a fairly systematic way. In this way, a system of communicating vessels was created: support for the Wallonian steel industry, for example, was automatically matched by support for the Flemish ports and textile industry. Since the 1980s, however, the limits of this highly expensive pacification technique appear to have been reached (Vilrokx and Van Leemput, 1992).

The socialist trade union movement: reformism and class struggle

Although Belgium was industrialized very early on, it was only quite late that a true trade union movement came into being. The first workers' associations in fact were production and consumer co-operatives dating from the years 1847-1852. The first trade unions for textile workers in Ghent, formed in 1857, were for a long time an isolated phenomenon. Under the influence of the First International Workingmen's Association (1864-1872/76), however, not only were new trade unions founded, but different socialist and anticlerical social views also began to be disseminated among them. From the years 1870s onwards, an ideological drift emerged between the more militant workers in the industrial centres in the south, opposed to centralization and politization, and the social-democrats which developed in Brussels and Ghent (Devreese, 1990). Nevertheless, due to another economic depression which started in 1873, until the 1880s, the trade union movement remained particularly small and mainly restricted to organizations of craftsmen or local occupational groups; there were no umbrella organizations and hardly any political links.

The politicization of the labour movement in the years 1870-fitted in with the growing politico-ideological polarization of Belgian society. In spite of this, the trade unions became involved only slowly in the political campaign for universal suffrage which was being pursued by the Belgian Workers Party (BWP/POB), founded in 1885 as a conglomerate of workers' organizations. It was not until 1898 that a Trade Union Committee was created within the party for the coordination of affiliated trade unions. However, before 1920 the trade unions were not of major importance in the party in comparison with the other political movements, socio-cultural associations, mutual health funds and, above all, cooperatives. By no means all the trade unions of that time joined the BWP/POB and the Trade Union Committee; in addition to the anti-socialist trade unions, which will be discussed in the following section, there were also politically neutral and revolutionary trade unions, which were often greatly influenced by anarchists (Moulaert, 1995). In 1906 the BWP/POB decided that unions which did not wish to join the party, but which were intended to continue the class struggle, could be admitted to the Trade Union Committee. However, several trade unions continued to operate outside the BWP/POB until the First World War, while the Trade Union Committee remained integrated within the socialist party.

The Belgian socialist labour movement was never renowned for its ideological purity. When the BWP/POB was founded, its programme was deliberately kept vague as a reaction against the ideological arguments which had resulted from the First International. In 1894 when, with an eye on the first elections on the basis of universal male plural voting, some ideological and programmatic clarity became necessary, the BWP/POB took up the so-called 'Charter of Quaregnon' as its manifesto (Destrée and Vandervelde, 1903). The Charter was in no way an ideologically homogeneous text, and betrayed influences from quite diverse quarters: progressive liberalism, free-thinking, Marxism, reformism and Proudhonism. The class struggle did, however, stand as the central issue, focusing on a 'socialist messianism'. In practice, the BWP/POB followed a pronounced reformist course. Nevertheless a variety of ideological ideas continued to exist within the party and in the many affiliated associations (Mommen, 1980; Liebman, 1979; Neuville, 1979). The immediate perspective of the BWP/POB remained universal suffrage, in practice restricted, with some minor exceptions, for men only - despite the relatively important role of women in the early years of the Belgian socialist labour movement, the BWP/POB adopted a clearly anti-feminist stance in this respect, in particular from 1901 onwards (for an in-depth account of the role of women in the early Belgian labour movement see Hilden, 1993).

Initially the trade unions, in particular, took up a very reserved, even dismissive position with respect to the parliamentarianism of the BWP/POB. Before the First World War, the trade union wing of the party was in any event weak and completely subordinate to the political struggle for universal suffrage. However, from the moment the 'one man one vote'-principle had been won in 1918, the position of the unions changed. Taken by the democratic mood after the war, they achieved a significant breakthrough in terms of increased recognition, power, and membership. With the foundation of the first joint industrial councils in 1920, they gained institutional status. However, they in fact remained excluded from politico-economical decision-making. Under those circumstances, the socialist trade union movement opted resolutely to chart a pragmatic course emphasizing its social action and striving for the extension of joint social consultation (Luyten, 1995b; Vanthemsche, 1993; Nauwelaerts, 1973). In 1924 the communists were excluded from the socialist trade unions.

Since the unions organized the unemployment insurance system, the economic depression in the 1930s led to a new influx of members - but also to an internal malaise (Vanthemsche, 1993, 1994b). In its economic policies the socialist trade unions did not resist technological innovation, but argued for a social redistribution of productivity gains and trade union participation - anticipating post-war labour regulations as described in the Productivity Act of 1954. They also underlined the necessity for joint organization of the economy. The Trade Union Committee opted firmly for participation by the BWP/POB in government, for consultation and for recognition of the trade union movement by the government and the employers. In 1936 it refused to join a popular front and followed the BWP/POB in its choice for the so-called 'Plan-De Man', which contained important new insights with respect to a more planned state intervention in the economy, with government controll over key industries and finance, but which also respected the bases of a free but regulated market economy.

In 1937 the Trade Union Committee was transformed into the Belgian Trade Union Federation (BVV), no longer as part of the BWP/POB, but as a separate body with its own manifesto, in which the emphasis was placed on economic democracy and the nationalization of basic industries. However, strong ideological as well as personal and structural links remained between the party and the trade union movement (Martin, 1989, pp. 167-169; Vanthemsche, 1993). During the war, however, the socialist trade union movement became deeply divided and fragmented. Together with the Flemish wing of the Christian trade union and with the liberal trade union, an important faction of the movement initially joined the unitary trade union organization, set up by the Germans (Steenhaut, 1993; Hemmerijckx, 1993).

After the war the Belgian Trade Union Federation attempted to set itself up as the focal point of the trade union landscape in restructuration. It thereby also sought to take the wind out of the sails of the leftist Mouvement Syndical Unifié (MSU) and the communist-controlled trade union fighting committees, which had arisen during the German Occupation. The Christian trade union movement declined the honour, however, and ultimately the BVV merged with the MSU and the union fighting committees to form the General Belgian Trade Union Federation (ABVV/FGTB). This led to a radicalization of the programme and a complete cut of the institutional links with the newly formed Belgian Socialist Party (BSP/PSB) - the successor of the former BWP/POB. However, in the sharp polarization in post-war Belgium between Catholics and non-Catholics the ties between the socialist unions and the party were soon restored and the ABVV/FGTB once again became an integral part of the socialist pillar, creating in 1949 a Socialist Common Action. The moderate, reformist wing succeeded, against the background of the Cold War, in having the communists expelled from socialist trade unions - though a militant left wing remained in Liège, under the leadership of André Renard (Hemmerijckx, 1986; Martin, 1989).

Ideologically, the ABVV/FGTB bolstered its position by insisting on structural reforms designed to lead to 'economic democracy' (Vandenbroucke, 1981). The extension of social security, made obligatory for all workers in December 1944, and of the joint consultative system in industrial relations in the next years, were largely influenced by the socialists and were in line with the views of the moderate wing of the ABVV/FGTB, though much less of the radical proposals of the leftists of Renard (Luyten, 1995b). The ABVV/FGTB programme for the following decade, as this was set out at the 1954 and 1956 congresses, argued primarily for greater economic planning, for the control of financial groups and holding companies and for the 'socialization' (i.e. taking into government administration) of the energy sector. The 'socialist state' was to be achieved through 'class struggle' and 'direct action'. This programme showed strong similarities to the pre-war 'Plan-De Man', while the strategy betrayed the influence of Renard's radical left wing.

In 1961 Renard would become the undisputed Walloon leader of the workers' 'uprising' against the so-called 'Unity Law'. Striving for structural reforms and, in a later stadium, for federalism when his plans proved to be impossible to realize within a national framework where the more moderate Flemings succesfully blocked the way to radical reforms (also within the socialist trade union movement itself), Renard symbolized the reaction of the Walloon workers to the general decline of Wallonia's heavy industries. His Mouvement Populaire Wallon, erected in 1962 as a pressure group for structural economic reforms and federalism, and open to everyone who subscribed to its principles (member of the socialist movement or not), emanated from the walloon socialist unions, but its development was hampered by the early death of its charismatic leader in 1962 (Deruette, 1991; Moreau, 1984; Neuville and Yerna, 1990; Kesteloot, 1988, 1993). The practice of the union action of the ABVV/FGTB in the 1950s and '60s remained emphatically reformist, however: together with the two other trade union federations, the ABVV/FGTB joined the employers as a 'social partner' in the joint consultative system, which reached its peak in the mid-1960s. Paradoxically, the left wing of the ABVV/FGTB favoured the system of social programming at interprofessional level, while the more traditional syndicalists disputed it, emphasizing sectoral bargaining (Luyten, 1995b).

At the end of the 1960s the motor of the economy suddenly sputtered, but a revival soon followed as well as a wave of social unrest at the start of the 1970s. For the first time since the 1954 and 1956 congresses the ABVV/FGTB decided in January 1971 to hold a major ideological congress to reflect on its fundamental aims and to redefine its position in the changed socio-economic climate. Consumption occupied a central position in the analysis: the core of 'neo-capitalism' was that consumption was determined by production, and not the other way round as suggested by the liberal credo 'The customer is always right'. This observation led to the inference of a new alienation of the worker. Consumption was ultimately a new means by which (neo) capitalism could exploit the masses. The social and material progress, achieved partly as a result of the socialist movement, was ultimately used by this neo-capitalism to safeguard the existing inequality and the privileged position of the capitalists. Socialism had to go further and 'contest the real aims of the regime in a global way'.[7] The conclusion was obvious: the trade union movement had to reject any integration with capitalism. However, the socio-economic consultation process remained for the ABVV/FGTB a means of gradually achieving the socialist society, characterized by total democracy on a wide political, economic, social and cultural front. The most important strategic options in this respect were above all the confirmation of the democratically planned economy, where social concerns had to be given priority over economic aspirations. Secondly, the ABVV/FGTB opted firmly for worker control rather than co-determination, which was after all based on the unquestioning assumption of the existence of social classes, and which could therefore not be an instrument for the class struggle. The ABVV/FGTB still wanted to accept responsibilities in certain cases but, as the saying went at that time, only in so far as it was able to decide freely on which responsibilities that should be and without accepting the fundamental logic of the capitalist system. For the ABVV/FGTB, the class struggle was by no means over. This decision undoubtedly pointed to a harder stance by the socialist trade union movement. Whether this led to more aggressive trade union action in the field, however, is very much open to debate.

The government played a crucial role in the socialist strategy of social transformation, not only through economic planning, but also through the development of collective services.[8] In contrast, with respect to social security the ABVV/FGTB was much more in favour of strengthening joint management by employee and employer organizations. One proviso here was that employees' contributions should not be increased, while the social security system had to become part of a broader social policy.

The ABVV/FGTB stuck to this policy also during the later 1970s. It considered the economic crisis a new phase in the class struggle, in which 'the working class', represented first of all by the socialist trade union movement, was engaged in a titanic struggle with 'the employers'.[9] This almost mythical proposition dominated the trade union discourse very prominently. The main lines of its programme, however, remained situated within the framework of the democratically planned economy, with attention focusing primarily on the financial sector. A public holding company had to become the key for determining economic and industrial policy in function of social objectives. The socialist trade union was also seeking to reform the industry itself, and put forward self-management as its ultimate goal. This self-management would only be possible, however, in a completely socialist society. In the meantime the ABVV/FGTB opposed the formation of an 'employees' council', as its Christian opponent saw it. On the contrary, it wanted to see the trade union delegation as the central body for handling disputes and consultations at company level, rather than the Works Council. A great deal of attention was focused on what was termed 'the quality of life': the living environment (and in the first place the working environment), physical planning and consumption. The degeneration of the environment was seen as a side-effect of the capitalist system, which only was interested in making profit.[10]

In addition to the democratization of the economy, the ABVV/FGTB also demanded the development of a global social policy. In particular the social security system was envisaged as an instrument for achieving a fairer redistribution of incomes. However, since the social security system was financed by social contributions, which in reality formed an indirect wage, they ought to be administered exclusively by the trade unions - even if, as was the case, the ABVV/FGTB argued for increasing the employer's share of the contributions. A reduction of working time was put foreward as the main direct instrument against unemployment.

It is noteworthy that in the second half of the 1970s women took on an increasingly prominent role in the development of the ABVV/FGTB programme. This does not so much mean that the commitment of the women's committee to achieving equal treatment for men and women in society, including at work and in the trade union itself, found more sympathy in the ABVV/FGTB - although that was the case to some extent.[11] More important would seem to be the fact that, in the debates on social security, on social policy in general, on the tax system and on the problem of unemployment, the feminine point of view came emphatically to the fore. Thus, for example, the ABVV/FGTB requested more collective services set up by the government, a demand inspired and stimulated not least by the women's committee. Women thus stimulated the commitment towards a broad vision of social security and social policy. The women's movement also laid a great deal of emphasis on the equal treatment of men and women in the social security system, something which led to the idea of individualization of the benefits and the abolition, or at least revision, of the term 'head of the family'. This same principle also lay at the basis of the resistance of the ABVV/FGTB to the so-called 'splitting' of taxes (a taxation technique whereby the income of both working partners was taxed together), which offered a tax advantage to women who remained at home. The stubborn resistance of the ABVV/FGTB to part-time work and flexible working hours was also partly (mainly ?) inspired by women, who were the main victims of the crisis. They perceived the new forms of employment purely as a considerable worsening of their already weak position on the labour market. Moreover, part-time work confirmed in practice the existing role patterns, and that was precisely what the women in the ABVV/FGTB wanted to see broken down. This last comment also points to the fact that the women in the ABVV/FGTB held a de facto somewhat broader view of trade unionism than the men: they perceived social issues less exclusively as part of a class struggle.

The 1980s were a particularly hard time for the ABVV/FGTB. It had difficulty finding answers to the challenges of a sombre economic climate and the neo-liberal offensive, and was thus confronted with demands for greater flexibility, deregulation and the introduction of new technologies. As regards flexible working hours and deregulation of conditions of employment, the ABVV/FGTB continued to adopt a very cautious stance, partly because it was afraid that the role of the trade union movement would be undermined if working conditions were tailored too closely to the individual worker. It also demanded attention for the social consequences of new forms of employment as well as of the introduction of new technologies. Workers had to be involved at the concept phase when new technology was being introduced. In December 1983 the ABVV/FGTB, together with the two other trade union federations, signed an interprofessional collective labour agreement (CAO 39), in which the protocols for introducing new technologies were established.

The state of the government finances drove the ABVV/FGTB to update its vision on the task of the government. Throughout the 1970s a great deal had been expected of the government: from a pronounced Keynesian perspective, the government, in a very selective way, had to boost the economy and put in place a new industrial policy. In practice, according to the ABVV/FGTB, in the 1980s virtually the opposite was happening: the State provided no stimuli - quite the reverse - but handed out all manner of fiscal 'gifts', without demanding anything in return in terms of job provision. However, the ABVV/FGTB did feel that the fiscal and parafiscal pressure on employment could not be increased any further, and consequently stated that more money should be taken from the rich.[12] In the sphere of social security, the ABVV/FGTB argued for a return to the 'basic principles' of the system: solidarity and insurance. The term 'solidarity' referred in concrete terms to solidarity - in the form of transfer of contributions - of the healthy with the sick, of those in work with the unemployed and of the active workforce with pensioners. The ABVV/FGTB was particularly opposed to the reduction of the social security system to a form of 'assistance' designed to combat poverty. For the ABVV/FGTB, the term 'insurance' did not mean a return to the capitalization system, but the linkage of benefits to contributions. This stance was not only a reaction to the systematic reduction of certain benefits, but was also an expression of a fundamental choice for the complete individualization of people's rights. With regard to taxation, too, the ABVV/FGTB opted for individualization. The emphasis on the insurance principle also recalled the fact that the workers themselves were paying for the risk of loss of income and that they were therefore fully entitled to claim benefits.[13]

Despite improvements in the economic climate and the political context in the last years of the 1980s - in 1988 the strongly neo-liberal tinted Martens government was replaced by a Catholic-socialist coalition - the ABVV/FGTB continued to face a legitimacy crisis, something which was reflected among other things in poor scores in the social elections and a continuing decline in membership numbers. The organization did make some progress among new employee groups, in particular among youth and white collar workers, but remained a prisoner of the decline of its industrial base in Wallonia. In spite of its emphasis on the solidarity within the working class and the permanent rhetoric of the struggle against 'the employers', the government and the ACV/CSC, the ABVV/FGTB could not escape the impression that the solidarity and unity of the working class were weakening.[14] The socialist union in fact also directed its ideas on solidarity towards the employers, in order that they would take up their responsibilities as 'employers' and 'entrepreneurs'. It felt obliged to refine its views on flexibility and deregulation at work, as a section of the workforce saw flexibility as an opportunity to achieve greater freedom of choice and was perhaps attracted by the view put forward by employers that excessive regulation and 'rigidity' were a threat to employment.[15] The ABVV/FGTB also came up against ideological difficulties when the ETUC put forward a model for co-determination for European companies, which was diametrically opposed to the ABVV/FGTB support for worker control.

From the late 1980s onwards, the climate in the ABVV/FGTB started to change. A new generation of trade union leaders, more technocratic and less rooted in the working class, put their stamp on the policy - the new president elected in 1989 was an intellectual with a universitary diploma and was formerly chairman of the white collar workers' union. The class struggle perspective as such was put at the background, as became strikingly clear at the ABVV/FGTB ideological congress of November 1990 - though the idea of 'abiding conflicts of interests' between employers and workers was sometimes raised, with the term 'class conflicts' being added as an explanatory qualifier. The international dimension became a key issue, with the choice for a more social and democratic Europe and international worker solidarity between East and West, North and South. The response of the ABVV/FGTB placed particular importance on 'solidarity' between workers. Apart from a new 'look', however, there was ultimately little in the way of innovation to be detected in the concrete action points. A substantial role was still accorded to the government in making society more geared to welfare. The plea for worker control, too, was taken up again, though from the basis of a 'new élan' on account of the 'growing conflicts of interest, commercialization and the shortage of critical opinion'. While it is true that more attention was given to the internal organization of the ABVV/FGTB, here too a choice was made for adaptations in continuity: the internal diversity (which was recognized more than in the past) led to greater centralization, without affecting the power basis of the affliated national unions.[16] As a side-effect of the cautious federalization of the confederative structures, the Flemish ABVV slowly adopted a more Flemish national stance - due to the French-speaking majority in the socialist movement, the socialists and in particular the socialist unions found themselves somewhat alienated from the Flemish issue. However, since the 1980s the balance between Flemish and Francophones in the socialist trade union movement has been reversed, the Flemish holding the majority.

In the 1990s internal tensions increased between the more technocratic leadership of the confederation, striving towards a broader union movement and therefore also towards more centralization, and, on the one hand, the more traditionnally class-based and highly bureaucratic affiliated unions, and, on the other, (partly coinciding) those arguing for more ideological 'correctness', in particular the leftist wing in Liège. These drifts came to the fore during the ABVV-FGTB congress of november 1994, which was particularly marked by sharp discussions and tensions between the leadership and the rank and file - which is too easily presented as an opposition between moderate leaders and radical militants. The congress once again appealed for a radical transformation of society in line with its options from 1971, revoking workers control and state intervention for job creation in particular. The tensions between de different fractions and views ran even higher in 1995 when both the president of the Flemish wing of the ABVV, who had opted for a political career, and the president of the confederation, who suddenly died on June 30th 1995, had to be replaced.

The Christian trade union movement: the consequences of anti-socialism

The Christian trade union movement came into being in the second half of the 1880s as a reaction against the growing socialist influence in the existing worker organizations. Due to the increasing polarization and the 'turning from the Church to the people' during the 1890s (Lamberts, 1991), those first anti-socialist trade unions got a confessional character. At about the same time new Christian trade unions were formed as well, initially often as mixed organizations of employers and workers, though quickly - before 1900 - developing into worker-only organizations. In 1912 the Christian Trade Union Confederation (ACV/CSC) was founded as a confederation of national occupational federations. From the start, however, it also had a regional 'inter-union' structure for common tasks. Although numerically not so far behind the socialists, the Christian trade union movement was unable to escape the shadow of its competitor until much later.

It would be difficult to claim that the early Christian trade union movement had a well-developed doctrine. In fact, the first anti-socialist trade unions adopted a politically and ideologically neutral stance. Their aim was to defend workers' interests and to offer protection against unemployment, while also seeking to achieve 'moral elevation' of the workers. They rejected the class struggle and opted for 'vigorous discussion' and arbitration based on the British model. Gradually the Christian trade union movement was to come under the influence of socio-Catholic corporatist views on society, though it would still continue to emphasise the need for an autonomous workers' organization. It should be noted here that, despite the importance of some clerics as Father Rutten during its formative years, the Christian trade union movement had originated as a lay organization and continued to push the interests of the workers as its central objective. Nevertheless, the unions were part of a broader Christian labour movement, which was rooted in the Catholic community and which in Flanders also was intertwined with the Flemish movement (see different articles in Gerard (ed.), 1993).

After the First World War, the ACV/CSC remained a long way behind its socialist counterpart, which enjoyed a true breakthrough. Partly with the support of the Church, and profiting from the unemployment insurance, however, the ACV/CSC was to undergo marked growth after 1925, and by 1939 it had a membership equal to more than 60 per cent of the number of members of the socialist trade unions (Pasture and Mampuys, 1990). Its influence was much greater than its numerical representative strength would suggest, though, partly as a result of its strong structural links with the Christian Democrats, the workers' wing of the Catholic party (Gerard, 1985, 1994).[17]

During the inter-war period the ACV/CSC gave priority to its organizational development. This organization was characterized by a marked centralization, although proposals for a complete interprofessional (re)organization were not accepted. The ACV/CSC also strengthened its own ideological basis. Above all, it wanted to achieve a 'democratic industrial organization', which meant that it wished to democratise economic life via joint consultative committees at sector and interprofessional level. Trade unions and employer organizations would thus determine the socio-economic policy in a 'guided economy'. In touch with the spirit of corporatism, which met with great approval in the 1930s (*Quadragesimo anno*, 1931), this type of industrial organization also implied that some of the powers of parliament would be transferred to these joint committees. However, the ACV/CSC rejected anti-democratic forms of corporatism, such as in Italy, where a form of State corporatism existed which eliminated the power of the trade unions. During the German occupation, however, it became apparent how strong the seduction of corporatism could be (Mampuys, 1994, 1984; Luyten, 1992; Kwanten, 1984).

After the Second World War, the ACV/CSC achieved its definitive breakthrough, enabling it to bypass the ABVV/FGTB during the 1950s. In fact, this catching-up exercise was completed in Flanders immediately after the War, while in Wallonia the ABVV/FGTB remained the largest trade union (Mampuys, 1994; Pasture, 1992, p. 170; Pasture and Mampuys, 1990). The ability of the ACV/CSC to outstrip its socialist counterpart was a unique 'achievement' for a Christian trade union in Europe (Pasture, 1994). This success was due to a host of factors, both structural (its actual implantation in Flanders and in new industries, both of which proved to be growth areas) and ideological and cultural (the Flemish image) in nature; it was also a result of sound strategic choices (Pasture and Mampuys, 1990; Pasture, 1992; Spineux, 1981).

The rebuilding of the Catholic pillar after the War was nevertheless far from an obvious process, particularly in the Christian workers' movement. As early as the period 1947-1949, however, the Christian labour movement - within which the trade union played a crucial role - was once again strongly anchored in the Catholic pillar. Strong (but informal) links were also built through the formation of the renewed Christian People's Party (CVP/PSC), successor to the old Catholic Party. This rapid reintegration was due primarily to the ideological polarization which divided the country into two ideological blocks since the Liberation (Pasture, 1995c, 1992, ch. 1).

The post-war restructuring of socio-economic life, with the introduction of compulsory social security and the expansion of the consultative structures at national, sector and company level, met - at least in principle - with the demands and expectations of the ACV/CSC, even if the situation on the field was for a long time far short of what was wanted. However, the ACV/CSC was unable to put into practice its model for co-determination in the companies, with joint representation on the management boards. Its proposal met with fierce resistance, not only from the employers but also from the socialist movement, which opposed any kind of co-management and common responsibility in the companies and emphasized workers' control (Dambre, 1985; Pasture, 1992, ch. 3; Luyten, 1995b). The basic philosophy of the ACV/CSC was a Christian-inspired personalism, which sought to follow a 'third path' as an alternative to both liberal capitalism and socialism. In its own words, the ACV/CSC aimed to achieve 'the recovery of the value of the human being and of human labour in all its forms and multitude of interhuman relations which make up society'.[18] It was an approach which involved a rejection in principle of the class struggle. This Christian personalism cannot simply be equated with the Catholic social doctrine, however: on issues such as co-determination and the recognition of the welfare state the ACV/CSC was a long way ahead of the Church (Pasture, 1991b). In addition, under pressure from the Flemish issue, the ACV/CSC had since the 1950s been in favour of (regional) economic planning or 'expansion'. During the 1960s social and economic 'programming' was to break through completely. Nevertheless, it was not until after 1968 that the ACV/CSC dared to use the term 'planned economy'.

In the course of the 1960s, the Christian workers' movement became thoroughly convinced that the world had changed dramatically. From as early as the end of the 1950s, particularly in the Catholic Workers Ligues (Katholieke Werkliedenbonden - KWB) (the suborganization of the Christian workers' movement which concentrated on the religious-moral and, later, on the socio-cultural training of adult workers), questions were being raised regarding the continued existence of workers as a separate social entity or class, not only as a result of the increased prosperity, but even more because of the greatly increased diversity in jobs (Pasture, 1992, pp. 305-316; 1995b). This does not alter the fact, however, that during the same period the KWB was preaching the class struggle on the basis of a personalistic criticism of capitalism. Furthermore, in the 1960s the upscaling and internationalization of the economy, technological developments and innovations in the organization of labour and labour relations brought considerable changes. Moreover, the right of existence of Christian social organizations as such was disputed. In 1964 the French Christian trade union CFTC was deconfessionalized, a fact which did not go unnoticed (Pasture, 1992).

In 1968, the ACV/CSC confirmed its aspiration to be a Christian trade union, though this was a decision which, in the light of the new views of the Vatican on the relationship between the Church and the secular world, was motivated mainly by pragmatic considerations, and certainly did not mean that the ACV/CSC was to take up an exclusively Christian standpoint. In fact, explicit references to Catholic social doctrine became more and more absent from the programme.[19] Moreover, the ACV/CSC adopted the personalistic-spiritualist manifesto of the World Confederation of Labour (WCL), the successor to the deconfessionalized International Federation of Christian Trade Unions (IFCTU) (Pasture, 1994a).[20]

Within its personalistic human vision, however, a great deal of attention was reserved for collectivity: collective welfare took priority over individual welfare. The ACV/CSC was in favour of a democratic 'service economy', in which the government would ensure that all fundamental human needs were met. Workers would have to be involved at all levels of the decision-making process. On a social level, the ACV/CSC wished to 'humanize' labour. It saw social security as a force for redistributing incomes - something which was a relatively recent view within the Christian labour movement as such - and wanted to give it a more active function in the promotion of general welfare. In this context the ACV/CSC wished to bypass the idea of income being related to the working wage as such, and argued in favour of a guaranteed income. In certain cases, it even pleaded for removing the link between work and income altogether. The attention for the 'less well off' was from that time on a new, recurrent element in the programme of the ACV/CSC, though it was emphasized that the financial costs of this should not be borne by the social security system, but by the State. Education, training and leisure time also received wide attention from the perspective of similar concerns for the emancipation of the worker.

1968 was also the year in which the female militants in the ACV/CSC pronounced their 'Statute of the female worker'.[21] At least since the 1950s the ACV/CSC had demanded 'Equal pay for equal work' - which didn't prevent it to believe until the early 1960s that the place of the mother was at home. New was the argument for equal access to employment and training, and for measures to ease the combination of motherhood and paid employment. These measures had to include legal steps (waiting period before receiving benefit, re-entry into the labour market) and collective services such as creches and accessible public services. At the same time, the female militants demanded a broadening of the 'Head of the family' concept in the social security system. However, the ACV/CSC continued to hold firm to the idea of a premium for mothers which 'took into account the income and outgoings of the family'. The basic principle of the entire Christian labour movement was that there ought to be sufficient freedom of choice for mothers to remain at home and bring up their children or to perform work outside the home. The implication of this was that in both cases women should be able to maintain a similar standard of living (Pasture, 1992, pp. 323-334; Dresse, 1990).

Partly as a result of the social unrest of the early 1970s, the ACV/CSC radicalized its programme. The most striking change was perhaps the new view on the commercial company. While the Christian labour movement had in the 1960s distanced itself somewhat from the principle of co-determination[22], now the ACV/CSC, partly inspired by experiments in Yugoslavia, opted resolutely for self-management as the final objective of its reforms. As necessary intermediate steps, the ACV/CSC wished to strengthen workers' control, as well as to organise consultation at work on various levels. During the transitional period it was above all important that the power of the Works Council was increased.[23]

The social security system, the primary function of which was to guarantee a minimum level of security, was also seen as forming part of a broad social policy. In principle, everyone had the right to a subsistence minimum. The level of benefits had to be uncoupled from the contributions paid and determined on the basis of need. Nonetheless, the benefits ought to be tailored to ensure the preservation of the acquired living standard and the development of prosperity, which in concrete terms meant that they had to be linked to the consumer price index and to pay levels. In the context of a genuine social policy, a system of 'democratic planning' had to form the basis for the development of a network of collective facilities in which attention was focused primarily on the needs of the lowest income groups.[24]

Alongside old themes which were dressed up in new clothes, the ACV/CSC also took a number of relatively new themes to heart. In the first place the consumer issue, although this, too, had been very emphatically present in 1968. In addition, living conditions and quality of life were important new areas for attention, though the resolutions did not go beyond the level of declarations of principle and did not really force their way through to the actual priorities in the trade union programme, let alone being translated into action. The radicalization of the Christian labour movement and the federalization of political life, with the split of the Christian democratic party CVP/PSC into two separate parties, the Flemish Christelijke Volkspartij (CVP) and the Francophone Parti Social Chrétien (PSC) in 1969, caused a shift in the

ACV/CSC's attitude towards politics. The French-speaking part of the Christian labour movement in 1972 decided to give up its exclusive support for the PSC (Pasture, 1992, 1993b). Since that moment the ACV/CSC in Wallonia and Brussels has remained very cautious with its political stance, giving only limited moral support to the political experiments of the French-speaking Christian labour movement (Pasture, 1991c; 1995c). In Flanders, the ACV/CSC continued to rely on the CVP for its political aims, albeit (at least theoretically) via the umbrella organization of the Christian labour movement ACW (Algemeen Christelijk Werknemersverbond) and while safeguarding its autonomy.

The radicalization of the programme of the ACV/CSC did not lead to a rapprochement to the ABVV/FGTB, on the contrary. In the first place, the latter rejected the ACV/CSC's argument for self-management, consultation at work and a strengthening of the Works Council. There were also differences on the issue of social security, among other things on the question of whether unemployment benefits should be paid at a fixed rate or as a function of pay. Above all, however, the views of the two unions differed on the issue of collective facilities. While both wanted to see an extension of collective services, the ACV/CSC felt that this could best be organized by the social organizations themselves, albeit with government support, while the ABVV/FGTB argued that the organization of collective services was the full responsability of the State. This difference in views had its roots partly in the ideological 'foundations' (the Christian-democratic subsidiarity principle), but had in our view at least as much to do with tradition and the far better development of Catholic social services. The ABVV/FGTB explicitly continued to argue for a common action - but it bore some responsability for the degrading relations too.[25] In spite of these differences, however, the trade union front held firm in the 1970s.

The economic crisis which began in 1974 did not lead to a fundamental realignment - though naturally, a number of new priorities appeared, particularly with respect to unemployment. The ACV/CSC plea for a third employment circuit, focusing on the easing of general human and social needs, was used by the government as an additional employment alternative in the framework of its employment policy (Pasture, 1991a). Like the ABVV/FGTB, the ACV/CSC had to offer a response to the continuing crisis, the renewed offensive from the employers' side and the neo-liberal tinted political context. The subgroups within the movement - women, migrants, middle managers and more than ever also pensioners and job-seekers - strengthened their structural position and representation.[26] Although the implicit support of the ACV/CSC leadership for the government policy was not undisputed even within its own circles, a broad consultation throughout the whole Christian labour movement on the relation with the CVP led in 1986 to a reaffirmation of the 'conditional confidence' in that party (Gerard, 1994b; Pasture, 1991a). The ACV/CSC adopted a very reticent stance with respect to new technologies - slightly less exclusively dismissive than the ABVV/FGTB - and stressed the need for an effective voluntaristic government policy. The government also had to guarantee the protection of democratic liberties and private life. Together with the ABVV/FGTB, the ACV/CSC demanded that the trade unions should be involved in the introduction of new technologies and that more attention should be devoted to the social consequences of those technologies. The ACV/CSC considered - at least theoretically - the protection of the weakest and the preservation of employment to be the main priorities. In terms of employment, it concentrated mainly on the public services.[27]

The relations between the ACV/CSC and ABVV/FGTB became particularly difficult during the 1980s (Mampuys, 1991, p. 485 ff., 1994; Pasture, 1992, ch. 7). As the CVP, with which the Christian labour movement maintained close contacts, had formed a government coalition since 1981 together with the liberals, and helped to form the crisis policies, the ACV/CSC, in spite of all the fine words on the independence of the trade union movement, was inhibited in its reaction against government policy. Moreover, its leadership, and especially its Chairman Jef Houthuys, was convinced of the need for an overhaul of government finances and for major savings. Up to the end of 1983, the government pursued an active employment policy in exchange for its austerity policy; the former policy was largely inspired by the ACV/CSC. After that date, only the austerity option remained (Pasture, 1991a). The ABVV/FGTB considered the lukewarm stance taken by the ACV/CSC to be a betrayal of the working class.

Although there was no question of a collapse of the trade union movement such as occurred in other countries, the ACV/CSC felt that the position of the movement was weakening. As a result of the downward trend of labour relations and the increasing pressures at interprofessional level serious stresses within the confederation arose. Attention was given to both the functioning of companies and the interprofessional activity, while the political dimension was not neglected either. Moreover, the ACV/CSC decided to develop a Local

Belgium: pragmatism in pluralism

Interprofessional Operation, to integrate the 'special groups' in the ACV/CSC policy and, finally, to promote greater democracy and participation from the base.[28] By opting for a full development of the local interprofessional operation, focusing among other things on training, the ACV/CSC was seeking to make clear that it saw its task as a broad one. Whether these options had many consequences in practice is open to serious doubt, however.[29] This also applies to the greater participation of specific groups, a standpoint with which the ACV/CSC sought to accommodate the growing diversity within the movement. In particular, the demand for greater recognition of the special groups in society, particularly migrants and job-seekers, appears to have reached at an impasse since the second half of the 1980s. It may be that the internal stresses and the need to have its own voice were felt less intensely as a result of the improvement in the economy. But the consequences of this standstil may prove to be serious on the long run, since it was particularly thanks to this strategy that the ACV/CSC had realized its breakthrough among relatively new categories of workers in the 1970's.

As regards flexibility, the ACV/CSC in the late 1980s gradually opted for a different course: in addition to the traditionally reticent stance, which did not in practice produce much in the way of results, the ACV/CSC attempted to reverse the roles and emphasized the freedom of choice of the worker. A similar approach was chosen for the new forms of participative management, which addressed the workers directly and ignored the unions. Against this the ACV/CSC placed its own model of consultation at work. Although the neo-liberal offensive against the State did not leave Christian Democratic circles unaffected, the ACV/CSC continued to support an extension of the government role in industrial policy and social facilities. In terms of social security, too, the ACV/CSC firmly rejected calls for the dismantling of the general security system with supplementary insurances.

In 1994 the ACV/CSC once again reflected on its aims and principles, as did the ABVV/FGTB. It presented itself as a union of personalistic 'values' (rather than principles) giving particular attention to social justice and public care, and to tolerance, solidarity and equality, which were threatened by the resurgence of racism.[30] The ACV/CSC recognized the family 'in all its existing forms' as basic cel of society. The Christian dimension of the ACV/CSC was underlined again, albeit cautiously, among other things because Christianity, in the eyes of the ACV/CSC, could give a reference scheme for social action and could provide a countervailing power (regarded as a major feature of trade unionism) against materialism, individualism, totalitarism, liberalism and all kinds of fundamentalism. By doing so, the ACV/CSC distanced itself de facto from the socialists, which in Christian democratic terms are labelled as materialistic (Pasture, 1995c). There was some talk about transforming the union into a broad social movement or 'civilians ligue' (*burgerbond*), which would not only defend workers but all weaker groups in society and which would not only be concerned with labour issues. However, the congress preferred to concentrate on the defence of workers' interests, albeit from a broad social perspective. For the general interests of the workers it decided to continue to rely on the other organizations of the Christian's workers movement. As to the delicate question of the relationship with the Flemish Christian democratic party CVP, which had deteriorated considerably since the latter's president had decided to push back the influence of the pressure groups within his party (Pasture, 1995c), this matter was referred to a common decision by the whole Christian labour movement, to be taken at a special congress of the Flemish Christian workers' umbrella organization ACW later in 1995. There, after the parliamentary elections of March 1995 won by the resigning Roman-red coalition, it was decided to retain a privileged relationship with the CVP, while, however, establishing more contacts with other political parties.

The middle class initiative: liberal trade unions

Apart from the socialist and Christian trade unions Belgium also experiences the existence of liberal trade unions, which must be unique in the world. Its influence, however, is rather limited, so we will only briefly evoke the main lines of its development and ideological options.

The initiative to stimulate the formation of liberal trade unions was taken by conservative liberal politicians at the end of the 19th century, in order to stem the tide to socialist progress and as a reaction against the introduction of universal suffrage, which had virtually wiped out the liberal party (Langendries, 1989; Miroir, 1982).[31] Middle class politicians created, in 1898, a liberal workers' party composed of cooperatives, friendly societies and some trade unions. These associations, mostly situated in the northern part of Belgium, hardly could gain foothold. In 1920 several of the liberal trade unions set up a liberal trade union Centre - in fact merely more than a common strike fund - the first of its kind in Belgium (Miroir, 1982). This common strike fund gradually fused with local unemployment funds and unions. It took ten years before this process of centralization was accomplished. As a result, the Liberal Centre was not composed of national (sectoral) unions, as do the other Belgian confederations, but consisted of regional unions, which remained a particular feature of liberal trade unionism until present day (Langendries, 1989; Rion, 1989; Miroir, 1982). Only the liberal workers in public service formed a separate trade union within this Centre, which in fact they only joined in 1927 (Miroir, 1982). In 1945 a 'social charter' was adopted with aims and principles (Rion, 1989, pp. 181-182) and the liberal Centre received its present name as General Federation of Liberal Trade Unions in Belgium (ACLVB/CGSLB) (Langendries, 1989; Miroir, 1982).

The liberal trade unions thus originated from the initiative of employers and liberal politicians, striving for an understanding between employers and employees, and even aiming at a collaboration between labour and capital. For the liberal trade unions this collaboration, however, was not possible without the recognition of the workers' human dignity and possibilities for individual development, which in turn postulated fundamental changes in the capitalist balance of power. In particular state intervention and the accession by the workers to individual and collective property was esteemed necessary. In the liberal-personalistic view the workers councils had to become the cornerstones of enterprise democracy. Therefore, they had to gradually obtain economic powers. Clear priority was given to reconciliation procedures and collective agreements, without refuting the right to strike (Rion, 1989; Miroir, 1982). In the 1950s the ACLVB/CGSLB adopted a clear Keynesian economic program with emphasis given to income redistribution through taxes and social security measures.

Although the Belgian liberals were fervent anticlericals, the liberal ideology and its brand of personalism converged with the Christian personalistic views and corporatistic ideas, which were found in the Christian trade unions from the 1920s to the 1950s. The ideology of the latter, however, was deeply rooted in a Christian *Weltanschauung*. And while the basic ideology of the Christian trade unions, as we have seen, secularized, it also radicalized, which was not or to a much lesser extent the case for the social liberalism of the ACLVB/CGSLB. Even more than the Christians, the liberal trade unions were often regarded by the workers and the other unions as strike breakers and 'yellow unions'. Christian and socialist unions opposed to collaboration with the liberals and refused their recognition in joint bodies, an attitude which only changed when socialists and liberals formed an anticlerical government coalition in 1954. Until today the other confederations ignore their

ACLVB/liberal competitor as much as possible; among other things, they block its way to the ETUC.

While middle class politicians and employers gave birth to the liberal trade unions, the relationship between this workers movement and the liberal party as well as the employers soon turned out to be a difficult one. In the interwar period in particular, liberal trade unions had to cope with yellow unions and social services in the enterprises, set up by local entrepreneurs to undermine unions' power. These initiatives threathened the credibility of the liberal trade unions (Miroir, 1982). Up to the present day the major employers' organizations in practice give priority to the *entente* with the two major confederations. Concerning the relationship with the liberal party, it is clear that the latter only used the union as an attraction pool for its own purposes. The party-union relations deteriorated completely since the transformation of the former highly anticlerical liberal party into the Party for Freedom and Progress (PVV/PLP) in 1961, which dropped its anticlericalism and expressed the desire to bring about a broad Centre-right front (Miroir, 1982). For years the ACLVB/CGSLB stressed its autonomy, while entertaining smooth relations with the other liberal organizations, such as the mutual health insurance fund. In the 1970s informal relations with the party improved, until the neo-liberal policy shift of the Flemish PVV (which in 1993 was transformed in Flemish Liberals and Democrats VLD) in the 1980s and the 'crusade' of the party's president Guy Verhofstadt against the role of the pressure groups in Belgian politics handicapped them again. Against neo-liberal mania for economics, direct democracy, privatization of the public services and the dismantling of social security and welfare provisions, saveguarding only minimal standards, the ACLVB/CGSLB put forward 'social liberalism', with recognizes the values of solidarity and the significance of social organizations for the well-being of society. However, the ACLVB/CGSLB also adhered to the principles of liberty, individual responsability and personal choice. In that sense it adopted a more positive attitude towards flexibility in labour relations and towards more personal responsability in social security than its competitors, also in order to decrease the tax level.

Conclusion: divergences in the convergence

It can at any event be deduced from the above summary of the programmatic/ideological development of the three trade union movements in Belgium that their programmes run largely parallel, even though we have focused attention in the selection of the themes discussed mainly on general social and 'ideologically sensitive' issues. Viewed over the long term it must be observed that after the years of foundation and early youth - roughly up until the First World War -, the different trade unions, while presenting very diverging ideological profiles to the outside world, did in fact hardly act differently in the practice of union action. The ACV/CSC projected itself as a Christian trade union and formed a strong buttress of the Catholic pillar. And yet it was a lay movement, which when it came down to it followed its own trade union logic rather than the abstract principles of the Catholic social doctrine. It certainly demanded no religious credentials from prospective members. In fact, the same applies to the socialist trade union movement, which verbally preached the class struggle and at times even supported the revolution, but which in practice opted for cooperation and consultation on the basis of a very reformist standpoint. The latter was essentially, and to a much larger extent, also the point of view of the liberal trade unions.

This highly pragmatic stance may have been largely due to the mutual competition: the prime issue for all the trade unions in their mutual relations was after all often the battle for members, which for the Christian trade union movement in particular came down to including as many workers as possible in its own ranks in order to protect them from 'Godless socialism'. The battle for members was fought partly with ideological means, but much more with pure union and practical means - as witnessed by the strong emphasis on service provision, particularly in the ACV/CSC.[32] In this context it should be noted that the Christian trade union movement faced no competition from a Protestant trade union, and consequently did not feel the need to work out its Christian principles (comp. Hellemans, 1988a; 1988b). In a similar way the socialist trade union movement was also virtually free of competition from dissidents and in particular from communists. Whenever that danger did threaten, for example immediately after the Second World War, the profile of the socialist trade union sharpened considerably. Ideologically the liberal trade unions never constituted a real threat to the others.

The ideological differences blurred still further in the 1960s. It seems to us that, in comparison with the ABVV/FGTB and the ACLVB/CGSLB, the ACV/CSC underwent a greater ideological evolution, although it also maintained the continuity of its development. This is abundantly clear from its views on the consumer society and the idea of a democratically planned economy. The ABVV/FGTB very slowly underwent an evolution, gradually replacing the class analysis with what can be labelled social personalism, which in fact becomes very similar to the 'secularized' Christian personalism of the ACV/CSC. Therefore the analysis of the consumption issue in the ACV/CSC and the ABVV/FGTB ran largely parallel. The analysis and the whole concept of a democratically planned economy which ensued from it, however, were more closely allied to a socialist view on society. In particular in response to new challenges - in concrete terms the introduction of new technologies and the demand for deregulation and flexibility - it is apparent that the three trade unions adopted the same stance. However, their approaches and the strategies in this respect were not really set in a broader social context. The desire to place the social dimension above the economy - the slogan 'an economy in service of the people' could be used by any of the three confederations - appears to be almost more of an elegant turn of phrase than a true vision of society.

The parallellism in the programmes was not due exclusively to a (natural and undeniable) ideological convergence, however. It was also related to the fact that while the programmes were developed, their feasibility to a large extent had been taken in account. The 'experience' of social consultation had unequivocally shown that only those programme elements were achieved which met with the fundamental agreement of both trade union federations and for which they were all fighting. In fact, this actually means that the programmes to some extent came into being together. In this respect, it should be borne in mind that the research departments, which also played a very influential role in the further achievement of the programme, were largely responsible for compiling the programmatic texts.

And yet this ideological convergence was only half the story. In line with their ideological traditions, the three confederations formulated fairly fundamental alternative society models at the end of the 1960s and beginning of the 1970s. In both the socialist and Christian society models workers and consumers controlled and planned the economic production for the benefit of the general welfare. But despite the highly comparable models, their elaboration clearly showed where the differences between the confederations were to be found.

Up to the end of the 1980s, the ABVV/FGTB continued to see the social reality essentially as a class struggle, a dichotomy between workers and employers, who stood against each other as two opposing camps and whereby the ABVV/FGTB and the socialist labour movement were projected as being the only true representatives of the working class. The differences within the working class were taken into account, but until late into the 1980s did not really affect the basic model. However, the ABVV/FGTB could not sustain this dichotomy completely. In particular, as it became interested in the consumer issue and, in part via the Consumer Council, came into contact with the consumer organizations, it became clear that the consumer and the worker could not automatically be seen as one and the same. The result was a very tense relationship between the ABVV/FGTB, which purported to represent the workers, and the consumer organizations.[33] The ACV/CSC undoubtedly also felt this tension, but reacted to it in a less rigid way, in our view mainly because its view of the world left more scope for variety, as well as for the 'general interest'. This latter aspect appears to be absent from the ABVV/FGTB perspective. In the whole of the period studied, the socialist movement virtually only had the interests of the workers at heart. A similar problem occurred with regard to the peace issue, where the ABVV/FGTB moreover had to deal with considerable internal tensions between those campaigning for disarmament, particularly in Flanders, and the employees of the arms factories. It would therefore seem that the perspective of the class struggle, at least as the ABVV/FGTB interpreted it, was less easily able to stimulate the socialist trade union movement to incorporate the new themes of the 1970s, in particular the peace question and the environmental issue, in its programme. When these new themes nevertheless found their way into the ABVV/FGTB programme, they were associated with the class struggle.

It should be noted that the attitude of the ABVV/FGTB in this respect is not representative for the whole socialist labour movement. The socialist party in particular, especially in Flanders, since 1978 has developed a strategy of modernization and broadening of its basis (Huyse, 1985). One can wonder why the ABVV/FGTB did not follow the party in this respect. A first element in our opinion is that political parties feel the need for new supporters sooner and more pregnant than trade unions. The electorate of the parties certainly is more versatile than the membership of the unions. Moreover, reactions against a loss of identity, essential in the opening up process, and opposition to change have more possibilities for expression in the unions than in political parties. In this respect one should note that the actual trade union policy is put into practice much more by the national (branch) unions than by the leadership of the confederations. This is particularly true for the ABVV/FGTB (more than is the case for the more centralized ACV/CSC). The national unions, in particular the mighty metalworkers federation, are very class based. Moreover the ABVV/FGTB, it should be kept in mind, still is a national organization which has its power basis among the Walloon heavy industries, the workers of which far from abandoned the idea of the class struggle. In fact, the socialist trade union movement has always more articulated the views of the walloon 'aristocratie ouvrière', even if tensions with the more moderate Flemings in the union sometimes ran high, as was the case for instance during the general strike against the Unity Law in 1961. Only very recently the Flemish ABVV started to follow its own course in this respect. As a federalized party since 1978 the SP is much less bound by this heritage.

The Christian labour movement has traditionally never seen the class struggle as the motor of history. On the contrary, until the 1960s the movement consistently rejected the class struggle as such. Its view of society has always been much more organic, with more of an eye for social differentiation. In the 1960s some in the Christian labour movement and many social scientists, feared the disappearance of workers as a 'class' altogether - a development which, strangely enough, appears to have bypassed the socialist trade union movement (but not the socialist party!) to a large extent. During the 1960s and early 1970s the idea of the class struggle did make its way into the thinking of the Christian labour movement, however, albeit mainly in the Young Christian Workers and the Catholic Workers' Ligues (KWB), and to a lesser extent in trade union circles. Even then, however, the term did not have entirely the same meaning as in a traditional socialist interpretation, but was much more concerned with the recognition of fundamental conflicts of interests. The whole mythology surrounding the 'working class' as a revolutionary force was not adopted. In contrast to the ABVV/FGTB, the image of a class struggle was not reinforced during the crisis years - quite the contrary. The ACV/CSC saw new fault lines emerge, between those in work and the unemployed, between permanent contracts of employment and sham statutes, etc.

The more differentiated view of society held by the ACV/CSC had consequences which worked to its advantage. Thus, for example, it concentrated its trade union strategy more on new employees and weak groups. This strategic choice gave it a structural advantage to the ABVV/FGTB which remained closely attached to the traditional 'aristocratie ouvrière' and whose class-based thinking left little scope for such differences, which were in any event considered to be subordinate to the more fundamental class oppositions (Spineux, 1988; Holderbeke, De Witte and van der Hallen, 1992).[34] The ACV/CSC also gave significantly more attention to the individuality of the different groups within the union itself. This was in particular true for migrant workers. The ABVV/FGTB set itself against any form of 'discrimination' - including positive discrimination - and accordingly had practically no specific structure for them - and when it did set this up, it did so much later than its Christian competitor. As a result, the ACV/CSC acquired a more 'migrant-friendly' image in the post-war period than the socialist trade union movement - itself a striking reversal of the situation in the inter-war period when, partly on the basis of a Flemish nationalist attitude, the Christian trade unions adopted a much more hostile stance than the socialist unions to 'foreigners' (Aerts and Martens, 1978, pp. 57-75). Basicly the same also applies for women, who - notwithstanding the traditional negative attitude of the Catholic community towards female labour in general - acquired their own voice in the highest administrative bodies in the ACV/CSC earlier than in the ABVV/FGTB.[35] Nevertheless, it should also be noted that a woman, Mia De Vits, in 1989 managed to become General Secretary of the ABVV/FGTB. Moreover, at least theoretically, the ABVV/FGTB found itself more in line with the feminist movement. The ACV/CSC - together with the related mass movement of Ligues of Christian Working Class Women - always had a very difficult relation with radical feminists because of the latters' opinions concerning the legalization of abortion.

The present-day view of society held by the ACV/CSC is undoubtedly still rooted in its 'Christian past'. Aside from its name and the (virtually invisible) presence of a chaplain, however, there is now little which points explicitly to a Christian dimension. Explicit or implicit references to Catholic social doctrine have in fact been absent since the 1960s. When the ACV/CSC pronounced the environment to be a new trade union priority in 1990, in contrast to the Confederation of Christian Trade Unions in the Netherlands (CNV), for example, the environmental issue was not expressed in Christian terms of 'stewardship' or 'concern for the Creation'. However, a strong orientation towards the human person has remained. Based on that historical tradition, there is a great deal of attention in the ACV/CSC for the individual as a whole, and not just for the worker in his work; the Christian trade union movement has always been open to a wider thematic approach. In this context it is also important to note that the more confederalist structure of the ACV/CSC also makes this more possible than the structure of the ABVV/FGTB, where the affiliated national trade unions - and thus the actual trade union action - carry much more weight.

The distance which the ACV/CSC took from 'traditional' Catholic social doctrine is also apparent in its attitude towards the State. The subsidiarity principle and the classic Catholic fear of the State have as good as disappeared from the ACV/CSC's views (which does not rule out the possibility of a rediscovery of this fear in the future).[36] Characteristic of this attitude is the call for the development of strong collective facilities. Women have played a not inconsiderable role in this latter development. It was after all women who pressed most strongly for collective facilities which would make it possible for them to perform work outside the home. The choice in principle for the mother who stayed at home had been abandoned by the Christian labour movement as early as the beginning of the 1960s, a decision in which women Christian trade unionists played a leading role (Pasture, 1992, pp. 323-324). The influence of women in the ABVV/FGTB since the 1970s is also striking, and is not restricted to typical women's demands such as equal pay for equal work - demands which for that matter prove difficult to realize. In our view women played a decisive role in the demand for collective services, in the call for individualization of both the social security system and the tax system, and in the strong resistance to deregulation and flexibility of labour.

The significance of women for the ideological development of the unions is surprizing. Trade unions are not exacly known for their woman-friendly charachter. However, the facts are there: women have managed to influence on the trade union agenda. But one should bear in mind that this happened only on a central level. Most national (branch) unions appear to be much less open to 'feminization' as the confederations - even though the concept of feminization is much too strong to describe the relative influence of women on certain general themes, in particular if we take in account the underrepresentation of women in all decision bodies. After all, although equal pay for equal work makes part of the unions' programmes for the whole post-war period, it still is far from realization. Wage negotiations are in daily practice much more in the core of trade union action than social security and taxation issues.

The ACLVB/CGSLB, finally, always has, as its Christian competitor, rejected the class struggle. Its basic ideology can be labelled as personalism or social liberalism, but its major feature really seems to be pragmatism. It kept out of the ideological disputes of the 1970s, and concentrated more on the particular defence of interests, without putting them into perspective. It also left much more room for individualism and personal responsability for the workers. In that sense the

ACLVB/CGSLB politics approached the categorial unions in other countries. From the results of social elections it can be deduced that the liberal trade unions draw their supporters mainly from SME's and among white collar workers indeed (Chlepner, 1956; Miroir, 1982).

Exception made for middle management (although even in this category the Christian trade union for middle management, affiliated to the ACV/CSC, is the most representative union), Belgian trade unions do not face similar competition from categorial unions as in most other European countries. This is not so much due to the salience of the Church/state cleavage, but in our view has to be attributed mainly to the fact that the Belgian unions did not organize themselves on an industrial basis. Notwithstanding continuous pressures from the blue collar workers unions, in the major two confederations (for the ACV/CSC see Pasture and Mampuys, 1990) the unions for civil service employees and white collar workers in the private sector remained autonomous and benefited from statuary guarantees concerning internal and external representation.

One should not overestimate the impact of the ideological choices, however, for union practice. Of course, putting principles into practice never has been easy. But the gap between words and deeds was never so wide as since the 1970s. The radicalization of the early 1970s hardly left any concrete trace in the collective agreements, and this was not only due to the economic depression. The whole system of collective bargaining hardly gives any opportunities for more fundamental orientations. If the unions since the 1970s were not able to enforce an effective redistribution of work by reducing working time measures, it was not only because of their weakened position on the labour market, but also, and in the first place, because of the priorities given by the national unions and their rank and file for saveguarding purchasing power. It is finally by similar contradictions between principles and practice that the orientations towards new groups and concerning new themes, both by the ACV/CSC and, in a different way, by the ABVV/FGTB, in the 1980s largely failed in practice, even when some special structures were realized. Indeed, if voting resolutions and even the creation of specific bodies are one thing, implementing policies remains something quite different.

In a general way, it can be concluded that the ideological dimension in the Belgian trade union movement - which has never been a major feature of it - has lost a great deal of its edge. The past still makes its presence felt, but this influence is also gradually coming to an end. As a result, the sustaining of trade union pluralism has become virtually exclusively a pragmatic and strategic option, even though every current has to a certain extent maintained a mentality and culture of its own. In other words, a merger between the trade union federations in fact depends to a large extent on the perspectives in the relatively short term, namely from the question of whether a merger might lead to an improvement in the position of the individual federations. In our view, this would not immediately appear to be the case. The question is also not on the agenda of any of the trade union confederations either (Pasture, 1994a, pp. 54-90). However, it may not totally be excluded that the current erosion of democratic institutions in Belgium finally leads to an implosion like in Italy. In that case, all possibilities remain open. But also another evolution is possible. The attention given in 1990 and 1994 by both ACV/CSC and ABVV/FGTB towards their basic options, may, against the flow, constitute a beginning of a reaffirmation of their ideological identities.

Table 3.1
Membership of Belgian trade unions (1900-1992) (x 1000)

	Christian	Socialist	Liberal
1900	11.0*	31.3	
1910	49.5	68.8	
1920	156.6	687.6	
1930	203.8	502.8	
1940	339.9	546.2	86.0
1950	471.5	525.9	75.7
1960	634.8	597.9	111.4
1970	812.0	697.5	123.7
1975	1042.3	885.5	160.9
1980	1151.8	939.0	199.5
1985	1190.6	902.9	210.9
1990	1246.7	888.5	213.1
1992	1317.6	901.1	210.1**

* 1901; ** 1991

Note: From 1945 onwards we deduced the propagandacoefficient for ACV/CSC and ABVV/FGTB (varying from 30% to 15%): see Pasture and Mampuys, 1990 and Pasture, 1993a. For the ACLVB/CGSLB, the propagandacoefficient is not known: its figures are therefore overestimated.

Source: Christian: ACV/CSC; Pasture and Mampuys, 1990.
Socialist: ABVV/FGTB.
Liberal: ACLVB/CGSLB; Miroir, 1982.

Table 3.2
Percentage of votes for works councils 1954-94

	ABVV/FGTB	ACV/CSC	ACLVB/CGSLB	NCK/CNC
1954	59.0	37.0	3.5	
1958	55.0	41.0	4.0	
1963	51.1	43.8	5.1	
1967	51.5	42.5	6.0	
1971	48.7	45.5	5.8	
1975	46.1	47.7	6.2	
1979	42.6	50.1	7.3	
1983	43.4	48.6	7.9	
1987	40.8	47.9	7.5	3.8
1991	37.9	51.5	7.5	3.1
1994*	37.8	52.1	7.9	1.2

* Provisional results

Source: Ministry of Labour and Employment

Abbreviatons

ABVV/FGTB	Algemeen Belgisch Vakverbond / Fédération Générale des Travailleurs de Belgique (General Belgian Trade Union Confederation)
ACLVB/CGSLB	Algemene Centrale van Liberale Vakbonden van België / Centrale Générale des Syndicats Libéraux de Belgique (General Confederation of Liberal Trade Unions in Belgium)
ACV/CSC	Algemeen Christelijk Vakverbond / Confédération des Syndicats Chrétiens (Christian Trade Union Confederation)
BSP/PSB	Belgische Socialistische Partij / Parti Socialiste Belge (Belgian Socialist Party)
BWP/BOP	Belgische Werklieden Partij / Parti Ouvrier Belge (Belgian Workers' Party)
CVP	Christelijke Volkspartij ([Flemish] Christian Democratic Party)
ETUC	European Trade Union Confederation
NCK/CNC	Nationale Confederatie voor Kaderpersoneel / Confédération Nationale des Cadres (National Confederation of Middle Management)
PSC	Parti Social Chrétien ([French-speaking] Christian Democratic Party)
PVV/PLP	Partij voor Vrijheid en Vooruitgang / Parti pour la Liberté et le Progrès (Party for Freedom and Progress)

Notes

1. With thanks to Johan Verberckmoes, Jozef Mampuys and Jan Moulaert for their critical comments on an earlier version of this chapter. References to trade union congress and activity reports mostly refer to the Dutch version. In priniple such documents have also a French version.
2. A more traditionally-minded generation of sociologists from the Catholic University of Leuven (J. Billiet, K. Dobbelaere), maintain that a common 'spirit' still exists, particularly in the Catholic 'pillar' (Billiet, 1988; 1993). Free-thinking authors have always laid the emphasis on the organization and power of the Catholic pillar and are therefore less inclined to speak of depillarization. See, for example, Raes, 1993 and Ponteur, 1993.
3. We concentrate in this chapter on the main currents. There have been attempts in the 1930s to create a Flemish nationalist trade union, but this did not succeed to gain considerable success. See De Wever, 1995.
4. The elections of 24 November 1991 humiliated the government coalition parties and gave a strong boost in Flanders to the extreme right-wing Vlaams Blok party. The poor service provided by the public services, which is being ascribed to the politicization, is seen as a major source of the discontent of the people which was reflected in the results of the election.
5. The mutual health insurance funds, however, also focus on other social classes and can therefore not be ascribed fully to the labour movement.
6. The schools funding question, the conflicts on social security and health insurance, and the cultural policy, were all settled in a similar way (the 1958 School Pact; the 1963 Leburton Act; the 1973 Culture Pact).
7. Janne, H., *Les mutations de la société moderne*, appendix to the Report to the extraordinary congress of the ABVV/FGTB 29-31, January 1971. There were also reports by Guy Spitaels on trade union aims and by a working group of trade unionists, sociologists and economists on worker control.
8. On both the examples cited, the ABVV/FGTB came into conflict with the Christian labour movement, which was much more in favour of the development of the collective services by the social movements. ABVV/FGTB-activity reports 1967-1971, p. 149 ff. (creches) and p. 165 ff. (annual holiday). For the backgrounds on the Christian side and for a concrete discussion of the problem of creches, see Pasture, 1992, p. 387 ff. I shall return to this issue later in this chapter.
9. See, for example, ABVV/FGTB-activity report 1975-1977.
10. *Voor een progressistisch alternatief*, ABVV/FGTB congress, 22 April 1977, in ABVV/FGTB-activity report 1975-1977, pp. 181-189 (Dutch version).
11. Although an informal women's working group had existed in the ABVV/FGTB since the mid-1960s, it was not until 1968 that an official women's committee was formed. From 1 January 1974 the two national responsibilities for women with an advisory role were incorporated into the administration of the ABVV/FGTB, and in March 1976 a separate administration for women was formed for the coordination of the women's action. On the development of the position of women in the ABVV/FGTB, see Dresse, 1990, pp. 9-17.
12. Delourme, *Pour une fiscalité plus équitable et plus efficace*, FGTB/ABVV Congrès extraordinaire 21-22 mars 1986. See also the resolutions and report of this extraordinary congress, 21-22 March 1986.

13. Based on the conference documents from the extraordinary congress of 21-22 March 1986, in particular M. De Vits, *Sociale zekerheid: geen afbraak! Zekerheid en rechtvaardigheid voor iedereen*.
14. ABVV/FGTB extraordinary congress, 21-22 March 1986, and statutory congress, 5-6-7 December 1986.
15. ABVV/FGTB statutory congress, 29-30 September 1989, esp. pp. 93-115.
16. *Samenleven in het ABVV/FGTB*, ABVV/FGTB (extraordinary) congress, 23-24 November 1990, p. 82.
17. The ACV/CSC was a constituent part of the Christian workers federation (Algemeen Christelijk Werkersverbond ACW - Ligue nationale des travailleurs chrétiens LNTC), which was founded in 1922 as the political expression of the Christian labour movement and which, alongside the farmers, middle class and the Conservatives constituted the Catholic Party. The term 'christian-democrat' was reserved for the the workers' wing of the Catholic Party; after 1945 it would gradually be used to describe the deconfessionalized Catholic political movement (Dewachter, 1995; Gerard, 1985; Pasture, 1991c).
18. *De christelijke vakbeweging: wezen en streven*, ACV/CSC congress 1951, p. 9.
19. *Het ACV verantwoordelijk voor de toekomst*. Working document for the XXIXth ACV/CSC congress, Brussels, 24-26 October 1968, worked up into a report commissioned by the congress and published in autumn 1969 (ACV/CSC socio-economic studies 13).
20. It can therefore no longer be claimed that the ACV/CSC (like some other Christian trade unions) aims to achieve a society based on 'Christian' principles, as is often readily assumed (e.g. Van Ruysseveldt and Harzing, 1992, p. 21).
21. The text of the statute is to be found in ACV/CSC-activity report 1966-68, pp. 110-113.
22. In particular since the so-called 'Manifest-action' of the Catholic Workers' Ligues KWB (1963-1964) and the ACV/CSC congress of 1964 about the trade unionism and the company (Pasture, 1992, pp. 201 ff.).
23. *Democratisering van de onderneming*, ACV/CSC Council, 19 January 1971, and *Van ondernemingsraad naar werknemersraad*, Extraordinary ACV/CSC congress, 1974. See also Mampuys, 1994 and Pasture, 1992, pp. 201-206 and 369-371.
24. *De maatschappelijke zekerheid*, Extraordinary ACV/CSC congress and ACV/CSC Congress 1972, pp. 40- 51 (and passim. to p. 75). See also Pasture, 1992, pp. 354-355.
25. The fact that the ABVV/FGTB itself bore some of the responsibility in the deteriorated relationship is apparent among other things from the ABVV/FGTB's uncooperative attitude with respect to the accession of the ACV/CSC to the ETUC (Pasture, 1994).
26. In 1981, for example, an unemployment department was set up, the structure for dealing with migrants was reorganized and the position of women in the ACV/CSC was analyzed, resulting in structural modifications.
27. Documents of the extraordinary congress held in Liège on 12-13 March 1983; Resolutions in ACV/CSC-activity report 1981-84, pp. 80-85.
28. In addition to the congress documents, see also V. Peeters, 'Vakbeweging. Terug naar af of nieuw élan', *De Gids op Maatschappelijk Gebied*, 1985, no. 1, pp. 11-30, for a general introduction.

29. See, for example, the commentary by C. Serroyen, 'Een 'schoon' congres overgedaan', *De Gids op Maatschappelijk Gebied*, 1987, nos. 8-9, pp. 671-676 on the ACV/CSC congress of 1987, where the resolutions passed in 1985 were evaluated.
30. ACV/CSC and ABVV/FGTB decided to exclude from their organizations active members of extreme-right organizations; the ACLVB/CGSLB on the contrary stated 'not to interfere with the political opinions of its affiliates'.
31. In a system of absolute representation, the liberal party was the great looser at the first elections for parliament with universal suffrage. When in 1900 proportional representation was introduced, however, the party could somewhat recover lost ground.
32. The claim by Valenzuela, 1992, p. 59, that 'in these cases, the various unions obviously do not compete with one another for the support of the workers, since each has its terrain cut out for it', however logical it may be, does not fit in with reality. On the contrary, competition was very fierce, leading among other things to 'closed shop' practices by both parties (e.g. the 'red or no bread'-actions of socialists directed against Christian unionized workers).
33. This tension is a fixed item in the activity reports of the ABVV/FGTB and also features in its militant sheet.
34. Also for historical reasons, since the socialist movement first organized the 'aristocratie ouvrière'. Cf. esp. Strikwerda, 1983. Compare the French communist party, which also failed to gauge the changes in the working class correctly and which, by concentrating almost exclusively on a rearguard 'type' of idealized workers' proletariat, helped to bring about its own downfall (Molinari, 1995).
35. In the ACV/CSC Sarah Masselang was appointed to the executive in 1965 in a consultative role; in the ABVV/FGTB it was not until 1974 that separate representation for women came into being. A summary of the union actions for women in the ACV/CSC and the ABVV/FGTB since 1945 can be found in Dresse, 1989; for the ACV/CSC see also Pasture, 1992, pp. 323-334. In 1989, however, the FGTB appointed a women, Mia De Vits, as General Secretary.
36. It should be noted here that the subsidiarity idea carries greater weight in other areas of the Christian labour movement, in particular in the umbrella organization ACW.

References

Aerts, M. and Martens, A. (1978), *Gastarbeider: lotgenoot en landgenoot ?*, Kritak, Leuven, pp. 57-75.
Bastians, J. (1994), 'Modern times: institutional dynamics in Belgian and French labor market policies', *West European Politics*, vol. 17, no. 1, January, pp. 98-122.
Beaupain, T., a.o. (1989), *50 jaar arbeidsverhoudingen*, Die Keure, Brugge.
Billiet, J. (1988), 'De katholieke zuil in Vlaanderen: ontwikkeling in het godsdienstig-sociologisch denken en onderzoek', in Billiet, J. (ed.), *Tussen bescherming en verovering. Sociologen en historici over zuilvorming*, KADOC-Studies 6, Universitaire Pers Leuven, Leuven, pp. 17-39.
Billiet, J. (1993), *Ondanks beperkt zicht. Studies over waarden, ontzuiling en politieke verandering*, VUB Press, Brussel.

Blom, J. C. H. and Lamberts, E. (1994), *Geschiedenis van de Nederlanden*, Nijgh & Van Ditmar/Infoboek, Rijswijck.

Brepoels, J. (1988), *Wat zoudt gij zonder 't werkvolk zijn ? Anderhalve eeuw arbeiderstrijd in België*, Kritak, Leuven.

Bundervoet, J. (1973), *Het doorstromingsprobleem in de hedendaagse vakbeweging. Kritische literatuurstudie en verkenning in de Belgische vakbonden*, Doctoral dissertation, Department of Sociology, Catholic University of Leuven.

Bundervoet, J. (1974), 'Vakbeweging in heroriëntering ?', *De Gids op maatschappelijk gebied*, vol. 65, no. 4, pp. 303-320.

Chlepner, B. S. (1972), *Cent ans d'histoire sociale en Belgique*, Editions de l'Université Libre de Bruxelles, Bruxelles.

Clement, P. (1993), 'Het Belgisch socialisme en de staat. Theorie en praktijk (1885-1940)', in Aerts, E. et al. (eds.), *Studia Historica OEconomica. Liber alumnorum Herman Van der Wee*, Leuven University Press, Leuven, pp. 81- 96.

Dambre, W. (1985), *Geschiedenis van de ondernemingsraden in België*, Kluwer, Antwerpen.

Deruette, S. (1991), *La grève de l'hiver 1960-1961. Lutte ouvrière et revendication wallonne*. Bruxelles, 1991.

Destrée, J. and Vandervelde, E. (1903), *Le socialisme en Belgique*, Paris.

Devreese, D. (1990), 'Belgium', in Van der Linden, M. and Rojahn, J. (ed.), *The Formation of Labour Movements 1870-1914. An International Perspective*. Brill, Leiden etc., pp. 25-56.

Dewachter, W., a.o. (eds.) (1995), *Les sociaux-chrétiens en Belgique*, Duculot, Louvain-la-Neuve, forthcoming.

De Wever, B. (1995), *Greep naar de macht. Vlaams-nationalisme en Nieuwe Orde. Het VNV 1933-1945*, Lannoo-Perspectief, Tielt/Gent.

De Witte, H. (1990), *Conformisme, radicalisme en machteloosheid. Een onderzoek naar de sociaal-culturele en sociaal- economische opvattingen van arbeiders in Vlaanderen*, HIVA series 12, HIVA, Catholic University of Leuven, Leuven.

Dhondt, J. (1960-69), *Geschiedenis van de socialistische arbeidersbeweging in België*, S. M. Ontwikkeling, Gent.

Dobbelaere, K. and Voyé, L. (1992), 'Godsdienst en kerkelijkheid', in Kerkhofs, J. a.o. (eds.), *De versnelde ommekeer. De waarden van Vlamingen, Walen en Brusselaars in de jaren negentig*, Lannoo/Koning Boudewijnstichting, Tielt.

Dresse, R., a.o. (1990), *Syndicalisme au féminin* (Le mouvement ouvrier en Belgique. Outils pédagogiques 9), Manuel 3: *Après 1945, reconnaissance et intégration dans les structures syndicales*, CARHOP, Bruxelles.

Ebbinghaus, B. and Visser, J. (1995), *The Development of Trade Unions in Western Europe, 1945-92. A Comparative Data Handbook*, Campus, Frankfurt/New York, forthcoming.

Gerard, E. (1985), *De katholieke partij in crisis. Partijpolitiek leven in België (1918-1940)*, Kritak, Leuven.

Gerard, E. (1994), 'Le MOC-ACW', in Gerard, E. and Wynants, P. (eds.), *Histoire du mouvement ouvrier chrétien en Belgique*, KADOC-Studies 16, Leuven University Press, Leuven, vol. 1, pp. 604-605.

Gerard, E. and Wynants, P. (eds.), *Histoire du mouvement ouvrier chrétien en Belgique*, KADOC-Studies 16, 2 vols., Leuven University Press, Leuven.

Hancké, B. (1991), 'The crisis of national unions: Belgian labour in decline', *Politics and Society*, vol. 19, no. 4, October, pp. 463-487.

Hancké, B. (1993), 'Trade union membership in Europe 1960-1990. Rediscovering local unions', *British Journal of Industrial relations*, pp. 593-613.

Hancké, B. and Slomp, H. (1993), 'A small difference with large consequences. Local and national unions in Belgium and the Netherlands', Harvard University, October (mimeo).

Hellemans, S. and Schepers, R. (1992), 'De ontwikkeling van corporatieve verzorgingsstaten in België en Nederland', in Hellemans, S. (ed.), *België en Nederland*, a special issue of *Sociologische Gids*, vol. 39, no. 5-6, pp. 346-364.

Hellemans, S. (1988a), 'Katholicisme en verzuiling in België, Duitsland, Nederland en Frankrijk', *Tijdschrift voor Sociologie*, vol. 9, no. 3, pp. 351-393.

Hellemans, S. (1988b), 'Verzuiling en ontzuiling van de katholieken in België en Nederland. Een historisch-sociologische vergelijking', *Sociologische Gids*, vol. 35, no. 1, pp. 43-56.

Hellemans, S. (1990), *Strijd om de moderniteit. Sociale bewegingen en verzuiling in Europa sinds 1900*, Kadoc-studies 10, Universitaire Pers Leuven, Leuven.

Hemmerijckx, R. (1986), *Le mouvement syndical unifié et la naissance du renardisme*, Courrier hebdomadaire du CRISP 1119-1120, Bruxelles.

Hemmerijckx, R. (1991), 'The Belgian Communist Party and the Trade Unions, 1940-1960', in Waller, M., Courtois, S. and Lazar, M. (eds.), *Comrades and Brothers. Communism and Trade Unions in Europe*, London.

Hemmerijckx, R. (1993), 'De Belgische socialisten tegen de Unie van Hand- en Geestesarbeiders', in *België 1940. Een maatschappij in crisis en oorlog*, NSGWO II, Brussel, pp. 481-496.

Hilden, P. (1993), *Women, Work, and Politics: Belgium, 1830-1914*, Oxford University Press, Oxford.

Holderbeke, F., De Witte, H. and van der Hallen, P. (1992), *Houding en verwachtingen van 'nieuwe werknemersgroepen' tegenover de vakbeweging. Een secundaire analyse van het onderzoek 'Vakbonden 2000'*, HIVA, Leuven.

Hondeghem, A. (1990), *De loopbaan van de ambtenaar. Tussen droom en werkelijkheid*, Vervolmakingscentrum voor overheidsbeleid en bestuur 8, KU Leuven.

Huyse, L. (1985), 'Het strategisch gevecht om een bredere basis', in Brepoels, J., a.o. (eds.), *Eeuwige dilemma's. Honderd jaar socialistische partij*, Kritak, Leuven, pp. 140-155.

Huyse, L. (1987), *De verzuiling voorbij*, Kritak, Leuven.

Kesteloot, C. (1988), 'Le Mouvement Populaire Wallon et la prise de conscience politique du mouvement wallon (1961-1965)', *Cahiers Marxistes*, no. 157-158, pp. 54-67.

Kesteloot, C. (1993), *Mouvement wallon et identité nationale*, Courrier hebdomadaire 1392, CRISP, Bruxelles.

Klijn, A. (1990), *Arbeiders- of volkspartij. Een vergelijkende studie van het Belgisch en Nederlands socialisme 1933-1946*, Universitaire Pers, Maastricht.

Kwanten, G. (1984), 'De bedrijfsorganisatie in de christelijke vakbeweging 1918-1930', *De Gids op maatschappelijk gebied*, vol. 75, no. 4, pp. 337-347.

Langendries, E. (1989), 'De niet-partijpolitieke organisaties: een liberale zuil ?', in Verhulst, A. and Hasquin, H. (dirs.), *Het liberalisme in België. Tweehonderd jaar geschiedenis*, Paul Hymanscentrum/Delta, Brussel, pp. 91-100.

Lehouck, F. (1978), 'De vakbondsontwikkeling in België', *Arbeidsblad*, vol. 79, pp. 505-538.
Liebman, M. (1979), *Les socialistes belges 1885-1914. La révolte et l'organisation*, Histoire du mouvement ouvrier en Belgique 3, Vie Ouvrière, Bruxelles.
Luykx, T. and Platel, M. (1985), *Politieke geschiedenis van België*, Kluwer, Antwerpen.
Luyten, D. (1993), 'Ontstaansvoorwaarden voor het corporatisme. Het model van het neo-corporatisme in het licht van de Belgische ervaring uit de jaren dertig', *Tijdschrift voor sociale geschiedenis*, vol. 19, no. 3, August, pp. 316-338.
Luyten, D. (1994), 'Crisis van het neo-corporatisme? Arbeidersbeweging en overlegeconomie sinds 1975', in *Democratie op het einde van de 20ste eeuw*, Koninklijke Academie voor Wetenschappen, Letteren en Schone Kunsten van België, Klasse der Letteren, Mededelingen, vol. 56, spec. no., pp. 169-194.
Luyten, D. (1995a), *Het corporatisme in België. Ontwikkeling en transformaties van het corporatisme als ideologisch-politiek verschijnsel*, Koninklijke Academie voor Wetenschappen, Letteren en Schone Kunsten van België, Verhandelingen, Brussel.
Luyten, D. (1995b), *Sociaal-economisch overleg in België sedert 1918*, Balans 6, VUB-Press, Brussel.
Luyten D. and Vanthemsche, G. (eds.) (1995), *Het sociaal pact van 1945: oorsprong, betekenis en gevolgen*, VUB-Press, Brussel.
Mabille, X. (1986), *Histoire politique de la Belgique: facteurs et acteurs de changement*, CRISP, Bruxelles.
Mampuys, J. (1984), 'Quadragesimo anno: corporatisme en christelijke vakbeweging 1930-1940', *De Gids op maatschappelijk gebied*, vol. 75, no. 5, pp. 395-418.
Mampuys, J. (1991), 'De christelijke vakbeweging en het Belgisch vakbondspluralisme', *De Gids op maatschappelijk gebied*, vol. 82, no. 5, pp. 467-492.
Mampuys, J. (1994), 'Le syndicalisme chrétien', in Gerard, E. and Wynants, P. (eds.), *Histoire du mouvement ouvrier chrétien en Belgique*, KADOC Studies 16, Leuven University Press, vol. 2, pp. 151-279.
Martens, A. (1994), '1983-'93 of ... de ononderbroken terugloop van de stakingen in België (kwantitatieve analyse van de stakingsvergoedingen uitbetaald door de ACV-weerstandskas)', *De Gids op maatschappelijk gebied*, vol. 85, no. 11, Nov., pp. 869-879.
Martens, A., Bundervoet, J. and Bosmans, W. (1984), 'Arbeid, arbeidsbeweging en verzorgingsmaatschappij', in Vrancken, J. and Hendrickx, E. (eds.), *Zorgen om de verzorgingsstaat*, Acco, Leuven/Amersfoort, pp. 154-184.
Martin, B. (1989), 'De totstandkoming van de socialistische gemeenschappelijke actie', in Witte, E., Burgelman, J.C. and Stouthuysen, P. (eds.), *Tussen restauratie en vernieuwing. Aspecten van de Belgische naoorlogse politiek 1944-1950*, VUB Press, Brussels, pp. 167-169.
Meynen, A. (1978), 'De grote werkstaking 1960-1961. Een inleidend overzicht van de ekonomische en socio-politieke achtergronden van de grote werkstaking 1960-1961', *Belgisch Tijdschrift voor Nieuwste Geschiedenis*, vol. 9, no. 2, pp. 481-516.
Miroir, A. (1982), 'Le syndicalisme libéral (1894-1961). Contribution à l'étude des familles politiques', *Revue Belge d'Histoire Contemporaine*, vol. 13, no. 1, pp. 59-82.
Mok, A. L. (1992), 'Werken in de prestatiemaatschappij', in Kerkhofs, J. a.o. (eds.), *De versnelde ommekeer. De waarden van Vlamingen, Walen en Brusselaars in de jaren negentig*, Lannoo and Koning Boudewijnstichting, Tielt.

Molinari, J. P. (1995), 'L'idéalisation de la classe ouvrière', in Deniot, J. (ed.), *Crises et métamorphoses ouvrières*, Logiques sociales, L'Harmattan, Paris, forthcoming.

Mommen, A. (1980), *De Belgische Werkliedenpartij. Ontstaan en ontwikkeling van het reformistisch socialisme 1880-1914*, Frans Masereelfonds, Gent.

Moreau, R. (1984), *Combat syndical et conscience wallonne. Du syndicalisme clandestin au Mouvement Populaire Wallon (1943-1963)*, Liège/Bruxelles/Mt.-S.-Marchienne.

Moulaert, J. (1995), *Rood en zwart. De anarchistische beweging in België 1880-1914*, Davidsfonds, Leuven (French translation Quorum, Bruxelles, 1996, forthcoming).

Nauwelaerts, M. (1973), 'De socialistische syndicale beweging na de Eerste Wereldoorlog (1919-1921)', *Belgisch Tijdschrift voor Nieuwste Geschiedenis*, no. 4, pp. 343-376.

Neuville, J. (1979), *Naissance et croissance du syndicalisme*, vol. 1: *L'origine des premiers syndicats*, Histoire du mouvement ouvrier en Belgique 1, Ed. Vie Ouvrière, Bruxelles.

Neuville, J. and Yerna, J. (1990), *Le choc de l'hiver 1960-1961. Les grèves contre la loi unique*, Pol-His, Vol. 3, De Boeck, Bruxelles.

Pasture, P. (1991a), *Omgaan met werkloosheid. Arbeidsmarktbeleid in crisistijd*, HIVA, Catholic University of Leuven (mimeo).

Pasture, P. (1991b), 'Het ACV en de katholieke sociale leer. Hoe hemel en aarde met elkaar verzoenen ?', *De Gids op maatschappelij gebied*, vol. 82, no. 5, pp. 447-465.

Pasture, P. (1991c), 'Le bras politique du mouvement ouvrier chrétien. Historique d'une relation turbulente', *La Revue Politique*, no. 5, pp. 7-29.

Pasture, P. (1992), *Kerk, politiek en sociale actie. De unieke positie van de christelijke arbeidersbeweging in België 1944-1973*, HIVA series 14, Garant, Leuven/Apeldoorn.

Pasture, P. (1993a), 'Syndicalisatiegraad: feiten en cijfers', *Nieuwsbrief WAV*, vol. 3, no. 1, April, pp. 31-32.

Pasture, P. (1993b), 'The April 1944 'Social Pact' in Belgium and its significance for the post-war welfare state', *Journal of Contemporary History*, vol. 28, no. 3, October, pp. 695-714.

Pasture, P. (1994a), *Christian Trade Unionism in Europe since 1968. Tensions Between Identity and Practice*, Avebury, Aldershot etc.

Pasture, P. (1994b), 'Diverging paths: the development of Catholic labour organizations in France, The Netherlands and Belgium since 1944', *Revue d'Histoire Ecclésiastique*, vol. 87, no. 1, pp. 54-90.

Pasture, P. (1995a), 'Liefde na datum. De christelijke arbeidersbeweging en het sociaal pact', in Luyten, D. and Vanthemsche, G. (eds.), *Het Sociaal Pact van 1944. Oorsprong, betekenis en gevolgen*, Balans 6, VUB Press, Brussel, pp. 305-323.

Pasture, P. (1995b), 'Où sont les travailleurs d'antan ? La perception de la classe ouvrière par le mouvement ouvrier chrétien belge dans la période d'après guerre', in Deniot, J. (éd.), *Crises et métamorphoses ouvrières*, Logiques sociales, L'Harmattan, Paris, forthcoming.

Pasture, P. (1995c), 'Entre Eglise et citoyen. Le PSC/CVP et le monde catholique organisé', in Dewachter, W. a.o. (eds.), *Un parti dans l'histoire. 50 ans d'action du Parti Social Chrétien*, Duculot, Louvain-la-Neuve, pp. 265-295.

Pasture, P. and Mampuys, J. (1990), *In de ban van het getal. Ledenanalyse van het ACV/CSC 1900-1990*, HIVA series 13, HIVA, Catholic University of Leuven.

Polasky, J. (1995), *The Democratic Socialism of Emile Vandervelde. Between Reform and Revolution*, Berg, Oxford/Washington.

'Politieke benoemingen: beterschap in een Belgische ziekte ?' (1993), *Kultuurleven*, no. 6, pp. 6-17.

Ponteur, L. (1993), 'Ontzuilen en vrijzinnige onmacht', in Demeyere, F. (ed.), *Over Pluralisme en Democratie. Verzuiling en integratie in een multiculturele samenleving*, VUB Press, Brussel, pp. 137-146.

Raes, K. (1993), 'Naar een lekenstatelijk verzekerde verdraagzaamheid of naar een verzuilde kolonisering van levensbeschouwingen of culturen ?', in Demeyere, F. (ed.), *Over Pluralisme en Democratie. Verzuiling en integratie in een multiculturele samenleving*, VUB Press, Brussel, pp. 125-136.

Rion, P. (1989), 'Het sociale vraagstuk', in Verhulst, A. and Hasquin, H. (dirs.), *Het liberalisme in België. Tweehonderd jaar geschiedenis*, Paul Hymanscentrum/Delta, Brussel, p. 175-182.

Shalev, M. (1992), 'The resurgence of labour quiescence', in Regini, M. (ed.), *The Future of Labour Movements*, Sage, London, pp. 102-149.

Slomp, H. and Van Mierlo, T. (1984), *Arbeidsverhoudingen in België*, Het Spectrum, Antwerpen/Utrecht, 2 vols.

Spineux, A. (1981), *Forces et strategies syndicales*, Doctoral dissertation, Department of Sociology, Université Catholique de Louvain.

Spineux, A. (1990), 'Trade Unionism in Belgium: The Difficulties of a Major Renovation', in Baglioni, G. and Crouch, C. (eds.), *European Industrial Relations: The Challenge of Flexibility*, Sage, London, pp. 42-70.

Steenhaut, W. (1993), 'De Unie van Hand- en Geestesarbeiders', in *België 1940. Een maatschappij in crisis en oorlog*, NSGWO II, Brussel, pp. 277-283.

Strikwerda, C. J. (1983), *Urban Structure, Religion and Language: Belgian Workers 1880-1914*, University Microfilms International, Ann Arbor (Mich.).

Stroobant, M. (1990), 'De overheid en het collectief overleg in België tijdens de sociaaleconomische crisis 1970-1988', in Beaupain, T. a.o. (eds.), *50 jaar arbeidsverhoudingen*, Die Keure, Bruges, pp. 79-83.

Valenzuela, J. S. (1992), 'Labour movements and political systems: some variations', in Regini, M. (ed.), *The Future of Labour Movements*, Sage, London, pp. 53-101.

Van de Kerckhove, J. (1979), 'De opstelling van de vakbeweging op de achtergrond van de industriële ontwikkeling in België', in *Politisering en professionalisering*, Antwerpen, pp. 179-208.

Van den Brande, A. (1987), 'Neo-Corporatism and Functional-Integral Power in Belgium', in Scholte, I. (ed.), *Political Stability and Neo-Corporatism. Corporatist Integration and Societal Cleavages in Western Europe*, Sage, London, pp. 95-119.

Vandenbroucke, F. (1981), *Van crisis tot crisis. Een socialistisch alternatief*, Kritak, Leuven.

Van den Bulck, J. (1992), 'Pillars and Politics', *West European Politics*, vol. 15, no. 2, April, pp. 35-55.

Van Ruysseveldt, J. and Harzing, A. W. K. (1992), 'Nederlandse en Belgische arbeidsverhoudingen in vergelijkend perspectief', *Arbeidsverhoudingen in Europa*, vol. 1: *Stelsels van arbeidsverhoudingen in West-Europa*, Netherlands Open University, Heerlen.

Vanthemsche, G. (1990), 'Unemployment insurance in interwar Belgium', *International Journal of Social History*, no. 3, pp. 349-376.

Vanthemsche, G. (1993), 'De Belgische arbeidersbeweging tijdens de crisis van de jaren 1930', in *België 1940. Een maatschappij in crisis en oorlog/Belgique 1940. Une société en crise. Un pays en guerre*, NCWOII, Brussel, pp. 201-225.

Vanthemsche, G. (1994a), *La sécurié sociale. Les origines du système belge. Le présent face à son passé*, De Boeck Université, Bruxelles.

Vanthemsche, G. (1994b), *Le chômage en Belgique de 1929 à 1940, son histoire, son actualité*, Labor, Bruxelles.

Vanthemsche, G. (1994c), 'De groeiende staat. Sociaal-economische functies van de Belgische staat in historisch perspectief', *De Gids op maatschappelijk gebied*, vol. 85, no. 11, November, pp. 847-868.

Verhulst, A. and Hasquin, H. (dirs.) (1989), *Het liberalisme in België. Tweehonderd jaar geschiedenis*, Paul Hymanscentrum/Delta, Brussel (=*Le libéralisme en Belgique. Deux cent ans d'histoire*).

Vilrokx, J. and Van Leemput, J. (1992), 'Belgium: a new stability in industrial relations ?', in Ferner, A. and Hyman, R. (eds.), *Industrial Relations in the New Europe*, Blackwell, Oxford/Cambridge (Mass), pp. 356-392.

Visser, J. (1991), 'Trends in union membership', *Employment outlook 1991*, OECD, Paris.

Wils, L. (1986), 'De historische verstrengeling tussen de christelijke arbeidersbeweging en de Vlaamse beweging', in Gerard E. and Mampuys M. (eds.), *Voor kerk en werk. Opstellen over de geschiedenis van de christelijke arbeidersbeweging (1886-1986)*, Kadoc-Yearbook 1985, Leuven University Press, pp. 15-40.

Wils, L. (1992), 'A brief history of the Flemish movement', in Hermans, T. (ed.), Vos, L. and Wils, L. (co-eds.), *The Flemish Movement. A Documentary History 1780-1990*, Athlone Press, London.

Witte, E., Craeybeckx, J. and Meynen, A. (1990), *Politieke geschiedenis van België van 1830 tot heden*, Standaard, Antwerpen.

4 The unattainable unity in the Netherlands

Patrick Pasture

Introduction

The Netherlands is without doubt a rewarding country for studying the impact of ideology on society, as is France, although for opposing reasons. Whereas France has been a breeding ground for secular thinking since the 18th century and is the stage for heated debates between intellectuals, the Netherlands, by contrast, seems to be a country of principles, where religion has infiltrated the whole of society and, in complete contrast to republican France, forms the basis of its democracy and forbearance. After all, the Dutch republic is a product of the Reformation, which led to a pronounced bourgeois society in which tolerance is seen as one of the basic values (Zahn, 1989).

Until the 1960s, the Netherlands was a typical example of a pillarized society (Hellemans, 1990, pp. 7-12). In the course of the nineteenth century three ideological communities had developed into major social movements, which had grown before the turn of the century into extensive and mutually integrated networks of organizations. They are usually referred to as 'pillars': protestant, socialist and Catholic respectively. The liberal political family never really developed into a pillar. Although the Catholics were in fact the last to make the move to 'pillarization' (close to 1900), from the 1920s until the 1950s the Catholic pillar was undoubtedly the most fully developed and most homogeneous pillar. It is therefore all the more surprising that it was the one to fall apart so quickly and completely. Right from the 1950s onwards, doubts grew within Catholic circles as to the wisdom of the ideal of a 'people's church'; that is why the fundamental social processes which led to the decline of the major social movements did not meet with a great deal of resistance - on the contrary (Thurlings, 1978). In the wake of industrialization also the socialists built up an entire network of their own organizations, but were never able to unite all workers behind their cause. After 1945, the socialist movement hoped for a breakthrough in the sense of a 'depillarization'. However, not only was socialist behaviour barely distinguishable from that among the other pillars, breakthrough thinking itself could actually be interpreted as a call to joining the socialist organizations. During the 1960s, the socialist identity became blurred and their network virtually fell apart in the following decade.

The protestant pillar was also lacking in stability: after all, it embraced a heterogeneous range of churches and denominations. The most important churches in the Netherlands are still the Dutch Reformed Church, which has its roots in the Reformation and clings to a rather Biblical humanist form of Christianity, and the Reformed Churches in the Netherlands, which unite several orthodox Calvinist secessions of the aforementioned Reformed Church. Moreover, especially in reformed circles, the principle of pillarization was disputed. Protestant pillarization was also never really 'complete' because there were always several political parties which appealed to protestant voters, especially the Christian Historical Union (CHU, 1906) and the Anti-Revolutionary Party (ARP, 1879). Paradoxically enough, most observers believe that the protestant pillar is the one that has remained most intact. For example, protestant press and newspapers remained largely in existence and, as will be documented later in this chapter, the protestant trade union movement refused to follow the socialists and Catholics into a federation. In 1980 the most important protestant political parties did, however, merge with the Catholic People's Party (KVP). Together, they formed the Christian Democratic Appeal (CDA) which, although it does not strongly stress its Christian dimension, nonetheless occupies a central position in protestant social life. In other respects, depillarization was also characterized from the 1960s onwards by the increase of non-pillarized organizations.

In the Netherlands, pillarization was partly responsible for the expansion of a corporative welfare state, within which the government and social organizations govern socio-economic life. State intervention, consultation between the government and the social organizations, and centralization form the three key characteristics of the Dutch system of industrial relations (Windmuller, De Galan and Van Zweden, 1990;

Visser, 1990, pp. 198-242; 1993, pp. 323-356). In essence, after the Second World War a factual agreement was reached under which the established trade unions acquired a high level of institutional recognition and participation in return for their cooperation in the reconstruction. Within this framework, the Dutch government was able to pursue a strict policy of low wages until 1963. Both government policy and the consultation system itself were based on the explicit 'feeling of co-responsibility' in the Dutch trade unions, which - surprisingly even so in the denominational camp - saw the government much more as an ally.

Until 1957, the Dutch trade unions grew steadily, despite the policy of low wages. The growth of the large confederations has been attributed to traditional feelings of loyalty, a strong identification with one's own religious or ideological community (Catholic, protestant, socialist) and the fact that the trade unions provided services which were not directly related to collective bargaining (Windmuller, 1969). However, this last factor was to be undermined by the expansion of national welfare packages in the 1950s. In this way, the organization of social security fell largely into the hands of corporative industrial insurance boards, on which the trade unions only played an administrative role.

In the late 1950s, the low wages policy led to tensions on the labour market and the trade union movement came under pressure. The large confederations faced heavy losses of members and competition from categorial trade unions which were politically independent and geared towards defending the material interests of members in the same sector. Consequently, the controlled wages policy had to be abandoned, resulting in a spectacular rise in the national wage. Social consultation was conducted at sectoral or intersectoral level, with the government remaining involved. The New Wage Bill of 1970 passed the main theme of wage negotiations to the social partners, with, however, the govenment keeping the right to impose a wage freeze. However, this did not really make the trade unions any more attractive. After all, the Dutch trade unions were as good as absent from the workplace, which meant that there was relatively little opportunity for direct contact with (potential) members. Trade union action mainly took place well above the heads of the workers. Moreover, as a result of the expansion of public social services, one of the trade unions' major attractions had disappeared. The trade unions also lost their spontaneous power of attraction as a result of the depillarization mentality. Nevertheless, the trade union movement was able to maintain its political role. In the 1960s and 1970s the Netherlands further developed into a generous welfare state, including a guaranteed minimum wage (collective labour agreement 1964, law in 1968), a general disability ruling (General Relief Act, 1964), automatic price indexing (1965 and 1974), guaranteed payment of 80% of the last wage in the event of disability (1968).

At the beginning of the 1970s, the Dutch trade union movement was infected by the socio-critical fire flickering all over Europe, but it did not really herald a renewed period of 'class struggle'. Nonetheless, the trade union movement stuck mainly to politics (Van der Linden and Schutjens, 1993). Besides, initiatives towards another strategy with respect to the company were launched, which led in 1971 to greater powers for the works council to represent the interests of workers. Until then, the works council had been more of a paternalistic body in the hands of the employer. In 1979, the employer himself was excluded from the works council, but the trade union movement did not subsequently gain a hold over the works councils either (Visser, 1994a).

The economic crisis from 1974 onward initially changed few of the basic features of the Dutch socio-economic and political system. The socialist-Catholic Van Uyl government, 'the most leftist government of the post-war period' (Hemerijck, 1995, p. 208), pursued an expansionist policy combined with wage restraint. The trade unions took a noticeably cautious line. In 1975, an agreement was reached on the introduction of new technologies (Leisinck, 1993). But consultation between the government and the social partners on wage restraint and budgetary control became increasingly difficult. Due to the weak position of the trade unions within companies the absence of a central wages policy put further downward pressure on wages. From the mid 1970s onwards the neo-corporatist system reached a real deadlock. Paradoxically, this was only broken after the new and anti-concertative 'no-nonsense' austerity coalition headed by Ruud Lubbers in 1982 threathened the social partners unilaterally to impose a strict price and wage freeze, which led to the so-called 'Wassenaar' accord between the social partners, opening the way to reinforced bipartite bargaining in the following decade. However, the phocus of the employers' perspective on industrial bargaining had definitivelly shifted to the company level. In the early 1990s, the government once again came to the fore as third partner in industrial relations practice, partly in response to the European integration (Hemerijck, 1995).

In the meantime, since the 1960s structural changes in the Dutch economy had a deep impact on employment. Among other things, a rapid increase in the participation of women in the labour market came about. Persistent mass unemployment in the 1980s plunged the trade union movement into a deep crisis, not least because the unemployed dropped out, which meant a spectacular nosedive in membership of the trade unions. Many working people found themselves in situations which prevented them from committing themselves, irrespective of how small the commitment, to a trade union: part-time work, job insecurity, etc. From 1982 onwards, moreover, the social security system was seriously slashed, undermining the foundations of the Dutch welfare state: even the minimum wage hung in the balance (Kloosterman, 1994).

Unity and diversity in the socialist trade union movement

The Dutch trade union movement developed at a relatively late stage, although the first Dutch trade unions in Amsterdam date back to the years 1860-1870. They combined social demands with social funds and were markedly moderate. After an initial attempt to coordinate the early labour organizations within the context of the First International Workers' Association (1869-1870) failed to get off the ground, a federation still followed relatively quickly, in 1871. This General Dutch Workers' Union (ANWV) wanted, on the one hand, to improve the employment conditions of the workers and expand their civil rights through peaceful action, and, on the other hand, achieve honest cooperation between labour and capital, between employers and employees. The federation embraced not only trade associations, but also a wide range of workers' associations. In addition to the fight for wage rises, cooperative action was its most important activity. However, the federation's attitude to politics was a bone of contention. When it spoke out in favour of universal suffrage and for public, neutral state education, the orthodox/protestant workers broke away and formed Patrimonium, the Christian Employees' Association (1877).

Several mainly socialist associations were never involved in the ANWV. In 1878, they formed their own union, which became a national organization in 1881 under the name of the Social Democratic League (SDB). These socialist organizations were initially only in style more radical than the ANWV and Patrimonium. In the SDB political and trade union action were very closely linked. However, while unable to reach unanimity on their political attitude, many socialists quickly became disillusioned with the lack of possibilities which the fledgling democracy offered the labour movement. Encouraged by the charismatic former minister Domela Nieuwenhuis, in the 1890s the SDB set off along an anti-parliamentary and revolutionary anarchic path. Under pressure of the Second International Workers' Association in 1893 within the SDB a National Labour Secretariat (NAS) was created as a national trade union centre, which in practice mainly was devoted to the organization of strikes. The protagonists of universal suffrage in 1894 split off the SDB and formed the Social Democratic Labour Party (SDAP). Despite attempts at cooperation, the revolutionary anarchists of the SDB and the social democrats of the SDAP soon grew apart, although both remained affiliated with the NAS (Perry, 1994; Hueting, De Jong Edz and Neij, 1983; Harmsen and Reinalda, 1975).

Around the turn of the century, the early Dutch labour movement was strongly divided. In general, however, as a result of the extension of the right to vote (the introduction of 'attributive' electoral rights, 1896) the social democrats, especially in the SDAP, gradually gained in confidence, as well as the Christians. Within the NAS tensions sometimes ran high between revolutionary syndicalists and those in favour of centralization and a more cautious stance. A failed strike movement in 1903 against the restriction of the right to strike (including a strike ban on public services and the railways), caused grave desperation in the socialist camp, but also sowed the seeds of the resurrection. Eventually, this led to the foundation of the Dutch Confederation of Trade Unions (NVV) in 1905. The experiences of the failed strike dictated its most important characteristics: a high level of centralization; emphasis on collective defence of interests at sectoral level (collective labour agreements); a fundamental choice for consultation (direct action was only considered acceptable in times of necessity and subject to thorough organization); attention to social legislation, but political autonomy. However, this last concept soon proved fictitious: as early as 1908 the NVV decided to support the SDAP in its fight for universal suffrage, which engendered a long lasting and very close relationship. In every sense, the NVV was in complete opposition with the old NAS, which remained the centre of the revolutionary syndicalists.

The First World War (which passed by the Netherlands) drove many workers towards the trade unions. In the restless climate of 1918 the socialist chairman P.J. Troelstra even predicted the (peaceful) 'revolution' but was not listened to, certainly not by the NVV. However, a number of important social measures were taken. In 1917 universal male suffrage was introduced, followed one year later by active electoral rights for women. However, this did not lead to an electoral breakthrough for the social democrats: the entire interwar period was dominated by the religious parties and their supporters. What was new was that the NVV was unveiling a wide social project, putting forward a form of statutory industrial organization, with the emphasis on employee participation - instead of consultation - in the running of the company as a transition to a more general form of socialization. Socialization or nationalization would put an end to exploitation as well as to the tyranny which allegedly turned the workers into objects. Socialization would secure more control to the people over production (Hueting, De Jong Edz and Neij, 1983).

Meanwhile, division within the non-denominational trade union movement had not abated. New forces had emerged, communists on the one hand, operating primarily within the existing organizations, the NAS as well as the NVV, and the General Dutch Trade Union Federation (ANV), on the other hand. The ANV was founded in 1919 as a neutral trade union and aimed mainly at white collar workers. Attempts at mergers or structured cooperation with the NVV failed. In 1930, the communists formed a 'red trade union opposition movement' which in fact acted as their own confederation. However, when, within the framework of the idea of a 'popular front', the communists began to work towards trade union unity, in November 1933 the NVV declared membership of the NVV incompatible with that of communist organizations. However, despite this division during the interwar period apart from the NAS all the trade unions were able to increase their membership, with the exception of a significant fall in 1920-21.

The Second World War shook the Dutch trade union movement. While the SDAP dissolved itself when it was placed under supervision by the occupiers, the NVV decided to keep going. When the denominational unions were liquidated, they were taken over by NVV mandataries. This action by the NVV opened up a deep rift between social democrats and supporters of religious parties, which could not be healed by the resignation of the NVV executive some time later, and dealt a heavy blow to the desire for trade union unity, which was also challenging the Netherlands at the time of the liberation. Initially, that desire had led to new initiatives which placed great importance on worker unity. During the occupation, 'unified trade unions' had been formed, with a hard core mainly of miners. At the end of 1944 and the beginning of 1945, this led to into a new national confederation, the Unified Trade Union Federation (EVC). In addition, the Dutch People's Movement (*Nederlandse Volksbeweging*) emerged at political level, uniting Catholics and socialists. This movement wanted to encourage a political alternative, strengthened by shared experiences during the occupation and based on a personalistic vision on man and world (Bank,

1978). Under its impulse, the prewar SDAP was transformed into a Labour Party (PvdA), open to Christians.

The PvdA resolutely distanced itself from the old class thinking and opted to expand its basis, both by presenting itself as a broad-based 'people's party' and by directly appealing to Christians (the idea of a 'breakthrough') (Bank, 1978; Klijn, 1990). The organizational links between the PvdA and the NVV were severed. The NVV, no longer an integral part of the party, did however fully agree with this change of ideological direction by the PvdA. It stressed that it was open to everyone, irrespective of their political or religious convictions. It even recognized the significance of faith and ideology for the trade union movement. Everything which could be termed dogmatic, marxist materialism was rejected. 'The potential gain in members was inversely proportionate to consistency of principles', was the cynical comment by the authors of the history of the NVV, *Naar groter eenheid* (Towards closer unity) (Hueting, De Jong and Neij, 1983, p. 158). In practice, the NVV would continue to see the PvdA as its political wing, and the party and the trade union movement stayed as close as two peas in a pod. Certainly, there was no trade union unity; conflicts between the confederations, heightened by the action of the NVV during the occupation, were too bitter for that. Nonetheless, as early as 1945 the three major confederations formed the Council of Trade Union Confederations (*Raad van Vakcentrales*) for mutual consultation, while together with the employers they created the Foundation of Labour (*Stichting van de Arbeid*) which was recognized by the government as its main consultative body in socio-economic matters - the rapidly growing EVC was not involved in this cooperation. Plans for a merger between the latter, in which the communists occupied a dominant position, and the NVV did indeed proceed to an advanced stage, but finally fell apart, mainly as a result of the NVV's fear of the communists. Initially, the EVC went with the spirit of the times, but as a result of the imminent Cold War and the stronger organization of the NVV, the tide turned and the EVC soon found itself completely out of the running.

In the 1950s, the NVV supported the controlled (low) wages policy and the statutory industrial organization. Nonetheless, the NVV had initially seen the statutory industrial organization differently, with more actual employee participation and state involvement, and as part of a democratically planned economy. In its final form, however, the workers did not have a say in the economic policy of the statutory industrial organization and the emphasis was on social aspects and the maintenance of social peace. In the last years of the 1950s, first the statutory industrial organization and then the controlled wages policy came under increasing pressure.

The NVV was looking chiefly for organizational modernization, but the far-reaching centralization which the trade union leadership had in mind found no favour among several of the affiliated unions. However, the new climate of labour relations and, not least, the increase in prosperity, led after much delay to a fundamental reflection on the role of the NVV in the Dutch system. Various unions still ran into financial difficulties in the course of the 1960s: the ever-rising costs of contemporary trade union action were not matched by a rise in income, on the contrary, as a result of stable or even falling membership.

Still, at the end of the 1960s, a fundamental reflection on the basic premises of the NVV took place. The statement of principles, which was approved in 1971, represented a new step towards a general trade union movement, following the first move in the immediate postwar period. Excessively abstract personalist concepts were scrapped as obsolete and old socialist basic concepts were referred to as dogmas. The NVV distanced itself from ideas concerning the need for economic planning and the transfer of the means of production to the community. As a basis for its action, the NVV from then on referred to the Universal Declaration on Human Rights. The trade union action of the NVV took as its basic premises not only the defence of the interests and demands of employees, but explicitly also the general interest as such. This shift has been referred to as from 'red' to 'pink' (Hueting, De Jongh and Neij, 1983, p. 347). More attention was also devoted to working women, but although there had been a committee for working women in existence since 1954, transformed into a permanent secretariat in 1959, in the 1960s the Women's Association was still directed purely at the home-working wives of affiliated men. Not until 1972 did the NVV congress decide that the Women's Association was open to all women, based on a general feminist viewpoint.[1]

In the early 1970s, the Netherlands was also lit by a left-wing, socio-critical flame. Although the NVV initially took a very negative view of the left-wing 'troublemakers', including within their own circles, it did begin discussions with the so-called Working Party for a socio-critical trade union movement (*Werkgroep Maatschappijkritische Vakbeweging*), set up by trade unionists of all collars in October 1970. This Working Party wanted far-reaching democratization at all levels of social and economic life - including in the company and the trade unions themselves. The 'established' Dutch trade unions did not succeed in reaching an agreement with it. However, the NVV did continue its reflection of its role and social vision.

In 1977, this resulted in the report entitled *Vakbeweging en maatschappij* (Trade union movement and society).[2] According to this report, the ideal society for which the trade union movement must strive is based on equality with the economy organized in the service of the people, not vice versa. From this markedly personalist perspective, the NVV was in favour of strong government control and a different division of wealth, based on fairness and social relevance. In this context, the NVV strongly emphasized social rights. The entire programme was set in a world context and was aimed not only at the traditional fields of trade union action - labour relations and social security in this case - but also at general welfare, the Third World, the significance of development and technology for the environment, culture and education. Strikingly absent, however, were proposals for company action, although from the late 1960s onwards, various aflliliated NVV-unions had made attempts to increase their presence within the companies.

In the meantime, the NVV entered into a federation in 1974, together with the Dutch Catholic Trade Union Federation (NKV). This federation would be converted into a genuine merger in 1981. It marked the start of a new phase in Dutch trade union history.

The denominational tradition

The origins of the denominational trade unions can be traced to the orthodox/protestant breakaway from the ANWV in 1877. However, Patrimonium cannot properly be called a trade union: it was an expression of protestant resistance to the secularization of society. It advocated a paternalistic solution to the social question and rejected both social legislation and the collective defence of interests as such. Change came gradually around 1891. In that year the protestants held the first Christian Social Congress, which included a recognition of the right to strike. Within Patrimonium the first protestant trade unions were formed around this time.

Trade unions also emerged around 1890 in Catholic circles (Roes, 1985, pp. 27 ff.). They quickly took on a blatantly Catholic character. In addition to mass trade union organization, the Catholics also wanted popular education and training - the way in which popular education and trade union action could be linked was to be a permanent area of tension for the Catholic labour movement. In addition, there was still tension between mixed organizations of workers, the petty bourgeoisie and craftsmen on the one hand and pure workers' organizations on the other hand. Division and organizational weakness put the Catholic trade union organizations in an unfavourable competitive position with respect to the socialist trade union movement in particular. Partly as a result of this, the Catholics sought contact with the protestants, resulting in the foundation of Unitas in Twente in 1896. This was an interdenominational union for textile workers, with both mixed and individual sections for Catholics and protestants. To the protestants, this interdenominationalism would remain the ideal, but in discussions on the Catholic side as to how to achieve more unity on the brightly chequered trade union landscape, the Roman Catholic episcopacy insisted on a purely Catholic trade union movement; from 1906 onwards, Catholic bishops forbade their subjects from joining interdenominational unions ex cathedra. In practice, it was some years before the protestant/Catholic divorce became absolute.

The CNV and the dream of a universal Christian trade union movement

The strike action of 1903 had been of major significance for the development of the Christian trade union movement. Christian (protestant) workers had helped break the strike, which made the chasm between them and the non-denominational, socialist trade union movement unbridgeable. However, this arrangement was also highly disputed within Christian circles; the trade unions' very *raison d'être* was again called into question. Given the prosperous development of the socialists, however, especially after the foundation of the NVV, a Christian (anti-socialist) reaction was inevitable.

This eventually came in 1909 with the foundation of the Federation of Christian Trade Unions in the Netherlands (CNV) as a national confederation. The CNV took as its foundation 'the Christian principles and consequently rejected the class struggle'. In its statement of principles, the CNV expressed its interdenominational structure: it appealed to all protestant churches and to Catholics, and included Catholic representatives among its leadership. As a result of the dismissive attitude of the Catholic bishops, however, the CNV became an exclusively protestant organization. The CNV did not have a detailed programme, but it did have a vague idea about 'industrial organization' and leaned heavily towards the Anti-Revolutionary Party (ARP) although at times it also hoped for a more socially oriented Christian party (Vos, 1986). Its first 'Social Policy Programme' dates from 1918 and contained a number of fairly specific action points relating to social security and a statutory industrial organization with binding collective labour agreements, arbitration committees and minimum wages.

After the Second World War the CNV, morally strengthened by its firm position during the occupation, shifted its emphasis. First of all, it expanded its vision of the social question: in particular, its new chairman, M. Ruppert, introduced a protestant Christian form of personalism and, from this perspective, devoted special attention to the dehumanization of work. On this basis, the CNV advocated co-management in the company and wage determination by industry - distancing itself from the controlled wages policy. Partly as a result of this new vision of the social question, the CNV grew somewhat apart from the ARP. Things were not going so smoothly with the churches either. For example, in 1946, the General Synod of the Dutch Reformed Church saw 'no reason' to 'dissuade' believers from becoming members of the NVV. Support for the Christian trade union organization, however, was forthcoming from Calvinist-reformed circles (Van den Toren, 1991, pp. 40-43; Dijkstra, 1979, pp. 107 ff.).

The subsequent postwar history of the CNV reveals some developments which may at first sight seem paradoxical. Secularization weakened the links with other Christian organizations, first and foremost with the protestant parties with whom the CNV always maintained a somewhat difficult relationship. At no point, however, had the bridges been burned. Becoming a member of the CNV was less and less evident to Christian employees and its Christian character was increasingly less of a criterion for choosing a trade union. Moreover, the work of the Council of Trade Union Confederations being restored in 1961, the CNV cooperated willingly and wholeheartedly with the other trade unions in the 1960s. On the other hand, however, the CNV somewhat surprisingly strengthened its ties with the churches and, above all, did not want to renounce its Christian identity. This was expressed especially in the Vision Programme and the resulting policy conclusions which the CNV laid down in 1970.[3]

In fact, this vision programme was a reaction to a sociological survey conducted in 1969 among members of the CNV, which showed that the singularity of the CNV was at the very least unclear and that a fair number of members could well envisage a merger of the CNV, preferably with the NKV. By contrast, the CNV explicitly defined its identity as 'being geared towards and wanting to take inspiration from the gospel'. The entire vision programme was in fact oriented towards a 'Biblical welfare society', with justice and charity as basic values. The CNV credited the government and the public service with a leading role in realizing these evangelical standards and values. Specifically, it advocated an index-linked pension and it wanted to remove health care from the domain of charity. However, the Christian trade union movement also attached great importance to personal responsibility and individual development, which were at the basis of the fundamental personal rights of man and of several policy visions, such as employee participation in companies and the insurance principle of social security. According to the CNV, the company was essentially a cooperative association in which all those involved should be able to contribute to policy in proportion to their responsibility. This cooperation was to be embodied in the board of supervisory directors or an equivalent top body, not in the works council. The CNV adopted a somewhat reserved position with respect to the introduction of new technologies, which was gradually becoming an important topic, since it threatened to control human beings.

With a view to the federation discussions with the NKV and the NVV, initiated by the NKV in 1969, the CNV placed even more emphasis on its singularity. It drew up a statement of principles, which was added to the statutes and which had to be signed by new members. In it, the CNV confirmed that it considered the gospel the source of its actions and it again rejected the class struggle as 'in conflict with joint responsibility and the shared task of employers and employees to bridge the gap in interests on the basis of justice and charity'.[4] It thus also immediately distanced itself from the dominant 'left-wing draught' blowing through the Netherlands.

Although the CNV sat at the negotiating table with the two other confederations between 1969 and 1973, it eventually decided not to join forces with them. Ultimately, the desire for its own identity was a strong factor in its decision. There was indeed a difference in vision and approach to problems between the CNV and the other confederations, but other factors also played a part. There was a definite lack of enthusiasm for a federation with the NVV and the NKV on the part of the unions for white collar workers and executives, because these groups would form only a small minority in the new federation.[5] Moreover, in the light of the opposition of the Catholic white collar workers to the federation, by remaining aloof the CNV - which never had burried its dream of an interdenominational movement - could hope to attract a number of Catholic white collar unions, including the Catholic teachers' and police officers' unions, which weren't affiliated to any confederation. These white collar unions were afraid, on the one hand, of being suppressed as small unions by the new federation, and on the other hand of not finding a place in the industry-structured FNV. All things considered, the CNV's decision not to join the federation did not do it any harm. After all, the worrying membership trend did subsequently take a positive turn and, a few years later, it was able to observe that more employees were joining for ideological reasons than was previously the case.[6] The federation partners, by contrast, who saw their ideal of a unified Dutch trade union movement go up in smoke, reacted bitterly and put an end to their existing cooperation with the CNV.

The merger of the NVV and the NKV was an important though not the only step in the depillarization process of the 1970s and 1980s. Of equal, if not more importance, was the merger of the Catholic and protestant political parties in 1982. The CNV as such was not involved in the restructuring of the political landscape. It did, however, implicitly support the formation of the CDA, which was after all also structured along interdenominational lines. Therefore the CNV considered the CDA as 'its most intellectually related political movement' (Albeda, 1986, p. 21) and its leaders would entertain implicit relations with individual CDA-politicians who favoured their views.

In terms of its programme, the CNV established some of its own emphases. One striking aspect was its firm stress on a welfare policy which included not only social work, but also education, the environment, public housing and social provisions - everything which could make 'situations and relationships in society' more human. Given the economic crisis, the CNV accepted a temporary halt to the rise in personal income and in collective provisions. In its own words, it gave priority to combatting inflation and unemployment.[7] In discussions on a restructuring of the social security system, it wanted both to maintain a branch-based order and a reinforcement of the regional organization, based on the principles of 'functional decentralization' and 'sovereignty in one's own circle'. There was at that time no question of handing over implementation of social security to the trade unions.[8] The demand for employee participation was still important. According to the CNV, in the long term employees had to achieve a majority on the board of supervisory directors. In 1980 the CNV even expressed itself in cautiously positive terms about employee self-management, not as an ideal but as a possible or acceptable form of business, which would perhaps never be widespread.[9] Employee participation also had to be achieved at branch level; specifically, the CNV chose joint consultation without direct government involvement in policy on employment conditions.

Bearing in mind the continuing economic depression of the 1980s, the CNV refused to pursue a contentious strategy. The Christian trade union movement was even ready to accept a reduction in purchasing power, although employees had to have a voice in wage restraint and the various groups of employees, especially working and non-working, had to be given equal treatment. On the whole the CNV remained in favour of a guided economy, geared towards 'controlled growth', taking into account the quality of life. The CNV advocated a redistribution of income and a levelling out of income differences, but argued against discrimination against the weakest groups and stated, so as not to alienate the middle classes, that income differences could be socially justified. It also insisted on maintaining the link between social security benefits and wage development.[10]

In 1984 the basic principles of the CNV and their application in a long-term vision were again subjected to thorough reflection. The passage relating to the rejection of the class struggle was deleted from the new statutes. The new version simply stated that the CNV accepted 'the Bible, which calls man to serve God and his neighbour' as the principle of its policy, objectives and activities.[11] A new Vision Programme further developed this principle. Responsibility before God and one's fellow man, charity, fairness and freedom formed the basic values of the CNV, inspired by and to be tested against the gospel. The vision programme described society as a responsible society, where people and organizations have to be given the space 'to develop in freedom and responsibility', bearing in mind the interests of others (p. 11). The CNV believed that this ideal could best be expressed in a mixed economy where the government had the task of promoting fairness and justice, which sounds more cautious than the leading role which the CNV ascribed to the government in the 1970s. Consultation and cooperation were to be the order of the day at all levels and strikes remained purely a last resort for the CNV. On an international level too the CNV wanted to work hard for peace. It described the arms race as being in conflict with the instructions of the Creator. Income policy had to be based on the family 'or other comparable living units' (p. 29). However, in terms of social security, the CNV took as its basis an individual right to benefits, but without making it a point of conflict.[12] The Christian trade union movement was also in favour of a thorough restructuring of social security, involving a reshaping of disability and unemployment insurance into one type of insurance against loss of income. Above all, the role of the social organizations in implementing social security had to be extended (Van den Toren, 1991). The CNV also (re)defined its position on technology and its consequences. It placed technological developments against the background of the biblical obligation to keep the earth habitable. The CNV believed that the trade union movement had a duty to make technology acceptable to society; the government had to ensure that technology was used in the service of the people.[13]

In the years to follow, the CNV worked out a complete 'division of labour' for the government and the social partners: primary and secondary conditions of employment, pensions and work insurance were deemed to be the field of the social partners (including the government as employer). In specific terms, that meant that wages policy and the implementation of employee insurance would have to be fully transferred to the social partners. National insurance, education, health care and employment policy would have to be jointly organized. Only an extremely limited number of fields, such as labour law and the protection of social minimums, would be the exclusive responsibility of the government. At intermediate level too, the CNV predicted a high degree of responsibility for the social partners, while the micro-level (the company) was seen expressly as a 'joint venture' in which the participating parties shared responsibility. In this vision, the employee representatives to the works council could not be considered mandataries of the trade union movement, but representatives of the industrial community.[14] This increased reticence with respect to the government was undoubtedly linked to the spirit of the times, but also, more specifically, to the CNV's disenchantment with 'politics' and more specifically the CDA (Albeda, 1986; Vos, 1986).

By the end of the 1980s, the CNV's policy priorities were the fight against unemployment, the protection of social security, the maintenance of the purchasing power of minimum wage earners and the fight against poverty.[15] This latter aspect was relatively new, but typical of the entire programme, which was intended to target the weakest in society. Incidentally, the CNV could identify itself with the Christian democrats' call for a 'caring society', devoting a great deal of attention to the personal responsibility of the individual for his welfare and for the value of the 'natural societies'. But it opposed the rethoric as it served as a way of whitewashing the destruction of social security.[16] The suppression of the public involvment should not imply that the individual was left to his fate, but for the CNV had to go hand in hand with a strengthening of civil society.[17]

In contrast to the ever-advancing secularization, the CNV - true to its tradition - first swam against the tide by emphasizing its Christian dimension and biblical inspiration and speaking out strongly in favour of an ideological contribution to society, for instance through education and the media. However, it was unable to prevent this Christian dimension becoming somewhat blurred in practice. In fact, the CNV brought its Christian inspiration less to the fore, but pointed primarily to its policy and the appeal of this to large groups of people, including non-Christians. It explicitly opened its doors to people with a non-Christian outlook on life, such is Islamic immigrants. In so doing, it followed a development which some other Christian trade unions had started many years earlier (Pasture, 1994b).

Two new topics made their entry into the CNV programme at the beginning of the 1990s. First, the environmental question. The CNV had devoted attention to the environment from as early as the 1970s onwards, as demonstrated by its working towards 'controlled' growth. Now, however, the environment was considered a policy priority. What is not clear is the extent to which this idea penetrated trade union practice and how the environment/work relationship was interpreted in practice. Noteworthy in this respect is that in particular CNV-participants (people who participate in CNV campaigns, without being core member) find themselves quite distanced from New Social Movements, including the Ecology Movement and the Peace Movement (Kriesi, 1993).

Another new theme is that of Europe. The CNV had many objections to the way in which the European Community employed the term 'subsidiarity' to demarcate and define powers: the CNV put its own responsibility first, in response to the European Community's efficiency ruling, thus referring both to the Catholic principle of subsidiarity and the protestant 'sovereignty in one's own circle'.[18] Nevertheless, it opposed the idea that a social Europe could only be achieved through a strongly controlling, centralizing European authority. In so doing, it referred to Dutch social security, advocating that the government ought to step back in favour of the social organizations. However, the weakness of the European trade union movement, especially the Christian trade union movement, and of democracy at European level, placed the CNV in a difficult position. It could only find a way out of this position if European decision-making became more democratic and the trade union movement became more powerful, with the ETUC making room for the individual identities of the affiliated organizations.[19] What this boiled down to was that the Christian trade unions within the ETUC would have to form a Christian faction (Pasture, 1994b).

The CNV consciously expanded its range of activities, especially its services, in an effort to deal with its declining membership.[20] 'Alternatively employed' were explicitly embraced.[21] Moreover, the CNV paid a remarkable amount of attention to immigrants as well as to female employees, which was something entirely new. The CNV had never shown a great deal of interest in female employees. In the Christian vision of the family, the mother's place was in the home. The CNV women's association had for that reason originally targeted non-working women. A committee on female labour was not set up until 1978(!), subsequently being transformed into a women's secretariat.[22] This women's secretariat certainly did not exert a great deal of influence, although the CNV did in principle accept the idea of equality between the sexes, especially in terms of wages and social security payments.

In 1993, the CNV set up a far-reaching reorganization process in order to make its trade union action more efficient and recognizable for the members.[23] A first policy line consists of a concentration of the professional action and its implementation up to the workplace - although the CNV did not attach great importance at the works councils: it even opposed the idea of works councils playing a role in the determination of terms of employment and the conclusion of collective agreements (Leisink, 1995, pp. 136-137). Secondly and perhaps more importantly, the CNV has decided to develop a regional organization for services and action support. Through this regional structure the CNV aims at reaching specific target groups and developing a broader movement through general political actions at regional level, in particular concerning consumer or environmental issues. Also a new vision programme is being elaborated, in which once again emphasis is put on personal responsability - the basis of its demand for participation -, on solidarity with the weakest, and on 'durability', emphasizing the stewardship of mankind for the environment.[24]

The Catholics: tensions in a clerical federation

From 1906 onwards, after the episcopal mandement banning interdenominationalism, a degree of clarity gradually emerged on the Catholic front. The episcopal intervention, however, only solved one problem. There was still the relationship between trade union action on the one hand and evangelization and education (the activities of the so-called *standsorganisatie*) on the other hand. In 1906 and 1909 two separate associations were founded for both activities, but then the mutual squabbling began in earnest. Again, the bishops had to intervene to settle the dispute, which led to the formation of the Roman Catholic Workers' Federation (RKWV) in 1925, combining trade union action and popular education (*standsorganisatie*) under one roof (Roes, 1985).

After the First World War, the Catholic labour movement saw its opportunity to achieve its programme of statutory industrial organization, with industry councils as cornerstone, but a counter-offensive by employers in 1920 made mincemeat of the movement's struggle and hit the Catholic trade union movement particularly hard. However, after this jolt, and stripped of its illusions, it was quickly able to pick itself up again and carved out a permanent position on the Dutch trade union map. From then on, it presented itself as more radical and explicitly began to wage war on capitalism. Human dignity and not profit-making were to be crucial to the production process, and co-management and statutory industrial organization were the logical consequences of this. The RKWV found support for its social vision in the Quadragesimo anno papal encyclical of 1931. The RKWV faithfully relied on the Roman Catholic National Party for the accomplishment of its programme, even when progressive Catholic intellectuals argued that the party was a long way from Catholic social doctrine and founded a dissident Catholic Democratic Party (Bank, 1985, pp. 296-297). Partly through their struggle for statutory industrial organization, the RKWV and the NVV certainly drew gradually closer to one another during the 1930s; the CNV accepted less state intervention in the statutory industrial organization than the RKWV, and in fact did not follow this rapprochement of the other confederations. Incidentally, the CNV remained much less willing to strike than the NVV or the RKWV, which stood between the two extremes on this matter (Roes, 1985).

After the Second World War, the RKWV reorganized itself into the Catholic Workers' Movement (KAB), merging the educational and trade union organizations into one movement. The KAB campaigned for a thorough reform of society, in the Catholic sense, and largely relied for this on the similarly modernized and more open Catholic People's Party (KVP) (Bank, 1985). It was convinced that the statutory industrial organization would be achieved in the new Dutch society and that emphasis could be placed on the apostolic and cultural action of the *standsorganisatie*, in an atmosphere of social peace. However, this analysis was fundamentally deficient as the statutory industrial organization as it took shape in practice - not entirely in accordance with the wishes of the KAB (Peet, 1994) - didn't match the Catholic expectations in the least.

Partly as a result of this failure, the virtual predominance of the *standsorganisatie*, of the pastoral and educational work in the KAB, proved a serious handicap. The statutory industrial organization also generated tensions with the white collar workers' unions, which did not want an industry-based structure in the KAB. In the early 1950s, the virtual predominance of the KAB in the politics of the Catholic People's Party also invoked strong resistance from a group of influential conservative intellectuals (Bank, 1985). Moreover, the bishops took control of the organizational problems, which only made a solution all the more difficult and long-term. The clerical nature of the KAB was underlined even more strongly in 1954, when the Catholic bishops again banned membership of socialist organizations. Although the KAB did essentially agree with the principle of political Catholic unity, it was irritated with this expression of sympathy because it caused a rift in relations between the three trade union confederations.[25] The strict controlled wage policy also caused dissatisfaction within the KAB with Dutch political policy at the end of the 1950s, and therefore with the KVP too.

This all led, in 1963, to yet another reorganization, in which the KAB was transformed into the Dutch Catholic Trade Union Federation (NKV), a trade union organization on an equal footing with the other confederations. In this new structure, pastoral and educational work would soon fade into obscurity. This was the result of a development, beginning in the last years of the 1950s, towards a more autonomous and radical organization of the KAB as a workers' and trade union movement (Roes, 1985; Peet, 1993). However, the new structure was unable to break the impasse in which the movement found itself and throughout the 1960s the NKV was plagued by interminable discussions on structure and identity. Its basis lay in the weakened industries, which was translated into hesitating and even falling membership. The NKV was faced - sooner and to a greater extent than the other federations - with the inability of the Dutch trade union movement to hold on to its members and attract new members. Moreover, the ideology of the movement was undermined by frustration, in particular after the failed statutory industrial organization and because of disillusionment with the politics of the KVP. Further below the surface, belief in the traditional Catholic values declined and tension increased between those traditional values and standards and the practices of believers. With respect to the trade union movement, we must mention increasing female labour in particular. The Catholic trade union movement did not give up its fundamental opposition to married women working outside the home until 1967. It did however express a preference for part-time work so as to make it possible to combine a job and a family and rejected the expansion of collective childcare facilities. At the end of the 1960s, this situation of ideological and organizational upheaval resulted in a fundamental change of course.

The political tensions of 1966-67 within the KVP, which lost a good deal of ground in the elections during those years, caused a breakdown in the exclusive relationship between the NKV and the KVP. An attempt by progressive Catholics to form a denominational labour party in 1968 was unable to rely on the support of the Catholic trade union movement and failed; in fact, the NKV had to recognize the political pluralism of its own supporters as a fact (Bank, 1985). Moreover, in the 1960s, the need for a denominational organization was increasingly being called into question. That is why the NKV took the initiative for far-reaching cooperation with the other confederations. After many setbacks, these discussions led to the agreement in 1973 to enter into a 'strong' federation, together with the NVV. The CNV had dropped out, incidentally much against the wishes of the white collar unions of the NKV.

In addition, the NKV radicalized its programme, also to the displeasure of the white collar workers' unions. This radicalism was expressed in what was known as the 'draft vision programme' dating from June 1975, *Een visie ter visie* (A vision for vision), confirmed two years later as *NKV-visie*. The NKV had become convinced that a dramatic change in the social order was imminent. However, the integration of the trade union movement into this social order - a main characteristic of the Dutch system - was considered co-responsible for the inability to enforce structural changes. Nonetheless, such changes were necessary, ran the diagnosis, because the prevailing capitalist system was at the root of the alienation of the employee. After all, he was governed by production. Employees' opportunities at social, economic and cultural level remained unequal and industrial relations continued to be characterized by what was explicitly recognized as 'the class struggle'. Nevertheless, both the employees and the trade union movement seemed resigned to this situation. To counteract this, *Een visie ter visie* advocated a thoroughly socio-critical reorganization of the trade union movement, although without renouncing consultation as a means of the collective defence of interests.

Despite some sudden and unexpected opposition of the bishops (Peet, 1994), in the 1970s the NKV continued along the road to unity with the NVV. The federation process progressed strikingly smoothly. The merger followed as a logical consequence in 1981.

Two in one: the Netherlands Trade Union Confederation

The merger of the NVV and the NKV into the Netherlands Trade Union Confederation (FNV), albeit initially as a federation rather than a merger, signalled the combination of two different traditions which had indeed moved very close to one another. This does not alter the fact that the federation more or less boiled down to the NKV joining the NVV, not only as a result of the imbalanced power relationships. The basic premises and objectives of the FNV fitted in mainly with the ideas of the NVV. Equality between the sexes, freedom, justice and solidarity were the basic premises of the FNV, which wanted optimum welfare for all. The Universal Declaration on Human Rights contained the basic values of its trade union action, while the federation explicitly acknowledged the significance of 'faith and ideology for trade union movement activities' (Article 3).[26] A protocol attached to the federation's statutes stated that, even in a merger, 'persons and groups should have space to make a contribution based on their faith or philosophy of life'. In specific terms, this led to the formation of an Ideology and Trade Union Secretariat (*Secretariaat Levensbeschouwing en Vakbeweging*), which organizes training activities and maintains contacts with the churches (and the Humanist Association) and can even formulate policy recommendations.

The FNV looking to strengthen its position among special groups in the workforce also envisaged 'secretariats' for young people, immigrants, female employees and intermediate and senior personnel. The latter secretariat was transformed in 1977 into the Centre for Intermediate and Senior Personnel (CMHP). Every intermediate and senior, regardless of the union to which he or she belonged, could take part in the activities of the CMHP. In this way, the FNV hoped to steal the thunder from the non-affiliated organizations (a brief description in Peet, 1985, p. 180).[27] The secretariat for women was the successor to the NVV Women's Association and the women made themselves clearly heard at the federation's congress, with the *Vrouw en arbeid* (Women and work) draft programme. The women's association saw itself as part of a broader female emancipation movement and endorsed the demands of the feminists, which were not always well-received in other FNV unions. In particular, the right to self-determination regarding abortion and a reduction of the working day remained important but strongly disputed demands right up to the 1980s.[28]

The FNV started out under difficult economic circumstances. This does not alter the fact that it offered an extremely wide programme. Far-reaching democratization, aimed primarily at the company, formed an initial central objective of this programme. A separate body for worker control, rather than the works council, was to become the linchpin of company democracy. Incidently, the NVV/FNV Industrial Union was experimenting with company committees from as early as the 1960s, but these did not prove terribly stable and were largely dependent on the trade union itself. At the same time, the FNV wanted to work towards an actively controlling and stimulating government policy as a function of welfare and selective growth, taking into account the environment, physical planning, international prosperity, and energy and raw material consumption. A reduction in working hours and early retirement were the accepted means of combatting unemployment. Curiously, in 1977 the FNV advocated an increase in individual employee choice regarding work, such as part-time working.[29] The FNV Women's Association in particular insisted on a reduction in working hours and the creation of possibilities so that everyone could make room for professional work, domestic work, caring activities and other social activities. This vision was not to be upheld, however, and in 1981 the FNV was to argue, following a workshop by the women's secretariat and a conference held by the CMHP, that part-time working was actually preventing an honest division of labour, incomes, knowledge and power. The FNV did retain the theoretical possibility of allowing working hours and incomes to vary according to individual situations and argued that part-time work should occupy a position equal to that of full-time work, but opposed the general promotion of part-time work.[30] In the 1980s the emphasis understandably lay on 'good, permanent work'. In terms of social security, the FNV asked for a legal statutory pension, the introduction of national insurance for medical expenses and the abolition of discriminatory definitions, such as the term 'breadwinner' (because it referred to males only). An integrated income and a consumption policy was to help reduce income differences.

Five years after the formation of the FNV, in 1981 the NVV and the NKV proceeded with a full merger. This step had to a large extent already been taken both in spirit and in practice; the opposition which remained in 1975 had quickly vanished. Nonetheless, the new federation did not radiate the hoped-for dynamics. On the contrary, the federation partners lost members in droves, especially in their traditional industrial strongholds. These were heavily hit by mass unemployment and the dramatic consequences of the second oil crisis of 1979, which affected the Dutch economy particularly hard.

The FNV merger congress devoted a great deal of attention to the ideological principles of the federation.[31] The congress acknowledged its dual inheritance - social democracy and 'the social movement in the Roman Catholic church'. Equality, solidarity, freedom and justice formed the basic values of the FNV, upon which it based its demand for democratization. The FNV assumed that, despite the increase in welfare and the expansion of the welfare state, little had changed in control relationships in the industrial community, politics and the government. The FNV believed that 'industrial democracy' meant that those working in the company had to have decision-making rights regarding the organization of labour. This also applied to the collective sector. At macro-economic level, the FNV was working towards democratic planning, with broad powers attributed to the government. In addition, the FNV devoted itself to a 'new world order' in which human rights, peace and development were the central themes. It was notable that, in these times of crisis, the federation stressed not only the right to work, but also the duty to work as a way of contributing to society. In order to achieve its fundamental objectives, it looked for a balance between social integration, the defence of interests and social reform. It resolved to devote more attention to the workplace and to demands relating to the quality of work. It did not want to look to one single political party, but to all 'progressive tendencies'. In practice, however, the FNV - like the NVV of old - lent towards the PvdA.

The women's programme *Vrouw en arbeid* (Woman and work) continued to cause problems. In addition, the FNV Women's Association only achieved voting rights in the federation council in 1982. Partly as a result of its dissatisfaction with the FNV's policy, at the end of 1984 the FNV women set up an FNV Women's Platform - an informal network of women cutting right across the unions and aimed at radicalizing and expanding female trade union action. Nevertheless, women did make a considerable contribution to the FNV programme, in particular in respect to social security and the tax system.

The FNV attached great importance to a reliable social security system and during the 1980s drew up proposals for reforming and adapting it to the economic crisis. It took as its basis the individual right to benefits and the equality of the sexes. More specifically, it sought an improvement in the position of the long-term unemployed, who were soon back on subsistence level benefits under the existing system. Nonetheless, it questioned a further increase in contributions. A reduction in working hours as a means of redistributing labour was to force the question about social security contributions, but it was also on the look-out for forms of income other than working and economizing.[32]

The basic principles individualization and consideration for the long-term unemployed, which formed the core of the FNV's plan for social security, were largely inspired by the FNV Women's Association. However, the Association strongly criticized their implementation. The FNV Women's Association put forward two basic premises for social security: the active promotion of the entry of women on the labour market and the individualization of social security, so that married women could become completely independent. In this respect the FNV proposals did not go far enough: the Women's Association was opposed to the inclusion of both employment history and age as criteria for the duration and level of benefits - this meant that women and those in the weakest positions in general were always at an added disadvantage. It was also against all forms of maintenance obligation for cohabitees. Moreover, it wanted a more active policy in favour of the 'forgotten' groups: school-leavers, those re-entering the labour market, part-time workers and those on social security. The Women's Association also noted that women were the only group amongst which the FNV was still making progress and that they were looking forward to the day when men and women would be equally represented within the federation.[33]

Discussions on equal treatment for men and women concerned not only social security. The problem was also raised with respect to a reform of the tax system. Howver, it proved extremely difficult to reconcile the principle of complete individualization with the principles of the fair distribution of costs according to ability to pay, equal rights and the fight to reduce income differences in society.[34]

In the end, virtually nothing came of the FNV's proposals: in its neoliberal policy to combat the economic depression the Christian democrat/liberal cabinet of R. Lubbers (1982-1986) cut deeply into the Dutch welfare state. In its defence, the FNV set its eyes first of all on the CDA. 'The CDA is in danger of degenerating into a Christian democratic demolition firm for social security,' was the opinion of deputy chairman Herman Bode, commenting when the CDA in principle accepted an end to the link between wages and benefits in 1983.[35] Even within the Ideology and Trade Union Movement Secretariat, views on government policy were particularly bitter. In other respects, highly radical positions were adopted within this secretariat. In 1983 it published a widely distributed and much-discussed 'hand-out' for training activities concerning 'the trade union movement, parliamentary democracy and civil disobedience,' which was highly critical of the Dutch political system and considered forms of civil disobedience acceptable, particularly in the battle against the dismantling of the welfare state.[36] The FNV did not adopt this radical language. On the contrary, while it fiercely defended the rights of employees to social security, it also placed emphasis on obligations and opposition to abuses.

Continuing mass unemployment, the political situation as well as the critics from the Women's Association on the implementation of the FNV's proposals on social security and the tax system led to some fundamental reflection on the relationship between paid and unpaid labour. This topic was in particular advanced by the FNV union of workers in the food industry, the *FNV-Voedingsbond*. The FNV chose a thorough redistribution of both paid and unpaid work, on the basis that everyone was entitled and obliged to provide for his or her own basic necessities through paid work.[37] This illustrates that the FNV fitted to the industrial model of full employment and consequently did not consider a fundamental reassesment of the significance of work in society (Valkenburg, 1995a). The above discussion about the individualization of taxes and social security benefits is thrown into clearer focus in the light of this attitude. The same applies for the demand for a reduction in working hours, which was (still) a central point in the fight against unemployment. Incidentally, not much came of this reduction: the employers' obsession with 'flexibility' ruled the social agenda in the 1980s, rather than the trade unions' demands for a reduction in working hours.

Given the economic developments, the FNV did recognize the need for a more flexible attitude to working conditions, which can include working hours. However, it did ask for a voice and generally applicable rulings, and opposed different rulings on legal status for individual (groups of) employees and the impending undermining of employees' legal protection. It also tried, although not very consistently, to put forward flexibility and the reduction of working hours as a form of 'exchange', assuming that some employees did actually want flexible or out-of-the-ordinary working hours. In any case, general rulings for certain groups of employees in the same company were taboo.[38] Virtually the same reasoning was followed regarding the discussion on the wage indexation system. Its abolishment was demanded by the employers, who considered it as one of the main handicaps of the Dutch economy and as a major cause of unemployment. In fact, the FNV was deeply divided on this issue, the public sector unions being anxious to maintain wage indexation and coupling provisions above all, while the more exposed unions of the private sector were ready to negotiate wage indexation for job creation (Hemerijck, 1995, p. 211).

The FNV believed that the technological developments in the economy underlying the demand for flexibility, were not irreversible. For this reason, the FNV wanted to create a framework, via interprofessional consultation, for driving and directing government policy on education, technology and the economic structure. Just as importantly, however, the FNV had to increase its impact within companies in order to be able to offer more of a response to employers. In the fight against the socially negative consequences of new technology, the call for more unity in the employee class and consideration for 'new employees' in propaganda and services were seen in a more positive light. In this context, the FNV was fully aware of the importance of the employee middle classes: they often made a significant contribution to the development of new technologies and could also play a part in making technology accessible to employees and the trade union movement.[39]

The above developments threw the spotlight on the importance of the company. The FNV gradually turned more towards the works council, coming back to its arguments from the 1970s, when it advocated worker control. After all, the works council had acquired an important role in practice in discussions on the introduction of new technologies and the adjustment of working conditions. In 1984, the FNV decided to make company operation a priority: the works council should develop into a 'company parliament'. In other respects, the FNV also saw an advantage in promoting production cooperation. In addition, the training of company delegates and services in companies had to be improved. No matter how difficult the actual implementation of these options was in practice, it provided the impulse for a new strategy (Visser, 1993a, 1994a).

The changed climate within the FNV is clearly visible from the mid-1980s onwards. This does not alter the fact that the lines of force of its socio-economic programme had not changed. The FNV remained an outspoken advocate of a neo-Keynesian-inspired policy with the government playing a major role, but bearing in mind the effects on the quality of work and life, the environment and the Third World.[40] Even the FNV's proposals for a better system of social security, put forward in January 1986, were entirely an extension of previous proposals.[41]

The new strategy as outlined in the major policy document *FNV-2000*, approved in June 1987, consisted primarily of a number of organizational and strategic options.[42] These were based largely on fundamental changes in the industrial structure and the labour market, and in mentality and society.

The FNV looked to the future chiefly as a time for strengthening the trade union movement itself. The main feature was more cooperation, both internally, between the various sections of the FNV itself and externally, with the other trade unions. In this respect, the FNV came back to the isolationist policy which it had pursued with respect to the CNV since the breakdown of the three-way federation discussions. Moreover, the FNV was looking for new forms of income, including in the form of a trade union premium - it wanted to be remunerated for the work it carried out for non-members. A new trade union culture had to replace the old symbols and often female-unfriendly and pathetic means of communication. With a more modern image, the FNV wanted to be boldly present and recognizable, first and foremost in the workplace, and easily 'accessible' via made-to-measure services and 'trade union shops'. The FNV wanted to be able to reach all employees, via 'target groups'; particular attention was devoted to young people, women, part-time workers, employees with flexible employment contracts, intermediate and senior personnel, ethnic minorities and those on social security benefit, for whom specific structures were organized or further developed.[43] This was successful in terms of women, who quickly permeated the various policy levels (table 4.1).

Table 4.1
Percentage of women in the FNV (1987-1991)

	Members	Paid officials	Policy collaborators	Federal council	Federal board
1987	17	12	31	8	19
1989	20	15	41	11	20
1991	21	24	43	13	26

Source: March 8-surveys. With thanks to Corrie van Eijl, IISG, Amsterdam.

Women members of the FNV were in any case on average younger and better educated than their male counterparts and felt - surprisingly - less attached to a church or ideology.[44] Specific women's demands found their way, via targeted action, into collective labour agreements, although with difficulty.[45] For the other groups, however, there was a yawning gap between theory and practice.

In sum, the FNV did not really consider the consequences of such a reorganization in terms of a redefinition of the demands for unity and solidarity on the one hand and of the recognition of differentiation and participation on the other (Valkenburg, 1995a, 1995b; Valkenburg and Zoll, 1995, pp. 138-140). In particular the recipients of benefit were the victim of this lack of logic and implementation (Van Berkel and Hindriks, 1991). In other respects, the FNV had to struggle against mounting tension between the confederation and the affiliated unions, as a result of the increasing differences in economic development between the industrial sectors and the decentralization of industrial relations, which inflated the significance of the central level.

The FNV also decided to develop new activities. Firstly, it wanted to take an active part in the field of vocational training, chiefly by providing information and support. Partly as a result of this, its second aim was to influence the labour market itself. Thirdly, its ambition was to change the organization of labour within companies, with more participation by employees and less centralization and hierarchy. Finally, it wanted to play a greater and more recognizable role in social security, by becoming more involved in its implementation and by providing certain advantages for trade union members. It should be clear that these latter proposals had nothing to do with a vision of the significance of social security and the role of the social organizations, and everything with the possibilities of social security rulings for membership recruitment and commitment.[46]

Influenced by new insights and objectives, the FNV adopted a more 'flexible' approach: partly as a result of its previous excessively dismissive attitude - so it thought - it had no concept of the development of new forms of industrial organization. In our opinion, the weak position of the FNV within companies was largely responsible for this. The FNV looked for ways of achieving a new distribution of paid and unpaid work - a drastic reduction in working hours with the preservation of gross wages and of the purchasing power of those on lower wages - without, however, questioning its ultimate goal of full paid employment. It no longer rejected part-time work, but did demand skilled jobs for at least twenty hours per week. In any case, from 1987 onwards, the trade unions received government support for their technology education and training efforts. A great deal of intensive attention was devoted to technology and the need for education and vocational training. In this respect the executive staff, via the Centre for Intermediate and Senior Personnel, fulfilled an important function.

On the whole however, the renewal of the FNV soon reached its limits. According to a recent evaluation of the implementation of the FNV-2000 policy, the proposals for renewal were hardly put into practice, mainly due to increasing internal tensions and the opposition of some major affiliated unions to a reorganization which might endanger their position in comparison with centralized and regional activities. The unions in the public and in the private sector seem to develop their proper cross-union service structures which might further undermine the confederal level. The reconsideration of the position of paid labour as the basis of trade union action as well as of welfare state arrangements was not implemented in recent policy documents, for instance on social security (Coenen, 1995; Beukema, 1995). Even the participation of activists in the regional structures and the broadening of the scope of the FNV in general was turned back in 1991 (Valkenburg, 1995b, p. 106; Valkenburg and Zoll, 1995, p. 139).[47]

Trade unions on the move

The history of the Dutch trade union movement is at first sight extremely colourful. Trade union pluralism is indeed a principal feature of the Dutch trade union movement. This pluralism is not only confined to the usual labour/capital, church/state or revolutionary/reformist cleavages, although these certainly are or have been present (Ebbinghaus, 1993). The presence of non-affiliated unions must after all be borne in mind in any evaluation of the ideological dimension of the Dutch trade union movement; these were explicitly opposed to a broad conception of the role of the trade union movement. The Dutch-born American specialist, John P. Windmuller believed as early as 1969 that the deepest fault line on the Dutch trade union landscape was (no longer) between the ideological confederations themselves, but between the ideological confederations and these non-affiliated, categorial organizations (Windmuller, 1969).

The Federation of Intermediate and Senior Personnel (MHP) (which changed its name to the Trade Union Federation for Intermediate and Senior Personnel MHP in 1980) occupies the most important position among these non-affiliated organizations. It was born in 1974 as a successor to the Dutch Federation for Senior Personnel, dating from 1966. MHP was recognized by the Socio-Economic Council (*Sociaal-Economische Raad*) as a representative confederation and, during the 1970s, rapidly accounted for a good 7-8 per cent of trade union members. In 1990 a federation of civil servants' unions was formed, also accounting for about 7-8 per cent of trade unionists. However, this was not recognized as a representative trade union organization for the whole economy because the overwhelming majority of its members were civil servants. In addition, a range of autonomous unions are also in existence, especially for teaching, caring and military staff.

The MHP represents employees from all areas of Dutch industry. It explicitly states that it is not entitled to make political or ideological pronouncements about social problems such as peace and security, nuclear energy, ethical and moral values, and therefore confines itself to the socio-economic interests of employees. In this respect, it gives priority to the interests of the individual and advocates far-reaching decentralization in industrial relations, in favour of companies. However, it also represents several Catholic or Christian white collar organizations, some of which left the NKV in protest at the formation of the FNV federation. With the exception of a few individual cases, these organizations felt not restrained from FNV and CNV by the ideological/political colours of these confederations, but because they opposed equalization and minorization in industrial unions dominated by manual workers. For this reason, the CNV is less affected by the competition of the MHP than the FNV. However, in the recent past the FNV has also attempted to make room for white collar workers and the intermediate and executive staff. To the extent that the ideological confederations succeed in doing this, they could knock the stuffing out of the non-affiliated categorial unions. To a large extent they indeed do. In the CNV workers only constitute a minority of 42 per cent of the ordinary members and even much less of the core members, which is comparable to the MHP. In the FNV, more rooted in traditional sectors of the economy, the share of the working class in the membership is 60 per cent and half of the active participants and core members (Kriesi, 1993, p. 157).[48] Incidently, one can argue that the individualistic and corporatist logic which inspires the categorial unions leads to a system of industrial relations where ultimately there is no room for them either.

Pluralism is an important factor in the Dutch trade union movement, as is the desire for unity, which has been a thread in trade union history. The desire for unity generated a great deal of vigour in the Dutch trade union movement. Recently, it led to a merger between the Catholic and social democratic trade unions and, linked to this, to a broadening of the denominational basis of the CNV, which saw its old dream of an interdenominational trade union movement become a reality. To a certain extent, however, this unification caused division. First of all because, after the failed three-way federation, the NKV and NVV almost completely reversed their cooperation with the CNV, arguing that the federation's aims included simplifying the decision-making procedure and that the advantage of a merger would be negated in a joint venture. Only in the late 1980s, under pressure due to its increasingly weak position, the FNV again started to work towards further cooperation. Secondly, the formation of the federation led to a regrouping of the trade unions for white collar workers and executives in the politically neutral MHP.

There was also movement in the rapidly changing position of the trade union movement: from growth as an opposition force, to far-reaching integration as a 'co-responsible partner' in the labour system - peaking with its mobilization in the controlled wages policy of the 1950s - to the 'back to basics' of the 1980s. This moving picture does not alter the fact that there were also some constants: the 'responsible' and pragmatic attitude of all Dutch trade unions, even in recent decades, the highly centralized organization of the unions, their commitment to central policy making, and the noticeably major significance of religion, despite secularization and the formation of a unified trade union movement, such as the FNV.

Ideological backgrounds remain significant in the most important trade union traditions, no matter how far they have evolved. The most striking case is the CNV, where a biblical consideration of objectives and policy continues to occupy an important position. Personal responsibility and respect for property are key aspects of this. The choice in favour of a harmonious society was expressed in a reticent attitude to trade union action, which also had practical repercussions. Moreover, as CNV members became more permeated by CNV ideology, they took a more reticent attitude to trade union action (Klandermans and Visser, 1995, pp. 139-157; Van der Veen and Klandermans, 1990, pp. 86-94; Van der Veen, 1992). The attention which the CNV devotes to problems relating to public order, safety and military questions, as well as concerning possible 'conscientious objections' which employees could have to deal with in their working environment is also significant and very characteristic of the CNV.[49] Its biblical inspiration is even clear when the CNV takes up relatively 'new' topics, especially development cooperation, the peace issue and concern for the environment, which made their way into the trade union agenda in the late 1980s. Within that framework, a relatively 'new' term is even introduced: the idea of 'stewardship'. Christian social thinking also provides a frame of reference with respect to European unification. Nonetheless, an important development is taking place: in the second half of the 1980s the basic premises are less obvious and the emphasis is placed on policy, where the CNV explicitly aspires to expansion, which inevitably leads to a loss of identity. Incidentally, ideological options allow specific policy options to be interpreted extremely flexibly: for example in the 1970s the CNV supported much more active government involvement in social and economic life than in the neo-liberal climate of the 1980s.

The FNV is the continuation of two traditions - socialist and Catholic. The historiographers of the NVV have adequately demonstrated that the socialist trade union movement in the Netherlands set sail on a pronounced reformist course and little remained of the original socialist starting points against the merger. The ideological core of the NVV, which was also handed down in full to its successor the FNV, was a belief in the fundamental equality of men and the resulting Human Rights. The NKV could also endorse these principles, having let go of its belief in an organic society based on harmonious cooperation and adopted into its basic vision aspects of the class struggle against social inequality and social injustice. The NKV and NVV were able to meet each other in a personalist human vision, with human dignity as central principle.[50] Nonetheless, personalism, in all its vagueness, can hardly be considered the underlying 'ideology' as a mobilizing force of the FNV. In fact, especially in recent policy documents as FNV-2000 (1987) or *Veelkleurige perspectieven* (Colourful perspectives, 1993), the FNV hardly succeeded in formulating a coherent view on society, appealing on 'solidarity' without specifying what this can signify in terms of concrete trade union action (Valkenburg and Zoll, 1995, p. 131). The Catholic legacy is quite explicitly continued in the FNV in the Ideology and Trade Union Secretariat, though the latter's radical views contrast heavily with the traditionally moderate and co-operative Catholic approach to society.

A number of striking differences emerge from a comparison of the programme and policy statements of the FNV and CNV. Although both the FNV and CNV are concerned about general social problems, we believe this is the case to a more pronounced extent for the Christian trade union movement than for the FNV. However, the latter seems to be more integrated with the new social movements (Kriesi, 1993). The more traditional and religion-based authoritarian attitude of the CNV members might provide an explanation for the reticence of CNV-members and especially participants regarding these movements

(Kriesi, 1993;[51] comp. Klandermans and Visser, 1994). The FNV also seems more developing towards an new enterprise approach than is its Christian counterpart. In this respect, it is also noticeable that discussions on flexibility, still the theme of the 1980s, are scarcely mentioned in the CNV, unlike the FNV. Perhaps this is partially due to the lack of influence of female employees in the CNV. Although a more thorough analysis than this is necessary before firm statements can be made, it still seems to us that in the FNV unions, it was mainly the female employees who took action in this respect. In the CNV, by contrast, a specific female contribution is virtually non-existent, at least until the end of the 1980s.[52] A similar reflection can be made with respect to discussions on a revision of the social security system: under pressure mainly from its female militants, the FNV registered the individualization of social security as one of its policy priorities. Within the CNV no trace of this debate is to be found, at least not at the highest level.

Despite the secularization and 'depillarization', trade union pluralism has persisted in the Netherlands; in any event, there are still significant differences in programme and approach between the two large confederations. A pronounced ideological dimension is demonstrable and vigorous, particularly in the CNV. However, there are also signs of a rapprochement, now that the FNV has given up its isolation strategy vis-à-vis the CNV and, for its part, the CNV is opting for a more open policy, albeit cautiously. Parallels are striking in the orientations the confederations take in order to modernize their organizational structures and in the significance attached to regional services and action support. The implementation of these reorientations, however, remains extremely doubtful, at least for the time being. Moreover, none of the unions studied seems ready to question its basic principles in the light of the fundamental changes of the industrial system and contemporary values: as such the position of the unions on the long term has fundamentally altered, however. Once the advance guard of the proletarians, they have become the interest group of the privileged employees with a stable paid job, only a minority of which belong to the traditional working class. Therefore, a new dawn for the Dutch unions has certainly not arrived yet, notwithstanding curent upheaval of membership rates.

Table 4.2
Membership of Dutch trade unions 1900-1974 (absolute numbers)

	ANWV	NVC[2]	NAS	NSV[3]	NVV	Patri-monium	CNV	NKV	Non-affiliated
1900	±2,500[1]	-	12,444	-	-	±13,000[1]	-	-	-
1910	-	-	3,454	-	40,660	-	6,587	11,650	122,724
1920	2,468	39,903	51,570	-	247,748	15,739	66,997	141,002	136,248
1930	-	36,434	17,361	2,748	251,487	13,410	71,300	130,894	114,295
1940	-	50,750	10,330	1,614	319,099	12,050	121,179	186,943	111,481
1950	-	2,790	163,278	-	381,533	7,953	155,627	296,410	160,655
1960	-	11,700	-	-	486,743	-	219,019	400,396	236,297
1970	-	-	-	-	562,548	-	238,542	400,032	323,200
1974	-	-	-	-	670,709	-	231,426	397,886	-

1 1894
2 NVC and following white collar workers' unions
3 Nederlands Syndicalistisch Vakverbond: revolutionary syndicalist break-away of the (by then) communist dominated NAS.

Source: Harmsen and Reinalda, 1975, pp. 430-433.

Table 4.3
Membership of Dutch trade unions 1970-1990 (x 1000)

	FNV	CNV	MHP	AVC	Non-affiliated
1970	(1,013)	238	32	39	
1975	1,059	226	106	89	
1980	1,054	302	114	112	
1985	903	299	107	103	
1990	1,025	308	132	102	
1993	1,104	337	154	109	140

Source: Visser, 1995a, p. 32. Please note these figures are not completely identical to those in table 4.1.

Abbreviations

ANV	Algemeen Nederlands Vakverbond (General Dutch Trade Union Federation)
ANWV	Algemene Nederlandse Werklieden Vereniging (General Dutch Workers' Union)
ARP	Anti-Revolutionaire Partij (Anti-Revolutionary Party)
CDA	Christen-Democratisch Appèl (Christian Democratic Appeal)
CHU	Christelijk Historische Unie (Christian Historical Union)
CMHP	Centrum voor Middelbaar en Hoger Personeel (Centre for Intermediate and Senior Personnel) (FNV)
CNV	Christelijk Nationaal Vakverbond (Federation of Christian Trade Unions in the Netherlands)
EVC	Eenheidsvakcentrale (Unified Trade Union Federation)
FNV	Federatie Nederlandse Vakbeweging (Netherlands Trade Union Confederation)
KAB	Katholieke Arbeidersbeweging (Catholic Workers' Movement)
KVP	Katholieke Volkspartij (Catholic People's Party)
MHP	Federatie voor Middelbaar en Hoger Personeel (Federation of Intermediate and Senior Personnel); since 1980 Vakcentrale voor Middelbaar en Hoger Personeel MHP (Trade Union Federation for Intermediate and Senior Personnel)
NAS	Nationaal Arbeids Secretariaat (National Labour Secretariat)
NKV	Nederlands Katholiek Vakverbond (Dutch Catholic Trade Union Federation)
NVV	Nederlands Vakverbond (Dutch Confederation of Trade Unions)
PvdA	Partij van de Arbeid (Labour Party)
RKWV	Rooms-Katholieke Werkliedenvereniging (Roman Catholic Workers' Federation)
SDAP	Sociaal-Democratische Arbeiders Partij (Social Democratic Labour Party)
SDB	Sociaal-Democratische Bond (Social Democratic League)

Unattainable unity in the Netherlands

Notes

1. *Ieder een eigen inkomen. Terugblik op één eeuw vakbeweging en vrouwenarbeid*, FNV, Amsterdam, 1990.
2. *Vakbeweging en Maatschappij*, Draft social vision, NVV, Amsterdam, January 1977 and *Vakbeweging en Maatschappij*, Resolution approved Federation Meeting 1 December 1977 and adopted NVV Federation council 6 February 1978, NVV, Amsterdam, 1978.
3. *Visieprogram van het CNV*, adopted by the general meeting held on 19 October 1970 and *Beleidsconclusies van het CNV over positie en beleid*, approved by the general meeting of the CNV on 19 October 1970; CNV activity reports 1969-71, pp. 19-20. See also Van den Toren, 1991, pp. 44-45 (and passim) and Pasture, 1994b, pp. 42-43.
4. CNV act. 1972-74, pp. 76-78. See also Pasture, 1994b, p. 44.
5. This factor is not mentioned in the relevant literature and must therefore be considered a hypothesis (in our view a highly probable one). Only a thorough survey based on internal source material from the CNV can produce a decisive conclusion but such a study has not been conducted. In 1971, the percentages of non-manual workers among members of the NVV, NKV and CNV were 24.3%, 10.8% and 27.9% respectively (Visser, 1984, p. 55).
6. *Wat willen de leden van de vakbeweging?*, CNV, Utrecht, September 1982. See further Pasture, 1994b.
7. *Sociale groei. Sociaal-politiek program voor de jaren 1977-1981*, CNV, Utrecht, 1977.
8. Ibid. and Van den Toren, 1991, which gives a summary on pp. 83-109 of the CNV's vision on the design of social security (with much attention to technical aspects).
9. *Vormen van werknemerszelfbeheer*, CNV, Utrecht, 1980 and various CNV notes on co-management and statutory industrial organization. Van den Toren, 1992, pp. 53-78 gives a summary of the CNV's attitudes to worker participation.
10. *Om werk en welzijn. Sociaal-politiek programma CNV 1981-1985*, CNV, Utrecht, 1981.
11. *Doelstellingen, arbeid en structuur van de christelijke vakbeweging*, CNV, Utrecht, 1984, pp. 4-5.
12. *Visieprogram*, CNV, Utrecht, 22 September 1984, pp. 29-30. The term 'individualization' does not appear in the CNV texts. The Vision Program argued that 'every person who finds him or herself or is likely to find him or herself under the same socio-economic circumstances has, in principle, irrespective of gender, the right to the same protection on the basis of social security legislation.' Moreover, it considered 'equal treatment of women and men in professional rulings, such as pensions, a condition'. Van den Toren (1991) does not deal with this question.
13. *Visieprogram*, CNV, Utrecht, 22 September 1984, pp. 17-18; *CNV en de automatisering*, CNV, Utrecht, 1985; *In actie voor morgen ...; CNV in de tijd*, CNV, Utrecht, May 1986, pp. 23-25.
14. *CNV in de tijd. Brochure over de identiteit van de christelijke vakbeweging*, CNV, Utrecht, May 1986; *In actie voor morgen. Sociaal-politiek program 1986-1990*, CNV, Utrecht, 1986.
15. *In actie voor morgen. Sociaal-politiek program 1986-1990*, CNV, Utrecht, 1986.

16. See for example the closing speech by H. Van der Meulen during the takeover of the chairmanship, Saturday 27 September 1986.
17. Various documents in World Confederation of Labour documentation service (Brussels), Files Documentation CNV and specifically *Toekomst in banen. Sociaalpolitiek program voor de periode 1990-1994*, CNV, Utrecht, July 1989.
18. The CNV took care to distinguish between the Catholic and protestant visions: the Catholic principle of subsidiarity stated that the government could only intervene as a supplementary measure and that decision-making had to take place at the lowest possible level. The protestant 'sovereignty in one's own circle' did not recognize this hierarchic vision, but said that all forms of community relations have their own function and right. See *Het CNV bouwt aan de structuur van Europa*, CNV, Utrecht, 1990.
19. Ibid.
20. See especially *Doeltreffend. De toekomst maken we samen*, CNV, Utrecht, 1989. The organizational modernization of the CNV is analysed by Paauwe and De Jong, 1992.
21. *Doeltreffend*. For the women's question we also refer to the CNV activity reports.
22. *Leidraad*. Intended for the sections of the CNV women's association, CNV Women's Association, Utrecht, 1980, p. 5.
23. 'Het CNV na(ar) 2000. Vakcentrale en bonden in beweging', *CNV-Opinie*, 1, febr. 1994; H. Brüning, 'CNV gaat eigen weg. Politiek en sociaal-economisch landschap sterk veranderd' and E. Hees, 'De oogst van over de schutting kijken. CNV zet nieuwe regiostructuur in de stijgers', *CNV-Opinie*, 6, July 1994, pp. 4-10.
24. Brüning, 'CNV gaat eigen weg. Politiek en sociaal-economisch landschap sterk veranderd', CNV-Opinie, 6, July 1994, pp. 4-5.
25. Remarkable was the reaction of the CNV to the bishop's mandement. CNV chairman Ruppert declared that he did not see how a Christian could live under the prevailing socialism. By rubbing salt into the wounds in this way, it was he who actually blew up the existing interconfederational consultation, rather than the KAB.
26. Brochure *Federatie Nederlandse Vakbeweging - Confederation Netherlands Trade Union Movement*, FNV, Amsterdam, February 1976. Note that the NVV had also recognized this significance.
27. The activities of the CMHP are described in the FNV activity reports, but - of course - these give little indication of its success.
28. *Ieder een eigen inkomen. Terugblik ...*, Amsterdam, FNV, 1990.
29. *Vier jaar vooruit. Kernthema's voor een sociaal en economisch beleid in de jaren 1977-1981*, Amsterdam, FNV - May 1977; *Werken aan werk*, FNV Congress 1978, FNV, Amsterdam, 1978; *Wat de FNV ervan vindt. Het FNV-beleid in hoofdlijnen*, FNV Information Office, Amsterdam, September 1980.
30. *FNV. Een deel van het geheel. FNV-visie op deeltijdarbeid*, FNV, Amsterdam, July 1981.
31. *FNV-grondslag*, FNV, Amsterdam, January 1982 (FNV congress 29 September-1 October 1981) (Statement of aims and ideals of the Netherlands Trade Union Confederation FNV, adopted by the FNV Congress Amsterdam 29-30 September and 1 October 1981, FNV, Amsterdam, March 1982).
32. It is impossible here to discuss in detail the structure and reform proposals of the social security system. In the *Werknemersverzekeringen* (Employees' insurance sys-

tem: guaranteeing an income in the event of involuntary loss of earnings) the benefits were determined at a rate of 80% of the daily wage and these were therefore not discriminatory; only minimum daily wages were determined for breadwinners, which was counter to the principles of non-discrimination and individualization. In the *Volksverzekeringen* (national insurance system: envisaging a replacement income in old age or in the event of long-term disability), in particular, benefits were based on the family situation. The FNV note *Sociale zekerheid*, a discussion document on system review for the FNV special congress of 25 October 1983, provides detailed information.

33. Reports of FNV special congress 25 october 1983 (FNV, Amsterdam, 1984); FNV Annual Report 1981-1984; FNV Women's Platform, Amsterdam September 1983 and report *Vrouwen pas op*, day of action 1 October 1983 (FNV, Amsterdam), as well as *FNV-grondslag*.

34. *FNV-grondslag*; FNV action programme 'Women and Work', FNV, Amsterdam, 1981; FNV special congress 25 October 1983 (especially note *Draagkracht, gelijkberechtiging en individualisering in relatie tot de loon- en inkomstenbelasting*, Discussion note for the FNV special congress of 25 October 1983) (FNV, Amsterdam, 1983); *Arbeid en solidariteit*, Note for the FNV Congress of 2, 3 and 4 october 1984, FNV, Amsterdam, June 1984; FNV Women's Platform, Amsterdam, September 1983 and FNV Annual Report.

35. Brief report of the 8th session of the FNV congress ... Tuesday 25 October 1983, Amersfoort. As former president of the NKV, Bode goes further here, in our view, than the usual 'opposition rhetoric'.

36. *Waar ligt de grens ? Over vakbeweging, parlementaire democratie en burgerlijke ongehoorzaamheid*. FNV Ideology and Trade Union Movement Secretariat hand-out, Amsterdam, 1983; FNV act. 1983 (Also on the study day 'Quality and future of the welfare state in a declining economy'). In September 1984 a new file was published, *Waar ligt de grens ? Parlementaire democratie en burgerlijke ongehoorzaamheid*, Amsterdam, with a report of the discussions on and reactions to the handout. On this secretariat, see also Wentholt, 1984, pp. 129-149 and Salemink, 1991, p. 189.

37. *Met z'n allen roepen in de woestijn. Een tussenrapport over het losser maken van de band tussen arbeid en inkomen*, Voedingsbond FNV, Utrecht 1981; *Arbeid en solidariteit*. Note for the FNV Congress of 2, 3 and 4 October 1984, FNV, Amsterdam, June 1984; Valkenburg, 1995a.

38. FNV Annual Reports, in particular 1985 (passim).

39. FNV Annual Report 1985, passim. Within the FNV the Centre for Intermediate and Senior Personnel probably fulfilled a pioneering role. See, for instance, FNV Annual Report 1982, pp. 50-51.

40. See, for example, *Kiezen voor nieuwe kansen*, FNV programme 1986-1990, FNV, Amsterdam, 1986 and *Het kan anders, beter*, FNV programme for the years 1990-1994, FNV, Amsterdam, 1990.

41. *Voor alle zekerheid. Het FNV-voorstel voor een beter stelsel van sociale zekerheid*, FNV, Amsterdam, January 1986. For the union's actions for the environment issue see *Vakbondsbasis voor milieubeleid*, FNV, Amsterdam, 1988 and *Het licht op groen*, FNV, Amsterdam, 1989. See also Leisink, 1995, pp. 128 ff.

42. For the following, we rely on the brochure *FNV 2000 - The renewal of the FNV*, FNV, Amsterdam, June 1987.

43. A separate secretariat had already been set up for recipients of benefit as early as 1984, which was placed under the responsibility of the federation management. FNV Annual Report, 1984 ff. The activity reports show the will of the FNV to align its policy to various categories of employees.
44. They were also less likely to be married and more active in part-time work. *FNV 2000 - The renewal of the FNV*, FNV, Amsterdam, June 1987, p. 6.
45. *Draaiboek CAO-onderhandelingen gericht op de verbetering van de positie van vrouwelijke werknemers*, FNV, Amsterdam, first edition September 1985.
46. Comparative research has demonstrated that rulings in which the trade unions are involved in implementing social security, as in Belgium, Denmark and Switzerland, strongly favour trade unionism. For a summary and evaluation of the literature see Visser, 1991, pp. 97-134.
47. *FNV op weg naar 2000*, FNV, Amsterdam, 1991; *Minder beter*, FNV, Amsterdam 1991.
48. These percentages are based on interviews on a representative sample of the Dutch population conducted in 1987. For the metholdology see Kriesi, 1993.
49. The CNV was thinking of moral dilemmas for employees in siting nuclear weapons, printing racist or pornographic literature, insuring fur coats, providing sexual information, using aggressive chemical agents in farming, etc.. *Gewetensbezwaren voor werknemers*, CNV, Utrecht, April 1983.
50. For the Dutch socio-democratic vision of personalism, see Klijn, 1990. There is no need to examine the Catholic personalist tradition. Specifically on the NKV, see Salemink, 1991, 189 ff.
51. Unfortunately, Hanspeter Kriesi's assessment does not allow a profound comparison of the different trade unions' attitudes in this respect
52. See the brochure *CNV Toen-Nu-Toekomst*, CNV, Utrecht, 1989, p. 18 and Dijkstra, 1979, p. 262 and passim.

References

Albeda, W. (1986), 'Regeringsbeleid en CNV. De spanningsvolle relatie tussen CNV en Nederlandse overheid (1977-1986)', in Looise, J.C., Paauwe, J. and Van Zuthem, H. J. (eds.), *Vakbeweging in verandering. Dilemma's en uitdagingen*, Kluwer, Deventer, pp. 21-36.
Albeda, W. and Dercksen, W. J. (1994), *Arbeidsverhoudingen in Nederland*, Samson, Alphen a/d Rijn.
Amelink, H. (1950), *Met ontplooide banieren*, CNV, Utrecht.
Amelink, H. (1950), *Onder eigen banier. Beknopt overzicht van het ontstaan en de ontwikkeling der christelijke vakbeweging (...)*, CNV, Utrecht.
Bank, J. (1978), *Opkomst en ondergang van de Nederlandse Volksbeweging (NVB)*, Cahiers Nederlandse politiek, Deventer.
Bank, J. (1985), 'De broederlijke relaties tussen KAB/NKV en KVP (1945-1981)', in Roes, J. (ed.), *Katholieke arbeidersbeweging. Studies over KAB en NKV in de economische en politieke ontwikkeling van Nederland na 1945*, Ambo, Baarn, pp. 293-342.
Beukema, L. (1995), 'Differentiatie van belangen als uitgangspunt voor nieuw beleid', in Coenen, H. (ed.), *De vakbeweging na 2000*, Van Arkel, Utrecht, pp. 142-168.

Blom, J. C. H. and Lamberts, E. (eds.) (1994), *Geschiedenis van de Nederlanden*, Nijgh & Van Ditmar/Infoboek, Rijswijck.

Buiting, H. (1990), 'The Netherlands', in Van der Linden, M. and Rojahn, J. (eds.), *The Formation of Labour Movements 1870-1914. An International Perspective*, Contributions to the History of Labour and Society 2, Brill, Leiden, vol. 1, pp. 57-84.

Coenen, H. (1995), 'De crisis van de vakbeweging', in Coenen, H. (ed.). *De vakbeweging na 2000*, Van Arkel, Utrecht, pp. 14-47.

Coenen, H. (ed.) (1995), *De vakbeweging na 2000*, Van Arkel, Utrecht.

Coenen, H. and Leisink, P. (eds.) (1993), *Work and Citizenship in the New Europe*, Aldershot.

De Liagre Böhl, H. (1991), 'Hoofdlijnen in de politieke ontwikkeling van het moderne Nederland', in Becker, U. (ed.), *Maatschappij, macht, Nederlandse politiek: een inleiding in de politieke wetenschap*, Het Spinhuis, Amsterdam, pp. 111-138.

Dijkstra, K. (1979), *Beweging in beweging. Het CNV na 1945*, CNV, Utrecht.

Ebbinghaus, B. (1993), *Labour Unity in Union Diversity. Trade Unions and Social Cleavages in Western Europe 1890-1989*, European University Institute, Florence.

Hagaart, R. (1955), *De christelijke-sociale beweging*, T. Wever, Franeker.

Harmsen, G. (1985), 'De arbeiders en hun vakorganisaties', in Van Holthoon, F.L. (ed.), *De Nederlandse samenleving sinds 1815. Wording en samenhang*, Van Gorcum, Assen/Maastricht, pp. 261-282.

Harmsen, G. and Reinalda, B. (1975), *Voor de bevrijding van de arbeid. Beknopte geschiedenis van de Nederlandse vakbeweging*, SUN, Nijmegen.

Hazenbosch, P. (red.) (1989), *Het CNV nader bekeken. Schetsen uit 80 jaar CNV-geschiedenis*, Kok, Kampen.

Hellemans, S. and Schepers, R. (1992), 'De ontwikkeling van corporatieve verzorgingsstaten in België en Nederland', in Hellemans, S. (ed.), *België en Nederland*, Spec. no. *Sociologische Gids*, vol. 2., no. 4, pp. 346-364.

Hellemans, S. (1990), *Pleidooi voor een internationale en tegen een provincialistische benadering van verzuiling*, Sociologisch Onderzoeksinstituut, KU Leuven.

Hemerijck, A. C. (1995), 'Corporatist Immobility in the Netherlands', in Crouch, C. and Traxler, F. (eds.), *Organized Industrial Relations in Europe: What Future?*, Perspectives on Europe, Avebury, Aldershot, pp. 183-226.

Hueting, E., De Jong Edz., F. and Neij, R. (1983), *Naar groter eenheid. De geschiedenis van het Nederlands Verbond van Vakverenigingen 1906-1981*, De Nederlandse arbeidsbeweging 13, Van Gennep, Amsterdam.

Klandermans, B. and Visser, J. (eds.) (1995), *De vakbeweging na de welvaartsstaat*, Van Gorcum, Assen.

Klijn, A. (1990), *Arbeiders of volkspartij. Een vergelijkende studie van het Belgische en het Nederlandse socialisme 1933-1946*, Universitaire Pers, Maastricht.

Kloosterman, R.C. (1994), 'Three worlds of welfare capitalism? The welfare state and the post-industrial trajectory in the Netherlands after 1980', *West-European Politics*, vol. 17, no. 4, October, pp. 166-189.

Kriesi, H. (1993), *Political Mobilization and Social Change. The Dutch Case in Comparative Perspective*, Public Policy and Social Welfare 12, Avebury, Aldershot etc.

Leisink, P. (1993), 'Is Innovation a Management Prerogative? Changing Employment Relationships, Innovative Unions', Leverhume Public Lecture, University of Warwick, May, (mimeo).

Leisink, P. (1995), 'Vakbondswerk in de onderneming: tussen ledenwerving en participatie', in Coenen, H. (ed.), *De vakbeweging na 2000*, Van Arkel, Utrecht, pp. 109-141.

Paauwe, J. and De Jong, J. A. (1992), 'Dutch Trade Union in Transition: an Organizational Development-approach', Mimeo, 9th World congress of the International Industrial Relations Association, Sydney, 30 Aug.-3 Sept.

Pasture, P. (1994a), 'Diverging paths: the development of Catholic labour organizations in France, the Netherlands and Belgium since 1944', *Revue d'Histoire Ecclésiastique*, vol. 88, no. 1, pp. 54-90.

Pasture, P. (1994b), *Christian Trade Unionism in Europe since 1968. Tensions between Identity and Practice*, Avebury, Aldershot.

Peet, J. (1985), 'Tussen aanpassing en vernieuwing. Hoofdlijnen in de geschiedenis van het Nederlands Katholiek Vakverbond, 1963-1981', in Roes, J. (ed.), *Katholieke arbeidersbeweging. Studies over KAB en NKV in de economische en politieke ontwikkeling van Nederland na 1945*, Ambo, Baarn, pp. 133-201.

Peet, J. (1993) (Mertens, P., coll.), *Katholieke arbeidersbeweging* (J. Roes, ed.), vol. 2: *De KAB en het NKV in de maatschappelijke ontwikkeling van Nederland na 1945*, KDC Bronnen en Studies 25, Arbor, Baarn.

Peet, J. (1994), 'De zeven magere jaren van het katholiek corporatisme. Katholieke Arbeidersbeweging en sociaal-economische orde in Nederland (1945-1952)', *Trajecta*, vol. 3, no. 1, pp. 61-84.

Perry, J. (1994), 'De jaren 1894-1919', in Brinkman, M., De Keizer, M. and Van Rossem, M. (eds.), *Honderd jaar sociaal-democratie in Nederland 1894-1994*, Bert Bakker, Amsterdam, pp. 9-61.

Righart, H. (1985), 'De ene ongedeelde KAB, vrome wens of werkelijkheid ? Een historische schets van de Katholieke Arbeidersbeweging, 1945-1963', in Roes, J. (ed.), *Katholieke arbeidersbeweging. Studies over KAB en NKV in de economische en politieke ontwikkeling van Nederland na 1945*, Ambo, Baarn, pp. 79-131.

Roes, J. (1985), 'Katholieke arbeidersbeweging in historische banen. Inleidende beschouwingen over achtergronden, fasen en aspecten', in Roes, J. (ed.), *Katholieke arbeidersbeweging. Studies over KAB en NKV in de economische en politieke ontwikkeling van Nederland na 1945*, Publikaties van het Katholiek Documentatiecentrum 25, Ambo, Baarn.

Salemink, T. (1991), *Katholieke kritiek op het kapitalisme 1891-1991. Honderd jaar debat over vrije markt en verzorgingsstaat*, Acco, Leuven/Amersfoort.

Thurlings, J. M. G. (1978), *De wankele zuil. Nederlandse katholieken tussen assimilatie en pluralisme*, Publikaties van het Katholiek Documentatie Centrum 1, 2nd. edition, Ambo, Baarn.

Valkenburg, B. (1995a), 'Trade unionism in the Netherlands: back to the future', *Transfer*, vol. 1, no. 1, pp. 64-79.

Valkenburg, B. (1995b), 'Participatie in de vakbeweging', in Coenen, H. (ed.), *De vakbeweging na 2000*, Van Arkel, Utrecht, pp. 88-108.

Valkenburg, B. and Zoll, R. (1995), 'Modernization, individualization, and solidarity: two perspectives on European trade unions today', *European Journal of Industrial Relations*, vol. 1, no. 1, pp. 119-144.

Van Berkel, R. (1995), 'Anders-actief in de vakbeweging: zoeken naar wegen uit de 'cultuur van ontevredenheid'', in Coenen, H. (ed.), *De vakbeweging na 2000*, Van Arkel, Utrecht, pp. 169-199.

Van Berkel, R. and Coenen, H. (1995), 'Het arbeidsbestel in de overgang van industriële samenleving naar risico-maatschappij', in Coenen, H. (ed.), *De vakbeweging na 2000*, Van Arkel, Utrecht, pp. 48-71.

Van Berkel, R. and Hindriks, T. (1991), *Uitkeringsgerechtigden en vakbeweging. Over de modernisering van het arbeidsbestel*, Van Arkel, Utrecht.

Van den Toren, J. P. (1991), 'Van loonslaaf tot bedrijfsgenoot'. *100 jaar christelijk-sociaal denken, medezeggenschap en sociale zekerheid*, Kok, Kampen.

Van der Linden, M. and Schutje, J.W. (1992), *De Nederlandse vakbeweging, haar basis en de staat. Een lange-termijnperspectief*, IISH Research Papers 6, IISG, Amsterdam.

Van der Veen, G. (1992), *Principes in praktijk. CNV-leden over collectieve acties*, Kok, Kampen.

Van der Veen, G. (1995), 'Vakbondsleden over acties', in Klandermans, B. and Visser, J. (eds.), *De vakbeweging na de welvaartsstaat*, Van Gorcum, Assen, pp. 139-157.

Van der Veen, G. and Klandermans, B. (1990), *Tussen overleg en strijd. CNV en collectieve acties*, Kok, Kampen.

Van Kersbergen, K. (1991), 'De Nederlandse verzorgingsstaat in vergelijkend perspectief', in Becker, U. (ed.), *Mens, macht, Nederlandse politiek: een inleiding in de politieke wetenschap*, Het Spinhuis, Amsterdam, pp. 265-294.

Van Kersbergen, K. and Becker, U. (1978), 'The Netherlands. A passive social democratic welfare state in a christian democratic ruled society', *Journal of Social Policy*, no. 4, pp. 477-499.

Van Rij, C. (1995), 'Naar de bond: vakbondsloopbanen en beroepsloopbanen', in Klandermans, B. and Visser, J. (eds.), *De vakbeweging na de welvaartsstaat*, Van Gorcum, Assen, pp. 67-86.

Visser, J. (1984), *Dimensions of Union Growth in Postwar Western Europe*, EUI Working Papers 89, European University Institute, Florence.

Visser, J. (1990), 'Continuity and change in Dutch industrial relations', in Baglioni, G. and Crouch, C. (eds.), *European Industrial Relations. The Challenge of Flexibility*, Sage, London, pp. 198-242.

Visser, J. (1991), *Trends in Trade Union Membership*, OECD-Employment Outlook, OECD, Paris, pp. 97-134.

Visser, J. (1992), 'The Netherlands. The end of an era and the end of a system', in Ferner, A. and Hyman, R. (eds.), *Industrial Relations in the New Europe*, Basil Blackwell, Oxford, pp. 323-356.

Visser, J. (1993), 'Works councils and unions in the Netherlands: rivals or alies ?', *The Netherlands Journal of Social Sciences*, vol. 29, no. 3 , pp. 64-92.

Visser, J. (1994), 'From paternalism to representation. Works councils in the Netherlands', in Rogers, J. and Streeck, W. (eds.), *Works Councils in Europe and America*, University of Chicago Press.

Visser, J. (1995a), 'Het profiel van de vakbeweging', in Klandermans, B. and Visser, J. (eds.), *De vakbeweging na de welvaartsstaat*, Van Gorcum, Assen, pp. 31-65.

Visser, J. (1995b), 'Vakbeweging en welvaartsstaat', in Klandermans, B. and Visser, J. (eds.), *De vakbeweging na de welvaartsstaat*, Van Gorcum, Assen, pp. 1-17.

Vos, C.J. (1986), 'Christelijke vakbeweging en politiek. De CNV-CDA controverse: broedertwist of koude oorlog ?', *Tijdschrift voor Arbeidsvraagstukken*, vol. 2, no. 1, pp. 4-12.

Wentholt, G. M. J. (1984), *Een arbeidersbeweging en haar priesters. Het einde van een relatie (...)*, Dekker en Van de Vegt, Nijmegen, pp. 129-149.

Windmuller, J. P. (1969), *Labour Relations in the Netherlands*, Cornell University Press, Ythaca.
Windmuller, J. P., De Galan, C. and Van Zweden, A. F. (1990), *Arbeidsverhoudingen in Nederland*, Het Spectrum, Utrecht/Antwerpen.
Zahn, E. (1989), *Regenten, rebellen en reformatoren. Een visie op Nederland en de Nederlanders*, Contact, Amsterdam (orig. *Das unbekannte Holland: Regenten, Rebellen und Reformatoren*, Siedler, Berlin 1984).

5 Germany: Inner trade union diversity

Johan Verberckmoes

Introduction

Since the Second World War, the Federal Republic of Germany has attached particular value to the institutional structures intended to guarantee its survival as a democratic, free state. Some people believe this represents a logical continuation of the ancient Prussian class-based state. The pluralist democracy which Germany has become nonetheless initially developed by turning its back on the recent past. The dangerous political extremism of National Socialism was strenuously rejected. Anti-communism, too, had its heyday against the backdrop of Soviet Russian expansion and domination in Eastern Europe and parts of Central Europe. The result was the expansion of a social consensus model of institutionalized cooperation between the State and major social forces. The economic success of the rejuvenated German nation provided a strong boost for this integration and helped ensure that the trade union movement became a significant partner in public life.

The principles of the consultative structures in the field of German industrial relations lie in the democratic legislation which, immediately after the Nazi era and the end of the war, created the framework within which the employees were involved in developing the free, socially corrected market economy. The collective memory of the fatal Weimar Republic and the pernicious Nazi regime made sure that from the start the trade union movement positioned itself within that logic, even if the political context was not always favourable towards it. Moreover, a unified trade union was created as early as 1949, the Deutscher

Gewerkschaftsbund (DGB), which had as its stated objective the permanent elimination of ideological diversity within the trade union movement.

The conditions were thus created for the development of a system of industrial relations which is seen by many as exemplary. However, that ultra-strong German consultative model seems to have been eroding rapidly for more than a decade. Following a stagnation in membership during the 1980s and an abnormal peak as a result of the merger of the memberships from the eastern and western *Länder* in 1991, membership figures have continually fallen since, in particular in the eastern *Länder*. New forms of employee participation proposed by the employers eat away at one of the foundations of the model, i.e. the organization of industrial relations by branch of industry. The same can be said of the increasing trend towards decentralization in collective bargaining, in favour of negotiation at company level. Moreover, the increasing internationalization of the economy made it difficult to maintain the specific postwar German system of industrial relations. Indeed, in German public opinion, the moral weight of Germany's own historic past is put into perspective more than previously. Undoubtedly, however, the most important cause of the recent radical changes was the fall of the Wall in 1989.

Influenced by all these developments, German trade unions are now being forced to thoroughly rethink their significance, influence, impact, structures and the way forward in terms of content. In this chapter, I assume that a clear understanding of the range of current options can only based on a consideration of the ideological traditions of the past. After all, even in what is one of the most officially un-ideologized trade union movements in Europe, many kinds of ideological contrasts still exist under the surface. In the course of its history, new challenges have repeatedly changed the face of the trade union movement. My argument will be that the relative success of the German consultative model can be attributed at least as much to the integration of these tensions as to its institutional roots.

For a clear understanding of the text, I should mention that it will focus mainly on the broad social significance of the trade union movement and of the DGB in particular as an umbrella organization. Industrial relations at company and industry level are hence left out of the picture somewhat. It should also be understood that the DGB is a fairly weak central body. The affiliated federations or *Industriegewerkschaften* (industry-wide unions) actually carry the German trade union movement. German unions are indeed mainly organized on the principle of one plant, one union. DGB unions comprise more than 80 per cent of all trade union members in Germany. The decision nonetheless to carry out this analysis at the level of the DGB is based partly on pragmatic considerations and partly on the observation that the latent ideological tensions are often activated precisely by the annual DGB congresses. First, the major institutional frameworks of German industrial relations will be reviewed in brief.

German industrial relations are characterized by a very low level of state intervention and a correspondingly high level of independence among the industrial actors (Thelen, 1991; Jacobi, Keller and Müller-Jentsch, 1992; Fuerstenberg, 1993; Lane, 1994). In particular, the principle of *Tarifautonomie* (free collective bargaining) protects the relatively strong position held by the trade union movement: trade unions and employers enter into mutual negotiations and conclude collective labour agreements (*Tarifverträge*), especially in matters concerning wages and working hours, without state intervention. Negotiations are held at the level of the branch of industry and the region. Once an agreement is reached, it applies to all companies in that branch of industry and region, irrespective of a trade union presence in those companies. Provided an agreement is valid, peace and compliance are compulsory. It must also be noted that this system of collective labour agreements cannot be directly associated with trade union membership. While approximately 90 per cent of employees are covered by a collective labour agreement, only about one third of the employees are members of a trade union. National, interprofessional negotiations do not exist, except in the public services. By contrast, the employment conditions of civil servants or *Beamte* are settled by parliamentary legislation. The Deutscher Beamtenbund (DBB), whose 800,000-strong membership is made up almost entirely of civil servants, is therefore more of a lobby organization than a genuine trade union (Keller, 1983).

A key element of the German consultative model is the duality between the trade union and the works council (*Betriebsrat*). Many authors believe that this dual system has contributed most to the stability of German industrial relations. While trade unions and employers' organizations hold collective negotiations at levels higher than that of the company, within the company itself this role is fulfilled by the independent *Betriebsrat*, which is formally separate from the trade union. The *Betriebsrat* was created by the *Betriebsverfassungsgesetz* (Industrial Constitution Law) of 1952. It represents the employees in the company and negotiates directly with the employer concerning working hours, holiday arrangements, bonuses, recruitment, selection and dismissal, company training and other employment conditions. The *Tarifverträge*, however, negotiated per branch of industry, always take precedence over the conditions negotiated in the company.

Since the 1970s the agreements reached at company level by the *Betriebsrat* have increasingly gained in importance vis-à-vis the *Tarifverträge*, in the sense that they adapt the general rules to the local situation. When the *Betriebsverfassungsgesetz* was revised in 1972, a central works council or *Gesamtbetriebsrat* was created at concern level, which gives employees the opportunity to exert influence on global policy relating to employment conditions in companies with more than one establishment. From an institutional point of view, the trade union does not intervene in negotiation procedures at company level. The union shop stewards, or *Vertrauensleute*, confine themselves to recruiting members for the trade union. In practice, however, the formal distinction between *Betriebsrat* and trade union delegation is largely fictitious, because the same people usually act via both channels. In 1994, provisional figures from the DGB showed that 76 per cent of the members of the *Betriebsräte* were also DGB members. Non-trade union members (20 per cent) were their major competitors.[1]

A third major component of German industrial relations is concerned with employee codetermination. The most far-reaching ruling in this context is the *Mitbestimmungsgesetz* (Law on Codetermination) dating from 1976. This states that in companies with more than 2000 employees, half of the seats on the *Aufsichtsrat*, or supervisory board, must be given to employee representatives, on the understanding however that at least one of them must hold a managerial position in the company. This *Aufsichtsrat* appoints and supervises the management. Its chief role is to defend company interests. The DGB has, however, always aimed for a more radical solution, after the model of the codetermination ruling applied to the coal, iron and steel industry in 1951 (known as the *Montanindustrie*: hence *Montanmitbestimmung*). At the time, the principle of joint representation was implemented in the *Aufsichtsrat* of companies employing more than 1000 people in these sectors. Since then, the German trade union movement has championed the expansion of this principle of equality, but in fact the genuine significance of that form of co-management has been increasingly undermined by the continued weakening of both industries.

One important consequence of all this is the often-praised stability of West German industrial relations, which is also reflected in the actions of the trade unions themselves. The democratic creed of the new Federal German Republic of 1949 implied a high level of mistrust, on the part of the employees too, of all political extremism - both right and left wing. In fact, the trade unions have always taken great care to explicitly distance themselves from any form of fascism or communism. Although not entirely insignificant, communist beliefs have nearly always been marginalized in the German trade union movement. As far as strikes are concerned, caution has always been the watchword. Strikes (and lockouts) are only legally permitted within the framework of rounds of collective bargaining on the basis of pronouncements by the Federal Labour Court. Within the company, mediation and arbitration procedures and binding pronouncements by the *Arbeitsgericht* (labour court) are in force. Strikes may only be used as a last resort. Even the strategy of *Schwerpunktstreike* (selective strikes) exudes an atmosphere of moderation. These are strikes which the trade unions call in a limited number of key companies, aimed at forcing an agreement for the whole sector. Wild, illegal strikes occur relatively infrequently. On the other hand, lockouts are also legally regulated by the employers, so that these occur in Germany more frequently than in most other European countries.

Another important consequence of the far-reaching legalization and institutionalization of industrial relations is that, since the Second World War, the West German trade union movement has always adopted an attitude of reserve with respect to far-reaching integration into State structures. The organizational cohesion between party and trade union in the former German Democratic Republic was until recently a negative counter-example in that respect. This independent attitude on the part of the West German trade union movement is expressed in its cautious view of the world of politics, at least in theory. Although almost all members of the West German parliament (*Bundestag*) from the Sozialdemokratische Partei Deutschlands (SPD) are members of a DGB trade union, the DGB sticks by the unwritten rule that its party-political independence is guaranteed as long as there are no top officers from the trade union sitting in parliament. Nevertheless, the DGB has many from its own ranks in the civil service and even at top government level, although numbers have fallen systematically since the 1970s. After all, in this period the SPD and DGB began to adopt a critical distance from each other, particularly when the social democratic party tapped new layers of the electorate over the course of the 1980s. Compared to the social democrats, the Christian democrats have always occupied a weak position within the DGB, although they have never become marginalized. At present, approximately 50 per cent of the DGB members are also members of the SPD. In the case of the Christlich-Demokratische Union (CDU) and the Christlich-Soziale Union (CSU), this number is between one quarter and one third. Among DGB *Vertrauensleute* at the beginning of the 1980s, 82 per cent were members of the SPD and only around 12 per cent members of the CDU or CSU (Mielke, 1983, p. 374). According to research in 1993, these figures have fallen to 64 per cent and 9 per cent respectively (Hege, 1994). An alternative to the critical but broad mutual support between the DGB and the SPD seems to be ruled out for the time being (Pelinka, 1980; Müller-Jentsch, 1992; Langkau, Matthöfer and Schneider, 1994).

The historical legacy of ideological pluralism[2]

The trade union movement in Germany was born out of the civil and democratic ideals of the 1948/49 revolution, the search for solutions to 'the social problem' on the part of social Christian thinkers and the advent of revolutionary social movements after the publication in London of Marx and Engels' Communist Manifesto in February 1848. To begin with, associations were mobilized chiefly by skilled craftsmen, such as printers or cigar makers. They ensured the continuity of the workers' movement, whose raison d'être was continually under threat, in the form of medical insurance funds and educational associations. After a short period during which workers' organizations were legally banned, in the 1860s and 1870s numerous profession-based unions were founded, often as a result of strikes. The major impetus for national trade union movements, on the other hand, came from the policital parties. Ideological diversity was therefore institutionalized right from the start. The Allgemeiner Deutscher Arbeitverein (ADAV), the first workers' party, founded in 1863 by Ferdinand Lassalle, provided the decisive incentive. At a congress in 1868, the ADAV founded the Allgemeiner Deutscher Arbeiterschaftsverband, a federation of 'free' social democratic trade unions. At the same congress, a group of dissidents, dissatisfied with the trade union movement's links with the social democratic party, formed the liberal Hirsch-Duncker trade union (the name referring to two liberal leaders). But also the Marxist-inspired, anti-Prussian social democrats broke away from the *lassalliens* and founded the Sozialdemokratische Arbeiterpartei (SDAP) in 1869, under the leadership of August Bebel and Wilhelm Liebknecht. In 1875, the two tendencies within German social democracy united into one party, the Sozialdemokratische Partei Deutschlands (SPD) and one trade union. On the sidelines of this development in social democracy,

Catholic and protestant priests confined themselves to founding religious and charitable workers' associations (Ritter, 1990; Fleck, 1994).

The increased pace of industrialization after the middle of the century and the domination of the military-aristocratic Prussians in the *Reich*, unified in 1871 under the leadership of an authoritarian *Kaiser*, heightened social contrasts. The further development of the trade union movement was seriously obstructed by the opposition of many employers, the legislative initiatives of chancellor Bismarck for the social protection of workers, which encouraged moderation, and the proscription of social democracy between 1878 and 1890. On the other hand, this meant that the workers' movement gained in independence. At the end of the nineteenth century, the rapidly growing German trade union movement consolidated its position in society as well as its ideological pluralism (Scharrer, 1990; Marks, 1989). In 1892 the first national congress of free social democratic trade unions was held. From 1894 onwards, interdenominational Christian trade unions were formed, which opposed social democratic principles (Schneider, 1982). Although the Christian trade union movement would remain the little brother of social democracy, it quickly became more important than the even smaller liberal Hirsch-Duncker trade unions. The Christliche Gewerkschaften Deutschlands (CGD), founded in 1899, was the first national Christian trade union in Europe. Despite opposition from the bishops, it maintained its interdenominational character. By the eve of the First World War, the trade unions had become an important though not very powerful force in German society. They were also the exponents of the diverse beliefs harboured by the workers. While the State and the employers reinforced trade union pragmatism by making concessions and concluding collective labour agreements, for its part the majority of the trade union movement rejected all revolutionary possibilities. The support of most trade unions for the war effort during the First World War reinforced their integration into the State and the economic structures.

Although the trade unions in the Weimar Republic adopted parallel, reformist positions, they continued to portray themselves as ideologically opposed to one another. They had particularly close ties with the political parties. The free trade unions regrouped themselves in the Allgemeiner Deutscher Gewerkschaftsbund (ADGB), where socialist rhetoric went hand in hand with reformist practice and the marginalization of revolutionary communism. This federation represented mainly manual workers. At political level, the ADGB was supported primarily by the moderate majority SPD and, to a lesser extent, by the radical Unabhängige Sozialdemokratische Partei Deutschlands (USPD). Incidentally, the marginalization of revolutionary tendencies within the workers' movement was also evident in the first codetermination ruling, which was introduced in 1920. It reinforced both the integration of employees in the company and the institutional position of the trade unions. The Christian national trade unions in the Deutscher Gewerkschaftsbund (DGB), the successor of the CGD, wanted to transcend class thinking. They believed in an organic, historical 'national community' giving employees the right to a share in the ownership and management of the means of production. The religious portion of their programme was emphasized chiefly by Catholics, the national component more by protestants. Its major political ally was the *Zentrum* and its members included both blue collar and white collar workers. The small Hirsch-Duncker trade unions, united in the Gewerkschaftsring, rejected the class struggle, declared themselves independent from all political parties and religiously neutral and had their ideological roots in socially oriented liberalism. The Deutsche Demokratische Partei (DDP) was their political equal. Their members were chiefly white collar workers.

On 2 May 1933 the Nazis stormed trade union buildings all over Germany. Trade union leaders were persecuted, joined the opposition against the Nazi-regime or fled abroad (Mommsen, 1993). The independent trade unions were disbanded and replaced by the Deutsche Arbeitsfront (DAF) which, according to the nationalist and corporatist ideology of Hitler's Nationalsozialistische Deutsche Arbeiterpartei (NSDAP), saw industrial relations purely within the context of the shared task of employers and employees in the service of the German fatherland. The national socialist labour charter removed all advisory and participation options from employees. After the Second World War, the refoundation of the German trade union movement was not without difficulties, although grassroots enthusiasm was high. Already during the last phase of the war against Nazi Germany, in the spring of 1945, local workers' organizations appeared on German territory, which followed the tradition of independent trade unionism as it had existed before 1933. However, the various allied occupation forces had differing ideas about the organization of the trade unions. Furthermore, trade union work was hampered by food shortages, wage freezes and mass unemployment.

Faced with the vicissitudes of reconstruction, the foundation of a non-partisan, industry-based trade union (*Einheitsgewerkschaft*) seemed imperative to many trade unionists. The idea was widely circulated -

not least among metalworkers - that blue collar and white collar workers could best be organized together and by branch of industry. That would increase unity among employees. On the other hand, the weak position of the trade union movement under the Weimar regime provided proof, according to many postwar trade union leaders, that ideological diversity necessarily led to immobilism.[3] But, contradictorily, perhaps the most important factor promoting the *Einheitsgewerkschaft* was the spread of anti-communism in the English, American and French occupation zones (Schönhoven, 1993). In 1945/46 the Freie Deutsche Gewerkschaftsbund (FDGB) was founded in the Soviet occupied eastern zone and soon lost its autonomy. The American policy of communist containment, on the other hand, fostered cooperation between all the other tendencies in the Western zones (Markovits, 1986, pp. 61-72). This way, two blocks were formed and anti-communism quickly eclipsed the anti-fascist and anti-capitalist ideals of the re-emerging trade union movement in these Western zones. Yet, anti-communism was not simply a product of the Cold War. It definitely also had pre-war origins (Macshane, 1992, pp. 187-237 and 289-294). In terms of trade union organization, the Anglo-Saxon model was copied. In the British occupation zone, an *Einheitsgewerkschaft* was founded in 1947, followed by industry-wide unions, or *Industriegewerkschaften*, in the American and French zones. In 1949, these merged together and the Deutscher Gewerkschaftsbund (DGB) held its founding congress from 12 to 14 October 1949. The federation incorporated 16 *Industriegewerkschaften*. From the start, a large majority of members and officers of the DGB were also members of the SPD. Christians were in the minority. Communists were marginalized, but retained significant influence in the works councils of the Ruhr mining industry and of some regions of the metal industry (Schönhoven, 1993, p. 266). The DGB declared its independence from all political parties.

If trade union unity thus seemed guaranteed at ideological level, unity among the various categories of employees was proving much more difficult to achieve. Both the Deutsche Angestellten Gewerkschaft (DAG) for white collar workers and the Deutscher Beamten Bund (DBB), for civil servants, remained outside the DGB. Their most important reason for doing so was historical: both professional categories had also had their own organizations during the Weimar Republic. Since collective bargaining for civil servants is forbidden in Germany, the DBB is little more than a lobby group. In 1951, the DAG represented 35 per cent of all unionized white collar workers and, by 1981, only 21 per cent (fewer than half a million members). Its members are chiefly senior officials and civil servants. Ideologically, the white collar trade union saw itself in the shadow of the DGB, on the understanding however that it was reluctant to adjust wage scales through collective labour agreements. The majority of the DAG leadership was social democrat. The congresses and programmes of the DAG did not deviate a great deal from the themes broached by the DGB. From the 1980s onwards the DAG began to coordinate its activities more effectively with the DGB, whereas the two trade unions had previously been rivals. This took place during a period when the public service trade unions within the DGB considerably strengthened their position (Markovits, 1986, p. 11; Pelinka, 1980, pp. 124-125; Halberstadt, 1991).

Even within the DGB itself, the oft-repeated motto that the pernicious diversity of the Weimar period had been conquered was not entirely true. In the late 1940s and the early 1950s the DGB and the Kommunistische Partei Deutschlands (KPD) embarked on a confrontational course. The unions, and especially IG Metall, the powerful metal and steel industry union, increasingly expelled communist officials from their ranks, until the KPD was officially banned in 1956 (Schönhoven, 1993). Concerning contacts with the FDGB in the German Democratic Republic, the majority in the DGB, and in particular IG Metall, opted for a similar tough stance, rejecting all communication, as this would imply a recognition of the communist regime. IG Metall would stick to this position until the end of the 1960s. Only a minority of mainly communists in the DGB favoured a normalization of relations between the DGB and the FDGB. This minority was led by IG Druck und Papier (Schroeder, 1993).

An even more cumbersome problem was the relationship between social democrats and Christians in the DGB (Pelinka, 1980, pp. 95-99; Markovits, 1986, pp. 11, 82-83 and 88; Schroeder, 1990, 1991 and 1992; Pasture, 1994, pp. 58-63). The Christian socialist-inspired trade union leaders sometimes had a hard time within the industry-based trade union, where their ideas and symbols were marginalized. They were predominantly Catholic. After 1945 protestants were virtually extinct in the trade union movement. On the whole, the *Einheitsgewerkschaft* was the best provisional solution for the Christians immediately after the War. Nonetheless, the tensions remained, in particular because young people who had not been active in the trade union movement before 1933 wanted to place more emphasis on Christian identity, if necessary by setting up a separate Christian trade union. The rapidly expanding CDU, however, saw any split in the industry-based union chiefly as a threat to the reconstruction of the country.

At the beginning of the 1950s, calls were increasingly made within Catholic circles for the foundation of a separate Christian trade union, distinct from the DGB, which, it was said, was continually sucking employees into the nets of social democracy. In this respect, the Katholische Arbeitnehmer-Bewegung (KAB), an educational association, played a leading role, initially supported by some bishops. The open support of the DGB for the SPD during the campaign for the *Bundestag* elections of 1953 and possible financial support from the trade union for the party provided the incentive for the KAB to demand more strict application by the DGB of the principle of party-political independence, otherwise the foundation of an independent Christian trade union would be the result. Two years later, the threat was carried out. In response to the action programme of the DGB, which combined a radical plea for economic democracy with powerful demands for an active wages policy, and as a result of the growing opposition within the federation to the rearming of the Federal Republic, in 1955 the Christliche Gewerkschaftsbewegung Deutschlands (CGD) was founded. It advocated worker co-ownership in the prevailing economic system and supported Adenauer's rearmament policy within the framework of Germany's increasing integration into the Western Alliance. In 1959, the CGD was transformed into the Christlicher Gewerkschaftsbund (CGB).

However, the CGB never succeeded in playing an important role in West German industrial relations. This impotence was largely the result of the lack of unity within Christian socialist circles in the 1950s. The whole controversy surrounding the question of whether or not Catholics should join the DGB had produced organizational diversity, which had a paralysing effect. Neither the Catholic hierarchy nor the evangelical church pledged its undivided support to the CGB - on the contrary. However, the major reason why a Christian trade union did not get off the ground in Germany was the fact that many Catholic employees simply did not want to leave the DGB. This must not be explained purely in terms of an advancing process of secularization. After all, the DGB had expanded into an organization with a permanent place in West German democracy.

The breakaway and foundation of an independent Christian trade union is, however, only part of the story. Even after 1955, Christians continued to join the DGB. Until 1960, they were grouped together in the Christlich-Soziale Kollegenschaft, which wanted to put more emphasis on Christian identity in the trade union. Ironically enough, in the Kollegenschaft the DGB found an ally in its fight against the centrifugal forces of both breakaway social Catholicism and communism. In other words, in the long term the disunity surrounding the strategy to be pursued in organized social Catholicism strengthened social democracy within the DGB. Social Catholicism of the 1950s retained a system of proportional representation in the DGB, which always gave them a few seats in the trade union leadership, right up to the highest level, including one of the two acting national chairmen. Since 1959, the Christian officials in the DGB have come together in the Arbeitsgemeinschaft christlich-sozialer DGB-Gewerkschafter, part of the Sozialausschüsse or Christlich-Demokratische Arbeitnehmerschaft (CDA), itself an organization for employees' interests within the CDU. The Arbeitsgemeinschaft did not play an important mediating role in the DGB.

The construction of the welfare state

The regenerated German trade union movement adopted a blatantly anti-fascist position in 1945. Partly because many employers had collaborated with the Nazi regime, this position implied violent anti-capitalism. In specific terms, this meant that the burgeoning trade union movement in the immediate postwar years advocated economic democracy, to be achieved through the nationalization of the energy sector, steel and chemical companies and large banks, and through worker participation in the company, based on total equality at all levels. This would all be the forerunner of a universal democratization of the new German society. However, things did not come this far. The opposition of the occupying forces, especially the Americans, to a far-reaching planned economy and the re-emergence of anti-communism curbed potential revolutionary intervention. Furthermore, the acceptance of the Marshall Plan by the trade union movement meant that they fully backed the reconstruction of West-Germany. The free market economy was an essential component of that reconstruction (Markovits, 1986, pp. 61-72; Pelinka, pp. 45-46 and 50-51; Schmidt, 1981).

At its founding congress in 1949 the DGB proposed an ambitious programme, which was to serve as a guide for its future role in the new Federal Republic. Although somewhat overtaken by events, anti-capitalism, full *Mitbestimmung* and the nationalization of key sectors were explicitly defended. The satisfaction of social needs must replace the capitalist profit principle. In order to achieve this, central economic planning was considered indispensable. On the other hand, however, freedom in economic life was also emphasized, so that the trade union developed as champion of a 'third way'. It was not entirely clear what form this would take, but free democracy, the parliamentary system and the constitution were fully recognized as its principles. A European economic policy was strongly advocated. The constitutional granting of equal rights to men and women on the labour market was welcomed. In this way, the DGB's programme of 1949 reconciled the social democratic ideals of economic democracy with ideas from the Christian social doctrine of classless cooperation in the constitutional State. In his lecture to the founding congress, the social democrat Hans Böckler quoted approvingly from the *Rerum Novarum* and *Quadragesimo Anno* encyclicals. Moreover, he had Thea Harmuth elected as the first woman on the executive committee, partly to strengthen the position of Christians in the trade union.[4]

Initially it looked as if the DGB had begun to make its ideal of workers' democracy come true. In 1951, after a strike threat, the model of joint codetermination in the steel and coal industry, the *Montanmitbestimmung*, which had been in existence since 1947, was established by law. As early as the following year, 1952, however, the DGB found the further implementation of its democratization programme blocked by the *Betriebsverfassungsgesetz* (Thelen, 1991). The law was an undisguised attempt by the CDU government to check trade union influence within companies. An important reason why the DGB was powerless to resist that law was undoubtedly that the trade union had for too long lived off its moral victory of 1945, when the workers' organizations had given themselves a responsible role in the reconstruction of a democratic Germany. The DGB all too easily assumed that it was an indispensable collaborator in the political and economic decision-making processes. It did not therefore refuse to support the foreign policy of chancellor Adenauer, which was aimed at full German integration into the West. This trade union support was only useful to the conservative government in so far as it promoted the integration of the new German state. However, a strongly institutionalized trade union power as a component of parliamentary democracy was rejected by the CDU. Moreover, the employers went on the offensive against the trade unions. Although the DGB itself was outspokenly anti-communist, its loyalty to the existing economic order was questioned. That even led to legal restrictions on the right to strike. On 28 January 1955 the Federal Court decided that strikes could only be held if their main issue was a demand to which the other party could respond in a collective agreement. Strikes and lock-outs were also recognized as equal weapons.

Despite its weak position in the budding German democracy, in choosing the idea of *Mitbestimmung* and gradually abandoning its demands for nationalization and a planned economy, the DGB reinforced its internal cohesion. Both social democrats and social Catholics could back the principle of *Mitbestimmung*. After all, it implied the attempt to extend the economic power of the workers as well as the recognition of the equal rights of capital and labour. However, unity within the DGB was still fragile. This was expressed not only in the conflict surrounding the foundation of the CGD, which later became the CGB. Indeed, new ideological dividing lines were drawn in the mid-1950s when, after the debacle of the previous years, the DGB embarked upon a reorientation of its overall policy (Deppe a.o., 1969; Markovits, 1986). The 'third way' which the trade union had wanted to achieve was quietly dropped as a project. In practice, the German democratic constitutional State, constructed by a conservative government, had become the framework within which the DGB wanted to operate.

Encouraged by the left-wing social democrat, Viktor Agartz, director of the DGB's research institute, and Otto Brenner, the new leader of IG Metall, the federation focused its operations increasingly on achieving maximum results on wages and worker protection - via collective bargaining. In this concept, the trade union was an independent force within the capitalist system and it had to use this position to benefit the workers as much as possible. On 1 May 1955 the DGB published an action programme in which the trade union established the objectives which would define its agenda for social action in the short term. It advocated a 40-hour working week, higher wages, equal pay for men and women, equal medical insurance for blue collar and white collar workers, an extension of social security, guaranteed employment, sufficient support in the event of unemployment, accident, sickness or old age, an extension of codetermination, better safety regulations at work and improved vocational training and education for young people. This was the first in a series of action programmes which would serve as a guide in collective bargaining per branch of industry and per region. From the end of the 1950s onwards, this joint strategy of decentralized negotiations based on a centrally established, general package of demands became the principal means of action employed by the German trade union movement.

Many of the programme points from 1955 were achieved over the following decade, chiefly under pressure from the largest trade union, IG Metall. As first union, it reached agreements on the gradual introduction of the 40-hour week, using the strike weapon at critical moments. However, the willingness of IG Metall to take action was not aimed purely at implementing the action programme; in the long term it wanted to guarantee the position of the trade union as an opposition force against capitalism. The DGB's founding programme from 1949 remained its point of reference. This was not an unambiguous position, since the IG Metall at the same was virulently anti-communist. A counter-reaction to the dominating, activist role by the IG Metall also emerged within the DGB. The trade unions in the mining, building and textile industries portrayed themselves as outspoken advocates of constructive cooperation in the further development of democracy in the Federal Republic. They did not consider the trade union movement as a *Gegenmacht* (opposing force), but as an *Ordnungsfaktor* (factor for order). To them the trade unions were social partners which recognized the individual rights of employers and expressly identified with the existing democratic and capitalist State. It boiled down to promoting the integration of the workers into the free democracy.

This ideological rift within the DGB was deep-rooted. Its historical predecessors lay in the Weimar Republic, where there had been a similar conflict within the ADGB. The supporters of a confrontational strategy towards the employers and of worker control of the economy via workers' councils had been pitted against the proponents of corporatist cooperation between trade unions, employers and the state. The return of this ideological conflict in the 1950s was partly caused by the undermining of the umbrella federation. After all, the DGB took no part in collective bargaining, which was handled solely by the *Industriegewerkschaften* and which continually increased in importance in this period to enable the workers to share the benefits of the *Wirtschaftswunder* (economic miracle). The variations in commitment, depending on the branch of industry and relative strength of each trade union, led to differing strategies. However, external factors were also at play. The advance of the proponents of the social partnership strategy was fostered by the SPD's soul-searching following a third successive defeat in the 1957 parliamentary elections. In the 'Bad Godesberg reform' the social democratic party threw out its Marxist social analysis and recognized the organic pluralism of the parliamentary democracy. The class struggle still predicted by the IG Metall seemed therefore increasingly anomalous. Incidentally, the level of trade union membership fell during this period from 38.6 per cent in 1951 to 32.6 per cent in 1965 (although numbers of members rose in absolute terms). Strike activity systematically declined. The antagonistic option, as defined in the 1949 programme, was in urgent need of correction in the eyes of many within the DGB.

Following intense debate, in 1963 the DGB plotted a course for a broad social project with its new basic programme.[5] Although it was those in favour of the social partnership option who insisted on the elaboration of this programme, the text itself was a careful compromise between both tendencies within the DGB. Freedom, self-determination and the Universal Declaration of the Rights of Man formed the basis of the programme. The position of Brenner and his followers was embodied in the observation that the capitalist economic order perpetuated the inequalities and dependence of the employees. On the other hand, it was stipulated that the prime objective of the trade union movement was to work towards the development of the social constitutional State and the democratization of society. State planning in the economy and nationalization were not overlooked, but were included in a long list of instruments to promote economic growth and to guarantee full employment and the employees' share in the increase in prosperity. Much interest was devoted to the State's financial and fiscal policy. Since this basic programme attempted to reconcile two very diverse options, these economic proposals were far from consistent. Only one principle was clearly put forward - that of the expansion of full, joint *Mitbestimmung* to the entire industry.

The 1963 programme was not entirely characterized by its vague economic policy, even if both ideological tendencies within the DGB did talk of a victory for their option. Rather, the trade union movement defined its own role in very broad social terms. The trade union movement promoted the independence and freedom of the employee at every level. It worked hard for peace and was against nuclear weapons. It worked towards the granting of equal rights to women and called upon young people to join the trade union. Through improved vocational training, a policy of continuing education and the judicious use of modern technology, it wanted to improve the position of workers in the economy. It advocated social housing construction as well as the democratization of culture and education. In short, the trade union movement wanted to do more than just improve the employees' material situation. It explicitly championed their further integration into society. These social and cultural dimensions were further embodied in a new action programme, which was proposed in 1965. In addition to the payment of a 'thirteenth month' in wages and a minimum of four weeks' holiday, it included demands such as adequate legal protection for tenants and paid study leave.

The choice of a broad social position which was adopted by the DGB was also reflected in its opposition to the *Notstandsgesetze* (emergency laws) - a package of measures designed to increase the powers of the government in times of serious domestic unrest. In 1960 the government submitted a proposal in this respect to change the constitution, but this was immediately rejected by the trade union movement. During the 1960s the topic dominated public debate and the DGB revealed itself generally opposed to it. The trade union continued to reinforce its position as a broad-based social movement, even though a restricted package of emergency measures was eventually approved by the government in 1968. Nonetheless, no unity could be achieved within the DGB on this matter. A moderate wing with a more pragmatic attitude counterbalanced the views of IG Metall and other hard-line trade unions, which unconditionally rejected the *Notstandsgesetze*.

Yet, the redefinition of the DGB's ideological profile along *Gegenmacht / Ordnungsfaktor* lines must also be qualified. When gender issues are taken into account, an entirely different picture emerges. The *Wirtschaftswunder* was exclusively happening to men (DGB, 1993; Buchholz-Will, 1995). Immediately after the war, German women were directed towards their moral obligation to do their bit for reconstruction. In December 1945, approximately 3 million women were in employment (30.3 per cent of the workforce). By September 1948 this figure had risen to 3.8 million (28.5 per cent), but male employment increased proportionately much more rapidly. The latter was the forerunner of a reconfirmation of the traditional division of tasks between men and women. Once the economy was on its feet again, the employment of women outside the home was called into question, even by female trade union officers. The most important subject of trade union policy regarding women in the 1950s and 1960s was therefore the protection of the woman as mother and core of the family, exemplified in cookery and cosmetics courses, tips for home decoration and fashion shows.

Nevertheless, right from the start the DGB also championed the equal treatment of men and women (DGB, 1993; Leminsky and Otto, 1974, pp. 365-381). The motto of equal pay for equal work was permanently etched into its programmes. However, in practice in the first half of the 1950s collective labour agreements with wage reduction clauses were still being concluded by predominantly male joint committees. The DGB had a separate department for women and, from 1952 onwards, *Bundesfrauenkonferenzen* (Federal Women's Conferences) were held but, when it came to decisions, the male-dominated DGB always had the last word. The men proved to be protective and condescending towards the women or ignored their complaints. Women were led to believe that whether or not their demands would be heard depended on their own contribution. In terms of content, too, women's work remained subordinate to the logic of the male-dominated labour market. It was thus frankly claimed that women first had to be properly trained and educated before they could fully participate in working life. Not until the *Programm für Arbeitnehmerinnen* (Female Workers' Programme) of 1969 was it fully acknowledged that a woman's work contributes to her personal development - in other words, that it is equal to a man's work.

Economic crisis and the limits of trade union power

By 1966 the first crisis of the postwar capitalist growth model hit the German economy. Apparently, the *Wirtschaftswunder* had its limits. Nonetheless, this observation did not lead to pessimism within the DGB, quite the contrary. Indeed, in December 1966 the SPD entered the Federal government for the first time since the Second World War, in a coalition with the CDU/CSU. The trade union movement therefore began to hope that reforms in the economy would be implemented, in accordance with its ambitions. The new government did indeed follow a Keynesian policy, which closely matched what the DGB had asked for in 1963. Within the framework of government economic planning, reference figures could be compiled for wage development which could serve as a framework for collective bargaining.

The government even went a step further. It set up the *Konzertierte Aktion*, a forum for State representatives, employers and trade unions organized several times each year to discuss economic problems. This was an attempt to better integrate the trade union movement into the State. The trade unions themselves agreed to it, although they declared that on no account would they accept any infringement of the independence of collective bargaining. Although in the long term they hoped to be able to implement radical changes towards greater codetermination, via the *Konzertierte Aktion*, the DGB would soon become disillusioned. The meetings proved to be formal gatherings involving no discussion whatsoever. In 1977 the DGB was to leave the *Konzertierte Aktion*, which immediately signalled the end of this form of corporatist consultation.

The formation of an SPD/FDP government in 1969 put the trade union in a more optimistic mood about the possibility of turning policy in the desired direction. Sound progress was made too. The welfare state was further expanded, with a pension reform, a more flexible retirement age and the legal harmonization of sickness benefits for blue collar and white collar workers. The *Arbeitsförderungsgesetz* (Labour Promotion Law) of 25 June 1969 provided an active labour market policy via improved vocational training and employment agencies. However, things went awry with the DGB's oldest theme, *Mitbestimmung*. The DGB stuck to its demand for joint worker representation in the *Aufsichtsräte* of all large companies, but was ultimately not rewarded in the *Mitbestimmungsgesetz* of 1976 (Thum, 1991; Müller, 1991). The 1972 *Betriebsverfassungsgesetz* was also a disappointment to the trade unions. Although they acquired more rights under the new law, the 1952 stipulation remained in force that the members of the works council could not strike (*Friedenspflicht* - obligation to keep the peace) and could not make any information public which could harm the company (*Schweigepflicht* - obligation to maintain secrecy). In other words, the weak institutional position of the German trade unions in the company itself was yet again perpetuated.

Nevertheless, optimism was running high within the trade union movement during the first half of the 1970s. Results were after all not bad. Sharp wage increases were exacted, partly as a result of increased strike activity after 1969. The metalworkers strike in Baden-Württemberg set an example. *Vertrauensleute* in the companies, on the other hand, pleaded for a more combative trade union style and challenged the position of the *Betriebsrat*, without, however, succeeding in altering the dual system. Many qualitative demands from the previous decade were met via collective agreements, including the 40-hour week in the industry and the tirteenth month pay (in 1971). The key to trade union policy during these years was the theme of the 'quality of life', launched by IG Metall in 1972. In the light of the introduction of new technologies, the effects of them on employees were critically evaluated by the trade unions, especially in terms of aspects such as enhanced safety at work, a reduction in working hours, longer holidays, better pension schemes and other social benefits. In the 1972 DGB action programme, the protection of the environment was mentioned for the first time.[6] At the time, this theme still followed on first and foremost from criticism by IG Metall of the capitalist growth economy.

In the late 1960s and the first half of the 1970s the DGB had considerably enhanced its influence at social and political level. This was for a large part due to the successful incorporation of the various ideological tendencies which had shaped the labour movement since the mid-

1950s. In particular Heinz Oskar Vetter, the new President of the DGB after 1969 (until 1982), played an important role in reconciling the *Gegenmacht* and *Ordnungsfaktor* options in the DGB. He did this by launching a raft of proposals and convening congresses on special topics such as the 'humanization of labour' or environment protection. Moreover, the lifting of the ban on the communist party in 1968 signalled the waning of Cold War anti-communism, although the DGB unions would retain a critical distance form political communism. The employers, on the other hand, launched an ideological offensive against the 'trade union state' via court cases and pamphlets. This campaign was supported by the FDP and, to a lesser extent, the CDU and CSU. The DGB was accused of having expanded its position of power to such an extent that it threatened the smooth operation of democracy. In this way, the privileged collaboration between the DGB and the SPD was exposed as well. In 1978/79 Franz Josef Strauss from the CSU would even propose to form party political groups in the DGB unions or, otherwise, to strengthen the CGB (Deppe, Hensche, Jansen and Rossmann, 1980). Both proposals were firmly rejected by the DGB. In contrast with the allegations, however, tensions rose between the DGB and the social democratic party, particularly once the SPD/FDP government led by chancellor Helmut Schmidt began to pursue an austerity policy.

The economic crisis of the mid-1970s made the DGB face up to the limits of its own influential position within the West German establishment. Indeed, the economic recession brought to an end a period during which high wage increases could be exacted. Structural problems in the shipbuilding industry and the steel and textile sectors pointed to deep-seated changes in the labour market. High unemployment was to became the main bugbear of the trade union movement. Initially, the movement counted primarily on the government's regional and sectoral investment policy to create new jobs.[7] In this respect, the DGB advocated investment which would lead to a new growth model and which would be aimed at energy-saving projects, social housing construction, public transport, environmental protection, training and the promotion of research and technology. The social democratic government did implement this type of investment programme between 1977 and 1981, but when the CDU/CSU/FDP government came to power in 1982, this policy was abandoned (Tofaute, 1993). The trade union movement was from then on forced to rely on its own strength.

Collective bargaining became increasingly decentralized in the course of the 1970s and 1980s, although the trade union federations continued to define the agenda. Moreover, under pressure from the economic crisis, the traditional central agreements on wage increases linked to an increase in productivity had to be abandoned. Other bargaining themes gained prominence, in particular job preservation and a reduction in working hours (to combat unemployment). The 'right to work' became a key concept (Streeck, 1984; Hegner and Landenberger, 1988). Two models to reduce working hours were put forward in the DGB. Trade unions such as IG Metall and the left-wing IG Druck und Papier defended the 35-hour week from 1977 onwards. Their belief was that the reduced volume of available work had to be redistributed among all workers to neutralize the increasing inequality between the employed and the unemployed. The Gewerkschaft Nahrung-Genuss-Gaststätten, the Gewerkschaft Textil-Bekleidung, the IG Chemie-Papier-Keramik, the IG Bau-Steine-Erden and the IG Bergbau und Energie, on the other hand, were in favour of pre-pension schemes (*Tarifrente*) as a way of redistributing labour.

In the revitalized action programme of the umbrella DGB published in 1979, the 35-hour week was included as a demand. The employers, for their part, were strongly opposed to the 35-hour working week and have fought the principle ever since, while showing more interest in pre-pension arrangements. The 38.5-hour working week with variable individual working hours was only introduced in the metalworking and paper industries in 1984, after the longest strike in German postwar history. In subsequent years, the working week was further reduced in the metalworking sector and the principle was also discussed and introduced in other sectors. It became increasingly more difficult, however, to call for reduced working hours with full wage compensation. In February 1995 the DGB officially agreed, for the first time, to negotiate a reduction in working hours with a partial loss of earnings. In August 1995, a two year old 'model' agreement at Volkswagen on the 28.8-hour (or four days) working week turned out to have been a Pyrrhic victory, as drastic job losses were announced by the management.

In return for collective agreements on the reduction of working time, often obtained as a result of highly publicized strikes, the trade unions agreed to flexible, company-adapted formulas of the reduction in working hours and a more flexible labour market. This deregulation of the labour market was formalized in the *Beschäftigungsförderungsgesetz* (Employment Promotion Law) of 1985. However, the most important concession was that since 1990 18 per cent of all employees in a company have had the right to retain their 40-hour working week on a voluntary and individual basis. This was a step closer to an individualization of industrial relations. Previously, 'quality control groups' and the idea of *Mitbestimmung am Arbeitsplatz* (codetermination in the workplace) had gained importance in the companies. Considering that increased (individual) freedom of employees to determine their working conditions and working hours could respond to their personal expectations, the DGB has taken seriously the idea of worker *Zeitsouveränität* (time sovereignty) since the mid-1980s.

In the mean time, in 1979 the DGB had put forward a new action programme and, in 1981, a new basic programme (Pfromm, 1982; Markovits, 1986, pp. 152-157; Müller-Jentsch, 1990; Brunner, 1989). Essentially, the earlier programmes were retained and further expanded, although their reformulation and reorganization pointed to more fundamental changes taking place in the eonomic and social context. The topic of job security unquestioningly dominated the agenda. The labour factor was said to be crucial to the expansion of a satisfactory social life. From this point of view, issues such as environment protection, housing, social security, training and cultural development were slotted into the trade union programme. Economic growth as such was not advocated, rather qualitative growth. The request for *Mitbestimmung* at all levels and in all fields of both labour and leisure activities ran like a thread through the new basic programme, but the term was so generally used as a synonym for the 'right to participation' that it seemed to lose its mobilizing force. Finally, the pluralist DGB explicitly ruled out any ideology which 'would misuse the unions for its own ends'. This was aimed at both right-wing and left-wing extremists. The DKP (Deutsche Kommunistische Partei) in particular was prevented from pursuing its own policy within the DGB. Communist and other left-wing trade unionists would remain active in the DGB, however, especially in the IG Druck und Papier.

In search of a new identity ?

In its 1963 basic programme the DGB had defended the integration of the trade union movement in a socially corrected market economy. Consequently, the codification and regulation of industrial relations had been widely accepted by the unions. Their traditional approach to collective action can be characterized as 'institutionalized class conflict'. Strike threats and strikes themselves take place on the basis of demands which are accurately in tune with economic reality. Before the trade unions take action, they have carefully weighed up how far they can go without undermining the competitive position of the companies. Despite mass unemployment, events in the 1970s and 1980s showed that the 'German model' of regulated industrial relations was still successful for employees and employers alike. Yet, changes to the model became inevitable. In the 1980s trade union action extended beyond the traditional large-scale coercive strike to include token strikes (*Warnstreik*), while the general level of mobilization accompanying wage negotiations rose. Until the beginning of the 1970s, collective bargaining had served primarily to exact higher wages and to demand more jobs. Since then, qualitative requirements have been first and foremost on the agenda, relating to the 'humanization' of labour, although it must also be stressed that there have been few concrete results in that respect. As the labour market deteriorated over the course of the 1970s and 1980s, the trade union movement was forced on to the offensive. The emphasis shifted to the preservation of existing jobs and the creation of new jobs via the redistribution of labour and a shorter working week.

Also with respect to ideology serious shifts were taking place in the 1980s. IG Chemie-Papier-Keramik, the third largest trade union within the DGB, developed from its *Gegenmacht* position during the 1950s/1960s to an *Ordnungsfaktor* position during the 1980s/1990s. The public services trade union, on the other hand, the Gewerkschaft Öffentliche Dienste Transport und Verkehr has developed more a *Gegenmacht* attitude since the 1980s. The traditional lines of ideological division in the DGB also led to diverging future scenarios with respect to the prevention of social dumping at European level (Markovits and Otto, 1991; Däubler and Lecher, 1991; Lecher and Platzer, 1994). From the early 1980s IG Metall has been advocating more European cooperation between national trade union movements, but on condition that they aim for a more equal distribution of wealth. To achieve this, the metalworkers' trade union believes that increased investment must be made in weak member states such as Portugal, Greece and Ireland, and in the Third World. The *Ordnungsfaktor* unions, on the other hand, are enthusiastic advocates of an integrated European market, aimed at harmonizing employment conditions and forms of worker participation. In order to protect their own workers from competition from low-wage countries, they urge more training programmes so that Germany can remain strong as a result of its well-qualified labour force. These scenarios have remained largely fictional, however, and the European unification has been a marginal issue in the DGB, mainly because of the dominant role of Germany in the European Union (Hoffmann, 1995).

Nonetheless, other ideological accents have also been stressed within the DGB, which only partially reflect the aforementioned dichotomy. Since the 1980s a major debate has been underway within the DGB about the central part played by work in the social lives of workers. In 1988, when even the *Ordnungsfaktor* trade unions within the DGB had fully backed the demand for a reduction in working hours, Oskar Lafontaine, the social democratic prime minister from Saarland, launched a proposal against giving civil servants wage compensation for a reduction in working hours (Swenson, 1992). The entire DGB reacted negatively and, by defending better-paid workers, emphasized its attachment to the traditional central role of paid employment for its members. Even though this reaction was largely the consequence of IG Metall's desire to maintain its dominant position within the DGB, the call within the trade union movement for action in more areas than just that of employment conditions persisted (Lattard, 1992, p. 130). This entire episode also revealed that the DGB was not afraid of pursuing its own course with respect to the social democratic party.

Even more remarkable in ideological terms was the gradual incorporation of topics supplied by the green movement, feminism and the new social movements (*Bürgerinitiativen*) into the DGB programming and operations. As far as ecological themes are concerned, since the 1980s the trade union movement has taken many initiatives.[8] In the 1970s it was still afraid that the emphasis on ecological effects would have a negative impact on unemployment. However, in the 1980s, when studies appeared which pointed to the favourable effects on employment of better environmental protection, the DGB let go of its reticence. It began to advocate ecologically sound businesses and ecologically sound economic growth. IG Chemie-Papier-Keramik is thus the party requesting company rulings relating to ecological production, waste disposal and transport of hazardous goods. The fact that a *Ordnungsfaktor* trade union is playing a pioneering role in this case is probably to do with defending this branch of industry with respect to the outside world. IG Metall has already been actively trying for many years to remove substances harmful to the environment and to health from the production process in as far as possible. In this way, the trade union is breathing new life into its age-old demand for codetermination, under the term *Produktmitbestimmung* (product codetermination). Smaller trade unions, such as the Gewerkschaft Nahrung-Genuss-Gaststätten (NGG) or IG Druck und Papier try to implement quality control and ecological awareness within the companies.

Only since the end of the 1980s, however, the DGB has emphasized wholeheartedly the future importance of environmental protection. Whereas ecological concerns were previously quickly pushed on to a back burner as soon as employment was under threat, now the arguments were more or less reversed. Sustained employment, it is said, can now only be created if investment is put into means of production which do not waste energy or raw materials. Otherwise, the waste-weary economy runs the risk of destroying itself in the long term.[9] All this means that the German trade unions have sought their own path as far as the environmental question is concerned, rather than following the Green Party. However, there is no coherent DGB policy at this level. According to a recent study, the debate on nuclear energy which has been going on since the mid-1970s demonstrates that the ideological discussions within the DGB are all but at a standstill (Jahn, 1993). Trade unions such as IG Metall, the Gewerkschaft Handel, Banken und Versicherungen, IG Medien and, to a lesser extent, the Gewerkschaft Öffentliche Dienste, Transport und Verkehr are openly advocating an alternative economic policy and denouncing the use of nuclear energy. *Ordnungsfaktor* trade unions such as IG Chemie and IG Bergbau und Energie, on the other hand, believe nuclear energy is indispensable to sustained economic growth.

From 1969 onwards, women's demands gained in importance in the DGB (DGB, 1993; Buchholz-Will, 1995). An expansion of vocational training for women was advocated, together with part-time work to give women the opportunity to combine their tasks of housewife and wage-earner. Women also asked for maternity leave, higher child benefits, better pensions and more socio-educational facilities, such as creches and nursery schools. At the 1982 DGB congress, a resolution was adopted in favour of the abolition of the separate treatment of spouses in fiscal legislation, which encouraged a partner, usually the woman, not to work. Moreover, voices were raised in favour of more women trade union executives, since despite their increasing share of membership, they remained under-represented in union institutions and committees. Positive action had to be taken in companies to correct the structural prejudice against women. In 1990, at the 14th congress of the DGB, it was observed that the achievement of all these objectives still left a great deal to be desired (Naumann, 1992; von Camen, 1993). New, specific demands were put forward, including those related to leave to look after sick children and relatives, parental leave or working hours adapted to suit the needs of parents. For the first time, it was decided to include positive action in favour of women on the list of subjects for collective bargaining.

As far as immigrant workers are concerned, the picture is not currently a very positive one. In 1971, the DGB officially decided that foreign employees had the right to equal treatment (Leminsky and Otto, 1974, pp. 351-364). However, a genuine DGB immigration policy did not emerge until the 1980s, chiefly as a reaction to the conservative restriction policy. The DGB now demanded the right of residence and municipal voting rights for immigrants and advocated measures especially to integrate young foreign workers into the labour market. The fact that immigrant workers were additionally motivated to take collective action, for example during the round of negotiations on the 35-hour working week in 1984, undoubtedly contributed to these proposals attracting a great deal of sympathy, including among the trade union public. However, in terms of achievements, trade union immigration policy still leaves much to be desired (Kühne, Öztürk and West, 1994; Kühne, 1992). Immigrants are under-represented in both trade union structures and in works councils. If a company cuts down on staff, immigrants are often the first victims, often without opposition from the works council. Initiatives to promote further training for immigrants are virtually non-existent. Moreover, the DGB takes scarcely any action against legal restrictions on immigration. The trade union has, however, always strongly condemned the rise of neo-fascism and violence against immigrants. The latter was incidentally also an argument for continuing to exclude all forms of political extremism, of whatever colour.[10]

At the end of the 1980s, as a result of a deep financial crisis which shook the very foundations of the organization, the DGB embarked on a reform debate (Hoffmann, 1995; Leif, Klein and Legrand, 1993; Uellenberg-van Dawen, 1994). Initially, structural changes and mergers were planned and implemented. Even at the 1994 congress, which was to hold an initial interim evaluation of the reform process, the merger question attracted almost all the attention so that no thorough debate could take place for the time being. The aim of the mergers is to respond to the changes on the labour market. Thus in 1989 a new media trade union was formed, IG Medien (the former IG Druck und Papier, plus employees from the arts and journalism). IG Chemie-Papier-Keramik, IG Bergbau und Energie and the Gewerkschaft Leder formally merged in 1995. The second largest DGB trade union, the Gewerkschaft Öffentliche Dienste, Transport und Verkehr (ÖTV) wants to coordinate its negotiation policy more closely with the independent DAB white collar union, although without holding joint negotiations.

The ultimate goal of the reform process is however much more ambitious, as the DGB was increasingly accused of lacking in ideas and vision. IG Metall set the spark to the flame with a series of 'congresses for the future' starting in 1988. The trade union movement wanted to modernize its ideology against the background of the approaching new millennium. The latter was clearly expressed when IG Metall launched its *Tarifreform 2000*.[11] However, a notable paradox is concealed behind that explicit objective. Specifically, the DGB is attempting to secure its national umbrella role as coordinator of the German trade union movement, while it is faced with a serious financial crisis, which leads to cuts in expenditure and deep cuts in the number of staff. In other words, the DGB seems to be using the prospect of the magic year 2000 as a cover-up to foster the re-establishment of its postwar role as reconciler of the different ideological tendencies within the trade union movement. As yet there were no signs, however, that the unions wanted to reinforce the federation. Moreover, the reform debate has been strongly criticized by both left-wingers looking for more revolutionary perspectives and conservative trade unionists who want to return to the 'core' issues of bargaining policies (Hoffmann, 1995, p. 112).

The elucidation of a new, global trade union ideology is chiefly driven by the trade union executives and goes hand in hand with the mobilization of intellectuals via the *Wirtschafts- und Sozialwissenschaftliches Institut* (WSI) of the DGB, the *Hans-Böckler-Stiftung* (HBS), the *Gewerkschaftliche Monatshefte* and a series of publications by the trade union publishers, Bund-Verlag (Hoffmann a.o., 1993; Leif, Klein and Legrand, 1993; Meyer, 1994: Markovits and Hess, 1991).[12] At first sight, this would seem to confirm the well-worn stereotype that ideologies are products of the mind and are therefore empty boxes should it come to social action. However, the DGB knows all too well that the proposed ideas can only prove their substance if they become the guiding principle of trade union action. In this sense, the entire reform debate has acquired its own agenda which stipulates that a special programme congress will be held in 1996 and that a final decision on the structural reforms will be taken in 1998. Moreover, the reform debate was given a special boost by the fall of the Wall in 1989. After all, the integration of former East Germany into the Federal Republic presented the DGB with even greater challenges. In terms of content, the DGB is advancing a *neue Politik* (new policy) vis-à-vis business logic, which is based on ecological imperatives for producer and consumer and which wants to neutralize gender differences and new social inequalities.

The fall of the Wall

The reunification of German rudely interrupted the process of ideological remodelling within the DGB. Aspects such as ecology, working hours and female and immigrant jobs were suddenly pushed into second place. Still, the DGB was slow to react to the events (Jander and Voss, 1991; Hege, 1991). It waited and had virtually no contacts with the civilian movement, which was behind the fall of the communist regime. The only important decision which the DGB took, after much hesitation, was not to reform the former state trade union in the DDR, the FDGB (Freier Deutscher Gewerkschaftsbund), from the inside. Over the 1980s, the DGB had attached growing importance to good relations with the FDGB, but once the change of power was completed, it seemed at the least imprudent to strive for continuity with the communist trade union.[13] On 30 September 1990 the FDGB was formally disbanded.

The DGB then transplanted its own organizational structures and West German collective bargaining arrangements into the eastern *Bundesländer* (Kittner, 1994). Since that took place without much participation, this reconstruction was not always as successful or undiscussed. For example the Gewerkschaft Öffentliche Dienste, Transport und Verkehr, transplanted to the east, attempted to clean up its act with a radical defence of existing jobs but, in so doing, undertook to defend the position of the former bureaucrats of the Democratic Republic. The expansion of an umbrella federation in the east was hindered because the trade unions refused to release financial resources. In short, we are still a long way from a unique DGB strategy for the integration of the eastern *Länder*. Incidentally, the *Gegenmacht* trade unions within the DGB chiefly emphasized the difficulties experienced by East German workers in adjusting to the capitalist system after the *Wende*. The *Ordnungsfaktor* trade unions, on the other hand, stressed more the opportunities that were gained (Martens, 1994). Prospects for the DGB in the eastern *Länder* are not very bright, however, since union density rates there have fallen from 60.2 per cent in 1991 to 43.1 per cent in 1994.

One point on which the DGB did agree was to achieve wage equality between East and West as soon as possible (Sadowski, Schneider and Wagner, 1994; Jacobi, Keller and Müller-Jentsch, 1992, pp. 252-253; Schroeder, 1994)). An agreement was reached on this matter in the metalworking and electricity sectors in 1991, which would bring about equality by 1994. In the spring of 1993, however, this agreement was revoked by the employers and replaced by a new agreement with 1996 as its target date and the additional clause that wage reduction (with the consent of the trade union) is not ruled out. It is clear from this that it is by no means certain that the trade unions of the DGB will succeed in acquiring the same authority in the eastern *Bundesländer*, in the process of collective bargaining, as they have enjoyed in the West for decades. An important consequence of the difficulties in implementing wage equality via collective agreements was that also in West Germany employers started to plead for more exception and opening clauses to adapt the sectoral agreements to specific company needs.

Moreover, not all the effects of the equality policy are wholly favourable. For example, since reunification many women have been forced out of the labour market and chiefly out of qualified jobs in the eastern *Bundesländer*. Indeed, the economic restructuration is hitting women much harder than men (Gensior, 1995). In December 1992 the unemployment rate in the East was 9.7 per cent for men and 18.6 per cent among women. Moreover, former East German measures relating to the compatibility of professional and family life have been scrapped. In this way, the inequality between men and women on the labour market has also been transferred from West to East.[14] Or, in other words, the incorporation of female demands in the DGB proved not that deep-rooted after all.

Through the reunification the DGB is again confronted with 'core' issues such as wage demands and the protection of employment. It proves difficult to reconcile these demands with the 'qualitative' issues which the federation has been incorporating in its policies and practices since more than a decade: a redistribution of the balance between working hours and free time; equal opportunities for men and women; an industrial policy which takes ecological effects into consideration. At the level of ideological discourse, however, the challenge of the *Einigungsprozess* has given the DGB a new opportunity to stress the indispensable role of the unions in preventing social disaster at times of radical economic change.[15]

Table 5.1
Membership and density rate of the DGB, 1950-1994

	Total DGB membership	Percentage of women in the DGB	Union density rate
1950	5,449,990	16.4%	37.9%
1955	6,104,872	17.2%	34.6%
1960	6,378,820	17.1%	31.8%
1965	6,574,491	15.7%	30.4%
1970	6,712,547	15.3%	30.3%
1975	7,364,912	17.8%	33.6%
1980	7,882,527	20.3%	34.3%
1985	7,719,468	22.1%	34.8%
1990	7,937,923	24.4%	31.2%
1991*	11,800,413	33.0%	35.7%
1994	9,774,663		31.2%

* Since 1991 figures apply to Eastern and Western *Ländern* together.

Source: Hemmer and Schmitz, 1990, p. 463; DGB, 1993, p. 87; the figures for 1994 are provisional and come from the DGB Bundesvorstand.

Notes

1. *IDS European Report*, no. 394, October 1994. I wish to thank Patrick Pasture and Jozef Mampuys for their comments on a first draft of this chapter.
2. Overviews in Schneider, 1991; Grebing, 1985; Schuster, 1985; Borsdorf, 1987; Armingeon, 1988; Hemmer and Schmitz, 1990.
3. During the congress on the DGB's history on 12 and 13 October 1979 the question of whether the trade union movement could not have saved itself by playing a more active role in the Weimar regime was hotly debated; see Vetter, 1980 and Müller-Jentsch, 1990, pp. 390-391.
4. *Protokoll Gründungskongress des Deutschen Gewerkschaftsbundes, München 12-14 Oktober 1949*, Bund, Köln, 1950, p. 199 (the encyclicals) and pp. 337-338 (the right to work and equal pay for women). Overviews of the DGB's history in Schuster, 1985; Schneider, 1991; Markovits, 1986; Deppe, Fülberth and Harrer, 1978; Thelen, 1991; Armingeon, 1988; Hemmer and Schmitz, 1990.
5. *Grundsatzprogramm des Deutschen Gewerkschaftsbundes*, DGB, Düsseldorf, 1963.
6. The 1972 action programme in the *Protokoll des 9. Ordentlichen Bundeskongresses, Berlin 25. bis 30. Juni 1972*, DGB, Düsseldorf, 1972; H.O. Vetter (ed.), *Humanisierung der Arbeit als gesellschaftspolitische und gewerkschaftliche Aufgabe: Prokoll der*

DGB-Konferenz vom 16. und 17. Mai 1974 in München, Europäische Verlagsanstalt, Frankfurt am Main, 1974.
7. *Vorschläge des DGB zur Wiederherstellung der Vollbeschäftigung*, DGB, Düsseldorf, 1977.
8. See, for example, 12. *Ordentlicher Bundeskongress Berlin 16.-22.5.82. Parlament der Arbeit. DGB. Anträge*, DGB, Düsseldorf, 1982, A 33-34; DGB (ed.), *Umweltschutz und qualitatives Wachstum. Bekämpfung der Arbeitslosigkeit und Beschleunigung des qualitativen Wachstums durch mehr Umweltschutz*, DGB, Düsseldorf, 1985; Schneider, 1986; Hildebrandt and Schmidt, 1991.
9. See, for example, IG Metall (ed.), *Umweltschutz zwischen Reparatur und realer Utopie. Wege aus der Bedrohung*, Köln, 1988; IG Metall (ed.), *Auto, Umwelt und Verkehr. Umsteuern, bevor es zu spät ist !*, IG Metall, Frankfurt am Main, 1990.
10. *12. Ordentlicher Bundeskongress Berlin 16.-22.5.82. Parlament der Arbeit. Anträge*, DGB, Düsseldorf, 1982, A 43.
11. IG Metall (ed.), *Tarifreform 2000. Ein Gestaltungsrahmen für die Industriearbeit der Zukunft. Diskussionsvorschläge für wichtige tarifpolitische Handlungsfelder*, IG Metall, Frankfurt am Main, 1991.
12. The view from the employers' research institute in Neidenhoff and Wilke, 1993.
13. *Herausforderung Ostdeutschland*, special issue of the *Gewerkschaftliche Monatshefte*, vol. 44, no. 1, 1993.
14. *Ein Schritt vorwärts - zwei Schritte zurück ? Gleichberechtigungspolitik in Ost und West*, special issue of the *WSI Mitteilungen*, vol. 45, no. 4, 1992.
15. DGB Bundesvorstand Grundsatzabteilung (ed.), *Thesen zur programmatischen Debatte im DGB: Leitbilder zur sozialen Einheit Deutschlands*, DGB, Düsseldorf, April 1995.

References

Armingeon, K. (1988), *Die Entwicklung der westdeutschen Gewerkschaften, 1950-1985*, Campus, Frankfurt/New York.

Borsdorf, U. (ed.) (1987), *Geschichte der Deutschen Gewerkschaften. Von den Anfängen bis 1945*, Bund, Köln.

Brunner, G. (1989), *Grundwerte als Fundament der pluralistischen Gesellschaft: eine Untersuchung der Positionen von Kirchen, Parteien und Gewerkschaften in der Bundesrepublik Deutschland*, Herder, Freiburg.

Buchholz-Will, W. (1995), 'Wann wird aus diesem Traum Wirklichkeit ? Die gewerkschaftliche Frauenarbeit in der Bundesrepublik Deutschland', in Hervé, F. (ed.), *Geschichte der deutschen Frauenbewegung*, 5th ed., PapyRossa, Köln.

Däubler, W. and Lecher, W. (eds.) (1991), *Die Gewerkschaften in den 12 EG-Ländern. Europäische Integration und Gewerkschaftsbewegung*, Bund, Köln.

Deppe, F. a.o. (1969), *Kritik der Mitbestimmung: Partnerschaft oder Klassenkampf ?*, Suhrkamp, Frankfurt.

Deppe, F., Fülberth, G. and Harrer, J. (eds.) (1978), *Geschichte der deutschen Gewerkschaftsbewegung*, 2nd. ed., Pahl-Rugenstein, Köln.

Deppe, F., Hensche, D., Jansen, M. and Rossmann, W. (1980), *Strauss und die Gewerkschaften. Texte, Materialien, Dokumente*, Bund, Köln.

DGB (ed.) (1993), *"Da haben wir uns alle schrecklich geirrt ...". Die Geschichte der gewerkschaftlichen Frauenarbeit im Deutschen Gewerkschaftsbund von 1945 bis 1960*, Centaurus, Pfaffenweiler.
Fleck, H.-G. (1994), *Sozialliberalismus und Gewerkschaftsbewegung. Die Hirsch-Dunckerschen Gewerkvereine 1868-1914*, Schriftenreihe der Otto Brenner Stiftung 56, Bund, Köln.
Fuerstenberg, F. (1993), 'Industrial relations in Germany', in Bamber, G.J. and Lansbury, R.D. (eds.), *International and Comparative Industrial Relations. A Study of Industrialised Market Economies*, Allen & Unwin, St. Leonards (Australia), pp. 175-196.
Gensior, S. (ed.) (1995), *Vergesellschaftung und Frauenerwerbsarbeit. Ost-West-Vergleiche*, Sigma, Berlin.
Grebing, H. (1985), *The History of the German Labour Movement: A Survey*, Berg, Leamington Spa.
Halberstadt, G. (1991), *Die Angestellten und ihre Gewerkschaft. Stationen einer bewegten Geschichte*, Rudolf Haufe, Freiburg.
Hege, A. (1991), 'Un syndicalisme unique pour deux systèmes sociaux ? Enjeux et perspectives de l'unification syndicale en Allemagne', *Travail et emploi*, vol. 50, no. 4, pp. 67-74.
Hege, A. (1994), 'Allemagne: quelle réforme pour le DGB?', in IRES. *Chronique internationale*, vol. 29, pp. 19-23.
Hegner, F. and Landenberger, M. (1988), *Arbeitszeit, Arbeitsmarkt und soziale Sicherung: ein Rückblick auf die Arbeitszeitdiskussion in der Bundesrepublik Deutschland nach 1950*, Beiträge zur Sozialwissenschaftlichen Forschung 108, Westdeutscher Verlag, Opladen.
Hemmer, H.-O. and Schmitz, K.T. (eds.) (1990), *Geschichte der Gewerkschaften in der Bundesrepublik Deutschland. Von den Anfängen bis heute*, Bund, Köln.
Hildebrandt, E. and Schmidt, E. (1991), 'Ökologie und Ökonomie: ein neues Spannungsfeld der industriellen Beziehungen', in Müller-Jentsch, W. (ed.), *Konfliktpartnerschaft. Akteure und Institutionen der industriellen Beziehungen*, Rainer Hampp, München-Mering, pp. 275-299
Hoffmann, J. a.o. (eds.) (1993), *Jenseits der Beschlusslage. Gewerkschaft als Zukunftswerkstatt*, 2nd. ed., HBS/Bund, Köln.
Hoffmann, J. (1995), 'Trade union reform in Germany: some analytical and critical remarks concerning the current debate', *Transfer. European Review of Labour and Research*, vol. 1, no. 1, pp. 98-113
Jacobi, O., Keller, B. and Müller-Jentsch, W. (1992), 'Germany: Codetermining the future?', in Ferner, A. and Hyman, R. (eds.), *Industrial Relations in the New Europe*, Blackwell, Oxford, pp. 218-269.
Jahn, D. (1993), *New Politics in Trade Unions. Applying Organizational Theory to the Ecological Discourse on Nuclear Energy in Sweden and Germany*, Dartmouth, Aldershot.
Jander, M. and Voss, Th. (1991), 'Mangel an Perspektiven. Die bundesdeutschen Gewerkschaften im Vereinigungsprozess', in Gatzmaga, D., Voss, Th. and Westermann, K. (eds.), *Auferstehen aus Ruinen. Arbeitswelt und Gewerkschaften in der früheren DDR*, Schüren, Marburg, pp. 147-155.
Keller, B. (1983), *Arbeitsbeziehungen im öffentlichen Dienst. Tarifpolitik der Gewerkschaften und Interessenpolitik der Beamtenverbände*, Campus, Frankfurt.
Kittner, M. (ed.) (1994), *Gewerkschaften heute. Jahrbuch für Arbeitnehmerfragen 1994*, Bund, Köln.

Kühne, P. (1992), 'Gewerkschaftliche Ausländerpolitik - diesseits der Beschlusslage', *Die Mitbestimmung*, vol. 38, nos. 8-9, pp. 49-53.

Kühne, P., Öztürk, N. and West, K.-W. (eds.) (1994), *Gewerkschaften und Einwanderung. Eine kritische Zwischenbalanz*, Bund, Köln.

Lane, C. (1994), 'Industrial order and the transformation of industrial relations: Britain, Germany and France compared', in Hyman, R. and Ferner, A. (eds.), *New Frontiers in European Industrial Relations*, Blackwell, Oxford, pp. 167-195.

Langkau, J., Matthöfer, H. and Schneider, M. (eds.)(1994), *SPD und Gewerkschaften. Band 1: Zur Geschichte eines Bündnisses. Band 2: Ein notwendiges Bündnis*, Dietz, Bonn.

Lattard, A. (1992), 'Le syndicalisme des années 80; à la recherche d'une nouvelle identité', *Revue d'Allemagne et des pays de langue allemande*, vol. 24, no. 1, pp. 123-131.

Lecher, W. and Platzer, H.-W. (eds.) (1994), *Europäische Union - Europäische Arbeitsbeziehungen ? Nationale Voraussetzungen und internationaler Rahmen*, Bund, Köln.

Leif, T., Klein, A. and Legrand, H.-J. (eds.) (1993), *Reform des DGB. Herausforderungen, Aufbruchspläne und Modernisierungskonzepte*, Bund, Köln.

Leminsky, G. and Otto, B. (1974), *Politik und Programmatik des Deutschen Gewerkschaftsbundes*, Bund, Köln.

MacShane, D. (1992), *International Labour and the Origins of the Cold War*, Clarendon Press, Oxford.

Markovits, A.S. (1986), *The Politics of West German Trade Unions. Strategies of Class and Interest Representation in Growth and Crisis*, Cambridge U.P., Cambridge.

Markovits, A.S. and Hess, A. (1991), 'Intellektuelle und Gewerkschaften in der Bundesrepublik (1945-1989)', *Gewerkschaftliche Monatshefte*, nos. 42-48, pp. 473-485.

Markovits, A.S. and Otto, A. (1991), 'West German labor and Europe '92', in Espina, A. (ed.), *Social Concertation, Neocorporatism and Democracy*, Ministerio de trabajo y seguridad social, Madrid, pp. 155-180.

Marks, G. (1989), *Unions in Politics. Britain, Germany, and the United States in the Nineteenth and Early Twentieth Centuries*, Princeton University Press, Princeton.

Martens, H. (1994), 'Gewerkschaftlicher Organizationsaufbau und Mitbestimmung in Ost-Deutschland - 17 Thesen', in Hoffman, R., Kluge, N., Linne, G. and Mezger, E. (eds.), *Problemstart: Politischer und sozialer Wandel in den neuen Bundesländern*, Bund, Köln, pp. 311-330.

Meyer, H.-W. (ed.) (1994), *Beiträge zur Reformdiskussion im Deutschen Gewerkschaftsbund und seinen Gewerkschaften. Band 1: Aufbrüche - Anstösse. Band 2: Sozial gerecht teilen - ökologisch umsteuern*, Bund, Köln.

Mielke, S. (ed.)(1983), *Internationales Gewerkschaftshandbuch*, Leske & Budrich, Opladen.

Mommsen, H. (1993), 'Der 20. Juli 1944 und die deutsche Arbeiterbewegung', in Schönhoven, K. and Staritz, D. (eds.), *Sozialismus und Kommunismus im Wandel. Hermann Weber zum 65. Geburtstag*, Bund, Köln, pp. 236-260.

Müller, G. (1991), *Strukturwandel und Arbeitnehmerrechte. Die wirtschaftliche Mitbestimmung in der Eisen- und Stahlindustrie 1945-1975*, Klartext, Essen.

Müller-Jentsch, W. (1990), 'Gewerkschaftliche Politik in der Wirtschaftskrise II, 1978/9 bis 1982/3', in Hemmer, H.-O. and Schmitz, K.T. (eds.), *Geschichte der Gewerkschaften*, pp. 375-412.

Müller-Jentsch, W. (1992), 'Länderanalyse Bundesrepublik Deutschland', in Grebing, H. and Meyer, T. (eds.), *Linksparteien und Gewerkschaften in Europa. Die Zukunft einer Partnerschaft*, Bund, Köln, pp. 103-117.

Naumann, B. (1992), 'Frauen in DGB-Strukturen - die unzureichende Einbindung von Fraueninteressen', *WSI Mitteilungen*, no. 4, pp. 241-249.

Neidenhoff, H.-U. and Wilke, M. (1993), *Der neue DGB. Zur Reformdiskussion in den DGB-Gewerkschaften*, Deutscher Instituts-Verlag, Köln.

Pasture, P. (1994), *Christian Trade Unionism in Europe Since 1968. Tensions Between Identity and Practice*, Avebury, Aldershot.

Pelinka, A. (1980), *Gewerkschaften im Parteienstaat. Ein Vergleich zwischen dem Deutschen und dem Österreichischen Gewerkschaftsbund*, Beiträge zur Politischen Wissenschaft 37, Duncker & Humblot, Berlin.

Pfromm, H.-A. (1982), *Das neue DGB-Grundsatzprogramm: Einführung und Kommentar*, Olzog, München.

Ritter, G.A. (ed.) (1990), *Der Aufstieg der deutschen Arbeiterbewegung. Sozialdemokratie und Freie Gewerkschaften im Parteiensystem und Sozialmilieu des Kaiserreiches*, München.

Sadowski, D., Schneider, M. and Wagner, K. (1994), 'The impact of European integration and German unification on industrial relations in Germany', *British Journal of Industrial Relations*, vol. 32, no. 4, pp. 523-537.

Scharrer, M. (1990), *Organisation und Vaterland. Gewerkschaften vor dem Ersten Weltkrieg*, Bund, Köln.

Schmidt, E. (1981), *Die verhinderte Neuordnung 1945-1952. Zur Auseinandersetzung um die Demokratisierung der Wirtschaft in den westlichen Besatzungszonen und in der Bundesrepublik Deutschland*, 8th ed., Frankfurt am Main.

Schneider, M. (1982), *Die Christlichen Gewerkschaften 1894-1933*, Politik- und Gesellschaftsgeschichte 10, Neue Gesellschaft, Bonn.

Schneider, W. (ed.) (1986), *Arbeit und Umwelt. Gewerkschaftliche Umweltpolitik*, Hamburg.

Schneider, M. (1991), *A Brief History of the German Trade Unions*, Dietz, Bonn.

Schönhoven, K. (1993), 'Kalter Krieg in den Gewerkschaften. Zur Gewerkschaftspolitik von KPD und SPD nach 1945', in Schönhoven, K. and Staritz, D. (eds.), *Sozialismus und Kommunismus im Wandel. Hermann Weber zum 65. Geburtstag*, Bund, Köln, pp. 261-280.

Schroeder, W. (1990), *Gewerkschaftspolitik zwischen DGB, Katholizismus und CDU 1945 bis 1960. Katholische Arbeitführer als Zeitzeugen in Interviews*, Bund, Köln.

Schroeder, W. (1991), 'Zwischen Sozialkatholizismus und Parteiorientierung. Die christlich-sozialen Funktionäre im DGB von 1945 bis 1960', *Gewerkschaftliche Monatshefte*, no. 5, pp. 328-338.

Schroeder, W. (1992), *Katholizismus und Einheitsgewerkschaft. Der Streit um den DGB und der Niedergang des Sozialkatholizismus in der Bundesrepublik bis 1960*, Politik- und Gesellschaftsgeschichte 30, Dietz, Bonn.

Schroeder, W. (1993), 'Facetten der deutschlandpolitischen Diskussion des DGB in der Adenauer-Ära', in Schönhoven, K. and Staritz, D. (eds.), *Sozialismus und Kommunismus im Wandel. Hermann Weber zum 65. Geburtstag*, Bund, Köln, pp. 281-300.

Schroeder, W. (1994), 'Aktuelle Probleme der Tarifautonomie vor dem Hintergrund des deutschen Einigungsprozesses', in Stützel, W. (ed.), *Streik im Strukturwandel.*

Die europäische Gewerkschaften auf der Suche nach neuen Wegen, Westfälisches Dampfboot, Münster, pp. 73-78.

Schuster, D. (1985), *The German Trade Union Movement*, Friedrich-Ebert-Stiftung, Bonn.

Streeck, W. (1984), 'Neo-corporatist industrial relations and the economic crisis in West Germany', in Goldthorpe, J.H. (ed.), *Order and Conflict in Contemporary Capitalism: Studies in the Political Economy of Western European Nations*, Clarendon Press, Oxford, pp. 291-314.

Swenson, P. (1992), 'Union politics, the Welfare State, and intraclass conflict in Sweden and Germany', in Golden, M. and Pontusson, J. (eds.), *Bargaining for Change. Union Politics in North America and Europe*, Cornell University Press, Ithaca/London, pp. 45-76.

Thelen, K.A. (1991), *Union of Parts. Labor Politics in Postwar Germany*, Cornell U.P., Ithaca and London.

Thum, H. (1991), *Wirtschaftsdemokratie und Mitbestimmung. Von den Anfängen 1916 bis zum Mitbestimmungsgesetz 1976*, Bund, Köln.

Tofaute, H. (1993), 'Keynes und seine Bedeutung für wirtschaftspolitische Forderungen der Gewerkschaften', *WSI Mitteilungen*, vol. 46, no. 11, pp. 718-727.

Uellenberg-van Dawen, W. (1994), 'Programm- und Organizationsdebatte des DGB', in Kittner, M. (ed.), *Gewerkschaften heute. Jahrbuch für Arbeitnehmerfragen 1994*, Bund, Köln, pp. 96-113.

Vetter, H.O. (ed.) (1980), *Aus der Geschichte lernen - die Zukunft gestalten*, Bund, Köln.

von Camen, G. (1993), 'Zwei Schritte vor - ein Schritt zurück. Der DGB und seine Frauenpolitik', in Leif, T., Klein, A. and Legrand, H.-J., *Reform des DGB*, pp. 280-292.

6 The United Kingdom: Between policy and party

Johan Verberckmoes

Since more than a decade continental Europeans consider Great Britain a society that is not catching up with the latest developments. This perception has persistently yet contradictorily been matched by the rhetorics of the last two Conservative Prime Ministers of the country, who both have stressed the continuation of Great Britain as a great nation. Whereas the non-committal attitude towards the European integration process is on the continent widely regarded as contrary to history's course, many Tories and other Britains find in this resistance a source for national pride and firm political leadership. Scarcely less noticed is the unrelenting stress on better economic performance in the world's once first industrial nation, parallelled with a relative decline of welfare state provisions and increasing social tensions in the 1980s and 1990s. The different perceptions involved are, however, not as much the result of any British insularity, as has all too often been alleged, but refer to deep ideological divisions and debates within Britain itself. Perhaps more than in other European countries, new ideological fissures have been made in contemporary British society, not least because of the strong ideological approach of the successive Conservative governments since 1979. While institutionalized pluralism prevails in many continental countries, the British social and political system seems to have prompted a much more ideology-ridden debate about change in modern society. Focusing on the issue of industrial relations, I will describe in this chapter the way in which this debate has manifested itself in the position, attitudes and statements of the TUC since the 1960s. My main argument will be that British trade unionism seems only to have been able to redefine its ideology at times when its close ties with the Labour party were loosening.

Up to the 1970s an implicit consensus has prevailed in Great Britain about free collective bargaining between employers and the collectively organized employees.[1] Both parties pragmatically recognized each other's existence and claims and tried to resolve their conflicts by voluntary agreements. State intervention was considered unnecessary and even an impediment to free collective bargaining. Trade union leaders, managers and politicians, as well as many academics following in the footsteps of Sydney and Beatrice Webb, have favoured this system moulded by custom. It brings conflicts into the open, yet does lead to negotiated settlements. In trying to weaken the trade union's legitimacy the successive Thather- and Major-governments have drastically modified this classic British model of industrial relations. But also the rapidly changing economic context points to a new reality for the trade unions. Multi-employer bargaining is declining constantly, mainly under influence of foreign-owned firms. More and more wages are fixed by plant managers, often without previous collective bargaining. Between 1980 and 1990 the number of establishments that recognized trade unions for collective bargaining fell by almost 20 per cent to around 40 per cent. Especially private sector manufacturing was affected by this decline. The debate on derecognition of trade unions is still going on, but recent interpretations suggest union recognition in new establishments is the key problem (Beaumont and Harris, 1995; Disney, Gosling and Machin, 1995).Union density is estimated to have dropped from a peak of around 55 per cent in 1979 to 37 per cent in 1991. Since 1994 it is unlawful for employers to deduct union dues from the payroll without the employees' periodic consent (as used to be the case), therefore increasing the threshold for employees to join the union. Also the number of strikes has declined sharply during the 1980s, from 2,310 annually in the 1975-79 period to 630 in 1990, the lowest figure since 1935. In number of days lost during strikes, however, the level in 1980s was similar to that of the 1960s. Decline in strike activity mainly took place in the private sector and among blue collar workers, whereas public service workers in communications, prison, health and postal services tended to engage more in strikes. Overall, there were no signs that these downward trends were halted or reversed in the 1990s.[2]

The 'de-incorporation' policy of employers - 'management deunionizing their thinking' (Dunn, 1993) - and the withdrawal of legislative immunities for unions by state authorities in the 1980s and 1990s is considered by some to represent a radical breach with the past national consensus in industrial relations. According to Purcell, a shift in ideology from collective representation to market individualism is the main cause of this dramatic change (Purcell, 1995). Yet, one might ask whether the breaking down of the implicit collective bargaining consensus and the weakening of institutionalized trade unionism in postwar Britain is not due to a more long-term process of change, in which different factors are involved. At least since 1968 and according to some even since the late 1950s (Crouch, 1977), the pluralist system of collective bargaining came under pressure. It was the Donovan report which first drew attention to this evolution. In the first instance this led to more corporatist labour relations and a more active role of the state. Especially when a Labour government was in power, the TUC was eager to support this policy, which increasingly brought the unions political power. At the same time, however, shopfloor level bargaining gained ever more importance. In a way, the continuing decentralization of industrial relations as well as the strong involvement of the TUC-leadership in national politics paved the way for the Thatcherite response to the unions. But, although decline cannot be denied, the trade unions have in the 1980s and 1990s not been wholly unable to challenge neoliberal ideology. Perhaps this ideological resistance has deeper roots in British trade unionism than is hitherto recognized.

It must be stressed that in this essay the TUC's General Council's policy will be analyzed and not the ideological evolution of the British trade unions as such. Although, in 1989, there were 313 trade unions in Britian and only 78 of them were affiliated to the TUC, the TUC is and has been the only central confederation of any importance. The other unions are simply very small ones, for the 78 TUC affiliated unions comprised 85.2 per cent of all trade unionists. Certainly, differences between trade unions will be put in perspective in this chapter, but in order to achieve a comprehensive view of trade unions' ideologies, one would first need detailed analyses of at least the main trade unions involved. Moreover, the TUC is only a coordinating trade union body and does not take part in collective bargaining, nor does it conduct collective actions. On the other hand, while the TUC is not a centre in control of the British trade union movement, during its annual congresses and in the social action it sustains ideological strife is ubiquitous.

The home of the labour movement

With the exception of the new company-based staff associations established by employers and mainly found in the finance sector, British trade unions have developed as organizations independent from employers, governments, political parties and churches (Gospel and Palmer, 1993; Sheldrake, 1991; Pimlott and Cook, 1991). Historically, occupational, market-based skills have provided the first incentives to lasting organizational success. In the eighteenth century local trade societies of skilled craftsmen negotiated with the employers about wages and work methods, while securing mutual insurance benefits for unemployment, sickness and death among their members. In the mid-nineteenth century these craft trade unions developed into centralized, national organizations, like the Amalgamated Society of Engineers or the Amalgamated Society of Carpenters and Joiners. As they organized their members across firms and industries, their primary goal was the protection of their own trade by preserving a separate, 'aristocratic' status in the world of labour and promoting a sense of occupational identity. Craft associations have steadily declined, mainly as a result of technological innovations, the introduction of computerized print-setting in the 1980s being a recent major example. Generally speaking, craft trade unions favoured improvements in their terms of employment through parliamentary legislation.

In the face of a majority of unskilled, low-paid workers in the nineteenth-century industries, ideas about radical change in society prompted the creation of general unions from as early as the 1830s. The Grand National Consolidated Trades Union of Robert Owen, though unable to consolidate itself, emphasized the unity of workers' interests in industries and agriculture and aimed to provide assistance during strikes. Radical ideas and actions were mostly expressed on a political level, for example in the Chartist movement, which was not able, however, to assure the labourers of any lasting influence on the political system. It was not until the 1880s that general unions achieved some success, mainly in the gas industry and the docks, and partly as a result of militant industrial action in the Docklands area of East London. The heirs of these first industrial unions, the Transport and General Workers' Union (TGWU) and the General Municipal and Boilermakers' Union (GMBU), are still among the most important British trade unions today. In the meanwhile, the idea of one union for each industry had substituted the idea of uniting all workers across Britain. This way, many unskilled and female workers, until the 1880s largely unorganized, became unionized. The reason behind industrial unionism, also labelled 'new unionism', was that it would provide the unions more easily with sufficient power to achieve industrial and political objectives. The mineworkers union, for instance, established collective bargaining, but also pressed for direct political action calling for the nationalization of their industry, which was only achieved until after the Second World War. Because the majority of trade union leaders in the late nineteenth and early twentieth centuries favoured a moderate, parliamentary based approach to industrial relations, the choice for industrial unions actually implied a pragmatic acceptance of existing society. As some historians (Stedman Jones, 1983) have argued, this strategy would have been preceded by workers' deradicalization and relative integration in late Victorian society.

The rise of British trade unionism was accompanied by the extension of legislative immunities. The Employers and Workmen Act 1875 recognized the labour contract between employer and employee. The Trade Union Act 1871 and the Conspiracy and Protection of Property Act 1875 (complemented by the Trade Disputes Act 1906) took away most legal restrictions on industrial action. These laws did not grant the unions rights, but immunities from common-law prosecutions. Being an amalgamation of craft unions, industrial unions, general unions and later white collar unions, the British trade union movement displayed a large organizational variety and little political efficiency. Relatively tolerated, the different unions took no great interest in centralizing their efforts. Indeed, when a Trades Union Congress (TUC) first met in 1868, it started as an annual debating society. Even when the TUC later began coordinating some political activity, it remained a weak central institution. Only at the end of the nineteenth century its role increased, while the unions more and more chose to complement their industrial action with action in the political sphere. When, as a result of a resolution moved by the Amalgamated Society of Railway Servants at the 1899 TUC Congress, a Labour Representation Committee was established in 1900 (renamed the Labour party in 1906) it was supported by some unions, not in the first place because of its Socialist drive, but because it explicitly aimed at returning more workers to Parliament, something which the Liberal Party largely neglected to do (Marks, 1989, p. 66; Lovell, 1991). For years to come the trade unions were crucial for the survival of political Labour. Once twenty-nine independent Labour members were sent to Parliament in 1906, the new Labour party under the leadership of Keir Hardie pressed for further legislation favourable to organized labour, to be implemented by Liberal governments. These measures laid the foundations of the welfare state and included the development of unemployment insurance and the statutory imposition by Trade Boards or Wages Councils of minimum pay levels for groups of underprivileged workers (Trade Boards Act 1909, modified in 1918 and later replaced by the Wages Councils Act 1945).

In the years immediately preceding the First World War widespread and at times violent industrial action substantiated a renewed working class radicalism. French and Belgian inspired syndicalist ideas about the revolutionary overthrow of capitalist society and workers' control of industry challenged the moderation of the trade leaders. In the end, syndicalism was restricted to a minority in the British trade unions, yet continued to retain symbolic power. At the same time, shop stewards had begun to be active in certain industries. These are annually elected representatives of the employers and represent the workers as well as the trade union on the shopfloor. On the other hand, the government as well as most trade unions stimulated a spirit of conciliation in the industry as well as voluntary collective bargaining between employers and unions, a trend consolidated during the First World War. The wartime Whitley Committee (1916/18) tried to remodel industrial relations, but only had a substantial impact in the sector of municipal and government utilities. It called for the creation of national and district level joint councils consisting of representatives of the employers and the unions, as well as for the establishment of joint works committees on shopfloor level. As a result of both syndicalist influence and an extended collective bargaining practice trade union membership increased considerably and peaked at 8.3 million (or 45 per cent of the workforce) in 1920. The trade unions enhanced their status in British society, while providing the Labour party with vital support to develop into an alternative government. Trade union control over the Labour party was firmly established.

Industrial unrest continued after the First World War and culminated in the General Strike between 3 and 12 May 1926. The strike was called by an ill-prepared General Council of the TUC in support of the miners, who faced wage cuts. Trade union solidarity between the miners, the railwaymen and the transport workers and dockers, which had been growing since the rise of 'new unionism', had in the meanwhile weakened, however, under the influence of the early 1920s economic recession. By presenting the general strike as a direct attack on the democratically elected government, the government brought enough pressure on the General Council of the TUC to call off the national strike without much result. On the contrary, the miners' strike continued until November and then ended with longer working hours and lower wages for the miners. In general, after the strike, a mood of militant Leftism in the TUC was replaced by strategies of industrial cooperation. In this context, it must also be mentioned that Soviet efforts to infiltrate the British labour movement had never been very effective (Calhoun, 1976). Whatever Communist sympathies had arisen in Great Britain after the Russian Revolution of 1917, the TUC and the Labour party's Socialist unity had only marginally been affected by it. When during the 1930s economic crisis extremists of both left and right made great strides, the trade unions again had only weak links with them. The Trade Disputes and Trade Union Act 1927 made sympathetic strikes and strikes against the government illegal. Moreover, the bill obliged trade union members to contract in rather than out of the Labour party levy on their subscriptions, which means that instead of chosing not to contribute for the Labour party, as used to be the case, trade unions members now explicitly had to chose to support the Labour party financially when paying their trade union membership subscriptions. As a result of the 1927 Act trade union affiliations to the Labour party fell considerably, thereby shifting the balance by the mid-1930s in favour of individual membership. Yet, the pre-eminent role of the trade unions in the Party was certainly not numerically challenged and party-union links were firmly re-established by the late 1930s, although not without conflict with the constituency parties. In 1946 the postwar Labour government repealed the Trade Disputes and Trade Union Act 1927.

The British trade unions gained considerable political influence during the Second World War. In May 1940 the Labour party joined the Coalition government of Winston Churchill. Ernest Bevin, General Secretary of the TGWU and a leading trade unionist since two decades, became Minister of Labour and National Service. Bevin's views on the mobilization of labour, wages and industrial relations prevailed in the Cabinet. But on issues related to the reconstruction of postwar society trade union influence was much less outspoken. These included the reform of the education system as well as the re-organization of health services, and housing policies. The Beveridge Report on social insurance (1942), which would in time become guiding for the development of the postwar welfare state, was not even a high priority for the trade union movement. One major reason was that social welfare reforms had during the interwar period mainly been proposed by women in the labour movement and constantly been rejected by male majorities

(Graves, 1994). One could argue that during the Second World War and in the immediate postwar period the TUC-leadership invented the tradition of State-free, responsable unionism, narrowing down trade union concerns to labour market issues only. While full employment became the first objective of the postwar government's economic policy, and public expenditure was instrumental to achieving it, the TUC stressed the importance of free collective bargaining. It guaranteed the independence of a trade union movement, which, for the first time in its existence, was in close contact with the government.

The TUC had indeed developed a working partnership with the wartime Coalition government, a relationship which continued under the Labour government 1945-1951 and, in a more diluted form, the Conservative governments 1951-1963. Therefore, a cooperative mood between government and trade unions underpinned the free collective bargaining consensus, which, in this way, was redefined during the 1940s. In a context of having become national institutions because of their wartime won prestige, British trade unions refrained from producing alternative models for society, leaving the reconstruction of the country to the competence of the government. Thus, in 1944 the TUC, although asking for the nationalization of a whole range of industries including coal, gas, electricity, the railways and other public utilities, rejected all schemes for workers participation or co-determination in nationalized enterprises. For one thing, this stress on the trade union's autonomy and voluntarist principles owed much to the sectionalist trade union structure. The TUC simply did not possess the power to move industrial relations practices beyond voluntarism, neither did it envisage such a policy. On the other hand, TUC-leaders had become established members of a labour movement in control of the country (Taylor, 1993).

On an ideological level, the TUC's harmonious relationship with the Attlee government, the first Labour government ever with an overall majority in the House of Commons, was based on a mixture of patriotism and anti-Communism. Unofficial strikes were vigorously opposed by government and TUC alike, because of the damage it was said to cause to the national interest, in particular the peacetime economic recovery. Shopfloor militancy was rebuked because of alleged Communist agitation, especially after the onset of the Cold War in 1947 (Flanders, 1977, pp. 158-162). The strong anti-Communist position of the TUC was, however, definitely also a result of interwar anxieties about Soviet infiltration. The Cold War and the British Communist Party's open hostility to the Marshall Plan and the productionist stance of the Labour government after 1948 confirmed the existing deep divide between two concepts of Socialism (MacShane, 1992, pp. 144-186). In industrial relations' terms, the postwar years were years of full employment, increased strength of the shop stewards and growing plant-based bargaining. But the voluntarist system of industrial relations, which epitomized the trade union's newly acquired status, very soon was tested. Fear of inflationary pressures because of wage increases brought the government after 1946 to press for wage restraint on the part of the trade unions. By March 1948 the TUC agreed to a policy of conditional wage moderation, which was left only two years later. Subsequently, the TUC reiterated its attachment to free collective bargaining, an attitude appealing to a rank and file eager to reject any notion of control.

A role to play in society

Consensual industrial relations persisted into the 1950s. The Conservative government was benign to the trade unions. Trade union leaders did not press for excessively large pay rises. In 1955, however, a wave of strikes, mainly because of interunion rivalries, announced difficulties for a TUC which was unable to adapt itself to changing economic and political conditions. Inside the TUC, the leadership which had carefully guarded the postwar consensus, was challenged by left-wing unionists, who stressed the rights of labour to bargain on equal terms with the employers (Taylor, 1993, p. 101). Wage restraint was in their eyes not a full TUC-policy, nor could it ever become one. This new generation of left-wingers gradually penetrated to leadership posts in the TUC and by the end of the 1960s had largely replaced the former right-wing leadership. Underlying this organizational change, several tensions contributed to the relative stagnation which confronted the British trade union movement (Coates, 1991, pp. 162-171). First of all, the shop stewards' influence steadily rose from the 1950s onwards, as payment systems were increasingly fixed at shop-floor level. Communist sympathies remained active among the shop stewards, even though membership of the Communist party had weakened. But shop-floor representation implied also restrictive, sectionalist attitudes and the defence of local rather than general interests. On the other hand, the extension of national consultative procedures involved trade union officials, who became more and more conscious of their status. The widening gap between the leadership and the rank and file in the trade unions manifested itself in the ongoing discussions about the postwar nationalizations. Whereas the official TUC-policy was to oppose worker participation in the public sector, criticism of this principle persisted well into the 1950s among the miners, the railwaymen and the postmen.

In the early 1960s the trade unions refused to consent to the Conservative government's attempts at wage restraint. To bring Labour back to power, however, the unions were prepared to change that policy and support a future incomes policy, to be implemented by the Labour government, which was indeed elected in 1964. Notwithstanding the agreement that the incomes policy would be voluntary, Labour very soon advocated a statutory policy (which eventually would fail). The Labour government's drastic decision to move beyond voluntarism certainly owed much to the fact that the weak TUC seemed utterly unable to make a voluntary policy effective vis-à-vis its affiliating unions, but was at least as much also the result of the institutional inadequacy of employer organization (Fulcher, 1991). Only in 1965 the Confederation of British Industry (CBI) came into existence, but it did not become a truly nation-wide employers' organization. The consequence of the move to a statutory incomes policy was that the trade unions started opposing their 'natural' ally. Already in 1965 the powerful TGWU had voted against a TUC endorsement of the government's proposal of an immediate 3 to 3.5 per cent pay limit (albeit with important exceptions). By 1967 the TUC General Council did no longer approve of the government's incomes policy, without, however, openly confronting the government on the issue. Such a confrontation did come about in 1969, when Barbara Castle, the newly appointed Employment Secretary, proposed in her White Paper *In Place of Strife* to curb unofficial strike activity by introducing a conciliation pause in unofficial strikes. She also pleaded for power for the Employment Secretary to impose settlements in interunion disputes and compulsory strike ballots in certain circumstances. Major discontent in the parliamentary Labour party led to the withdrawal of the propositions and the government's acceptance of a 'solemn and binding undertaking' by the TUC to effectively settle interunion disputes and unofficial strikes. At a TUC Special Congress on 5 June 1969 an overwhelming majority in the TUC voted for the policy document *Programme for Action*, which rejected any statutory penalties concerned with disputes and unofficial strikes, while at the same time strenghtening the discretionary powers of the TUC General Council to deal more effectively with these issues (Panitch, 1976). The TUC had, for the time being, won its battle against legislative interference with the industrial relations system.

The TUC General Council's focus on voluntarism undoubtedly testified to the collective power and the political impact of the trade unions. However, the TUC's triumphant mood also partly obscured the fundamental transformations which the trade union movement as a whole was undergoing. Interunion disputes had been a recurrent problem in the highly fragmented trade union movement, but in the 1960s and 1970s needed urgently to be dealt with, as they were increasingly blamed as a source for poor economic performance (Coates and Topham, 1980, pp. 39-60; Undy a.o., 1981, pp. 68-70). Already in 1962 the TUC had announced the reorganization of trade union structures. A strong wave of amalgamations followed, although the TUC still recognized that diversity of structure was simply a characteristic of British trade unionism. Between 1962 and 1979 the number of TUC affiliated unions fell from 182 to 112. The average size of TUC unions increased from 45,675 to 108,286 members during the same period. A major example was the Amalgamated Union of Engineering Workers (AUEW), formed out of the Amalgamated Engineering Union, the Amalgamated Union of Foundry Workers, the Draughtsmen's Association and the Constructional Engineering Union. Craft identity, although weakening, retained its importance up to the 1970s. The trend towards general unions was irreversible, however.

Only partially related to these mergers was the extension and change in membership of the trade unions. Traditional unions like the mineworkers and railwaymen unions lost members because of declining employment in these sectors. White collar and public sector unionism, on the other hand, were on the rise. The National and Local Government Officers' Association (NALGO) as well as the National Union of Teachers (NUT) became important large unions and joined the TUC in the 1960s. In the early 1970s the Association of Scientific, Technical and Managerial Staffs (ASTMS) became the fastest growing white collar union. To a limited extent, the trade unions had also started to recruit among the immigrant workers (Pelling, 1981, p. 272). But the most telling change was the growing presence of women in the trade unions. The number of women trade unionists doubled between 1950 and 1974, bringing the proportion of women in the TUC from 15.4 to 26 per cent. This growth was linked up with the increase in white collar unionism (Soldon, 1978, pp. 164-165). Not that the growing unionization of women had an immediate impact on the trade union movement, rather the contrary. While women non-manual workers in the public sector secured equal pay and equality of opportunities in the 1960s, the absence of these in the private sector led to greater female dissatisfaction.

Although the TUC took up the demand in principle for equal pay, in practice it did hardly anything to get it implemented. This indifferent attitude prompted women in the TUC, and especially the Women's Advisory Committee, to focus attention on specific gender-related issues, such as the need for training opportunities for women or a better representation of women in the trade unions. Only in the late 1960s did women's initiatives gain some prominence. In 1970 the Equal Pay Act established equal wage rates for women and men working in the same or equivalent jobs, but also accepted a transition period of five years (Boston, 1987; Cunnison and Stageman, 1993).

Changes in membership were accompanied by a decisive move to work place bargaining. The Donovan commission (1965-68) analyzed industrial conflict as arising out of the discrepancies between the 'formal' system of industry level collective agreements between trade unions and employers' organizations, and the 'informal' system of shop-floor level bargaining in which the shop stewards were key figures. It was the latter model which was identified as having become the most important one and the Commission therefore pleaded for official recognition of the shop steward's status. The result was a dramatic increase in the presence of shop stewards in the 1970s and a parallel formalization of plant-level bargaining. One major consequence of their formal recognition was that leading shop stewards became closely involved in union decision-making. During the 1960s industrial conflict had steadily increased, the Donovan Commission stated, because of the growing capacity for independent, 'unofficial' action at shop-floor level. National agreements on wages therefore had less and less impact. Demands of day to day collective bargaining by far dominated the agenda. This implied that it became increasingly difficult for the trade unions to carve out the new vision on society it desperately needed in order to survive adverse political circumstances. Such a reflection was not absent, however.

Indeed, the most telling indication that British trade unionism was undergoing a deep transformation was the apparent existence of ideological divisions in some of the major unions in the 1960s and early 1970s. In the Amalgamated Engineering Union (AEU, since 1971 Amalgamated Union of Engineering Workers, AUEW) an unofficial two-party system remodelled the internal discussions on a left (Communist and left Labour) versus right (Labour) balance of power and had an influence on full-time officer elections. A growth in factionalism also took place in the ASTMS, NALGO and NUT. In these unions small groups of International Socialists challenged their respective leadership to take a tougher stance on such matters as incomes policy and industrial relations legislation (Undy a.o., 1981, pp. 55-57, 105-111 and 124-125). Moreover, traditional suspicion of Communist influence in the unions waned and in 1973 the TUC agreed to lift the old prohibition of Communists attending the annual conference as delegates. It was estimated that in the mid-1970s around 10 per cent of all officials in the unions were Communists (Taylor, 1978, p. 84). The relative strength of left-wing tendencies in the trade union movement definitely played a mobilizing role in the explosion of strike activity between 1968 and 1974. As the public sector was the hardest hit by the incomes policy, public sector discontent was another major factor of industrial unrest.

Although the sectionalism of the trade unions continued to prevent a clear-cut political identification with the struggle of the proletariat, around 1968 a new language pervaded the TUC. In the face of increased militantism among the rank and file left-wing union leaders pleaded for the formulation of 'ideas about the society it would ultimately like to see'. Jack Jones, the in September 1969 newly elected, influential General Secretary of the highly centralized and less faction-ridden TGWU, strongly favoured a decentralized trade unionism in which the shop stewards played a key role. Further integration of workplace realities in the union structures would secure a greater participation of workers in trade union democracy. Even more militant was Hugh Scanlon, elected President of the AEU in 1967. Scanlon passionately advocated industrial democracy on the way to a Socialist society. Worker's control in the industry was his recipe (Taylor, 1993, pp. 147-151). Although someone like Scanlon later repudiated his former radicalism, the new language which emerged in the TUC was a clear sign that, in a way, the postwar consensus period was undeniably and irrevocably over. The TUC would nevertheless hold firmly on to the idea of consensus.

Which way for strong unions ?

The 1970s were punctuated by a series of events which gained symbolic value, from the collective action 'to kill the Bill' in 1971 to the 'Winter of Discontent' in 1978/79. When the newly elected Conservative government introduced the Industrial Relations Bill (1971), the TUC immediately rejected this intervention in what it considered to be its internal workings. The Bill imposed a rigorous registration of trade unions, as well as strike ballots, if ordered by the Secretary of State, made collective agreements legally binding and illegal certain unofficial strikes. Except for the key registration issues, the other items were therefore not that much different from previous Labour proposals. The Bill would, however, never have much result, mainly because it lacked effectiveness when put in practice, and be repealed by the Labour government that came to power in 1974. What is important in this context, is that the nature of the response to the Bill was different in the TUC than in some of its affiliated unions. Massive industrial action was mounted 'to kill the Bill', but the TUC refrained from the general strike some called for. As a means of protesting the TUC called for refusing to register, but initially did not want to go as far, as the Left was demanding, as to consider deregistering a condition for remaining member of the TUC. At the 1971 TUC Congress the AUEW succeeded, however, against the TUC General Council, to pass a resolution which linked affiliation to deregistration (Taylor, 1993, pp. 195-196).

In the mid-1970s the TUC agreed to take part in a number of corporatist arrangements. At the instigation of the Conservative government a tripartite Manpower Services Commission was established in 1973, which would deal with unemployment and training issues and play an important role in the development of a coordinated labour market policy. When Labour came to power in 1974 the example was followed with tripartite commissions on health and safety at work, on conciliation and arbitration, and on sex and discrimination. Tripartism was not an unfamiliar item on the industrial relations agenda, with the National Economic Development Council (NEDC) in existence since 1962. As a tripartite planning body for the economy, the NEDC had not, however, gained much influence. It was the union's resistance to any statutory incomes policy as well as the little interest in tripartism on behalf of the employers which would restrict further moves on the path to corporatism.

The move to greater corporatist involvement by the TUC had been preceded by a revitalization of the entente between the unions and the Labour party. Although the political events of the 1960s had created tensions, the unions had retained an overwhelming impact on the party in terms of members and money. The unions still accounted for around 90 per cent of the votes cast at Labour's conferences. The unions were interested in making the alliance even more powerful. At the initiative of Jack Jones the TUC-Labour party Liaison Committee was created in 1972. It prepared the labour legislation later to be implemented when Labour was back in power. Moreover, the Liaison Committee made detailed proposals for economic and social policy, which would become known as the Social Contract. The envisaged implementation of these proposals and the repeal of the much hated Industrial Relations Act by the Labour government in 1974 gained the enthusiastic support of the TUC. The ties between the unions and the party were indeed never as close as during the 1970s, while also being formalized. Whereas in the 1950s and 1960s the TUC at least had always expressed the desire to stay aloof from party politics, as a means of enhancing the unions' influence, during the 1970s it was nearly the other way around. This should, however, not obscure the fact that not all union members supported the Labour party, rather the contrary. Even if around two thirds of the union membership voted Labour in general elections, this also means that one third voted Conservative. Due to persistent internal disagreements on how to deal with the unions, the Tories did, however, not do much to support, let alone institutionalize workers' interest in their party (Dorey, 1995). The main supporters of the Labour party were still the general and industrial unions, either by sponsoring Labour MPs, or by their members not contracting out of their levy to the Labour party. In the expanding white collar unions, on the other hand, contracting out became a regular practice in the 1970s. In 1974 only about one third of the ASTMS members paid the levy. Other unions, like the NALGO, NUT and the Civil and Public Services Association did not even affiliate to the Labour party (Taylor, 1978).

In the mid-1970s the trade unions seemed to some the most powerful political group in British society. Whether this was true or not, they were definitely a force to be reckoned with, as was also indicated by the rising membership figures in the 1970s. But union power did not necessarily mean enhanced prosperity for the workers, as became abundantly clear when the economic crisis broke out. In late 1974 and early 1975, with no statutory controls on wages existing any more, unions started to press for huge wage increases under the Labour government. On the other hand, unemployment figures kept rising and prices went up. Faced with the danger of economic catastrophe, the TUC accepted once again, in 1975/76, the principle of voluntary wage restraint. Its main result would be that wage differentials were squeezed, which enhanced shopfloor grievances. Moreover, although the Social Contract called for greater industrial and economic democracy through an extension of public ownership, price controls, the abolition of social service charges and policies to redistribute income and wealth, when put in practice by a reluctant Labour government these measures were of little importance. Non-government led ways of enhancing workers' interests were even hardly considered, as was shown by the general indifference in which the proposals for employee representation on company boards of a Labour Committee of Inquiry under the chairmanship of Lord Bullock were received (Hyman, 1986).

It seems that the radical ideological language which had erupted around 1968 hardly affected the TUC-policy during the next decade, keen as the organization was on achieving its goals through its political ally. It stuck to the Social Contract, rather than developing a policy of its own, and persistently weighed the political viability of its demands. Once the economic crisis deepened, however, and unemployment figures were pushed up, the TUC was confronted with the limits of its strategy. At the 1978 congress a further continuation of the incomes policy was rejected by a large majority. Sectional interests flared up again in the winter of 1978/79 in unprecedented wave of strikes for wage rises involving car workers, lorry drivers, dustmen and hospital ancillary workers. Low paid workers in the public service sector launched an unsuccessful attempt at substantially increasing their minimum wage. On 22 January 1979 1.5 million workers took part in a nationwide day of action. Overall, average real wages declined with around 2 per cent in 1978/79, despite the militant actions. A 'concordat' on all economic and social issues between the unions and the Labour party in February 1979 failed to convince everyone that the labour movement was still united. In fact, it proved deeply divided. In the end the major consequence of this 'Winter of Discontent' was that public opinion turned against a weak Labour party and the supposedly too powerful unions, as became clear in the Conservative victory in the May 1979 general election. In this election 33 per cent of trade unionists voted Conservative and 51 per cent Labour. The postwar political consensus collapsed.

Union decline and the resilience of ideology

With a series of Employment Acts in 1980, 1982, 1988 and 1990 and a Trade Union Act (1984) the Conservatives decisively changed British industrial relations (McIlroy, 1991).[3] Trade unions' legal immunities were substantially reduced and union power forcefully curbed. Strike ballots became obligatory in nearly all cases. Picketing was limited to the specific site of the dispute. Sympathetic and secondary industrial action by the unions was severely restricted. Trade unions were obliged to formalize their organization: membership lists, the right of members to inspect the union accounts, the secret ballot of union officials. Moreover, labour market flexibility became a tenet of the Conservatives. Closed shop agreements were first restricted and later declared unlawful; in 1978 25 per cent of all employees in Great Britain had worked under a closed shop agreement. Job control strategies, which reserve qualified functions for qualified workers, were being dismantled. Statutory tripartite bodies were seriously weakened and eventually abolished, like the NEDC on 1 January 1993. This was especially significant since tripartite contacts with the government had become more important since 1979 for a TUC which was faced with a rapidly shrinking influence in government circles (Mitchell, 1987). The Wages Councils, which had been in existence since the beginning of the century and set statutory minimum pay levels for some of the least protected workers, were initially reduced, later neglected and finally abolished in 1993. The Thatcher and Major governments also discouraged national collective bargaining and promoted individual and plant level agreements. Bargaining still takes place on a voluntarist basis, however, and its results are not legally binding.

What did matter to the Conservatives was not to establish an interventionist policy in collective bargaining - in that sense the Thatcher and Major governments have continued and even enhanced traditional voluntarism - but to weaken the unions (Hanson, 1991). This became patently obvious after Margaret Thatcher had asserted her authority with a first Cabinet reshuffle in September 1981 and the hard-liner Norman Tebbit became Secretary of State for Employment. An overt use of ideological propaganda supported the Conservative's effort to destroy public and official recognition of the trade unions, yet it must also be stressed that this ideology took shape under the influence of events and actions and only became a coherent philosophy in the latter half of the 1980s (Middlemas, 1991). A key element of this neoliberal or libertarian individualist ideology is the myth of equality which it conveys: employees are estimated to be free individuals when hiring their skills, talents and experience to employers. Unequal power relations are radically denied, although, ironically, the empowerment of individuals is one of the main arguments of the neoliberal creed. On an economic level, the free operation of market forces was imperative to the Tories. As far as community and social services are concerned, the Conservatives have persistantly discouraged public spending and the public organization of these services, favouring their exposure to competitive pressures. On the other hand, in order to protect the interests of free competition, the neoliberal ideology advocated a strong, autonomous state (Gamble, 1994). From the point of view of this ideology, trade unions were nothing less than a handicap to the individual's chances on the labour market and as a citizen. Against the background of postwar British history, the Conservatives easily found arguments to support their views. The close alliance between the Labour party and the trade unions, job control strategies, closed shop agreements and the defence of sectional interests through uncontrolled social action all contributed to paint the picture of a powerful trade union movement, which hindered the modernization of British industry and the introduction of new technologies and modern management techniques. In actual fact, although trade unions had been conservative forces resisting innovation at times, the British trade union movement never had the full abusive power neoliberal ideology astutely ascribed to it.

Although the employers' free initiative has been the sacred cow of neoliberal Conservative ideology, it is remarkable that the employers have taken few initiatives under the new laws to radically ban trade union influence from their companies (union busting). The majority among the employers is careful not to upset existing industrial relations at shop-floor level (Crouch, 1990). In some companies joint consultative committees on a voluntary basis are useful new instruments for an improved communication between the management and the employees (Lane, 1989). Ideas about industrial democracy have, however, disappeared from the scene. Yet, the continuing trend of decentralization in collective bargaining has given the employers a relative advantage. Moreover, a certain recentralization has taken place from the shop-floor to the company level, which has enhanced employers' negotiating strength. At the same time, job control and job demarcation strategies, specifically concerned with qualified labour and once the cornerstone of craft unionism, have been rolled back, as the employers regained full power over the organization of labour. This led to bitter disputes with the trade unions, particularly in the newspaper industry.

But, how did the trade unions and the TUC react to the Conservative onslaught ? In the first few years after 1979 their reaction was rather muted, relying as they did on an early return of a Labour government. Besides, the Conservatives at first proceeded rather carefully with their new labour legislation, anxious not to provoke concerted union action. The unions did indeed not mount a strong opposition, which in turn stiffened the Conservative resolve to introduce tougher measures. The Conservative government became less and less concerned about compliance. As a result, after 1981, and even more so after the Conservative's next election victory in 1983, the implacable Thatcherite response to the trade unions took shape. In the meantime, the creation of the Social Democratic Party signalled the labour movement's confusion; what was left of the Labour party moved to the left. Whatever threats against the government's policies the TUC issued in this period, they seemed more designed to rehabilitate the Labour party than to combat the Conservatives (Middlemas, 1991, p. 327). In the area of industrial relations the TUC faced a task for which it was ill-prepared after decades of cooperative-minded and full employment policies. In fact, the TUC would never seriously defy the new Tory legislation, which was introduced piecemeal and could rely on large public support, even among trade unionists. Moreover, rising unemployment, the decline of Britain's manufacturing base and falling union membership further weakened the position of the trade unions and the confidence of their leaders (Marsh, 1992).

Although, at first sight, the overall reaction of the trade unions was very moderate, strong ideological debate emerged among the TUC-members. Whereas during the 1970s debate had largely focused on militant shop-floor resistance to the national concertative policies cherished by the TUC-leadership, under influence of political developments the range of alternative options broadened during the first half of the 1980s. Three major views as to the appropriate response to Thatcherism in the TUC can be identified. Having been shaped during the late 1970s (Crouch, 1990), these three broad currents of thinking were decisively redefined after the 1983 Conservative election victory, which shattered the hope of an early return to consensual policies under a new Labour government. The first, pragmatic view was expressed by TUC General Secretary Len Murray at the 1983 TUC Congress.[4] In order to recover lost ground, Murray argued, the TUC had to be willing to start discussions with the new Conservative government, looking for a cooperation on the basis of a broad programma on wages, social, educactional, training and welfare matters. This policy, which became known as 'new realism', was doomed to failure as the Prime Minister became openly hostile to the trade unions and refused any form of cooperation. Behind Murray's appeal was a moderately successful attempt to reassert TUC-control over a divided trade union movement.

The second option, favoured by the right-wing EETPU, was originally close to the first one, in that it warned against the possible negative results of massive confrontation with the government. This best possible damage limitation[5] policy of the EETPU gradually changed to an American-style business unionism approach. Concerned with the growing employment capacities in their new high-technology sectors, the EETPU, followed by the AUEW, took the demand for flexibility by the employers seriously. They started signing special company agreements with individual firms, which included acceptance of flexible working methods, no strike deals, company-controlled forms of employee representation and single union recognition (Crouch, 1990; Bassett, 1987). For all its undeniable advantages, mainly in terms of union recognition and employment, this company-based option radically challenged established trade union practices. First of all, the single union agreements were square to traditional multi-unionism in the companies. As a result of the derecognition of other unions in companies covered by EETPU single union agreements and the recruitment policies of the EETPU in areas of industry covered by other unions, the EETPU was expelled from the TUC in 1988. Moreover, the resort to compromise, even to the point of forfeiting the right to strike, seemed a threat to the union's free choice of tactic. Last, but not least, this new conception of trade unionism silently abandoned the class struggle perspective, which, although it had always been largely rhetorical, was still very much a part of British trade unionism. Notwithstanding resistance from some other unions, business unionism made moderate progress in British industrial relations, without, however, developing into a 'new industrial relations' model as some foresaw (Millward, 1994). The EETPU and the AUEW merged in 1992 to become the Amalgamated Engineering and Electrical Union (AEEU).

The resurgence of the class struggle was at the core of the third reaction to Thatcherism. Arthur Scargill, the militant President of the National Union of Mineworkers (NUM), was the main proponent of the view that the Conservative government simply had to be brought down. He referred back to the old, marginal, but never completely vanished syndicalist ideas and called for direct action. Without holding a national ballot, and thus openly confronting the government, Scargill led his miners into a national strike (1984/85) with far-reaching consequences (Adeney and Lloyd, 1986; Marsh, 1992, pp. 119-125). Violent confrontation at the picket lines and the robust ideological posture of the two opponents, Scargill and Thatcher, made the miners' strike into a highly publicized event and gave it enormous symbolic value. In the end, it was the final blow for a conception of trade unionism which still looked back to the nineteenth century. After all, coal mining was irrevocably an industry in decline. In that context, a purely confrontational strategy ending without a negotiated settlement did not promise a good future for the trade unions. Scargill's uncompromising radicalism was therefore mistrusted in the TUC. The TUC-leadership attempted to mediate in the dispute, but failed. Although the 1984 TUC Congress supported the miners with a General Council Statement[6] about not crossing official picket lines (with coal, coke or oil for the power stations), the other unions, and particularly those in the electricity sector, expressed their unwillingness about taking action in support of the miners. The TUC was not prepared to enter into a direct confrontation with the government.

The miners' strike was probably the most important watershed in the history of postwar trade union ideology. Under strong ideological attack from neoliberalism it ended the fiction of a Socialist labour movement which had never fully embraced Socialism. Closely linked up with a party that was regularly in office, the trade unions had never developed any long-term goals or an alternative vision of society. Concern for the general interest of the workers had been left to the Labour party. The trade unions had always restricted themselves to the protection of occupational interests. The exception which proves the rule was typically an issue which had nothing inherently Socialist: the Campaign for Nuclear Disarmament. In the 1960s and, again, in the beginning of the 1980s, British unions, and especially the TGWU, were among the strongest supporters of the campaigns for unilateral disarmament (Pimlott, 1991). With a weak Labour party and unions losing members and influence the labour movement seemed therefore to run out of options after the miner's strike. But, it is exactly at this point in the latter half of the 1980s that a fundamental reorientation started to take shape along new fault lines and on the basis of issues relatively new to the trade union movement.

A new agenda[7]

After the policy alternatives of 'new realism' and open confrontation had failed, the focus of reform of the TUC gradually shifted inwards. Already in 1980-81 an internal TUC-inquiry had recommended provision of better services, restructuring of central headquarters and new project areas in training, collective bargaining, health and safety, and employment for women and ethnic minorities (Middlemas, 1991, p. 555). However, recruitment strategies turned out to be the first reform policy objective, as membership losses increased dramatically. From a peak of 13.2 million in 1979 TUC-membership fell to 8.4 million in 1989 (Fulcher, 1991, p. 248), mainly as a result of employment restructuring and rising unemployment (the unemployed tend to renounce their union membership in Britain). The burden of decline was almost completely on the manual workers' unions, whereas the public sector and white collar unions showed smaller losses and, in some cases, such as service occupations, even gains. These shifts led to a changed balance of power between the unions affiliating to the TUC. This was reflected in the 1983 TUC-decision on a new 100,000 member rule to qualify for a place on the General Council, which benefitted the white collar unions. Although recruitment campaigns have been targeted at professional and managerial staff as well as at low paid, unskilled workers on temporary or part-time contracts, success has been limited (Waddington, 1995). Another consequence of changed membership patterns (as well as of a need for modernization) was a wave of union mergers. The amalgamation of NUPE, NALGO and COSHE in 1993 made the new public sector UNISON the most powerful British union with nearly 1,5 million members, nearly two-thirds of them being women. Other major unions formed by mergers are MSF (1988) and GMPU (1991). These mergers represent an accelerated phase in an evolution which has been going on since the nineteenth century and which tries to reduce the negative effects of interunion rivalries. The financial and organizational powers of these new 'super unions' have to provide better services to the members. However, they also threaten the authority of the weak central trade union body which the TUC is.

Faced with questions about its ability to further represent the interests of all workers, the TUC affiliated unions embarked on campaigns targeted at hitherto largely neglected groups of workers, such as part-time, female, young and black workers. Assessments over their likely success range from slightly idealized optimism (Kelly, 1988) to qualified pessimism (Fulcher, 1991). Concerning the need to combat rapidly rising youth unemployment, the TUC lost much influence in the course of the 1980s on the decisions that were taken by a Conservative government that strongly emphasized the needs of industry and lower wages. As a result of the Conservative's open attacks on tripartite institutions training became the nearly exclusive competence of the employers, while remaining financed by the state (Marsh, 1992, pp. 125-134; Crouch, 1995). Its involvement in formulating youth unemployment policies being virtually reduced to nil, the TUC showed strong internal divisions over its response to the government's training policy and even stepped out of what was left of tripartite consultation on training. Overall, youth training was a low priority on the trade union agenda, notwithstanding official declarations (Ryan, 1995; Balchin and Ashton, 1995). To a limited extent, young people have been involved in alternative forms of mobilization, such as actions against racism.

A rather different story is told by the ever growing female membership of the TUC. For a very long time the achievement of equal pay legislation had been a major concern of women trade unionists, who often found very little support in their own unions. When the 1970 Equal Pay Act came to be implemented, however, women soon realized that the segregation and re-grading of jobs allowed for their continued discrimination on the labour market. Equal opportunities for women was the new issue of the 1970s, but again union policies and practices were often far apart. It was the legislation of the Labour government rather than sustained TUC lobbying which established equal opportunities (discrimination on the grounds of sex in employment, education, the provision of housing and services, and advertising was made illegal in the 1975 Sex Discrimination Act) and minimum paid maternity leave. In the unions themselves women were still under-represented. A major problem was that men and women had very different perceptions about women's rights. The right to free abortion, for instance, was only taken up by the TUC after strong pressure from women members. Incidentally, this issue also caused some tensions with Catholic trade unionists; a Catholic minority has always been active in the labour movement (Hornsby-Smith and Foley, 1993). Therefore, although serious progress was made in the 1970s in terms of legislation, women's issues were still confronted with male values and behaviour in the trade unions.

This situation almost reversed after 1978. At a time when worsening conditions on the labour market diluted the implementation of the equality legislation the TUC issued a flood of policy statements on women's rights. Women unionists' active concern to broaden the trade union agenda started to have an impact on the general ideology of the unions. In 1980, for instance, the TUC drafted a model equal opportunities clause in which also the discrimination against black workers was condemned. In order to make the model clause effective the TUC started positive action programmes. Policy initiatives were taken to provide better childcare facilities. Efforts were made to improve the representation of women in the trade unions. In 1989, on a total of fifty-five members on the TUC General Council, twelve seats were reserved for women (Boston, 1987; Cunnison and Stageman, 1993). Yet, although about a third of all TUC affiliated union members were women in the early 1990s, they still remain under-represented in all union functions. At the 1994 Congress three black members were elected on the General Council. One of these seats was reserved for a black woman.

Since the 1980s the TUC underwent a process of slow, but steady feminization, in the sense that there was a growing understanding for gender-related demands which went beyond wage and job preservation. When it published in 1990 an updated version of *A Charter for Equality for Women in the Trade Union Movement*, the TUC included such items as sexual harassment and discrimination against lesbians and gay men, or disabled women. Although hostile reactions at the annual Congresses against the inclusion of these issues persisted, an important shift was definitely taking place in trade union attitudes.[8] The combination of work and family commitments for both women and men ranked high on the list of TUC priorities for the 1990s.[9] Influenced by women's values, unions also adopted new, less confrontational ways of negotiating (Cunnison and Stageman, 1993). Several factors help to explain this ideological change. First, women themselves actively promoted their interests in the trade unions. The Women Against Pit Closures movement during the miner's strike of 1984-85 raised women's political consciousness and led some of them to challenge male behaviour in the unions, for instance by pleading for childcare facilities at union meetings (Cunnison and Stageman, 1993, pp. 113-117; Leonard, 1991). Second, reacting against new business unionism, some of the larger general and service unions, like the TGWU and the National Union of Public Employees (NUPE), stressed the defence of the interests of the lowest-paid groups as the primary goal of the trade union movement. Third, the growth of public sector grievances as a result of Conservative privatization policies affected unions with a proportionally large female membership.[10]

The most significant ideological change during the last decade has been that British unions have espoused European social policy. In the 1970s and the early 1980s most TUC-unions were either simply against EEC-membership of Great Britain, or at least expressed reservations about 'Europe'. However, because their traditional immunities from judicial intervention were being seriously undermined by the Conservative government and because the decentralization of free collective bargaining weakened the position of the unions vis-à-vis the employers, the trade unions increasingly turned to European 'directives' to legally enforce rights for the employers and the unions. Again, issues of non-discrimination and equal pay for women paved the way. In 1991 the right to paid maternity leave was significantly improved thanks to a European directive (Cunnison and Stageman, 1993, pp. 183-185), and the TUC has pressed for further improvements.[11] New protections concerning health and safety at the workplace were assured. The symbolic event which has marked the change of position of the TUC in becoming pro-Europe was the speech Jacques Delors, the President of the European Commission, delivered at the 1988 TUC Congress, in which he linked an integrated single market to high standards of social protection and guaranteed social rights.[12] Especially when the United Kingdom in 1989 as only EC-member refused to sign the Social Charter, the TUC found in the support for Europe a new means of fighting the Conservative government. Trade unions looked for closer cooperation with continental unions. The TUC started to play a leading role in the coordination of trade union activities at European level (Marsh, 1992, pp. 134-137; MacShane, 1991).

The adoption of the European social dimension prompted a new language in the TUC. A key element was the development of a 'social partnership' between unions and employers, not only within the enterprise and workplace, but also at national level. Two references are of crucial importance to understand the concept of social partnership. In the first place, the TUC referred to industrial relations practices in other European countries, especially France and Germany, where, it was alleged, successful economies were based on high standards of social protection. Secondly, the TUC gave this reference to the different approach in continental Europe a distinct national imprint by claiming that the British government refused to adopt such a consensus policy and therefore had put Britain behind the others.[13] To reverse this trend and promote industrial competitiveness a social partnership policy was the only way out. This implied redefining collective bargaining. Priorities changed to include demands which concerned employees and employers alike: flexible working hours, part-time work, better training, enhanced career development, health and safety. Moreover, under influence of especially the German example, renewed thinking about industrial democracy resulted in proposals about gain sharing, works councils and greater rights to information and consultation.[14] It is, however, still unclear to what extent this definitely ideological approach will change trade union practices (Stützel, 1994, pp. 156-183). Even the choice of topics remains highly selective. Environmental protection, for instance, is hardly on the TUC and the collective bargaining agenda.

Perhaps, what is at stake in the great ideological changes in the last decade is not as much the development of a new industrial relations system, but rather the general position of the TUC as a lobbying institution at national level. Acutely aware of the ongoing decentralization of industrial relations as well as of the rapid globalization of the economy beyond national boundaries the TUC has started in 1993-1994 a 'relaunch' under its new General Secretary John Monks. In his speech to the 1993 Congress Monk mentioned nothing less than the 'commitment to lift Britain again to the forefront of nations'. Strong, well organized unions, which also took care of the personal interests of their members through judicial services, training opportunities and even courses to enhance self-confidence, were needed in the battle against unemployment and bad economic performance. At the same 1993 Congress John Smith, the leader of the Labour party, voiced the same concern for strong unions in order to guarantee the basic workers' rights which the Conservative government was denying them.[15] Smith's successor, Tony Blair, has looked at the relaunch of the TUC from a different perspective, thus bringing into the open the altered relationship between the Labour party and the unions (Bassett, 1991; Marsh, 1992, pp. 139-163). After taking successful steps towards removing the famous clause 4 (on nationalizations) from the party statutes, Blair has also envisaged to reduce the union vote at policy-making party conferences to 50 per cent or less. It can be argued that in this way Blair echoes trade union concerns about autonomy, representativity and the need for change.

Table 6.1
Trade union membership, 1945-1992
(unions not affiliated to the TUC included)

	Total membership	Percentage of labour force
1945	7,875,000	42.2%
1955	9,741,000	42.4%
1965	10,325,000	41.6%
1970	11,179,000	45.8%
1975	12,193,000	48.6%
1980	12,947,000	51.8%
1985	10,716,000	45.0%
1990	9,947,000	38.0%
1992	8,900,000	34.0%

Source: Taylor, 1993, pp. 381-382; Morris, T. (1995), 'Annual review article 1994', *British Journal of Industrial Relations*, vol. 33, no. 1, pp. 117-135.

Abbreviations

AEEU	Amalgamated Engineering and Electrical Union
ASTMS	Association of Scientific, Technical and Managerial Staffs
AUEW	Amalgamated Union of Engineering Workers
CBI	Confederation of British Industry
COSHE	Confederation of Health Service Employees
EETPU	Electrical, Electronic, Telecommunication and Plumbing Union
GMBU	General Municipal and Boilermakers' Union
GMPU	Graphical, Paper and Media Union
MSF	Manufacturing, Science, Finance
NALGO	National and Local Government Officers' Association
NEDC	National Economic Development Council
NUM	National Union of Mineworkers
NUPE	National Union of Public Employees
NUT	National Union of Teachers
TGWU	Transport and General Workers' Union
TUC	Trades Union Congress

Notes

1. Introductions to British industrial relations in Clegg, 1979; Fox, 1985; Gospel and Palmer, 1993; Edwards a.o., 1992.
2. For the above figures and the debate on their interpretation see Beaumont and Harris, 1995; Disney, Gosling and Machin, 1995; Millward, 1994; Edwards et al., 1992; Geroski et al., 1995; Milner, 1995; Gall and McKay, 1994.
3. An overview of the Conservative legislation 1980-1990 in Marsh, 1992, pp. 74-80.
4. TUC Congress report, 1983, pp. 463-464.
5. Cf. the intervention of Erik Hammond of the EETPU in the TUC Congress report, 1982.
6. TUC Congress report, 1984, p. 653.
7. Taylor, 1994 is a book commissioned by the TUC as part of its 'renewal programme'.
8. TUC (1990), *Charter for Equality for Women in the Trade Union Movement*, TUC, London; cf. TUC Congress report, 1985, p. 636 for an unfriendly male reaction.
9. Cf. Employment Law: A New Approach, in TUC Congress report, 1990.
10. A case study about the National Association of Local Government Officers (NALGO) in Lawrence, 1994.
11. Cf. TUC Congress report, 1994.
12. TUC Congress report, 1988, pp. 568-570.
13. TUC Congress report, 1991 (e.g. composite motion 1 on p. 6) and TUC Congress report, 1992.
14. A final report on representation at work is scheduled for the 1995 Congress of the TUC, which had not yet taken place at the time of writing this chapter.
15. TUC Congress report, 1993.

References

Adeney, M. and Lloyd, J. (1986), *Loss Without Limit: The Miners' Strike of 1984-5*, Routledge & Keegan Paul, London.

Balchin, A. and Ashton, D. (1995), 'Les dispositifs d'insertion des jeunes au Royaume-Uni', *La Revue de l'IRES*, no. 17, pp. 135-164.

Bassett, P. (1987), *Strike Free: New Industrial Relations in Britain*, Macmillan, Basingstoke.

Bassett, P; (1991), 'Unions and Labour in the 1980s and 1990s', in Pimlott, B. and Cook, C. (eds.), *Trade Unions in British Politics*, pp. 307-327.

Beaumont, P.B. and Harris, R.I.D. (1995), 'Union de-recognition and declining union density in Britain', *Industrial and Labor Relations Review*, vol. 48, no. 3, pp. 389-402.

Boston, S. (1987), *Women Workers and the Trade Unions*, Lawrence & Wishart, London.

Calhoun, D.F. (1976), *The United Front: The TUC and the Russians, 1923-1928*, Cambridge U.P., Cambridge.

Clegg, H.A. (1979), *The Changing System of Industrial Relations in Great Britain*, Blackwell, Oxford.

Coates, D. (1989), *The Crisis of Labour*, Philip Allen, Oxford.

Coates, K. and Topham, T. (1980), *Trade Unions in Britain*, Spokesman, Nottingham.

Coates, K. (1991), 'The vagaries of participation 1945-1960', in Pimlott, B. and Cook, C. (eds.), *Trade Unions in British Politics*, pp. 156-172.

Crouch, C. (1977), *Class Conflict and the Industrial Relations Crisis. Compromise and Corporatism in the Policies of the British State*, Heinemann, London.

Crouch, C. (1990), 'United Kingdom: the rejection of compromise', in Baglioni, G. and Crouch, C. (eds.), *European Industrial Relations. The Challenge of Flexibility*, Sage, London, Newbury Park and New Delhi, pp. 326-355.

Crouch, C. (1995), 'Organized interests as resources or as constraint: rival logics of vocational training policy', in Crouch, C. and Traxler, F. (eds.), *Organized Industrial Relations in Europe: What Future ?*, Avebury, Aldershot, pp. 287-308.

Cunnison, S. and Stageman, J. (1993), *Feminizing the Unions. Challenging the Culture of Masculinity*, Avebury, Aldershot.

Disney, R., Gosling, A. and Machin, S. (1995), 'British unions in decline: determinants of the 1980s fall in union recognition', *Industrial and Labor Relations Review*, vol. 48, no. 3, pp. 403-419.

Dorey, P. (1995), *The Conservative Party and the Trade Unions*, Routledge, London.

Dunn, S. (1993), 'From Donovan to...wherever', *British Journal of Industrial Relations*, vol. 31, no. 2, pp. 169-187.

Edwards, P., Hall, M., Hyman, R., Marginson, P., Sisson, K., Waddington, J. and Winchester, D. (1992), 'Great Britain: still muddling through', in Ferner, A. and Hyman, R. (eds.), *Industrial Relations in the New Europe*, Blackwell, Oxford.

Flanders, A. (1977), *Trade Unions*, 7th ed., Hutchinson, London.

Fox, A. (1985), *History and Heritage: The Social Origins of the British Industrial Relations System*, Allen and Unwin, London.

Fulcher, J. (1991), *Labour Movements, Employers and the State. Conflict and Co-operation in Britain and Sweden*, Clarendon Press, Oxford.

Gall, G. and McKay, S. (1994), 'Trade union derecognition in Britain, 1988-1994', *British Journal of Industrial Relations*, vol. 32, no. 3, pp. 433-448.

Gamble, A. (1994), *The Free Economy and the Strong State: The Politics of Thatcherism*, 2nd. ed., Macmillan, Basingstoke.

Geroski, P., Gregg, P. and Desjonqueres, T. (1995), 'Did the retreat of UK trade unionism accelerate during the 1990-1993 recession ?', *British Journal of Industrial Relations*, vol. 33, no. 1, pp. 35-54.

Gospel, H.F. and Palmer, G. (1993), *British Industrial Relations*, 2nd. ed., Routledge, London and New York.

Graves, P.M. (1994), *Labour Women. Women in British Working-Class Politics 1918-1939*, Cambridge U.P., Cambridge.

Hanson, C. (1991), *Taming the Unions*, Macmillan, Basingstoke.

Hornsby-Smith, M.P. and Foley, M. (1993), 'British Catholics in the labour movement: a study of religious and political marginalization', *Social Compass*, vol. 40, no. 1, pp. 45-54.

Hyman, R. (1986), 'British industrial relations: the limits of corporatism', in Jacobi, O., Jessop, B., Kastendiek, H. and Regini, M. (eds.), *Economic Crisis, Trade Unions and the State*, Croom Helm, London, Sydney and Dover, New Hampshire, pp. 79-104.

Hyman, R. (1989), *The Political Economy of Industrial Relations*, Macmillan, London.

Kelly, J. (1988), *Trade Unions and Socialist Politics*, Verso, London.

Lane, C. (1989), *Management and Labour in Europe. The Industrial Enterprise in Germany, Britain and France*, Edward Elgar, Aldershot.

Lawrence, E. (1994), *Gender and Trade Unions*, Taylor and Francis, London.

Leonard, A. (1991), 'Women in struggle. A case study in a Kent mining community', in Redclift, N. and Sinclair, M.T. (eds.), *Working Women. International Perspectives on Labour and Gender Ideology*, Routledge, London and New York, pp. 125-148.

Lovell, J. (1991), 'Trade unions and the development of independent labour politics 1889-1906', in Pimlott, B. and Cook, C. (eds.), *Trade Unions in British Politics*, pp. 28-47.

McIlroy, J. (1988), *Trade Unions in Britain Today*, Manchester University Press, Manchester.

McIlroy, J. (1991), *The Permanent Revolution ? Conservative Law and the Trade Unions*, Spokesman, Nottingham.

MacShane, D. (1991), 'British Unions and Europe', in Pimlott, B. and Cook, C. (eds.), *Trade Unions in British Politics*, pp. 286-306.

MacShane, D. (1992), *International Labour and the Origins of the Cold War*, Clarendon Press, Oxford.

Marks, G. (1989), *Unions in Politics. Britain, Germany, and the United States in the Nineteenth and Early Twentieth Centuries*, Princeton U.P., Princeton.

Marsh, D. (1992), *The New Politics of British Trade Unionism. Union Power and the Thatcher Legacy*, Macmillan, Basingstoke and London.

Middlemas, K. (1991), *Power, Competition and the State. Volume 3: The End of the Postwar Era: Britain since 1974*, Macmillan, Basingstoke and London.

Millward, N. (1994), *The New Industrial Relations ? Based on the ED/ ESRC/ PSI/ ACAS Surveys*, Policy Studies Institute, London.

Milner, S. (1995), 'The coverage of collective pay-setting institutions in Britain, 1895-1990', *British Journal of Industrial Relations*, vol. 33, no. 1, pp. 69-91.

Mitchell, N. (1987), 'Changing pressure group politics: the case of the TUC, 1976-1984', *British Journal of Political Science*, vol. 17, pp. 509-517.

Panitch, L. (1976), *Social Democracy and Industrial Militancy: The Labour party, the Trade Unions and Incomes Policy, 1945-74*, Cambridge U.P., Cambridge.

Pelling, H. (1981), *A History of British Trade Unionism*, 3rd. ed., Penguin, Harmondsworth.

Pimlott, B. (1991), 'Trade unions and the second coming of CND', in Pimlott, B. and Cook, C. (eds.), *Trade Unions in British Politics*, pp. 200-222.

Pimlott, B. and Cook, C. (eds.)(1991), *Trade Unions in British Politics: The First 250 Years*, 2nd. ed., Longman, London and New York.

Purcell, J. (1995), 'Ideology and the end of institutional industrial relations: evidence from the UK', in Crouch, C. and Traxler, F. (eds.), *Organized Industrial Relations in Europe: What Future ?*, Avebury, Aldershot, pp. 101-119.

Ryan, P. (1995), 'Trade union policies towards the Youth Training Scheme: Patterns and causes', *British Journal of Industrial Relations*, vol. 33, no. 1, pp. 1-33.

Sheldrake, J. (1991), *Industrial Relations & Politics in Britain 1880-1989*, Pinter, London and New York.

Soldon, N.C. (1978), *Women in British Trade Unions 1874-1976*, Gill and Macmillan/Rowman and Littlefield, Dublin and Totowa.

Steadman Jones, G. (1983), 'Working-class culture and working-class politics in London, 1870-1900: notes on the remaking of a working class', in Stedman Jones, G., *Languages of Class. Studies in English Working Class History 1832-1982*, Cambridge U.P., Cambridge, pp. 179-238.

Stützel, W. (ed.) (1994), *Streik im Strukturwandel. Die europäischen Gewerkschaften auf der Suche nach neuen Wegen*, Westfälisches Dampfboot, Münster.

Taylor, R. (1978), *The Fifth Estate. Britain's Unions in the Seventies*, Routledge & Kegan Paul, London, Henley and Boston.

Taylor, R. (1993), *The Trade Union Question in British Politics. Government and Unions since 1945*, Blackwell, Oxford and Cambridge, Mass.

Taylor, R. (1994), *The Future of the Trade Unions*, André Deutsch, London.

TUC (ed.)(1993), *Working for your Future. The TUC 1868-1993. The First 125 Years*, TUC, London.

Undy, R., Ellis, V. a.o. (1981), *Change in Trade Unions. The Development of UK Unions since the 1960s*, Hutchinson, London.

Waddington, J. (1995), 'UK Unions: searching for a new agenda', *Transfer. European Review of Labour and Research*, vol. 1, no. 1, pp. 31-43.

7 Sweden: The emergence and erosion of a 'model'

Bo Stråth

The historical emergence

Since the 1950s there has been a great deal of talk about a specific Swedish model for the organization of the labour market. Its characteristics are described as including institutionalized high capacity to compromise and a low record of conflict in an order where labour organizes capital. The trade unions have a high status in this order. The model was argued, almost mythologically, to have arisen suddenly in the 1930s as a Social Democratic response to the Great Depression. Labour organized capital in a way which allowed for economic growth and social equality at the same time.

The approach in this chapter is one which problematizes concepts like 'model' and emphasizes a view on labour market organization much more in terms of gradual emergence and ongoing transformation. The discursive power over concepts and symbols for the production of interpretive frameworks is a key tool in processes of political problem resolution, where every solution is pregnant with new, unforeseen problems. In order to shed historical light on the emergence of the Swedish labour market organization and the role of the trade unions it is necessary to go back to the years after 1905 rather than to the 1930s.

Feelings of crisis had been gathering up since the early 1890s when the workers of the emerging industrial society had begun to build their own identity on the concept of 'class'. The first union federations at a national level emerged in the 1880s. The Social Democratic Party was founded in 1889, seven years before they won their first seat in Parliament. There were from the very beginning close relationships and overlapping memberships between the union movement and the Social Democratic Party. The unions fought for recognition by the employers and the party for parliamentary power. Early on a kind of division of labour between the party and the unions emerged. These strategies made the emerging labour movement look for compromizes with the employers and for votes from outside the working-class. The strategies could be labelled 'empirical opportunism' (Stråth, 1982, pp. 67-84, pp. 142-165). At the ideological level there were tight connections to the German labour movement and the second International. The class identity which created solidarity and unity in the movement was experienced in terms of every-day unjustices and inequalities rather than in chiliastic revolutionary terms. There was a clear development in a pragmatic and reformistic direction.

Yellow trade unions never constituted the same problem as in Germany. Neither emerged any scope for Christian unions. The Social Democrats and the unions at the beginning of the 1890s proclaimed religious neutrality quite compatible with the strategy of 'empirical opportunism'. This was one important factor contributing to the high degree of homogeneity in the Swedish labour movement.

The ruling elites and the employers initially stood firm against the claims of the Social Democrats and the trade unions. Their response to the challenge of organized labour was the mobilization of the concept of nation ('*folk*') as an alternative category of identity into which the protesting workers could be integrated.

The growth of manufacturing industries and the emergence of national business networks and finance markets had transformed the labour force and the labour market and brought with it intensified unionization in the 1890s, which, in turn, resulted in enhanced organization of employers' interest. The 1890s were a period of a dynamic, interactive, mutually reinforcing organization of interests at the national level of the labour market. A new pattern of organization of society emerged (Torstendahl, 1991). Interests became nationally organized not only in terms of economic and financial operations but also in the labour market, and strong central and hierarchical confederations for the employees (Landsorganisationen, LO, 1898) and employers (Svenska Arbetsgivareföreningen, SAF, 1902, in response to LO) became a key factor in the breakthrough of a national industrial relations framework.

This national organization of interests was accentuated after the Swedish-Norwegian divorce in 1905, when Norway left the union with Sweden (which had been established by military power in 1814 in the wake of the Napoleonic wars), and the feelings of national crisis it provoked among the conservative ruling elites. The reaction to the experienced stage of crisis can be described in terms of a conservative reform strategy, where earlier blockages against social and political reform were released. On the labour market the December Compromise of 1906 meant the employers' recognition of the trade unions. In 1907 the first steps towards universal male suffrage were taken after almost two decades of debate. In 1913 the old age pension (the *folk* pension) issue was solved after having been debated and investigated since 1884.

This capacity for absorbing change was facilitated by another factor - emigration. Emigration to North America became *the* symbolic question soon after 1905. It attracted and channeled the social energy released from the frustration experienced by the ruling classes over the loss of Norway. (Reconquest was never seriously considered as an alternative). One million people emigrated to North America between 1850 and 1925. This corresponded to one-fifth of the Swedish population in 1900, and was only exceeded in Ireland and Norway. Like these two countries Sweden was a poor agricultural country in the outskirts of Europe with a late industrialization. Emigration was basically a rural reaction to poverty and overpopulation.

Emigration as a social phenomenon had certainly already culminated before the turn of the century 1900. In this respect it was a decreasing problem after 1905, and rather a problem to be referred to the declining agrarian society than to the emerging industrial society. However, as a discursive and political phenomenon, it played its greatest role as a symbolic catalyst for responses to the crisis experienced after the divorce from Norway. A government commission on emigration was appointed in 1907 and its work, which went on until 1913, resulted in a 21-volume report. A special inquiry among industrialists, commercial and business corporations attempted to find out what was wrong with Swedish industry and to study its 'weak and slow development' in connection with emigration. The country was said to need a 'vigorous Swedish industrial policy' to counteract emigration. If the productive capacity and the work intensity could be raised, emigration would be stopped. Sweden needed a devoted labour force.

In the discursive field of the public debate on emigration, economic and social developments were perceived and experienced in terms of threats and opportunities. Rudolf Kjellén, Conservative political scientist and influential participant in the public debate on the problems of modernization, opposed class struggle socialism as a point of departure for political discourse. He argued for 'national' socialism, where the country was seen as a whole which involved all the people in political work and gave them responsibilities. The country was supposed to be a home for the whole people. The idea of the *'folkhemmet'*, in which society was organized as a family, with the home as a metaphor, subordinated the class struggle parole to the national welfare.

The concept of *folk* had great power of attraction both among the conservative ruling classes and the lower classes of the population. Of course, their interpretation of the concept went in different directions. For the Conservatives it was a concept expressing allegiance to the authorities and traditional values in opposition to rapid change. Among the lower classes the identification with the concept mediated progressive popular protests against the conservative authorities. These differences opened up for a political contest about the priority of interpretation of the concept. When the Social Democrats a few decades later took over the *folkhemmet* metaphor and made it their symbol, after a discursive struggle about its content with the Conservatives, they argued that the happiness of the lower classes, of which the working class was just one part, was based on their efforts to contribute to the *folkhemmet*. *Folk* and *folkhem* as expressions of traditional values were mobilized as linguistic instruments for modernization and reform (Trägårdh, 1990). Originally, however, the metaphor was constructed as a specific conservative response to the experienced state of crisis at the beginning of the 20th century with emigration as a kind of symbolic representation. In this broader discursive context the preconditions and scope of manoeuvre improved for the trade unions, which not least the recognition of them in December, 1906 demonstrates.

In Sweden, because of emigration, no dual labour market model like that in Germany developed. Economic and social development came about slowly in one important respect; it was not until the mid-1930s that the industrial sector gained a larger share of employment than the agricultural sector. The dynamic industrialization was not accompanied by a corresponding urbanization, as in Germany.[1] The relatively small share of the labour force working in industry and the quick accumulation of capital set up favourable conditions for absorbing change.

Instead of a rural reserve army, exerting a downward pressure on wages and serving as a labour market regulator and driving force of the iron wage law, in Sweden there was an upward pressure on wages. The upward wage pressure in the wake of emigration was certainly a problem for the export industries. On the other hand, it provoked not only an interest in capital intensive production and productivity gains but also increased purchasing power, increased consumer demand, and the development of alternative market strategies, targeted at the domestic market. The outcome was homogenization of the standard of living and far smaller differences between the modern and the traditional sectors than in many other countries (Sommerstad, 1992; for Germany, for instance, Lutz, 1986, pp. 132-133). An early basis developed for later mass consumption, in the framework of Fordist and Keynesian strategies, through increased purchasing power. Here, too, as in the case of the attraction of the concept of *folk*, an element of continuity is discernible.

Historically, processes of capital accumulation and economic integration have often meant political and social disintegration. In Sweden, capital concentration and economic integration proved to be compatible with political and social integration. The emerging bourgeoisie, the entrepreneurs, the farmers, and the workers established a discursive field, where, in crucial respects, they came very close to one another in the national processes of problem resolution. Deep cultural values, developed over centuries by a Lutheran state church orthodoxy and a centralized state administration in contradictory but consistent coexistence with peasant autonomy at the parish level, were transformed during the conservative crisis therapy after 1905, although the old institutions as such remained. The state church was reformed. Parliament got a new composition with a growing strength for the Social Democrats after the suffrage reform in 1907/1909. The state bureaucracy got new tasks and expanded. The conservative reforms provided a perfect soundingboard for Social Democratic politics a few decades later. It is not difficult to see the Social Democratic state from the 1930s as the extension of the conservative civil service bureaucracy, and Social Democracy as a form of secularized Lutheranism. The compromises of the parish meetings during centuries, based on handshake rather than contract, were transformed to the labour market.

The transformation of a conservative reform state to a Social Democratic one in Sweden is an excellent illustration of how the evolution in values and institutions takes place in modern societies with a mass communication capacity. Theories on society all too often see the political debate in terms of exclusive alternatives. However, positions taken by political parties overlap one another. Key concepts and metaphors have their central position beacause they attract different groups, although the interpretation varies from group to group and is controversial. As matter of fact, exactly the shared interest in the same symbolic representation is the motor of politics.[2] Hegemony means priority or even monopoly of problem definition. Hegemony determines what is possible to propose and what is ruled off the political agenda. However, this does not mean the existence of only one discourse ruling out all others. The intellectual space in which hegemony arises is a disorderly collection of ideologies. Together they constitute an ideological chorus, which, like the chorus in Greek drama, 'both participates and comments upon the scene around it', as Gluck argues in her discussion of the Meiji modernization in Japan a few decades before the Swedish folkhemmet modernization (Gluck, 1985). Social problems, social reform, social policy, social education, social revolution, social novels, socialism, sociology: the choric theme is clear. Hegemony as an overall feature does not exclude pluralism and competition and contradictions among different ideologies applying for attention from different points of departure. Instead, these are what constitutes the hegemony. Ideology and hegemony become elements of a discursive struggle for power.

'Hegemony' in this view is not a static concept but a matter of transformation, where many of the key concepts and value patterns remain, although they are transformed to cover new contexts, new problems, and new expressions of interests and identity. In this perspective the transformation from a Conservative to a Social Democratic reform state should be understood, with *folk* and *folkhem* as two of the key concepts.

When the workers began to unionize and to demand the right to conclude collective agreements, employers were faced with a choice of strategy. Basically, two different strategy options can be discerned: Crush the unions and integrate the workers individually in a patriarchal order of industrial relations, or integrate the workers collectively by letting the unions represent as many workers as possible, and negotiate with the unions to produce predictability and stability. The December Compromise of 1906 between LO and SAF, entered into in the prevailing post-1905 mood, meant the final breakthrough of this latter option after two major lockouts in the engineering industry in 1903 and 1905 (Stråth, 1982).

The December Compromise meant that the employers' prerogative to organize the work process was accepted by the unions in exchange for the recognition of basic trade union rights. This development fit very well with the strategy of the trade unions when they developed their organizations in the 1880s and the 1890s. The emphasis was on improvement of workers' conditions on the labour market, while the power over the work process was neglected. The nationally organized trade unions can be seen as 'open cartels' with the task of restricting price competition and other sales conditions on the labour market (Åmark, 1986). Mutual recognition at the central level curbed the fragmentation of the trade union movement and promoted the early emergence of hierarchical and centralized structures in the interest organization of the labour market, at the same time as the unions' presence at the workplace, guaranteed by the December Compromise, promoted decentralization. In 1903, for instance, bipartite employer-trade union arrangements were established at the local level in the case of employment offices (Rothstein, 1992).

The perception of a tight labour market, owing to emigration, during this crucial phase of industrialization in Sweden set the preconditions for the union strategy. The labour market situation gave specific strength to the unions. From their power basis they gave priority to the improvement of wages and other conditions on the labour market. Article 23 in the charter of the Swedish Employers' Association (SAF) determined the exclusive rights of the employers to 'direct and distribute the work' in the enterprises. Although the article was a thorn in the side of the union leaders until it was repealed through government legislation in 1976, it was never an energy-absorbing primary point of attack. A kind of 'basic compromise' emerged, where the unions accepted employers' authority over the work process in exchange for the employers' acceptance of the unions' influence on wages and other labour market conditions.

Between 1895 and 1910, the unions' open cartel strategy was victorious and was institutionalized into the collective agreement system. The turn of the century was a period of fast growth of union strength. Between 1902 and 1907, union membership increased by 260 per cent. The employers realized the advantages of controlled conflict and of collective bargaining as opposed to uncontrolled conflict and no agreements. It was a matter of establishing a balance of power with the aim of preventing conflict from exceeding an acceptable level. This approach on the part of the employers can be seen as one of the most important elements of the Conservative reform strategy emerging after 1905. Organized capital in Sweden was more an instrument of professional problem resolution than an instrument for ideological struggle. The

Swedish employers realized that the trade unions had rapidly grown very strong in the 1890s and the 1900s, and they drew conclusions from this insight that were only temporarily upset after the severe union defeat in the general strike in 1909.

Although the principle perspective implied that consensus was considered possible and desirable, the emerging order did not exclude fights and conflicts. The employers' strategy of recognition and integration was initially a consequence of the workers' militancy and combattive behaviour. The manoeuvring space of the union leaders was affected by steps taken by the employers and vice versa. Although the concept of 'common interests' was launched, the dualistic perspective remained as strong as ever in the interpretive frameworks of the unions. The balance of power meant a recognition of compromise as a principle from dualistic points of departure. The more resources the employers and the unions had, the more they had at risk in a conflict, the more interested they became in the institutionalization of compromises (Rothstein, 1992). Therefore, union strength was a crucial factor when the attempts were intensified to de-escalate the conflict level in the 1920s.

Most of the responsibility for dispute settlement in the order emerging after 1905 was left to the unions and the employers' organizations. However, in the 1920s the government's interest in institutionalized settlement increased, which had to do with the fact that Swedish labour market still was very strike-prone in comparison with other nations. Parallel to the institutionalization of the collective bargaining system, an increased government interest in abating the level of conflict gradually emerged as an instrument for improved productivity.

Social Democratic, Liberal and Conservative governments all demonstrated their interest in peace on the labour market. In 1921, the Social Democratic government appointed a committee on this issue. It was, however, shelved after just one year. In 1924, the committee was reestablished by the Conservative government. In 1926, a Social Democratic government appointed a new tripartite committee of inquiry. In 1928, a Liberal government passed a law on the Labour Court and collective agreements, implying the imposition of industrial peace when there was a standing agreement (Johansson, 1989, chapter 3). The view expressed in the Liberal bill was close to the one the Social Democrats had held in 1926. Sharp Social Democratic protests against the bill should be considered in the broader parliamentarian context of Social Democratic politics. The protests more concerned the fact that the Social Democrats had not been invited to participate in the preparatory work on the bill than the contents of the bill itself. Very soon after the implementation of the law, the Social Deocrats and the trade unions accepted it fully.

It would be a mistake to look for the precise point of time when this order of industrial relations broke through, because there is no such point in time, but rather a three to four decade long transitional period lasting from the reorganization of society after 1905 to the late 1930s, beginning in a conservative value framework and ending as a national order under Social Democratic primacy. This long transition was a period of trial and error with numerous advances and setbacks, not least at the local level, before a national category of identification, on the union side still class-based, and a national interpretive framework had been chiselled out and hierarchical and centralized organizations had grown strong enough to maintain the order. This happened to a great extent owing to an increasing legitimacy to discipline the members. This legitimacy, in turn, was gained through trade-offs in central bargaining. The distribution of the trade-offs produced both legitimacy and disciplined members in a mutually reinforcing process, which produced a unionization rate which is among the highest in the world, having grown almost continuously since the mid-1920s (Kjellberg, 1992, p. 118, cf the annex of this chapter).

At the political level this process meant a transition from a Conservative *folkhem* concept to the Social Democratic *folkhem* in the framework of the party's reformulation of itself from a class party to a *folk* party. At the end of the 1920s, there was a decisive debate on the concepts of *folk* and class in the Social Democratic Party. This transformation meant the definite redistribution of power from the Conservatives to the Social Democrats within the discursive and organizational framework established after 1905. The framework remained but the content shifted.

In 1932-1933 the Social Democrats secured a parliamentary basis through a red-green agreement with the farmers, the 'Cattle Trading Agreement' (*kohandeln*). This agreement marked the beginning of a period of almost uninterrupted Social Democratic government power lasting until 1976. It was a trade-off between increased unemployment benefits and customs protection for agricultural products. It was the consequence of a Social Democratic response to shop floor protests against unemployment. The leadership of the Social Democrats did what they felt politically obliged to do without too much consideration to what economic theory prescribed or to problems of financing and budget deficit. The agreement is a good illustration of the strategy of 'empirical opportunism' established around 1900.

Unemployment, which was 15 per cent in 1933, was still as high as 9 per cent in 1939. The effects of the cattle trading agreement were not, in that respect, particularly dramatic. Its political importance was of another kind, a new government approach to the old dispute about unemployment benefits at market wages. To the unions the new approach meant the prospect of an *entente cordiale* between a Social Democratic state and themselves.

One immediate form of impact of this intervention in 1932-1933 was that the government took responsibility for redundancies caused by rationalization. New prerequisites for the resumption of the labour market compromise were thus established. It was especially important that the trade unions were commissioned with the administration of the unemployment insurance funds, which increased the incitements for unionization considerably and became one of the key factors of the high unionization rate. This construction was a clear break with orthodox labour market theories about state neutrality in this respect. In order not to disturb the self-healing forces of the market the state had to refrain from intervention, according to orthodox theory. In January 1936, Prime Minister Per-Albin Hansson and Minister of Social Welfare Gustav Möller proposed tripartite negotiations under much more direct government leadership than in the tripartite talks initiated by the Conservative government in 1928, where the role of the government had been more passive. The Conservative initiative was taken in the prevailing mood of Mondism and in the framework of the conflictual labour market.

LO at first welcomed the Social Democratic government initiative in 1936, while SAF, the employers' federation, was reluctant. SAF proposed bilateral talks between themselves and LO. They feared dictates from the Social Democratic government. However, LO also experienced a potential political threat. The parliamentary situation was unstable and the long-term fate of the minority government was highly uncertain. A future Conservative-Liberal government might intervene with legislation to protect the third party's rights in industrial conflict and restrict the right to strike. The Conservatives had taken the offensive on this question and demanded legislation.

In this uncertain parliamentary situation, where both parties experienced threats from legislation, LO agreed to SAF's proposal about bilateral talks. The Social Democratic government received the LO decision with resentment but could not do much about it (Johansson, 1989, pp. 136-137, pp. 141-142). Under the threat of legislation, LO and SAF negotiated for two years before signing the Saltsjöbaden Agreement in 1938. A new agreement in 1942 on rationalization and industrial welfare confirmed the stability of the bipartite agreement.

The agreement at Saltsjöbaden was to become one of the most important elements of the Swedish labour market organization. The established pattern of bilateral rule-creation in the labour market was reinforced. The issue of industrial peace could finally be removed from the political agenda, and it remained so for the next three decades (Johansson, 1989, chapter 7. From the employers' point of view, see de Geer, 1978). The agreement at Saltsjöbaden was a response to changed supply and demand relations on the labour market in the wake of the Great Depression. It was a trade-off arrangement where the unions sold industrial peace and bought collectively bargained wage agreements, i.e. the recognition of the strategy of limited competition on the supply side implicit in the open cartel strategy. The guarantee of industrial peace by the unions was emphasized in the 1940s when balloting on collective bargaining outcomes was abolished and strikes involving more than a few per cent of the members of a union federation had to be approved by LO. This meant a fundamental shift of the right to strike from the shop floor to the higher echelons of the unions. One important precondition of the centralization of industrial relations in 1938 was the state responsibility for redundancy through the Unemployment Insurance Act of 1935 under union administration.

Given the LO-SAF basic agreement in Saltsjöbaden in 1938 on collective bargaining and industrial peace and the Social Democrats' permanent control of government power from 1936 to 1976, the focus of the order became economic policy. This necessarily had to involve the government, as opposed to bilateral rule-creation and wage formation. In the tripartite institutional framework which developed, a distribution of labour was established implying that the labour market and collective wage bargaining became the concern of bipartly organized capital and labour, which were increasingly hierarchically organized under the top federations of SAF and LO. The Social Democrats set the framework of the enterprises in a capitalist economy where productivity and profits increased the political power of distribution. While it is a well-founded argument that labour organized capital, the two branches of the labour movement stamped the model in a way that also took the interests of the employers into consideration. The formula which was gradually chiselled out included the promotion of a highly productivity capitalist economy, generating high profits. Although there was also contention between the unions and the employers as to the distribution of profits, there was still the protective cloak of a Social Democratic government which had an overall distributive responsibility and used taxes and budget transfers as important instruments of implementation.

The experiences of World War II reinforced and institutionalized the compromises of the 1930s. The Swedish labour movement accepted the overall responsibility of wartime management and eventually got the credit for this by and large successful undertaking. At the institutional level, the huge wartime administration was designed as an apparatus with competence and responsibility. At the political level the enormous resources mobilized because of the war opened up an entirely new perspective for the Social Democrats. The war demonstrated that the rates of taxation, public spending, public consumption, and compulsory accumulation of capital were far beyond the wildest dreams of the prewar Social Democrats, an insight they would never forget. Much more than being a break, World War II in neutral Sweden meant a transition to fulfillment of the visions implicit in the *folkhemmet* metaphor and a transgression of the limits set by the historical context of the 1930s. From that point on, every political alternative had to be formulated within the *folkhemmet* framework as this was conceptualized by the Social Democrats and the trade unions.

Self-reflection in the mirror of foreign interest: the perception of a 'model' emerges

The 'wage policy with solidarity' brought the privilege of interpretation and the initiative on the labour market to the unions. At the same time 'wage policy with solidarity' became an important driving force for the continued rationalizations of the industry. The 'wage policy with solidarity' was invented by the LO economists Gösta Rehn and Rudolf Meidner and presented as a union strategy around 1950. The policy meant pressure on low productivity enterprises. Threats of redundancy were met by means of general government measures to stimulate mobility (moving allowances, retraining courses, labour exchange offices) combined with selective employment incentives for stagnating regions, industries and enterprises (state orders, state enterprises or state subsidies for production and jobs).

The union 'wage policy with solidarity' meant that equal wages were paid for equal work. The implication was that less profitable enterprises which could not pay the stipulated wages would have to close down. The wage level in the profitable enterprises and industries was used as the gauge in central wage negotiations. Union wage policy was a powerful instrument for structural change and for the transfer of labour from low to high productivity industries. The unions even pushed for layoffs and contraction in less competitive industries such as textiles, and encouraged inter-regional and inter-industrial transfer of labour, especially to the engineering industry. The problem, according to union economists, was not how to avoid redundancy in unprofitable or low productivity industries, but how to create new jobs in more profitable industries for the workers who were made redundant.

The union strategy required centralized bargaining. Centralization was also an employer interest. In order to avoid wage explosions as a result of 'scissoring', in which indulgent employers' associations concluded collective agreements at different points in time, SAF imposed centralized wage bargaining in 1954-1956 (Kjellberg, 1992, p. 96).

As a consequence of centralized bargaining, government regulation of wages was never on the agenda in the following decades; the wage policy with solidarity functioned as an extra-governmental form of incomes policy. However, the 'active labour market policy' managed by the Labour Market Board (Arbetsmarknadsstyrelsen, AMS), created in 1948, played an increasingly important supplementary role. AMS was a government office where from the mid-1950s the economic and administrative resources grew rapidly. Organized labour and capital were represented on the supervisory board of AMS. Considerable resources were from the end of the 1950s allocated for labour market training centres. Initially, the LO strategy was not at all a strategy for dealing with unemployment, but a means for the flexible transfer of labour in order to promote high productivity, and to increase the wages of the lowest paid workers. The Labour Market Board and its retraining centres became the pivots of this new strategy.

Encouraging of geographical and occupational mobility allowed expanding industries to take on workers from declining regions and industries. The wage policy with solidarity accelerated the structural transformation by forcing up wages in low-paid industries such as textiles, while the automobile industry and other export industries benefited from relatively low wage increases. The combination of an active labour market policy and economic expansion made possible 'full employment', another prominent goal of the Swedish labour movement. Full employment and collective bargaining with solidarity legitimized the LO policy in the eyes of the union members (Kjellberg, 1992, pp. 96-97). These were the bonanza years of what was increasingly perceived as the 'Swedish model', which also included the broader context of welfare state arrangements.[3]

The image of a specific Swedish model took form under mutually reinforcing interaction between the increasing interest paid abroad to the Swedish labour market organization and self-reflection in the mirror of this foreign interest after World War II among the left-wingers in the US, Britain, Germany and France. The left-wing interest in Sweden in these countries was controversial. Sweden became a weapon in domestic policies, which only increased the interest. Foreign study delegations visited Sweden and the leaderships of LO and SAF made joint journeys to Britain and the US in order to present the 'Swedish model'. In the image that emerged, Sweden became the country of social peace and consensus. This image connoted to ideas of a specific world mission in a *Denkfigur* which also contained the concepts of 'neutrality' and 'third world' (Stråth, 1993, chapter 4).

History was used in this Social Democratic construction of a national identity with foreign assistance. A sharp demarcation was drawn between the pre-1930s and the post-1930s. In the Social Democratic language the myth emerged of an active labour market policy having been born in response to the crisis of the 1930s. References back to the 1930s and the Social Democratic salvation from unemployment were repeated in all election campaigns. Social Democratic politics were given historical legitimation. The Social Democrats were argued to have saved Sweden from unemployment and Social Democratic policy ever since was seen as a guarantee that this scourge would never return. Keynesian economic theory gave scientific legitimacy to the myth.

What was sold in the political market as a conscious general strategy launched in response to the crisis of the 1930s, was actually a gradually emerging process of muddling through, where the goals as they were perceived in the situations of decision-making had a much more limited scope than they appeared to have in retrospect. The retrospective perspective was not the perspective *ex ante facto* of the actors in the 1950s. There was no such a thing as a great strategy with an inherent logic of its own, but only short-term strategies of different actors responding to specific problems which were only brought together in retrospect to form what looked like the realization of an idea that had already been there from the start. However, the heuristic framework of full employment and perpetual growth since the early 1930s as the outcome of long-term strategies made sense to the Swedish population.

To describe this use of history in the 1950s as the construction of a myth is, of course, not to argue that nothing changed in the 1930s. The most obvious sign that something really *had* changed was the discursive power to establish the myth that everything had changed in the 1930s. The 1930s meant decisive steps from an order where capital organized labour to one where labour organized capital. The *Stoßrichtung* of sociopolitical and economic processes was increasingly initiated by organized labour rather than by organized capital. However, the differences between a society where capital integrates and organizes labour and one where labour integrates and organizes capital should not be exaggerated. In both cases concessions to the other side are important keys to success with the integration of the other party. The suit into which the Social Democrats stepped in the 1930s was tailored as a conservative response to the feelings of crisis after 1905. Of course, it looked different when the Social Democrats began to wear it instead of the Conservatives, but in many respects it was still the same suit, however. In this perspective the 1930s in Sweden must be described in terms of continuity and discontinuity, where continuity does not mean static but continuous gradual change, with some new elements constantly appearing and others remaining the same.

The use of history in the 1950s in order to produce meaning and describe how the 'model' emerged made the development seem like a masterpiece of social engineering and rational planning of politics and economy. This image took on gradually hegemonic proportions during the 1960s when economic growth, on the basis of a vigorous circle where mass consumption and mass production mutually reinforced one another, and Keynesian economic manipulation confirmed the success story.

As a matter of fact, it was only in 1957 that the Social Democratic government accepted the trade unions' 'wage policy with solidarity', and then hesitantly, as well as their ideas about a flanking 'active labour market policy'. Then they also consented to a union claim to strengthen the Labour Market Board. Although their were tight ties between LO and the Social Democratic Party since the 1890s, in a relationship which can be described as a division of labour between the industrial relations order and the wider economic political and welfare state arrangements, this division of labour occasionally produced tensions between the two branches of organized labour. The Social Democrats never hesitated to tell LO that they represented a wider constituency which gave them a wider responsibility. During the first half of the 1950s the Social Democratic Minister of Finance Gunnar Sträng refused to believe that the labour market theory of the LO economists was compatible with economic stabilization, although this was exactly what the theory pretended to be. Only in 1956 did the arguments of the LO economists convince the government.[4]

1957 was important also in one specific respect. The Social Democrats and the trade unions fought and won the battle about a pension system to supplement the age pension system of 1913. The labour movement suggested a compulsory system which placed the workers and low-paid white collar employees on an equal footing with large sectors of the salaried employees who had achieved supplementary pensions in the framework of collective bargaining. The Social Democratic proposal did not only attract the blue collar workers but also those white collar employees who still did not have any collective pension agreement. This attraction occurred in a way which did not provoke protests among those salaried employees who already had supplementary pension agreements, because according to the proposal the pension level varied with the income level instead of beeing fixed at one and the same level of basic social security.

The battle about public pension funds, to which the employers would have to deliver the money, was pursued in terms of confiscation of private property. The outcome meant a growing distance between the labour movement and the farmers, which had formed a welfare coalition since the cattle trading agreement in the 1930s, based on equal and universal benefits on a basic level of social security, and a rapprochement between the labour movement and the middle classes of salaried employees, where welfare was translated more into income guarantee than to basic social needs. This new coalition became the engine of Social Democratic politics in the 1960s.

The salaried employees had created their first trade union federation in the 1930s. In 1931 DACO was established for salaried employees in the private industry, and in 1937 TCO for the lower-grade officials in the public sector. In 1944 the two unions merged. Among the professional cadres with an academic degree particularly younger secondary school teachers and medical doctors were active when SACO was established in 1943-1947. While white-collar rate of unionization at first lagged behind manual, by the 1970s the gap had been eliminated (Kjellberg, 1992, p. 118). Politically TCO (Tjänstemännes Centralorganisation) and SACO (Sveriges Akademikers Centralorganisation) are as organizations neutral and never developed the corresponding close relationships to the Social Democratic party as LO did. However, at the same time there are at the personal level obvious ties between the TCO cadre and the Social Democrats. This ambiguity has exposed TCO to internal tension when the confederation has been requested to take a stand in controversial political questions like the pensions issue in 1957-1958 and the wage-earner-fund issue in the 1970s (below).

The interrelationships in the triangle of LO-TCO-SACO have varied over time in a complex pattern from cooperation and coordination of wage strategies to rivalry and conflict, where LO and TCO generally have been closer to one another under a certain demarcation to SACO. This pattern of triangular cooperation and conflict has off and on split the confederations internally, because of the emergence of bargaining cartels among the public sector and the private sector unions respectively, involving both blue collar and salaried employee unions in both cases. The rivalry between the private sector and the public sector employees is an important factor in Swedish labour market organization since the 1970s.

At the same time as the Social Democrats seemed to reach new heights in the 1960s potential strains were accumulated in the 'model'. These signs of strain were hardly paid attention to, however, in the general mood of social engineering. The signs came from two directions. There were increasing protests against enterprise closures and compulsory labour mobility in the wake of the 'active labour market policy'. There were also increasing signs of tension in the newly established coalition between the blue and white collar employees when the coordination of the wage policy with solidarity concerned not only LO but also TCO and, although to a less degree, SACO.

However, these signs of strain were suppressed until the late 1960s when they turned up in more dramatic forms. The hegemonic view during the first half of the 1960s emphasized the crucial role of the government and the Labour Market Board. With retraining programmes, labour was transferred from stagnating to prosperous industries, where problems of overheating were reduced. Bipartite bargaining about wages was supplemented with government responsibility for retraining courses and housing programmes. The government took care of the redundant workers so that they could be transferred, after retraining, from decreasing to expanding industries.

In the politics of the 1960s there were close links between stabilization policy, wage formation and labour market policy. Labour market policy was institutionalized as a necessary complement to general fiscal and monetary policy, necessary if the goals of full employment and price stability were to be realized. The active labour market policy, by virtue of which everyone either had a job or was being trained for one, became the pivot of the Social Democratic reform strategy and the core of the *folkhemmet* metaphor. The strategy appealed to the Swedish population, for whom diligence at work and devotion to one's job were virtues which had emerged culturally over centuries. Their origins were deeply rooted in the protestant ethics of the Lutheran state church. Here an obvious element of continuity is discernable in the Swedish organization of society.

One prerequisite for and consequence of the unions' success in influencing policy was their high status, achieved through their production and rationalization philosophy and through the general political and cultural environment in which the labour movement had achieved substantial power. The hegemony between the Social Democratic Party and LO, established on the basis of the concepts of *folk*, 'wage policy with solidarity' and 'active labour market policy' was, however, complex and problematic, not simple and monolithic (Heclo and Madsen 1987, pp. 322-323). It had nothing to do with a static concept of unilateral progress achieved through preconceived strategies. Although it is debatable to what extent wages really were equalized, the union members believed they were, which was the important thing. Employees in the high productivity industries were compensated through wage drift at the plant level for what they had given up in the name of solidarity in the centralized bargaining process. What was equalized at the central level was, at least to some extent, restored at the local level, where in particular the piecework systems promoted local wage increases beyond the control of central levels of bargaining.

The 1960s saw the culmination of the belief in tripartite economic management and social engineering, based on the labour market compromise. The effect was that labour organized capital, with a close association between macroeconomic policy, wage formation and labour market strategy.

The erosion of the 'model'

The general radicalization of the social debate in the wake of the events in 1968 put the trade unions' and the Social Democrats' solidarity and productivity model under strain. One prerequisite for the Social Democratic postwar policy was economic growth, implying full employment, increasing real wages and accumulation of capital.

The success of the Social Democrats was continually confirmed during the bonanza period of some 10-20 years in an almost self-fulfilling way, and was scientifically legitimatized through Keynesian theory. The 1960s brought this development to a head in the wake of economic growth. Structural rationalizations, stimulating the mobility of the production factors, meant rapid technological and economic progress. The reverse of this development, continually visible since the 1950s but increasingly apparent by the late 1960s, has already been touched upon: enterprise closures, layoffs and transfers. People found it more and more problematic to be forced to move from environments where they felt at home. The labour process changed, especially in the engineering industry where the new piecework systems were often called into question.

A wave of unofficial strikes in the engineering industry followed a long strike in the iron ore mines in Lappland in 1969-1970. Demands were made for co-determination and job protection. This outburst of protests was triggered off by imperfections in the functioning of the 'model', but was linked to the general dramatic radicalization, political and ideological, in the late 1960s all over the industrialized world. The compromise on the Swedish labour market established in the 1930s had reached its limit. As in the early 1930s, the grievances of the rank and file provoked political intervention. The radicalization of the late 1960s on the shop floors and in the social debate in general activated not only union leaders but also political leaders. The union movement, not least the Swedish Metalworkers' Union, was pushing for change in response to the strike wave. Where far-reaching agreements with the employers were impossible, legislation was used by the Social Democratic government as a tool, for the first time since 1936 on such a large scale. The Act on Employee Representation on Boards of Directors in 1973, the Act on Job Security in 1974 and the Act on Co-determination in 1976 are just a few examples. This development of Social Democratic policy was qualitatively new, since distribution policy had previously been in focus. The 'class' concept was reactivated in a way reminiscent of the 1930s. In this respect Sweden was part of an international trend, of course. The long-term unintended and unforeseen impact in the Swedish configuration was the undermining of the established balance in the tripartite institutional framework.

One important and intentional consequence, with unintended long-term implications, of the intensified 'class' performance around 1970, and the labour market legislation implemented in order to integrate and channel the shop floor protests, was the downward dislocation of power within the union movement towards the shop floor level.

The labour market legislation was generally seen as a victory for the militant fraction in the labour movement. This was the short-term scenario, however. Co-determination, employee board representation, job protection, and industrial welfare legislation meant new tasks for union cadres at the local level. The long-term implication was to undermine the hierarchical structure. The employers' response to the outburst of worker militancy and to the legislation was particularly crucial to this erosion of hierarchy. The employers' perception of increasing shop-floor militancy caused them to pay more attention to the enterprise level of industrial relations and correspondingly less to the established centralized bargaining culture. An ideological/discursive employers' counter-movement began, aimed to integrate and channel the outburst of militancy the centralized bargaining structure had failed to prevent. The target of this counter-movement was the shop-floor level.

New employer strategies emerged, based on identity construction around the concept of *medarbetare*, workmate which in English rather would be 'colleague', the white collar term translated to involve blue collar levels and to efface differences between blue collar and white collar occupations, as opposed to 'worker', as an alternative to the conveyor belt and piecework strategy for productivity gains. At the company level, the development was mirrored in phrases like *medarbetare*, 'teamwork', 'job design', 'meaningful work', 'employees' profit sharing', 'responsibility' and so on. The development of this new teamwork and team spirit strategy was certainly a phenomenon all over the world, which had to do with new production technology, where production of services, computors and robots increasingly replace manual labour at the conveyor belts. Although this development seemed to be part of a general trend, obviously similar to the development of industrial relations in Japan, in the Swedish case it had a very specific domestic origin as well.

The union problem involved in this employer approach was that old loyalties within the union movement were being supplemented and challenged by cross-loyalties and new feelings of identity with the company. Nationwide loyalty as a prerequisite for a 'wage policy with solidarity' broke down into local management-workforce loyalties. The 'class' concept which had been reactivated for a short while in the wake of the events of 1968 and the strike-wave in 1969-1970 was ever more diluted by the employers' decentralising integration strategy.

The new employer strategy meant an obvious management interest in effacing the union division between blue and white collar employees, because that division was disappearing in the work process. This change was much more than the outcome of an employer strategy to come to terms with shop floor militancy. Technological change in the wake of the transformation of the industrial society to the information and knowledge society brought robotization and computorization to the manufacturing industry, implying decreasing status for both blue collar and white collar occupations and dissolution of barriers between these two categories of employees. Management gradually (in the 1970s-1980s) developed an interest in having *one* collectively bargained agreement per company. At the same time the interest in plant as opposed to centralized bargaining increased in the framework of the emerging *medarbetare* strategy. This strategy had a tremendous impact on SAF which lost hierarchical strength, and in the 1980s was rapidly transformed from a powerful bargaining organization to a weak policy organization. This development, in turn, has affected and will continue to affect the union organization strongly. This development was the long-term outcome of a response to a mixture of technological change and shop floor militancy.

The new labour market legislation at the beginning of the 1970s was rooted in a period of economic growth. The increased union influence at the shop-floor level, and union efforts to integrate the protests was intended to be exerted in sharing an ever-larger pie, and in mastering many of the problems the very pace of growth had accentuated, such as high labour mobility. The fact that the laws would be applied to a situation of economic stagnation and major restructuring, emerging in the wake of the dollar collapse in 1971, the oil price shock in 1973, and the collapse of key industries such as steel and shipbuilding around 1975, only emphasized the difficulties to which the Swedish model was exposed.

The collapse of key industries occurred around 1975, a few years after the outburst of militancy and the integration of the protests by means of legislation. These included the shipbuilding and steel industries. Again political intervention was called for by militant workforce exposed to threats of layoff, with demands for job security. The mood from the years after 1968 returned. Massive subsidy packages were delivered in order to bridge the breakdown and avoid layoffs. The class concept was mobilized in this fight for jobs in the manufacturing industry at the same time as the concept was being undermined by developments in other sectors of the labour market, where the service occupations, particularly in public service, grew rapidly (Stråth, 1987, chapter 4). In these circumstances, emphasis in labour market policy shifted to saving jobs in industries in competitive difficulties rather than channeling labour into the rapidly expanding sectors. This produced powerful pressure for massive subsidies to steady the rapid decline of some sectors. The shift from concentration on mobility to concentration on job security occurred under the intellectual hegemony of the *folkhemmet* metaphor. The intellectual framework remained, while the content changed.

However, this mobilization of the 'class' concept for subsidies soon proved to be a rearguard action. The impact of the resource mobilization for ailing industries and their employees worked, in the long run, in the same decentralising direction as the labour market legislation. In the struggle for jobs, workforces of competing firms fought and were played off against each other. Sometimes local employee-management coalitions emerged in the fight for survival against corresponding coalitions in other enterprises. Rivalry increased within the union movement and the hierarchical ties were exposed to severe strain. In this scenario the class concept continued to disappear as an instrument for the expression of solidarity. At a more general level, the subsidies to declining industries resulted in increasing opposition in the early 1980s, when economic stagnation produced increased social rivalry. The fact that it was the various non-Social Democratic governments after 1976 which delivered these support packages did not prevent them from being increasingly associated in the public opinion with general inertia, and being seen as representatives of old-fashioned Social Democratic politics. High taxes began also in broad sectors of Social Democratic adherents to connote to waste with public money rather than distribution from the rich to the poor. The subsidy packages in combination with the 'wage-earner fund' proposal (see below) contributed to the neo-liberal discursive breakthrough.

The loss of jobs in the manufacturing sector, the development of new management strategies, and this deep transformation and dissolution of class identities must be referred to fundamental changes in enterprise organization and management strategies, and can be seen as a major aspect of the transformation from a society where industrial manufacturing production is the dominant contributor to employment towards a knowledge society with increased emphasis on R&D, service production, administration, communications technology, and transnational enterprise organization.

At the political level this development of dissolution of the 'model' and its underlying preconditions was speeded up in its Swedish context by two other processes. These, like the ones just mentioned, both seemed at first to provoke radicalization and militancy: the wage-earner fund proposal and the rapid increase of the rate of female participation on the labour market.

The Swedish 'model' as it developed in the 1950s had one long-term weakness. A 'wage policy with solidarity' required wage restraints for employees in the most profitable enterprises, in order to maintain the principle of equal wage for equal work. If the most profitable enterprises had been the gauge in the centrally determined wage level, too many companies would have to close down. The level had to be well above that of the low productivity companies but below the most profitable ones. This restraint meant increased profits for the employers in these enterprises. The concept of 'surplus profits' (*övervinster*) was a union invention to pedagocically describe this problem. The 'surplus profits' were of no benefit to the employees in enterprises with lower wage levels but only to the shareholders. Of course, under such conditions, the employees in the most profitable enterprises could not accept permanent wage restraints. These enterprises were concentrated in the engineering sector. Therefore this problem was experienced particularly strongly by the metalworkers' union. The outburst of militancy and strikes around 1970 in the engineering industries should be seen in this context.

In 1973 Rudolf Meidner, one of the architects of LO's 'wage policy with solidarity', was asigned to carry out a union inquiry into this problem which potentially threatened to expose the union movement to severe tension. His point of departure was that the expansive power of profitable enterprises had to be maintained. The Meidner Report, submitted in 1976, recommended that some of the profits be redistributed to the employees: not individually, which would have been a veiled wage increase in the profitable enterprises incompatible with the 'wage policy with solidarity', but collectively into central wage-earner funds (For a discussion of the wage-earner funds, Trautwein, 1986, 1994).

This proposal provoked massive employer protests. It was received by the employers as a conscious union attempt to change the rules of the game on the labour market with the same effect as the wave of legislation but much more profoundly. The funds were described in terms of mass nationalization of the Swedish economy and the end of private ownership. The employers formed a committee which came to be called the 4 October Committee, the date of a spectacular demonstration in Stockholm in which tens of thousands of employers rallied to protest against the proposal. They experienced growing support in the public opinion. Finally, the wage-earner funds proposal was a catalyst in a discursive transformation, where the Social Democrats and the unions lost their prerogative of problem formulation, established during the campaign for the supplementary pensions in 1956-1958, to a more neo-liberal rhetoric.[5]

The Social Democrats were squeezed between radical claims from the left in the unions, which were still getting fuel from the post-1968 mood, hoping for a decisive change of power from capital to labour under the class concept, without realising the deeper processes which were about to effectfully undermine this mood, and a growing opposition to or at least hesitation about radicalism. The militant tendency in the labour movement took verbal expression in a way that made the unions prisoners of their own language. This prevented them from seeing the development of deeper processes which were about to shake the foundation of the whole industrial society and totally undermine the prerequisites for a construction of identity around the concept of class.

The Social Democratic leadership was never particularly interested in the unions' wage-earner funds proposal. Soon it was clear to the leadership that instead of being a technical solution, the wage-earner fund idea had become a symbol and a catalyst for decisive changes of power in the existing order. They experienced the proposal as particularly embarassing when it was used as an element of grassroots militancy and as an argument for a socialist society. The Social Democratic leadership never had any interest in changing the model, whereby labour representatives organized a capitalist society.

The only interest of the Social Democratic government was in integrating the protests emerging in the wake of the general radicalization of the social discourse after 1968. Therefore, the government did not feel that it could ignore the fund proposal of the unions, just as it had not ignored the protests against unemployment in the early 1930s. A Government Commission was appointed before the Social Democrats were forced to resign from government in 1976. The commission worked under various non-Social Democratic governments and delivered its report in 1981. In 1983, the Social Democratic government, which had come back to power after the elections in September 1982, forced through Parliament a very diluted wage-earner fund bill. One of the first decisions of the new non-Social Democratic government in 1991 was to dissolve these funds.

The debate on the wage-earner funds produced a kind of discursive polarization unknown since the debate on the supplementary pension in the 1950s and the unemployment debate in the 1930s. While these two earlier discursive struggles were pivotal to the establishment of a Social Democratic/trade unionist problem formulation primacy and discursive hegemony, the wage earner funds was the most decisive symbolic factor when the primacy of problem formulation in the social discourse during the 1980s shifted from the Social Democratic to the neo-liberal camp. Social Democratic economic policy during their government period from 1982 to 1991 was the best reflection of this shift, as they moved in a clearly neoliberal direction.[6]

The mobilization of female labour

The dissolution of the Swedish model not only had to do with intensified labour market legislation, a struggle for job protection, the wage-earner-fund proposal, and new management strategies, however. The public sector increased its share of the GDP in Sweden from 30 per cent in 1960 to 67 per cent in 1983. Sixty per cent of this 67 per cent (i.e. 40 per cent of the GDP) was absorbed by public consumption and investment, whilst 40 per cent was accounted for by transfers.

The growth of the public sector brought high female participation in the labour market. In 1950 there were 800 000 women on the Swedish labour market. In 1970 the figure had grown to 1.2 milion, i.e. a 50 per cent growth in 20 years. During the following period of 20 years the growth was somewhat higher, 57 per cent, to 1.6 milion in 1980 and 2.1 milion in 1990. In 1960 30 per cent of the labour force was women. In 1990 the figure was over 45 per cent. The growth of female labour market participation from 1970 occurred exclusively in the service producing public sector. In manufacturing industry employment began to decline.[7] This development can be described in figures:

Table 7.1
Employment in per cent of the population 16-64 years

Year	Women in per cent of all women	Men in per cent of all men
1970	58.3	85.9
1980	73.4	86.9
1990	80.3	84.4

Source: Statistiska Centralbyrån, *Arbetskraftundersökningar*, SCB, Stockholm.

Overall, developments from 1960 onward increased employment from 3.3 million to 4.3 million by the mid-1980s. Table 7.2 demonstrates very clearly that the growth in employment terms occurred almost exclusively in the public service producing sector. Restructuring and decline in the manufacturing industry caused a loss of 10,000-15,000 jobs a year but this was more than compensated for by the expansion in the public sector.

Table 7.2
Employment in manufacturing and service production in Sweden in the private and public sectors respectively, 1963-1983
(Index 1963=100)

	Year	Private sector	Public sector
Manufacturing	1963	100	100
	1973	85	102
	1983	75	91
Service	1963	100	100
	1973	103	162
	1983	118	236

Source: Kuuse, 1986, pp. 36-38.

This expansion was achieved by political decisions to increase the social welfare, child care and educational services in the 1960s. This, in turn, must be related to the parliamentary situation. The Social Democrats realized at an early point that they had to build class alliances in order to gain and maintain parliamentary power. From the 1930s to the 1950s there was such an alliance with the farmers, but by the late 1950s agricultural decline had eroded the base of this alliance. In this situation the Social Democrats turned to the growing middle class of salaried employees for support. The furious political struggle over compulsory supplementary pensions in 1957-1958 should be seen in this context. This reform was the springboard for a new alliance between the Social Democrats and the middle classes.

The middle classes were attracted by qualitative changes in the Social Democrats' perception of the welfare state. The 'minimalistic' approach, practiced in the entente cordiale with the farmers since the 1930s, by which the poor were guaranteed a safety net of social security, was replaced by a 'maximalistic' strategy. The state would guarantee income security rather than basic security if an individual's regular income was not forthcoming for some reason. Rather than being shaped around the requirements of the working class, the 'new' welfare state was designed to meet the standards of the middle classes: a higher standard of service to which the working class could also gain access. The long-term effect, here too, was the gradual transformation of class-based identities into other categories of identity.

The reforms meant an explosive growth of social expenditure and taxes in the 1960s and 1970s in parallel with the radical increase in women's participation in the labour market. Women were absorbed in the rapidly growing social service sector at low levels of pay and, although this eased the escalating costs (for the households in the form of higher taxes and for the state in the form of increasing wage expenditures) somewhat in the short run, it posed serious long-term problems. The public sector came to take over the labour-absorbing role of the high productivity manufacturing enterprises in the active labour market policy model of the LO economists. This change of focus towards the public sector worked in the same direction as the shift in the 1970s from a concentration in the labour market organization on labour mobility to job protection.

The social welfare reforms generated their own internal dynamics and the growth of public sector employment should be regarded as coincidental with, rather than as a response to, the rapid decline in key industries such as steel and shipbuilding. The politics of industrial transformation had its own special logic, driven by the emergence of mass lay-offs across broad industrial sectors which stretched the active labour market policy to its limit. There was no strategy of exchanging jobs in the manufacturing industry for jobs in the public service sector. The decline in the industry was mainly managed by a rapid increase in the numbers of early retirements, which covered up much of what looked like a full-employment society. However, as a matter of fact, if the figures for early retirement are added to the figures for unemployment and retraining programmes, the Swedish figures in the 1980s came close to the unemployment figures of 10-20 per cent or more in most western European countries. This development not only brought long-term financial problems for the state budget but also considerable productivity losses as compared with the bonanza years of the 'model' with labour transfers to high productivity industries and enterprises. Table 7.3 sheds light on the interrelationships when the Swedish model began to go downhill. Decreasing income taxes, due to increasing unemployment and early retirement, resulting in increasing burdens on the social insurance systems, constituted an explosive mix.

Table 7.3
The Swedish labour force 1970-1993, thousands

	1970	1980	1990	1993
1. Unemployed	59	84	69	356
2. Labour market training	69	121	140	262
3. Pre-pension	188	281	354	403
4. Sum 1-3	316	486	563	1,021
5. Public sector employed	766	1,183	1,298	1,269
6. Private sector employed	2,763	2,553	2,670	2,289
7. Labour market (= sum 4-6)	3,845	4,222	4,531	4,579
8. 4 in per cent of 7	8.2%	11.5%	12.5%	22.3%

Source: Svenska Arbetsgivareföreningen (Swedish Employers' Confederation), *Strukturrapport 1995*, SAF, 1995, Stockholm.

The implication for the state budget was even worse owing to the dramatic increase of the number of old age pensioners, from 947 000 in 1970 to 1 362 000 in 1980 and 1 533 000 in 1990.

The labour force for the public sector was mainly recruited from the female labour market reserve. The women's entrance on the labour market under the motto of 'emancipation' meant an emancipation from traditional value patterns around the family which was accompanied by the general radicalization of the social discourse in the 1970s. Women's emancipation was among themselves and in the public debate at first rather unreflectedly interpreted as an element of the more radical 'class' politics of those days. However, in the 1980s it became increasingly clear that the real content of the 'emancipation' was the accumulation of cheap female labour in the public service sector. At the same time, their male colleagues in the manufacturing export industry enjoyed rapidly advancing wages, owing to ascending profits in the wake of a 16 per cent devaluation of the Swedish currency by the Social Democratic government at their comeback in 1982. This development was not readable in terms of employment but in terms of increasing wages for those who still had jobs in the manufacturing export industry.

The tension in the union movement increased. The public sector unions required wage increases of 10 per cent or more in order to keep pace with the development in the export industry. The labour market conflicts increased in the 1980s. The Swedish labour market was no longer as peaceful as it had been and, more importantly, a new pattern of conflict emerged. Instead of conflict between capital and labour a pattern emerged where public service sector unions fought against unions representing the workforces in the manufacturing export industry, i. e. women against men. Instead of being compatible with the 'class' concept, gender increasingly became a competing identity category. This emergence of increasing tension was visible both in LO and in TCO. This process had an effect on the unions in a more positive way, too, however. The female unionization rate, until the 1980s significantly below the male rate, had in 1990 overtaken it. At the same time the unionization rate in the public sector outstripped that in the private sector (Kjellberg, 1992, p. 118).

This gender emancipation not only from family values but also from class identity, under increasing unionization rates, was a factor working in the same direction and as strong as the employers' *medarbetare* strategy. Both processes worked in a centrifugal direction and exposed the 'model' to strong erosion in the 1980s.

The long-term impact was paralysis of the entire LO structure. Nothing demonstrates this paralysis better than the LO approach to the question of Swedish membership in the EU in 1994. In the intensive debate before the referendum in November the members of the public sector unions feared that a Swedish membership would mean budget cuts in order to make the Swedish economy compatible with the requirements of the EU. A reduction of the budget deficit would, in turn, mean decreased employment in the public sector. Therefore, these members were mainly against Swedish membership. The unions representing the employees in the manufacturing export industries argued that Swedish membership was necessary for competitive reasons. The consequence of these opposing views was that LO refrained from taking a clear position in one of (or perhaps the most) important question in Swedish politics since 1945.

Current perspectives

The processes in the labour market initiated in the 1970s, and at first accompanied by radical rhetoric and reactivation of the class concept, occurred in the 1980s, increasingly in a neoliberal discursive framework. At the same time, state finances deteriorated considerably because of changed productivity preconditions and increasing engagements in the wake of the restructuring of the labour market. This deterioration in real terms was also accompanied by the discursive transformation in a neoliberal direction. At the beginning of the 1990s the

Swedish 'model' no longer functioned in any reasonable sense of the concept of 'model'.

What had been piled up in the 1970s in the organization of the labour market now got full effect. The employers' *medarbetare* strategy, the increasing emphasis on finance and banking rather than production investments, and the discursive transformation of the problem formulations in neoliberal direction formed a framework for the economic policy of the Social Democratic government 1982-1991 when it broke with the subsidy politics of the non-social democratic governments 1976-1982 to crisis industries. The trade unions paralyzed by the conflict between public and private sector unions could not do much against this development.[8] The 1980s was a decisive decade for the collapse of the Swedish model.

The wage-earner-fund debate and its symbolic and discursive implications for the neoliberal turn was crucial in this development. The whole change of the work organization and composition of the labour force, owing to the transformation of the industrial society to an information and knowledge society brought increasing problems with the financing of the welfare production. The wage-earner funds served as the symbolic representation of this trend and the reaction it provoked. The economic policy of the Social Democratic government (1982-1991) favoured the capital owners in a vain attempt to get them to invest more in order to create more employment. This attempt to beseech the industrial society with full employment produced severe tension between the Social Democratic government and LO.[9]

These factors seemed to reinforce one another and form a kind of vicious circle, which emerged when in the 1980s the vigorous circle of the 1950s and 1960s was short-circuited and reversed. The most obvious change was the collapse of the hierarchical bargaining structures and of the centralized organization of the labour market, and it is difficult to see how they can be restored in the future.

In the mid-1990s a transformation of the Swedish labour market organization can be discerned as moving in basically three directions. The three scenarios or trends can be epitomized as follows:

1. The shrinking number of employees in the transnationally organized companies in the manufacturing industry will increasingly mean that their union activity is concentrated on the company level. The demarcation between white and blue collar occupations will cease. Wage bargaining and other negotiations about employment conditions in this sphere will increasingly occur in the company frame-

work. If the ongoing transformation will continue in the same direction, the organization of employee interests will occur in the framework of what could be called 'company unions', modelled on Japanese patterns of industrial relations. In the more distant future, these company unions may become more or less integrated parts of the personnel function of the companies.

The Metalworkers' Union was once the symbol of the Swedish union movement. Today their central position in LO has been replaced by the union representing the local government employees. The position of the metalworkers' union in LO is more marginalized, and a new cooperative pattern is emerging between the union of the metalworkers, the salaried employees in the manufacturing industry and the civil engineers. In many respects, the metalworkers' union seems to have more shared interests with these federations than with LO. The three union federations are organized in three different confederations, LO for the traditional blue collar occupations of 'workers', TCO for the traditional white collar occupations of 'salaried employees' and SACO for the employees with university degrees. If a merger between the three federations occurs in the long run, the impact on the confederative labour market structure will be great. A successful merger could mean the establishment of some kind of umbrella for the company unions which would prevent too great a differentiation of wages and employment conditions. The prospects of the emergence of such an umbrella for politics 'with solidarity' is extremely difficult to evaluate.

Basically, union politics in this sphere should be expansive, with or without an umbrella framework of solidarity. Although redundancy is obviously rising the kind of labour that will still be in demand in manufacturing is equipped with skill, training and other qualities management is prepared to pay for. Moreover, an increasing share of the welfare production may occur through bargaining trade offs in this sphere, in pace with the deteriorating public finances. Such a development would increase social differentiation, of course. However, at least one important curbing factor on expansive union politics is probably the transnational organization of companies, which means potential competition between employees in different countries about how to attract capital for investment. This is a matter not of attractive employment conditions but of attractive capital conditions.

2. The public sector unions will not have the same opportunities as the company-centred unions in manufacturing industry to pursue an expansive policy. The decline in employment in the public sector was obvious between 1993 and 1994 owing to the financial crisis of the welfare production. The number of female employees decreased from 1 065 000 to 1 002 000 and the number of male employees from 433 000 to 390 000. At the same time the number of jobs increased in the private sector for both women and men, from 758 000 to 788 000 for women and from 1 275 000 to 1 308 000 for men.[10]

The gloomy prospects of public finances will push the public sector unions in a defensive direction. The ideological/discursive framework of the public debate is hardly on their side. The growing attractive power in the concept of *vårdnadsbidrag*, the child maintenance allowance, in the political debate *can* be seen as ideological support for fewer women on the labour market. So far the decline in employment has not been gender specific, however. The participation rate figures for 1990 in table 7.1, 80.3 per cent for women and 84.4 per cent for men had in 1994 decreased to 70.7 per cent and 72.2 per cent respectively.[11]

One key question will probably be whether public employee interests, which are organized today in the traditional three confederations (LO, TCO and SACO), like interests in the manufacturing industry, will manage to merge or cooperate at a sectoral level, and form a corresponding umbrella of solidarity as discussed above. The alternative to union cooperation in the public sector is increased rivalry. There is an obvious risk that the limited scope for expansive union politics will trigger inter-union conflict rather than cooperation.

The impact of scenarios 1 and 2 would be continued erosion of the hierarchical power of the three union confederations, and a regrouping of the organized interests of the employees with a focus on the local workplace level. This local focus might be supplemented with sectoral (manufacturing industry and public sector) umbrella organizations where the historical labour market division between white and blue collar occupations has finally disappeared. How tightly or loosely such sectoral umbrellas would work if they emerge - on a scale from confederations to occasional joint ventures or bargaining cartels - is still an open question.

3. In the short run, at least, there is hardly any dramatic risk of decreased unionization rate in trends 1 and 2. This risk is evident in the

third scenario, where the focus is on changing labour markets in the direction of more subcontracting, employment restricted to specific projects, increasing part time work, and computer-based work increasingly being done in the home or at small workplaces far from urbanization. Money for investment in such small-scale workplaces is often mobilized from funds for regional politics. The employers can be anything from large transnational companies to small highly specialized entrepreneurs.

The implication of this trend under names such as 'flexibility' and 'small is beautiful', is fewer opportunities for employees to meet. In many cases they do not even know of one another. New occupations emerge in the borderland between entrepreneur and employee. Employment contracts are increasingly signed on an individual basis without union mediation. In many cases there are no employment contracts in the proper sense of the term but of contracts for time-limited specific projects.

It goes without saying that this third scenario will have tremendous long-term impact on the preconditions for trade unions in a conventional sense. The most important influence will probably be difficulties in convincing people to unionize. How strong this trend will be compared with scenarios 1 and 2 is still an open question. However, it seems clear that this third scenario is the one in which the trade unions have paid least attention to the development of counter-strategies.

The three scenarios or trends outlined here are universal for the transformation of industrial societies towards information and knowledge societies. However, the historical embeddedness in the form of the 'model' give them their specific Swedish shape, like other historical roots in other societies result in other kinds of responses.

Neither in Sweden nor in other societies are the three scenarios mutually exclusive. They exist in parallel. The question of which of the three trends in the long run will prove to be strongest, and will determine the general normative and regulative developments on the labour market, is still an open question. The answer will probably be different for different societies. In Sweden the historical legacy would speak for a combination of trends 1 and 2, especially in consideration of the erosion of the model today. However, the decreasing rates of unionization in the 1980s as they are reflected in tables 7.4-7.6 is an indication of more dramatic long-term changes.

Table 7.4
Unionization rate 1930-1990, per cent

Year	Workers	Salaried employees	Employees
1930	45	24	41
1940	66	35	58
1950	76	47	67
1960	78	50	68
1970	80	63	73
1980	83	84	83
1990	81	81	81

Source: Statistics compiled by the research project *Fackliga organisationer och medlemmar under 1990-talet* (Anders Kjellberg), Dept. of Sociology, University of Lund; Research report Anders Kjellberg, *Fackliga organisationer och medlemmar i dagens Sverige*, forthcoming 1995. The figures 1930-1970 in Kjellberg, 1983.

Table 7.5
Unionization rate 1975-1991, gender and
public and private sector, manual workers, per cent

	1975	1980/1981	1986/1987	1991
Men	84	86	87	80
Women	67	80	87	81
Both sexes	77	83	87	81
Private sector	78	82	84	77
Public sector	76	86	92	87

Source: Kjellberg, 1992.

Table 7.6
Unionization rate 1975-1991,
salaried employees according to gender, per cent

	1975	1980/1981	1986/1987	1991
Men	80	84	83	78
Women	78	84	85	83
Both sexes	79	84	84	80

Source: See table 7.5

Notes

1. The population grew from 3.5 million in 1850 to 5.2 million in 1900. Still, in 1850, 90 per cent of the population lived in the countryside. By 1900 this figure had only decreased to 75 per cent: the urbanization process was far less dynamic than in Germany, for instance. In 1850 75 per cent of the active population was in agriculture and 10 per cent were in industry and crafts. In 1900 these figures were 57 and 20 per cent, respectively.
2. For a theoretical development of this view, see Koselleck, 1985 and 1989. Cf Bo Stråth, 'Introduction' in: Stråth (ed), 1990, and Trägårdh, 1990.
3. For a discussion of the active labour market policy and the contradictions involved in it, see Martin, 1979, and Swenson, 1989.
4. Interview with Rudolf Meidner and several documents under wage policy with solidarity and active labour market policy files in the archives of LO, Stockholm. Cf Pontusson, 1988, on Social Democratic hegemony.
5. This conclusion is based on an extensive survey of the comprehensive press cutting files of the LO archives, Stockholm.
6. Interview with LO economist Dan Andersson.
7. Statistics compiled by Yvonne Hirdman, Institutet för Arbetslivsforskning, Stockholm.
8. Interview with LO economist Dan Andersson.
9. Ibid.
10. Statistiska Centralbyrån, Arbetskraftsundersökningar, SCB, Stockholm.
11. Ibid.

References

Åmark, K. (1986), *Facklig makt och fackligt medlemskap*, Arkiv, Lund.
Geer de, H. (1978), *Rationaliseringsrörelsen i Sverige. Effectivitetsidéer och socialt ansvar under mellankrigstiden*, SNS, Stockholm.
Gluck, C. (1985), *Japan's Modern Myths. Ideology in the late Meiji Period*, Princeton UP, New Jersey.
Heclo, H. and Madsen, H. (1987), *Policy and Politics in Sweden. Principle Pragmatism*, Temple UP, Philadelphia.
Johansson, A. L. (1989), *Tillväxt och klassamarbete*, Tiden, Stockholm.
Kjellberg, A. (1983). *Facklig organisering i tolv länder*, Arkiv, Lund.
Kjellberg, A. (1992), 'Sweden: can the model survive ?', in Ferner, A. and Hyman, R. (eds.), *Industrial Relations in the New Europe*, Blackwell, Oxford.
Koselleck, R. (1989), *Critique and Crisis*, Cambridge UP, Cambridge.
Koselleck, R. (1985), *Futures Past. On the Semantics of Historical Time*, Cambridge UP, Cambridge.
Kuuse, J. (1986), *Strukturomvandlingen och arbetsmarknadens organisering*, Stockholm.
Lutz, B. (1984), *Der kurze Traum immer währender Prosperität*, Campus, Frankfurt/Main.
Martin, A. (1979), 'The dynamics of change in a Keynesian political economy: the Swedish case and its implications', in Crouch, C. (ed.), *State and Economy in Contemporary Capitalism*, St. Martin's Press, New York.

Pontusson, J. (1988), *Swedish Social Democracy and British Labour: Essays on the Nature and Conditions of Social Democratic Hegemony*, Cornell UP, New York.

Rothstein, B. (1992), *Den korporativa staten*, Norstedts, Stockholm.

Sommestad, L. (1992), *Från mejerska till mejerist. En studie av mejeriyrkets maskulariseringsprocess*, Arkiv, Lund.

Stråth, B. (1982), *Varvsarbetare i två varvsstäder*, Svenska Varv, Göteborg (with an extensive English summary).

Stråth, B. (1989), *The Politics of Deindustrialisation*, Croom Helm, London.

Stråth, B. (ed.) (1990), *Language and the Construction of Class Identities. The Struggle for Discursive Power in Social Organisation: Scandinavia and Germany after 1900*, Gothenburg University.

Stråth, B. (1993), *Folkhemmet mot Europa*, Tiden, Stockholm.

Swenson, P. (1989), *Fair Shares. Unions, Pay, and Politics in Sweden and West Germany*, Adamantine Press, London.

Torstendahl, R. (1991), *Bureaucratisation in Northwestern Europe 1880-1985. Domination and Governance*, Routledge, London.

Trägårdh, L. (1990), 'Varieties of volkish ideologies. Sweden and Germany 1848-1933', in Stråth, B. (ed.), *Language and the Construction of Class Identities*, Gothenburg University.

Trautwein, H. M. (1986), *Arbeitnehmerfonds in Schweden - der dritte Weg ?*, Peter Lang, Frankfurt/Main.

Trautwein, H. M. (1994), 'Wage-earner funds', in Arestis, P. and Sawyer, M. (eds.), *The Elgar Companion to Radical Political Economy*, Edward Elgar, Aldershot.

Contributors

Giampiero Bianchi, researcher at the Fondazione Giulio Pastore in Rome.

Fondazione Giulio Pastore • Via Collina 24 • I-00187 Roma • Phone 39-6-4817850/4817860 • Fax 39-6-4815785

Colin Crouch, professor of comparative social institutions, Trinity College, Oxford and Istituto Universitario Europeo, Badia Fiesolana (Florence).

Istituto Universitario Europeo Badia Fiesolana • Via dei Roccettini • I-50016 San Domenico di Fiesole (Florence) • Phone 39-55-4685236 • Fax 39-55-4685201

Frans De Wachter, professor of ethics, Higher Institute of Philosophy, KU Leuven.

KU Leuven • Hoger Instituut voor Wijsbegeerte • Kardinaal Mercierplein 2 • B-3000 Leuven • Phone 32-16-32 63 13 • Fax 32-16-32 63 11

Hans De Witte, head of labour sector at the Higher Institute of Labour Studies, KU Leuven.

KU Leuven • Hoger Instituut voor de Arbeid • E. Van Evenstraat 2E • B-3000 Leuven • Phone 32-16-323340 • Fax 32-16-323344 • E-mail hans.dewitte@hiva.kuleuven.ac.be

Bernhard Ebbinghaus, assistant professor, Mannheim Centre for European Social Research, University of Mannheim.

Mannheim Centre for European Social Research • University of Mannheim • D-68131 Mannheim • Phone 49-621-292 8431/5318 • Fax 49-621-292 8435 • E-mail bebbing@mzes.sowi.uni-mannheim.de

Michael Gordon, professor of management, School of Business, Rutgers University.

School of Business • Rutgers University • Janice H. Levin Building • Rockefeller Rd. • New Brunswick, New Jersey 08903, USA • Phone 1-908-932 3279 • Fax 1-908-445 6329 • E-mail gordon@zodiac.rutgers.edu

Jean Hartley, senior lecturer in organizational psychology, Department of Organizational Psychology, Birkbeck College, University of London.

Department of Organizational Psychology • Birkbeck College • University of London • Malet St. • UK-London WC1E 7HX • Phone 44-171-6316394 • Fax 44-171-6316750 • E-mail ubjv642@bbk.cu@ac.uk

Anton Hemerijck, lecturer, Department of Public Administration, Erasmus Universiteit Rotterdam.

Vakgroep Bestuurskunde • Erasmus Universiteit • Postbus 1738 • NL-3000 DR Rotterdam • Phone 31-10-4082635/2526 • Fax 31-10-4527842 • E-mail hemerijck@bsk.eur.nl

Richard Hyman, professor of industrial relations, Industrial Relations Research Unit (IRRU), University of Warwick.

University of Warwick • IRRU • UK-Coventry CV4 7AL • Phone 44-1203-523840 • Fax 44-1203-524656 • E-mail irobrh@wbs.warwick.ac.uk

Bert Klandermans, professor, Department of Social Pyschology, Free University of Amsterdam.

Free University of Amsterdam • Department of Social Psychology • De Boelelaan 1081 • NL-1081 HV Amsterdam • Phone 31-20-444 88 50/88 65 • Fax 31-20-444 89 21

Albert Martens, professor of industrial relations and urban sociology, KU Leuven.

KU Leuven • Departement Sociologie • E. Van Evenstraat 2C • B-3000 Leuven • Tel. 32-16-32 31 68 • Fax 32-16-32 33 65

René Mouriaux, directeur de recherche CNRS, Centre d'Etude de la Vie Politique Française (CEVIPOF).

Centre d'Etude de la Vie Politique Française (CEVIPOF) • 10, rue de la Chaise • F-75007 Paris • Phone 33-1-45 48 63 18 • Fax 33-1-42 22 07 64

Patrick Pasture, senior research assistant of the National Fund for Scientific Research (NFWO), Higher Institute of Labour Studies and Department of History, KU Leuven.

KU Leuven • Hoger Instituut voor de Arbeid • E. Van Evenstraat 2E • B-3000 Leuven • Phone 32-16-323330 • Fax 32-16-323344 • E-mail patrick.pasture@hiva.kuleuven.ac.be

Werner Reutter, Hochschulassistent, Philosophische Fakultät, Humboldt-Universität zu Berlin.

Humboldt-Universität zu Berlin • Philosophische Fakultät III • Fakultätsinstitut Sozialwissenschaften • Institut für Politikwissenschaft • Unter den Linden 6 • D-10099 Berlin • Phone 49-30-2843 1431 • Fax 49-30-2843 1429

Bo Stråth, professor, Historiska Institutionen, Göteborgs Universitet.

Historiska Institutionen • Göteborgs Universitet • S-41298 Göteborg • Phone 46-31-7734502 • Fax 46-31-7734456 • E-mail bo.straath@history.gu.se

Magnus Sverke, research assistant, The Swedish Institute for Work Life Research.

Swedish Insitute for Work Life Research • Box 12670 • S-11293 Stockholm • Phone 46-8-617 0332 • Fax 46-8-653 1750 • E-mail magnus_s@alc.se

Gerrita van der Veen, program leader, SWOKA, Institute for Consumer Research.

SWOKA • Instituut voor Consumentenonderzoek • Alexanderstraat 14 • NL-2514 JL Den Haag • Phone 31-70-3469225 • Fax 31-70-3603963

Johan Verberckmoes, senior research assistant, Department of History and Higher Institute of Labour Studies, KU Leuven.

KU Leuven • Hoger Instituut voor de Arbeid • E. Van Evenstraat 2E • B-3000 Leuven • Phone 32-16-323330 • Fax 32-16-323344 • E-mail johan.verberckmoes@arts.kuleuven.ac.be

Jelle Visser, lecturer, Department of Sociology, Universiteit Amsterdam.

Universiteit Amsterdam • Vakgroep Sociologie • Oude Hoogstraat 24 • NL-1012 CE Amsterdam • Phone 31-20-5252231 • Fax 31-20-5252179 • E-mail visser@sara.nl

Lode Wils, professor emeritus, Department of History, KU Leuven.

KU Leuven • Departement Geschiedenis • PO Box 33 • B-3000 Leuven • Tel. 32-16-40 55 20